Modeling and Simulation in Engineering, 2nd Edition

Modeling and Simulation in Engineering, 2nd Edition

Editors

Camelia Petrescu
Valeriu David

MDPI • Basel • Beijing • Wuhan • Barcelona • Belgrade • Manchester • Tokyo • Cluj • Tianjin

Editors

Camelia Petrescu
Technical University of Iasi
Iasi, Romania

Valeriu David
"Gheorghe Asachi" Technical
University of Iasi
Iasi, Romania

Editorial Office
MDPI
St. Alban-Anlage 66
4052 Basel, Switzerland

This is a reprint of articles from the Special Issue published online in the open access journal *Mathematics* (ISSN 2227-7390) (available at: https://www.mdpi.com/si/mathematics/Model_Simul_Eng_II).

For citation purposes, cite each article independently as indicated on the article page online and as indicated below:

LastName, A.A.; LastName, B.B.; LastName, C.C. Article Title. *Journal Name* **Year**, *Volume Number*, Page Range.

ISBN 978-3-0365-8288-7 (Hbk)
ISBN 978-3-0365-8289-4 (PDF)

Contents

About the Editors

Camelia Petrescu

Camelia Petrescu received her MSc degree in Electrical Engineering (1982) from the Technical University of Iasi and Ph.D degree in Electrical Engineering from Politehnica University Bucharest, Romania (1994). She is a full professor at the Technical University of Iasi. Her areas of interest include analytical and numerical electromagnetic field analysis, optimization methods and electric power quality.

Valeriu David

Valeriu David received his M.S. and Ph.D. degrees in electronic/electric engineering from the "Gheorghe Asachi" Technical University of Iasi, Romania in 1983 and 1998, respectively. He is a full professor at the Technical University of Iasi and a Senior Member of IEEE. His teaching and research activities include electric and electronic measurements, estimation of biomedical and environmental parameters, survey of the electromagnetic environment and electromagnetic absorbers/shields.

mathematics

Article

The Dual Characterization of Structured and Skewed Structured Singular Values

Mutti-Ur Rehman [1,2,†], Jehad Alzabut [3,4,†], Taqwa Ateeq [5], Jutarat Kongson [6,*] and Weerawat Sudsutad [7]

1   Department of Mathematics, Akfa University, Tashkent 111221, Uzbekistan; m.rehman@akfauniversity.org
2   Department of Mathematics, Sukkur IBA University, Sukkur 65200, Pakistan
3   Deparment of Mathematics and General Sciences, Prince Sultan University, Riyadh 11586, Saudi Arabia; jalzabut@psu.edu.sa or jehad.alzabut@ostimteknik.edu.tr
4   Department of Industrial Engineering, OSTİM Technical University, 06374 Ankara, Turkey
5   Department of Applied Mathematics, Arab American University, Jenin 44862, Palestine; taqwa.ateeq@jenin.edu.ps
6   Research Group of Theoretical and Computation in Applied Science, Department of Mathematics, Faculty of Science, Burapha University, Chonburi 20131, Thailand
7   Department of Statistics, Faculty of Science, Ramkhamhaeng University, Bangkok 10240, Thailand; weerawat.s@rumail.ru.ac.th
*   Correspondence: jutarat_k@go.buu.ac.th
†   These authors contributed equally to this work.

Abstract: The structured singular values and skewed structured singular values are the well-known mathematical quantities and bridge the gap between linear algebra and system theory. It is well-known fact that an exact computation of these quantities is NP-hard. The NP-hard nature of structured singular values and skewed structured singular values allow us to provide an estimations of lower and upper bounds which guarantee the stability and instability of feedback systems in control. In this paper, we present new results on the dual characterization of structured singular values and skewed structured singular values. The results on the estimation of upper bounds for these two quantities are also computed.

Keywords: eigenvalues; singular values; structured singular values; skewed structured singular values

MSC: 15A18; 15A03; 05B20; 15A23

Citation: Rehman, M.-U.; Alzabut, J.; Ateeq, T.; Kongson, J.; Sudsutad, W. The Dual Characterization of Structured and Skewed Structured Singular Values. *Mathematics* **2022**, *10*, 2050. https://doi.org/10.3390/math10122050

Academic Editors: Adolfo Ballester-Bolinches and Carlo Bianca

Received: 15 April 2022
Accepted: 6 June 2022
Published: 13 June 2022

Publisher's Note: MDPI stays neutral with regard to jurisdictional claims in published maps and institutional affiliations.

1. Introduction

The structured singular value (SSV) was first introduced by J. C. Doyel [1] and Safonov [2] as a mathematical tool, which is widely used to investigate the robustness, performance and stability of linear feedback systems in control. In control system analysis, the problem associated with the determination of stability and robustness in the presence of uncertainties is among the most fundamental issue in control and it has attracted a reasonable amount of researchers in the last three decades. Much of the research work has been done in robustness analysis for two different class of problems from system theory which involves the uncertainties. For this purpose, two different kinds of approaches has been developed.

One of the approach is based upon the frequency-based robust stability conditions in the form of the small gain condition. The small gain condition is most useful for analyzing those problems from system theory which are associated with the norm bounded unstructured or complex structured uncertainties. An example of such an approach is based upon the structured singular values introduced in [1,3].

An another approach is largely inspired by Kharitonov work [4]. The main aim of the work by Kharitonov is to determine the stability robustness with a finite number of conditions. This approach also aims to study the problems in control when real parametric uncertainties consisting of real-valued uncertain parameters are involved, for a more details see, e.g., [5–7].

In principle, both types of methodologies can be modified to deal with real and complex parametric uncertainties. Indeed, the early developments in structured singular values deals with the uncertainties which are only pure complex. However, the extensions have been made so that the real-valued uncertainties can also be considered [8,9]. The Kharitonov type approaches deal with the μ-value problems while considering the real-valued uncertainties [10–12].

The exact computation of SSV is impenetrable which makes it NP-hard [13]. The NP-hard nature of SSV broach to foster methods for approximation of its lower and upper bounds. However, the SSV lower bounds are computed using the generalization of power method [14,15]. Moreover, the balanced AMI technique developed by [16] is the utilization of bounds introduced by [17] and is particularized in a preeminent style in [16]. The given matrix, under consideration, is first balanced while imploging a variation of Osborne's [18] generalized to crank the repeated real/complex scalars and the number of full blocks. Further, Perron approach is a determination for balancing the given matrix. The Perron eigenvector methodology is established on the idea apt by Safonov [2].

The D-Scaling upper bound presented in [1] is the most extensively used paper for the approximation of the upper bound of structured singular values. The D-Scaling for complex structures acquiring full complex blocks is close to the original SSV. For more details, we suggest the reader to consult [19] and the reference therein. Meanwhile, for non-trivial complex structures, the D-Scaling upper bound turns out to be more flexible [1,19].

The SSV theory for mixed real/complex cases is an extension of SSV that acquiesce the structure to consist of real and complex parts. The computation of upper bounds for the mixed SSV presented by [17] is also known as (D, q)-Scaling upper bound of skewed structured singular values ν, and is quite apart from actual mixed SSV [20].

The investigation for the non-fragile asynchronous H_∞ control while considering the stochastic memory systems with Bernoulli distribution has been recently studied by [21]. An efficient algorithm for the computation of budget allocation procedure for the selection of top candidate solution for objective performance measure has been extensively studied by [22].

In this article, we give an analytical treatment for the dual characterization of structured singular values and skewed structured singular values. We present some new results for the computation of an upper bounds of these quantities.

The rest of the paper is organized as: In Section 2, we provide the preliminaries of our article. In particular, we give the Definitions of the block diagonal structure, structured singular values and skewed structured singular values for a set of block diagonal matrices and subset of positive definite matrices. In Section 3, we present new results on the computation of the dual characterization of structured singular values and skewed structured singular values. The computation of upper bounds of skewed structured singular values are also presented in Section 3 of our article. Finally, Section 4 is about the conclusion of our presented work.

2. Preliminaries

Before we proceed, we give some essential definitions that will act as prerequisites for the subsequent results.

Definition 1 ([23]). *The set of block diagonal matrices X is defined as*

$$X \quad := \quad \left\{ diag(\alpha_i I_i; \beta_j I_j; C_t) : \alpha_i \in \mathbb{R}, \beta_j \in \mathbb{C}, C_t \in \mathbb{C}^{m_t \times m_t} \right\},$$

where $\alpha_i I_i$, $\beta_j I_j$, and C_t denote the number of repeated real scalar blocks with different sizes for all $i = 1, \cdots, r$, the number of complex scalar blocks with different sizes for all $j = 1, \cdots, c$ and the number of full complex blocks with different sizes for all $t = 1, \cdots, k$, respectively.

Definition 2 ([1]). *For a given n-dimensional complex valued matrix $M \in \mathbb{C}^{n \times n}$, the structured singular value with respect to X is defined as*

$$\mu_X(M) := \begin{cases} 0, & \text{if } det(I - M\Delta) \neq 0, \, \forall \Delta \in X \\ \dfrac{1}{\min\limits_{\Delta}\{\|\Delta\|_2 \colon \Delta \in X, \, det(I - M\Delta) = 0\}}, & \text{else.} \end{cases} \tag{1}$$

The matrix valued function Δ is an uncertainty that occurs in the linear feedback system.

Definition 3 ([23]). *The sets D_X and G_X*

$$D_X := \left\{ diag(P_1, \ldots, P_r; P_1, \ldots, P_c; P_1, \ldots, P_t) \right\}$$

and

$$G_X := \left\{ diag(H_1, \ldots, H_r; O_1, \ldots, O_c; O_1, \ldots, O_t \right\}$$

contains positive definite matrices P_i for all $i = 1, \cdots, r$, P_j for all $j = 1, \cdots, c$ and P_t for all $t = 1, \cdots, k$ and Hermitian matrices H_i for all $i = 1, \cdots, r$, and repeated null complex scalar blocks O_j for all $j = 1, \cdots, c$ and number of null full complex blocks O_t for all $t = 1, \cdots, k$, respectively.

Definition 4 ([23]). *For a given n dimensional complex valued square matrix $M \in \mathbb{C}^{n \times n}$ and $\beta \in \mathbb{R}$, the matrix-value function $f_\beta(D, G)$ is defined as*

$$f_\beta(D, G) := M^H D M + i(GM - M^H G) - \beta^2 D,$$

where matrices D, G belongs to D_X and G_X, receptively.

Definition 5 ([23]). *The upper bound of $\mu_X(M)$ is denoted by $\nu_X(M)$ and is defined as*

$$\nu_X(M) := \inf_{\beta > 0} \left\{ \beta : \exists \, D \in D_X \text{ and } G \in G_X \text{ s.t. } f_\beta(D, G) < 0 \right\}.$$

Let $M \in \mathbb{C}^{m \times n}$ be a given matrix and (m_r, m_c, m_C) represent an m-tuples of positive integers and let

$$K = (k_1, \ldots, k_{m_r}, k_{m_r+1}, \ldots, k_{m_r+m_c}, k_{m_r+m_c+1}, \ldots, k_{m_C}), \tag{2}$$

where $\sum_{i=1}^{m} k_i = n$.

Definition 6 ([23]). *The set of block diagonal matrices is defined as*

$$X_K := \{\Delta = diag(\delta_1 I_1, \ldots, \delta_r I_r, \delta_1 I_1, \ldots, \delta_c I_c, \Delta_1, \ldots, \Delta_t)\}.$$

In Definition 6, $\delta_i \in \mathbb{R} \, \forall i = 1, \cdots, r$, $\delta_j \in \mathbb{C} \, \forall j = 1, \cdots, c$, $\Delta_t \in \mathbb{C}^{t \times t} \, \forall t = 1, \cdots, k$. The set X_K is pure real if $\delta_j = 0$ and pure complex if $\delta_i = 0$, otherwise it is with mixed real and complex block perturbation. For $\Delta_t \in \mathbb{C}^{t \times t}$, the set X_K turns out to be a set of full complex blocks perturbation.

Definition 7 ([1]). *For given matrix $M \in \mathbb{C}^{m \times n}$ and X_K, the structured singular value; denoted by $\mu_{X_K}(M)$ and is defined as*

$$\mu_{X_K}(M) := \begin{cases} 0, & \text{if } det(I - M\Delta) \neq 0, \Delta \in X_K \\ \dfrac{1}{\min\limits_{\Delta \in X_K}\{\|\Delta\|_2 \colon det(I - M\Delta) = 0\}}, & \text{else,} \end{cases} \tag{3}$$

where $\|\Delta\|_2$ denotes the largest singular value of Δ.

Definition 8 ([23]). *The set Y_K of block diagonal structure is defined as*

$$Y_K : \{\Delta_v = diag(\delta_1 I_1, \ldots, \delta_r I_r, \delta_1 I_1, \ldots, \delta_c I_c; \delta_1 I_1, \ldots, \delta_c I_c; \Delta_1, \ldots, \Delta_t)\}.$$

In Definition 8, $\delta_i \in \mathbb{R}$ $\forall i = 1, \cdots, r$, $\delta_j \in \mathbb{C}$ $\forall j = 1, \cdots, c$, $\Delta_t \in \mathbb{C}^{t \times t}$ $\forall t = 1, \cdots, k$.

Definition 9 ([23]). *The secondary set $Z_{\hat{R}}$ of block diagonal structure is defined as*

$$Z_{\hat{R}} : \{\Delta_v = diag(\delta_1 I_1, \ldots, \delta_r I_r, \delta_1 I_1, \ldots, \delta_c I_c; \Delta_1, \ldots, \Delta_t)\}.$$

In Definition 9, $\delta_i \in \mathbb{R}$ $\forall i = 1, \cdots, r$, $\delta_j \in \mathbb{C}$ $\forall j = 1, \cdots, c$, $\Delta_t \in \mathbb{C}^{t \times t}$ $\forall t = 1, \cdots, k$.

Definition 10 ([23]). *The set Z_K is restricted to the unit ball and is defined as*

$$BZ_{\hat{2}} = \left\{ \Delta_f \in Z_{\hat{R}} : \|\Delta_f\|_2 \leq 1 \right\}.$$

Definition 11 ([23]). *The block structure $W_{K,\hat{R}}$ is defined as*

$$W_{K,\hat{R}} = \left\{ \Delta = diag(\Delta_f, \Delta_v) \right\}, \tag{4}$$

or

$$\Delta = \left(\begin{array}{c|c} \Delta_f & 0 \\ \hline 0 & \Delta_v \end{array} \right). \tag{5}$$

Definition 12 ([23]). *For given matrix $M \in \mathbb{C}^{m \times n}$ and $Z_{\hat{R}}$, the skewed structured singular value is denoted by $\mu_{Z_{\hat{R}}}(M)$ and is defined as*

$$\mu_{Z_{\hat{R}}}(M) := \begin{cases} 0, & \text{if } det(I - M\Delta) \neq 0, \Delta \in W_{K,\hat{R}} \\ \dfrac{1}{\min\limits_{\Delta \in W_{K,\hat{R}}} \{\|\Delta_v\|_2 : det(I - M\Delta) = 0\}}, & \text{else.} \end{cases} \tag{6}$$

3. The Main Results

In the section, we present some new results on the computation of structured singular values and skewed structured singular value.

3.1. Dual Characterization of $\mu_X(M)$ and $\nu_X(M)$

We give a dual characterization of $\mu_X(M)$ and $\nu_X(M)$. The characterization is the dual in the sense that they act as an application for duality argument in convex sets. The following result given by Boyed [24] is considered as a standard result for the separation of the hyper-planes.

Lemma 1 ([24]). *Let $P(E) \in \mathbb{C}^{m \times m}$ and P depends affinely on $E \in \mathbb{C}^{n \times n}$. Let γ be the some convex subset of $\mathbb{C}^{n \times n}$. Then, there exists no $E \in \gamma$ such that the Hermitian part of $P(E)$ becomes negative, that is,*

$$He(P(E)) < 0$$

if and only if there is some non-zero matrix W, that is, $W = W^H$ and is non-negative such that

$$Re(Tr(WP(E))) \geq 0.$$

We make use of the following assumptions to prove our main result for dual characterization of $\nu_X(M)$.

Assumption 1. *The matrix $E \in \mathbb{C}^{n \times n}$ in $D_X + G_X$ is Hermitian, that is $E = E^H$.*

Assumption 2. *The matrices* $(M - \beta I), (M^H + \beta I)$ *are Hermitian, that is,*

$$(M - \beta I) = (M + \beta I)^H$$

and

$$(M^H + \beta I) = (M^H + \beta I)^H.$$

Theorem 1 (Dual Characterization of $\nu_x(M)$)**.** *Let $M \in \mathbb{C}^{n \times n}$ and X be the set of block diagonal matrices, as defined above. The quantity $\beta \in \mathbb{R}$ is lower bound of an upper bound of $\mu_X(M)$*

$$\beta \leq \nu_X(M) \Leftrightarrow \exists\, W = W^H \geq 0$$

such that

$$\eta_i[(M - \beta I)W(M^H + \beta I)E] \geq 0, \forall E \in D_X + iG_X.$$

Proof. The matrices $(M - \beta I)$, $(M^H + \beta I)$, W and E are Hermitian. The unitary diagonalization of the matrix $((M - \beta I)W(M^H + \beta I)E)$ implies that

$$(M - \beta I)W(M^H + \beta I)E = Q\Lambda Q^*$$

or

$$\Lambda = diag(\lambda_1, \ldots, \lambda_z, \lambda_{z+1}, \ldots, \lambda_n) = Q^*((M - \beta I)W(M^H + \beta I)E)Q \tag{7}$$

We construct matrices M_0, M_+, which pack $\lambda_1, \cdots, \lambda_z$ as zero eigen-values and $\lambda_{z+1}, \cdots, \lambda_n$ as strictly positive eigen-values.

$$M_0 = \begin{pmatrix} 1 & & 0 \\ & \ddots & \\ 0 & & 1 \end{pmatrix} \in \mathbb{C}^{n_z \times n_z},$$

and

$$M_+ = \begin{pmatrix} \frac{1}{\lambda_{z+1}^{1/2}} & & 0 \\ & \ddots & \\ 0 & & \frac{1}{\lambda_n^{1/2}} \end{pmatrix} \in \mathbb{C}^{n_p \times n_p},$$

and then assemble all eigen-values into matrix $\mathbb{B}$ as

$$\mathbb{B} = \begin{pmatrix} M_0 & 0 \\ 0 & M_+ \end{pmatrix}.$$

A simple calculation shows that

$$(Q\mathbb{B})^*((M - \beta I)W(M^H + \beta I)E)(Q\mathbb{B}) = \mathbb{B}^*\Lambda\mathbb{B} = \begin{pmatrix} O_z & 0 \\ 0 & I_p \end{pmatrix}. \tag{8}$$

In Equation (8), O_z and I_p are of dimensions n_z and n_p.

Suppose that there exists an Hermitian matrix $\hat{H}$, which is a similar matrix to $((M - \beta I)W(M^H + \beta I)E)$ such that

$$Q_{(M-\beta I)W(M^H+\beta I)E}, \mathbb{B}_{(M-\beta I)W(M^H+\beta I)E} = (M - \beta I)W(M^H + \beta I)E, \tag{9}$$

and

$$Q_{\hat{H}}, \mathbb{B}_{\hat{H}} = \hat{H}. \tag{10}$$

In a similar manner,

$$(Q_{(M-\beta I)W(M^H+\beta I)E}\mathbb{B}_{(M-\beta I)W(M^H+\beta I)E})^*[(M-\beta I)W(M^H+\beta I)E]$$

$$(Q_{(M-\beta I)W(M^H+\beta I)E}\mathbb{B}_{(M-\beta I)W(M^H+\beta I)E}) = \begin{bmatrix} O_z & 0 \\ 0 & I_p \end{bmatrix} = (Q_{\hat{H}}\mathbb{B}_{\hat{H}})^*\hat{H}(Q_{\hat{H}}\mathbb{B}_{\hat{H}}).$$

In turn, the quantity $(M-\beta I)W(M^H+\beta I)E$ implies that,

$$(Q_{(M-\beta I)W(M^H+\beta I)E}\mathbb{B}_{(M-\beta I)W(M^H+\beta I)E})^{-1} = (Q_{\hat{H}}\mathbb{B}_{\hat{H}})^*\hat{H}(Q_{\hat{H}}\mathbb{B}_{\hat{H}})(Q_{\hat{H}}\mathbb{B}_{\hat{H}})^{-1}. \tag{11}$$

Thus, finally we obtain the following expression for the quantity $(M-\beta I)W(M^H + \beta I)E$, that is,

$$(M-\beta I)W(M^H+\beta I)E = TV.$$

Here the matrix $T = (Q_{\hat{H}}\mathbb{B}_{\hat{H}}\mathbb{B}^{-1}_{(M-\beta I)W(M^H+\beta I)E}Q^{-1}_{(M-\beta I)W(M^H+\beta I)E})^*$, and the matrix $V = \hat{H}(Q_{\hat{H}}\mathbb{B}_{\hat{H}}\mathbb{B}^{-1}_{(M-\beta I)W(M^H+\beta I)E}Q^{-1}_{(M-\beta I)W(M^H+\beta I)E})$. The result in above equation implies the existence of some invertible matrix Z such that

$$(M-\beta I)W(M^H+\beta I)E = Z^*\hat{H}Z.$$

Reduce $(M-\beta I)W(M^H+\beta I)E$ and $\hat{H}$ to the form of Equation (8) as:

$$(Y\Omega)^*((M-\beta I)W(M^H+\beta I)E)(Y\Omega) = \begin{pmatrix} O_z & 0 \\ 0 & I_p \end{pmatrix},$$

where $Y = Q_{(M-\beta I)W(M^H+\beta I)E}$ and $\Omega = \mathbb{B}_{(M-\beta I)W(M^H+\beta I)E}$ and hence, we have that,

$$(Q_{\hat{H}}\mathbb{B}_{\hat{H}})^*\hat{H}(Q_{\hat{H}}\mathbb{B}_{\hat{H}}) = \begin{bmatrix} O_{\hat{z}} & 0 \\ 0 & I_{\hat{p}} \end{bmatrix}. \tag{12}$$

Next, we intend to show that $z = \hat{z}$ and $p = \hat{p}$. However, since, $(M-\beta I)W(M^H + \beta I)E = Z^*\hat{H}Z$ and from Equation (12), we get

$$(ZY\Omega)^*\hat{H}(ZY\Omega) = \begin{bmatrix} O_z & 0 \\ 0 & I_p \end{bmatrix}. \tag{13}$$

Equations (12) and (13) have two similar transformations for $\hat{H}$. We write these as

$$Y^*\hat{H}Y = \begin{pmatrix} O_z & 0 \\ 0 & I_p \end{pmatrix}; \quad \hat{Y}^*\hat{H}\hat{Y} = \begin{pmatrix} O_{\hat{z}} & 0 \\ 0 & I_{\hat{p}} \end{pmatrix}$$

where matrices Y and $\hat{Y}^*$ are invertible. We show $z = \hat{z}$ and skip to show $p = \hat{p}$ to avoid redundancy in working rules.

Let

$$W = \mathcal{N}(Y^*\hat{H}Y), \quad \dim(\mathcal{W}) = z.$$

Take $w \in \mathcal{W}$, then we get $Y^*\hat{H}Yw = 0$. As the matrix Y is invertible, so $Y^*\hat{H}w = 0$. For $\hat{Y}^{-1}Yw \in \hat{Y}^{-1}Y\mathcal{W}$, then we have

$$\hat{Y}^*\hat{H}\hat{Y}x = \hat{Y}^*\hat{H}\hat{Y}w.$$

Furthermore, $\hat{Y}^{-1}Y\mathcal{W} \subset \mathcal{N}(\hat{Y}^*\hat{H}Y)$ and by making use of the fact that Y and $\hat{Y}$ are invertible,

$$\hat{z} = dim(\mathcal{N}(\hat{Y}^*BY)) \geq dim(\hat{Y}^{-1}Y\mathcal{W}) = dim(\mathcal{W}) = dim(\mathcal{N}(Y^*\hat{H}Y)) = z.$$

Finally, by switching the roles of $Y^*\hat{H}Y$ and $(\hat{Y}^*\hat{H}\hat{Y})$, it follows that $z \geq z^*$, so, $z = z^*$. $\square$

Assumption 3. *For $t \in \mathbb{C}^{n \times 1}$, the matrix $tt^H = W$ with $W = W^H \geq 0$.*

Theorem 2. *(Dual Characterization of $\mu_X(M)$). Let X be any set of block diagonal matrices as defined in* (8)*. Then, $\mu_X(M) \geq \beta$ if and only if there exists $t \in \mathbb{C}^{n \times 1}$ such that*

$$Re\ tr[(M - \beta I)tt^H(M^H + \alpha I)E] \geq 0, \forall E \in D_x + iG_x.$$

Proof. The proof is similar to that of Theorem 1 by making use of Assumption 3. $\square$

Theorem 3. *For $W \in \mathbb{C}^{m \times n}, W = W^H \geq 0$ there exists $B \geq 0$ s.t. $W^{1/2} = B$.*

Proof. The proof is followed from spectral decomposition Theorem. Indeed, we do have $W = QDQ^*$ with $QQ^* = I = Q^*Q$ and

$$D = diag(\lambda_1, \lambda_2, \ldots, \lambda_n),\ \forall i = 1, \cdots, n.$$

For all $i \in [1, \cdots, n]$, $\lambda_i(W) \geq 0$. Set $B := Q\tilde{D}Q^*$ with $\tilde{D} = diag(\lambda_1^{1/2}, \lambda_2^{1/2}, \ldots, \lambda_n^{1/2})$. In turn, this implies that

$$W^{1/2} = B,\ or\ , B^2 = W. \tag{14}$$

The proof is done. $\square$

Lemma 2. *If $M \in \mathbb{C}^{m \times n}$ has rank one, then $\mu_X(M) = \nu_X(M)$.*

Proof. It is sufficient to show $\nu_X(M) \geq \beta$ implies that $\mu_X(M) \geq \beta$ for $\beta \in [0, \infty)$. For this purpose, consider that $\nu_x(M) \geq \beta$, then from Theorem 3.1, there is a nonzero non-negative definite matrix W such that $W = W^H \geq 0$, which satisfies matrix inequality

$$(M - \beta I)W(M^H + \beta I)E \geq 0,\ \forall E \in DX + iG_X.$$

Next, we pick the largest rank-1 piece of M, that is, $\sigma_1 u_1 \theta_1^H$

$$M = u_1 \left(\begin{array}{c|c} \sigma_1 & 0 \\ \hline 0 & 0 \end{array} \right) \theta_1^H,\ \sigma_1 > 0, u_1, \theta_1 \in \mathbb{C}^{n \times 1}$$

Factorize W as

$$W = tt^H + \hat{W}. \tag{15}$$

In Equation (15), $\hat{W}$ is chosen such that $\hat{W}\theta_1 = 0$, $\hat{W} = \hat{W}^H \geq 0$, $t \in \mathbb{C}^{n \times 1}$. If $B\theta_1 = 0$, then $W = \hat{W}$ for $t = 0$. The PSD-matrix B is defined in Theorem 3. If $B\theta_1 \neq 0$, then take $t = \frac{1}{(\theta_1^H W \theta_1)^{1/2}} W\theta_1$, $\hat{W} = W - \frac{1}{(\theta_1^H W \theta_1)^{1/2}} W\theta_1\theta_1^H W$. This shows that

$$\begin{aligned}
(M - \beta I)tt^H(M^H + \beta I) &= (\sigma_1 u_1 \theta_1^H - \beta I)(W - \hat{W})(\theta_1 u_1^H + \beta I) \\
&= (M - \beta I)W(M^H + \beta I) + \beta^2 \hat{W}.
\end{aligned}$$

Since, by Theorem 3, we have that

$$(M - \beta I)W(M^H + \beta I)E \geq 0,\ \forall E \in D_X + iG_X,$$

then so does

$$(M - \beta I)tt^H(M^H + \beta I)E$$

as the factor $\beta^2 \hat{W}$ is non-negative. $\square$

3.2. Computing Upper Bound of Skewed Structured Singular Value

In this section, we present some new results on the computation of the upper bounds of structured singular values, that is, $\mu_s(\cdot)$.

Theorem 4. *For a given matrix $M \in \mathbb{C}^{m \times n}$ and block diagonal structure*

$$S = \left(\begin{array}{c|c} I_f & 0 \\ \hline 0 & v^t v \end{array} \right).$$

The inequality holds true, that is, $\mu_s(M_s(v)) \leq \sigma_1(M_s(v))$ with

$$M_s(v) := S^{-1} M = \left(\begin{array}{c|c} M_{11} & M_{12} \\ \hline \frac{1}{v} M_{21} & \frac{1}{v} M_{22} \end{array} \right).$$

Proof. For given matrix $M \in \mathbb{C}^{m \times n}$, there exists unitary matrices $U \in \mathbb{C}^{m \times n}, V \in \mathbb{C}^{m \times n}$ such that

$$M = U \left(\begin{array}{c|c} \sigma_1 & 0 \\ \hline 0 & T \end{array} \right) V^H.$$

Take σ_1 and $\theta_1 \in \mathbb{C}^{n \times 1}$ such that $\sigma_1 = \|M\theta_1\|_2 = \|M\|_2$ and $\|\theta_1\|_2 = 1$. Let $u_1 = \frac{M\theta_1}{\sigma_1}$, then $\|u_1\|_2 = \frac{\|M\theta_1\|_2}{\sigma_1} = \frac{\|M\theta_1\|_2}{\|M\|_2} = 1$. Take $U_2 \in \mathbb{C}^{m \times m-1}, V_2 \in \mathbb{C}^{n \times n-1}$ so that, U and V become $U = (u_1 | U_2)$ and $V = (v_1 | V_2)$ with U, V being unitary matrices. Then, the product of matrices $U^H M V$ takes the form as:

$$(u_1 | U_2) M (v_1 | V_2) = \left(\begin{array}{c|c} u_1^H M\theta_1 & u_1^H M V_2 \\ \hline U_2 M\theta_1 & U_2^H M V_2 \end{array} \right) = \left(\begin{array}{c|c} \sigma_1 u_1^H u_1 & u_1^H M V_2 \\ \hline \sigma_1 U_2^H u_1 & U_2^H M V_2 \end{array} \right) = \left(\begin{array}{c|c} \sigma_1 & w^H \\ \hline 0 & B \end{array} \right),$$

with $u_1^H u_1 = 1, U_2^H u_1 = 0, w = V_2^H M^H u_1$, and $B = U_2^H M V_2$.

By taking $w = 0$, we have that

$$\sigma_1^2 = \|M\|_2^2 = \|U^H M V\|_2^2 = \max_{x \neq 0} \frac{\|U^H M V x\|_2^2}{\|x\|_2^2} = \max_{x \neq 0} \frac{\left\| \left(\begin{array}{c|c} \sigma_1 & u^H \\ \hline 0 & B \end{array} \right) x \right\|_2^2}{\|x\|_2^2}.$$

Replace $x \longrightarrow w$, we get

$$\sigma_1^2 \geq \frac{(\sigma_1^2 + w^H w)^2}{(\sigma_1^2 + w^H w)} = \sigma_1^2 + w^H w.$$

In turn, this implies that $w = 0$ and

$$U^H M V = \left(\begin{array}{c|c} \sigma_1 & 0 \\ \hline 0 & B \end{array} \right) \quad \text{or} \quad M = U \left(\begin{array}{c|c} \sigma_1 & 0 \\ \hline 0 & B \end{array} \right) V^H. \tag{16}$$

To see the fact that $\mu_s(M_s) \leq \sigma_1(M_s)$, we have

$$M_s(v) := S^{-1} M = \left(\begin{array}{c|c} M_{11} & M_{12} \\ \hline \frac{1}{v} M_{21} & \frac{1}{v} M_{22} \end{array} \right).$$

The largest singular value $\sigma_1(M_s)$ depends upon v. Furthermore,

$$\left(\begin{array}{c|c} I & M_s(v) \\ \hline M_s^H(v) & I \end{array} \right) > 0 \iff I - M_s(v) I^{-1} M_s^H(v) \geq 0.$$

It follows that

$$\lambda_i(I - M_s(v) M_s^H(v)) \geq 0, \ \forall i$$

or

$$1 - \lambda_i(M_s(\nu)M_s^H(\nu)) \geq 0, \forall i$$

or

$$\lambda_i(M_s(\nu)M_s^H(\nu)) \leq 1, \ \forall i.$$

Finally, we have

$$\sigma_1(M_s(\nu)) \leq 1.$$

The proof is done. $\square$

4. Conclusions

We have introduced some new results for upper bounds of structured singular values and skewed structured singular values along with their dual characterizations. The characterization is defined in the sense that they act as an application for some duality argument in the given convex sets. The accomplished results on the dual characterization of structured and skewed structured singular values can be used to obtain the new direction for the computation of lower bounds of both of these quantities. The numerical treatment on the dual characterization of both structured and skewed structured singular values is our future work. The interested researchers may use this opportunity to carry out their research while making use of this contribution.

Author Contributions: Conceptualization, M.-U.R., J.A. and T.A.; methodology, M.-U.R., J.A. and T.A.; software, M.-U.R., J.A. and T.A.; validation, M.-U.R., J.A. and T.A.; formal analysis, M.-U.R., J.A., T.A., J.K. and W.S.; investigation, M.-U.R., J.A. and T.A.; resources, M.-U.R., J.A. and T.A.; data curation, M.-U.R., J.A. and T.A.; writing—original draft preparation, M.-U.R., J.A. and T.A.; writing—review and editing, M.-U.R., J.A., T.A., J.K. and W.S.; visualization, M.-U.R., J.A. and T.A.; supervision, J.A.; project administration, M.-U.R., J.A. and T.A.; funding acquisition, J.K. and J.A. All authors have read and agreed to the published version of the manuscript.

Funding: This work was financially supported by the Faculty of Science, Burapha University, Thailand (Grant no. *SC06/2564*).

Institutional Review Board Statement: Not applicable.

Informed Consent Statement: Not applicable.

Data Availability Statement: Not applicable.

Acknowledgments: Alzabut is thankful and grateful to Prince Sultan University and OSTİM Technical University for their endless support. J. Kongson would like to gratefully acknowledge Burapha University and the Center of Excellence in Mathematics (CEM), CHE, Sri Ayutthaya Rd., Bangkok, 10400, Thailand, for supporting this research.

Conflicts of Interest: The authors have stated that they have no competing interest.

References

1. Doyle, J. Analysis of feedback systems with structured uncertainties. *IEE Proc. D-Control Theory Appl.* **1982**, *129*, 242–250. [CrossRef]
2. Safonov, M.G. Stability margins of diagonally perturbed multivariable feedback systems. *IEE Proc. D (Control Theory Appl.)* **1982**, *129*, 251–256. [CrossRef]
3. Hinrichsen, D.; Pritchard, A.J. Real and complex stability radii: A survey. In *Control of Uncertain Systems*; Birkhäuser: Basel, Switzerland, 1990; pp. 119–162.
4. Kharitonov, V.L. Asymptotic stability of an equilibrium position of a family of systems of linear differential equations. *Differ. Uraveniya* **1978**, *14*, 1483–1485.
5. Barmish, B.R. New tools for robustness analysis. In Proceedings of the 27th IEEE Conference on Decision Control, Austin, TX, USA, 7–9 December 1988.
6. Polls, M.P.; Olbrot, W.; Fu, M. An overview of recent results on the parametric approach to robust stability. In Proceedings of the 28th IEEE Conference on Decision Control, Tampa, FL, USA, 13–15 December 1989.
7. Siljak, D.D. Parameter space methods for robust control design: A guided tour. *IEEE Trans. Autom. Control* **1989**, *34*, 674–688. [CrossRef]

8. de Gaston, R.R.E.; Safonov, M.G. Exact calculation of the multiloop stability margin. *IEEE Trans. Autom. Control* **1988**, *33*, 156–171. [CrossRef]

9. Fan, M.K.H.; Tits, A.L.; Doyle, J.C. Robustness in the presence of mixed parametric uncertainty and unmodeled dynamics. *IEEE Trans. Autom. Control* **1991**, *36*, 25–38. [CrossRef]

10. Barmish, B.R.; Khargonekar, P.P. Robust stability of feedback control systems with uncertain parameters and unmodeled dynamics. *Math. Control Signals Syst.* **1990**, *3*, 197–210. [CrossRef]

11. Chapellat, H.; Dahleh, M.; Bhattacharyya, S.P. Robust stability under structured and unstructured perturbations. *IEEE Trans. Autom. Control* **1990**, *35*, 1100–1108. [CrossRef]

12. Hollot, C.V.; Looze, D.P.; Bartlett, A.C. Unmodeled dynamics: Performance and stability via parameter space methods. In Proceedings of the 26th IEEE Conference on Decision and Control, Los Angeles, CA, USA, 9–11 December 1987.

13. Braatz, R.P.; Young, P.M.; Doyle, J.C.; Morari, M. Computational complexity of μ calculation. *IEEE Trans. Autom. Control* **1994**, *39*, 1000–1002. [CrossRef]

14. Packard, A.; Fan, M.K.; Doyle, J.C. A *Power Method for the Structured Singular Value*; 1988.

15. Young, P.M.; Doyle, J.C. Computation of mu with real and complex uncertainties. In Proceedings of the 29th IEEE Conference on Decision and Control, Honolulu, HI, USA, 5–7 December 1990; pp. 1230–1235.

16. Young, P.M.; Newlin, M.P.; Doyle, J.C. Practical computation of the mixed μ problem. In Proceedings of the 1992 American Control Conference, Chicago, IL, USA, 24–26 June 1992.

17. Fan, M.K.; Tits, A.L.; Doyle, J.C. Robustness in the presence of joint parametric uncertainty and unmodeled dynamics. In Proceedings of the 1988 American control Conference, Atlanta, GA, USA, 15–17 June 1988.

18. Osborne, E.E. On pre-conditioning of matrices. *J. ACM (JACM)* **1960**, *7*, 338–345. [CrossRef]

19. Packard, A.; Doyle, J. The complex structured singular value. *Automatica* **1993**, *29*, 71–109. [CrossRef]

20. Young, P.M.; Newlin, M.P.; Doyle, J.C. Let's get real. In *Robust Control Theory*; Springer: New York, NY, USA, 1995; pp. 143–173.

21. Luo, J.; Tian, W.; Zhong, S.; Shi, K.; Chen, H.; Gu, X.M.; Wang, W. Non-fragile asynchronous H_∞ control for uncertain stochastic memory systems with Bernoulli distribution. *Appl. Math. Comput.* **2017**, *312*, 109–128. [CrossRef]

22. Kou, G.; Xiao, H.; Cao, M.; Lee, L.H. Optimal computing budget allocation for the vector evaluated genetic algorithm in multi-objective simulation optimization. *Automatica* **2021**, *129*, 109599. [CrossRef]

23. Meinsma, G.; Shrivastava, Y.; Fu, M. A dual formulation of mixed/spl mu/and on the losslessness of (D, G) scaling. *IEEE Trans. Autom. Control* **1997**, *42*, 1032–1036. [CrossRef]

24. Boyd, S.; El Ghaoui, L.; Feron, E.; Balakrishnan, V. *Linear Matrix Inequalities in System and Control Theory*; SIAMIn: Philadelphia, PA, USA, 1994.

 *mathematics*

Article

A Novel Surrogate Model-Based Solving Framework for the Black-Box Dynamic Co-Design and Optimization Problem in the Dynamic System

Qi Zhang, Yizhong Wu * and Li Lu

National Center of Technology Innovation for Intelligent Design and Numerical Control, School of Mechanical Science and Engineering, Huazhong University of Science and Technology, Wuhan 430074, China
* Correspondence: cad.wyz@hust.edu.cn

Abstract: When encountering the black-box dynamic co-design and optimization (BDCDO) problem in the multidisciplinary dynamic system, the finite difference technique is inefficient or even infeasible to provide approximate numerical gradient information for the optimization algorithm since it requires numerous original expensive evaluations. Therefore, a solving framework based on the surrogate model of the state equation is introduced to optimize BDCDO. To efficiently construct the surrogate model, a sequential sampling method is presented on the basis of the successive relative improvement ratio. Meanwhile, a termination criterion is suggested to quantify the convergence of the solution. Ultimately, the newly proposed sampling strategy and termination criterion are incorporated into the BDCDO solving framework to optimize two numerical examples and two engineering examples. The results demonstrate that the framework integrating the proposed sampling strategy and termination criterion has the best performance in terms of the accuracy, efficiency, and computational budget compared to the existing methods.

Keywords: black-box dynamic system; co-design and optimization; surrogate model; sequential sampling; termination criterion

MSC: 93-10

Citation: Zhang, Q.; Wu, Y.; Lu, L. A Novel Surrogate Model-Based Solving Framework for the Black-Box Dynamic Co-Design and Optimization Problem in the Dynamic System. *Mathematics* **2022**, *10*, 3239. https://doi.org/10.3390/math10183239

Academic Editors: Camelia Petrescu and Valeriu David

Received: 19 August 2022
Accepted: 2 September 2022
Published: 6 September 2022

Publisher's Note: MDPI stays neutral with regard to jurisdictional claims in published maps and institutional affiliations.

1. Introduction

Differing from the dynamic optimization problem (DOP), also known as the optimal control problem, in which only the control strategy decision is optimized to improve the performance of the dynamic system [1–3], the dynamic co-design and optimization (DCDO) problem accounts for the bi-directional dependency of physical system design and control system design and includes two types of design variables: plant (or physical) and control [4]. Two categories of co-design methods, nested (or multi-layer optimization) method and simultaneous method, are developed and deployed on the DCDO problem in the engineering applications [5–8]. In those two co-design methods, though the optimization structures are different, the DCDO problem should be transcribed into a finite-dimensional nonlinear programming (NLP) problem via direct transcription [9] to optimize.

However, when solving the DCDO problem of the sophisticated dynamic systems involving multiple disciplines or multiple subsystems, co-design schemes inevitably encounter obstructions such as high computational consumption incurred from the time-consuming system simulations [10]. Moreover, in some engineering practices, dynamic system models are constructed by industrial simulation software or platforms, and the explicit equations of the state in dynamic systems expressed by differential algebraic equations cannot be extracted directly from the dynamic models [11]. The DCDO involving such dynamic system models is referred to as the black-box dynamic co-design and optimization

(BDCDO) problem. Due to the lack of explicit state equation, the finite-difference technique, rather than the automatic differentiation technique, provides approximate Jacobian information matrices for NLP solvers to iteratively optimize BDCDO, which demands significant computational resources to evaluate the dynamic systems and definitely further increases the computational budget of the co-design schemes.

The response surface methods (RSMs) have been proven to be effective tools to address computationally expensive problems in complex static black-box systems [12–16]. Therefore, RSMs are introduced to approximate the black-box dynamic system to alleviate the number of the original system valuations and save computational costs. In attempting to reduce the modeling difficulty and preserve the dynamic properties of the dynamic system, Deshmukh et al. [17] presented the derivative function surrogate modeling methodology to construct surrogate models for the derivative functions of the dynamic system rather than construct surrogate models of the whole system responses [18–20]. In order to build high-fidelity model surrogate models of the derivative functions, Deshmukh et al. [17] used the Latin Hypercube Sampling (LHS) method for sequential sampling in the minimal hypercube space containing the current optimal trajectory to update the surrogate model. Lefebvre et al. [21] averaged the errors of the KRG model after integrating the errors along the current optimal trajectory and then used the values of state variables obtained by inverse error integral of each segment as new samples to update the KRG model. Qiao et al. [22] proposed EFDC sampling method based on KRG model to filter the current trajectory discrete points after error analysis, combine the spatial distance to cluster these discrete points, and select the points with the largest prediction error to update the model. At the same time, some reasonable solution termination criteria also have been investigated to avoid redundant iterations, which contribute little to the accuracy improvement of the solution result. Deshmukh et al. [17] determined whether the solution process stops or not based on the discrepancy between the current and previous iterates. Lefebvre et al. [21] proposed a new metric, dynamical mismatch, to identify whether the solution process is terminated or not. However, computing the dynamical mismatch needs additional sample points and consumes more computational resources. Qiao et al. [22] adopted the accuracy of the surrogate model and the successive relative improvement of the objective function as the stopping plan to assess the convergence of the solution process more comprehensively.

Admittedly, the BDCDO solving framework combined with the above-mentioned sampling strategies and termination criteria indeed reduce the number of samples for constructing the surrogate models of derivative functions to different degrees, but the efficiency of modeling and the robustness of the optimal solution still require further improvement. To this end, a new sequential sampling strategy based on the successive relative improvement ratio of the discrete trajectory points and maximizing distances between the nearest sample points, called SRIRMD, is proposed in this work to effectively improve the accuracy of the surrogate models by selecting the points with a large successive relative improvement ratio among the discrete trajectory points as new samples. Meanwhile, maximizing the minimum distances between new samples and existing samples can ensure the uniform distribution of all sample points. In addition, according to the fundamental observation that the state trajectories tend to coincide during the solving process of dynamic optimization problems, a new termination criterion, named the state trajectory overlap ratio (STOR), is presented to quantify the convergence and intuitively reflect the convergence trend of the solution in the iterative process. Finally, two numerical examples, one 3-DOF robot co-design and optimization problem and one horizontal axis wind turbine co-design and optimization problem, are solved by the means of the BDCDO solving framework integrated with the SRIRMD sampling strategy and the STOR termination criterion. The results demonstrate that the BDCDO solving framework combining the SRIRMD sampling strategy and the STOR termination criterion has the best performance compared to existing methods and can obtain more accurate and robust solutions with fewer sample points, improving the solution efficiency and reducing the computational budget.

The rest of this paper is organized as follows. Section 2 reviews the dynamic optimization problem and its direct solving method and the Kriging technique. Section 3 introduces the BDCDO solving framework combining the new sampling strategy and termination criterion. Section 4 verifies the feasibility and efficiency of the BDCDO solving framework through two numerical examples and two engineering examples. The conclusions are revealed in the last section.

2. Background

2.1. Dynamic Co-Design and Optimization Problem and Its Direct Solving Method

The objective of the dynamic co-design and optimization (DCDO) problem is to solve the optimal input vectors of physical design parameters $\mathbf{x}_p^*$ and control variables $\mathbf{u}^*(t)$ that minimizes the system performance index. The standard form of DCDO based on the simultaneous method is described as follows [23,24]:

$$\min_{\mathbf{x}_p, \mathbf{u}(t)} \quad J(\mathbf{x}_p, \mathbf{u}(t)) = \phi(\mathbf{x}_p, \xi(t_0), \xi(t_f), t_0, t_f) + \int_{t_0}^{t_f} L(\mathbf{x}_p, \xi(t), \mathbf{u}(t), t)dt$$

$$s.t. \quad \dot{\xi}(t) = \mathbf{f}(\mathbf{x}_p, \xi(t), \mathbf{u}(t), t)$$
$$\Psi(\xi(t_0), t_0, \xi(t_f), t_f) = 0 \tag{1}$$
$$\mathbf{g}(\mathbf{x}_p, \xi(t), \mathbf{u}(t), t) \le 0$$
$$\mathbf{u}_L \le \mathbf{u}(t) \le \mathbf{u}_U$$
$$\mathbf{x}_L \le \mathbf{x}_p \le \mathbf{x}_U$$

where J is the response of a cost function that consists of a Mayer term $\phi(\cdot)$ and Lagrange term $L(\cdot)$. $t \in [t_0, t_f]$ denotes the time horizon, and t_0 and t_f are initial time and terminal times. $\xi(t_0)$ and $\xi(t_f)$ indicate the initial and terminal states of the system, while $\xi(t)$ and $\mathbf{u}(t)$ are vectors of the state variables and control inputs at moment t. DCDO is subject to several different constraints such as state equations $\dot{\xi}(t) = \mathbf{f}(\mathbf{x}_p, \xi(t), \mathbf{u}(t), t)$, boundary constraints Ψ, and path constraints $\mathbf{g}$. Among these three constraints, the state equations and path constraints are continuous constraints that must be satisfied during the entire time period, while the boundary constraints are discrete constraints that only need to be satisfied at the moments t_0 and t_f. Finally, the vectors of the physical design parameters $\mathbf{x}_p$ and control inputs $\mathbf{u}(t)$ enforce the interval constraints $[\mathbf{x}_L, \mathbf{x}_U]$ and $[\mathbf{u}_L, \mathbf{u}_U]$, respectively.

In the direct solving approach of the DCDO, the vectors of the state variables $\xi(t)$, plant design parameters $\mathbf{x}_p$, and control inputs $\mathbf{u}(t)$ are discretized at the time grid nodes by means of the DT. Thus, the DCDO is transformed into an NLP, as shown below.

$$\min_{\mathbf{x}_p, \Xi, \Theta} \quad J(\mathbf{x}_p, \Xi, \Theta) = \phi(\mathbf{x}_p, \xi(t_0), \xi(t_f), t_0, t_f) + \sum_{k=0}^{N} \omega_k \cdot L(t, \mathbf{x}_p, \Xi(k), \Theta(k))$$

$$s.t. \quad \mathbf{D} \cdot \Xi = \mathbf{f}(\mathbf{x}_p, \Xi, \Theta) \tag{2}$$
$$\Psi(\xi(t_0), t_0, \xi(t_f), t_f) = 0$$
$$\mathbf{g}(\mathbf{x}_p, \Xi, \Theta) \le 0$$

where Ξ and Θ are the discrete matrices of the state variables and control inputs in the time domain, ω_k is the integration weight, and $\mathbf{D}$ is the differential matrix specified in different pseudospectral methods [25,26]. When solving the BDCDO of the dynamic system based on the surrogate models of the derivative functions, the right hand-side functions of the state equations are approximated by the surrogate models. Hence, replacing the derivative function $\mathbf{f}(\cdot)$ in Equation (2) with the surrogate model $\hat{\mathbf{f}}(\cdot)$ forms a computationally inexpensive expression:

$$\mathbf{D} \cdot \Xi = \hat{\mathbf{f}}(\mathbf{x}_p, \Xi, \Theta) \tag{3}$$

2.2. Kriging Technique

In view of the efficiency and effectiveness of the Kriging technique in approximating low-dimensional problems, as well as providing prediction errors at arbitrary points [27], the Kriging technique is adopted to construct the surrogate model in the BDCDO. When training the model, the state variables, physical design parameters, and control variables $\mathbf{X} = [\mathbf{x}_p, \xi, \mathbf{u}]^T$ are fed into the model, and the output are the valuations of the derivative functions $\mathbf{f}(\mathbf{X})$ in the state equation.

The standard Kriging model has two main components: the regression function and the stochastic process [28]. The expression is formulated as follows:

$$\hat{f}(\mathbf{X}) = \mathbf{F}^T(\mathbf{X})\beta + z(\mathbf{X}) \tag{4}$$

where $\mathbf{F}^T(\mathbf{X})$ contains a series of regression functions, and β is a trend coefficient vector. $z(\mathbf{X})$ denotes a random process with a mean of 0 and variance σ_z^2. The spatial covariance function between the stochastic processes $z(\mathbf{X}_i)$ and $z(\mathbf{X}_j)$ can be expressed as

$$\text{cov}[z(\mathbf{X}_i), z(\mathbf{X}_j)] = \sigma_z^2 \mathbf{G}(\theta, \mathbf{X}_i, \mathbf{X}_j) \tag{5}$$

where $\mathbf{X}_i$ and $\mathbf{X}_j$ are two different points in the design space, $\mathbf{G}$ is the Gaussian spatial correlation function, and θ is the corresponding vector of correlation coefficients. The values of $\mathbf{G}$ and $\mathbf{F}$ at sample points constitute matrices $\mathbf{R} = \mathbf{G}(\mathbf{X}_i, \mathbf{X}_j)$ and $\mathbf{S} = \mathbf{F}(\mathbf{X}_i)$. According to the unbiased estimator theory, the least squares solution of the regression model is

$$\hat{\beta} = (\mathbf{S}^T \mathbf{R}^{-1} \mathbf{S})^{-1} \mathbf{S}^T \mathbf{R}^{-1} \mathbf{Y} \tag{6}$$

and the maximum likelihood estimation of variance is

$$\hat{\sigma}_z^2 = \frac{1}{m}(\mathbf{Y} - \mathbf{S}\hat{\beta})^T \mathbf{R}^{-1}(\mathbf{Y} - \mathbf{S}\hat{\beta}) \tag{7}$$

where $\mathbf{Y} = [\hat{f}(\mathbf{X}_i)]$, $i = 1, 2, \ldots, m$.

Thus, Equation (4) is translated into

$$\hat{f}(\mathbf{X}) = \mathbf{F}^T(\mathbf{X})\beta + \mathbf{r}^T(\mathbf{X})\mathbf{R}^{-1}(\mathbf{Y} - \mathbf{S}\hat{\beta}),\ \mathbf{r}(\mathbf{X}) = [\mathbf{G}(\theta, \mathbf{X}, \mathbf{X}_1), \ldots, \mathbf{G}(\theta, \mathbf{X}, \mathbf{X}_m)]^T \tag{8}$$

Suppose $\mathbf{d} = \mathbf{S}^T \mathbf{R}^{-1} \mathbf{r} - \mathbf{S}$, the predictor of the mean square error (MSE) is calculated as follows:

$$MSE = \sigma_z^2(1 + \mathbf{d}^T(\mathbf{S}^T \mathbf{R}^{-1} \mathbf{S})^{-1}\mathbf{d} - \mathbf{r}\mathbf{R}^{-1}\mathbf{r}) \tag{9}$$

3. The BDCDO Solving Framework

The BDCDO solving framework based on the surrogate model of the derivative function mainly consists of two parts: refining the surrogate model for the right hand-side function of the state equation and solving the black-box dynamic co-design and optimization (BDCDO) problem based on the surrogate model. In the loop of approximating the derivative function, the initial model is built according to the initial samples set and then updated by the sequential sampling method. In the loop of solving the BDCDO, the BDCDO is discretized into NLP at time grid nodes, then the approximate Jacobian information matrices based on the model are delivered for the SQP algorithm to solve the NLP. For the purpose of efficiently constructing the surrogate model of the derivative function, the new sampling method based on the successive relative improvement ratio of the discrete trajectory points and maximize the distances between the sample points, termed SRIRMD, is elaborated in this section. Meanwhile, to quantify the convergence and intuitively reflect the convergence trend of the solution, a new termination criterion on the basis of the fact that the state trajectories tends to coincide during the solving process, called the state trajectory overlap ratio (STOR), is also introduced in this section. Finally, the newly proposed sampling strategy, SRIRMD, and termination criterion, STOR, are integrated into the solving framework of BDCDO.

3.1. Adaptive Sequential Sampling Strategy

In the static optimization problem, the optimal result is a point; hence, single sampling strategies that focus on improving the accuracy of the surrogate model near the current optimal point are widely used, while batch sampling strategies are evidenced to be unable to enhance the performance of updating model [29]. However, the scenario is quite different in the dynamic optimization problem since the optimal results are time-dependent control curves and the corresponding state trajectories. Adding a new sample point during each iteration contributes less to improving the convergence rate of the state trajectory but instead increases the number of modeling and optimization throughout the solution process and consumes more computational resources.

Motivated by the sequential sampling strategy in the static optimization problem, the adaptive sampling strategy applied to the DOP should concentrate on how to improve the accuracy of the local region where the current state trajectory is located in order to avoid redundant sampling in the uninteresting area. To this end, it is necessary to pick informative points in the vicinity of the current trajectory to update the surrogate model of the derivative function. Fortunately, the discrete trajectory points (DTPs) on the current state trajectory offer a large number of candidate samples. However, it is not wise to add all DTPs to the samples set, because (a) the expensive evaluation of all DTPs requires a lot of computational effort, and (b) closer DTPs are less helpful to improving the accuracy but increase the complexity of the model. Hence, a new sequential sampling strategy based on the successive relative improvement ratios of the DTPs and maximizing the distances between the sample points, called SRIRMD, is presented in this work. The SRIRMD sampling strategy prioritizes picking the points with large successive relative improvement ratios among the DTPs as new samples to refine the surrogate model. Meanwhile, maximizing the minimum distances between new samples and existing samples can guarantee that all sample points are distributed uniformly. The specific steps of the SRIRMD method are listed below.

Step 1: Obtain the initial values V_I and the optimal values V_O at the discrete points of the current state trajectory and calculate the successive relative improvement ratios (srir) of all discrete points.

$$SRIR = \left\{ srir \middle| srir = \left| V_O^i - V_I^i \right| / \left| V_O^i \right|, i = 1, 2, \ldots, m \right\} \tag{10}$$

where m is the number of discrete points of the current trajectory.

Step 2: Generate the candidate samples set S_{SRIR} by eliminating the points whose srir is smaller than the allowable deviation factor β from the DTPs.

$$S_{SRIR} = \{DTPi | sriri \geq \beta, sriri \in SRIR\} \tag{11}$$

Step 3: Calculate the distance matrix $\mathbf{D}_{min}$ of all candidate samples in S_{SRIR} to the nearest point in the existing samples set $S^{(l)}$.

Step 4: Select new sample x_{new} by the following sampling criterion.

$$\max srir(x_{new}) \cdot \mathbf{D}_{min}(x_{new}) \tag{12}$$

Step 5: Add the new sample x_{new} into samples set $S^{(l)}$ and delete x_{new} in S_{SRIR}.

Step 6: Repeat Step 3–5 until the required number of samples are picked, and the samples set is updated to $S^{(l+1)}$.

Step 7: Terminate the current round of sampling.

Figure 1 exhibits the process of selecting new sample points from the DTPs employing the SRIRMD strategy. The dotted lines are the previous state trajectories, the dots are the discrete points of those previous state trajectories, and the red solid lines are the current optimal state trajectories. The new points sampled by SRIRMD method are plotted in the form of black stars, and these samples are mainly distributed in the areas with large successive relative improvement ratios while being evenly spread.

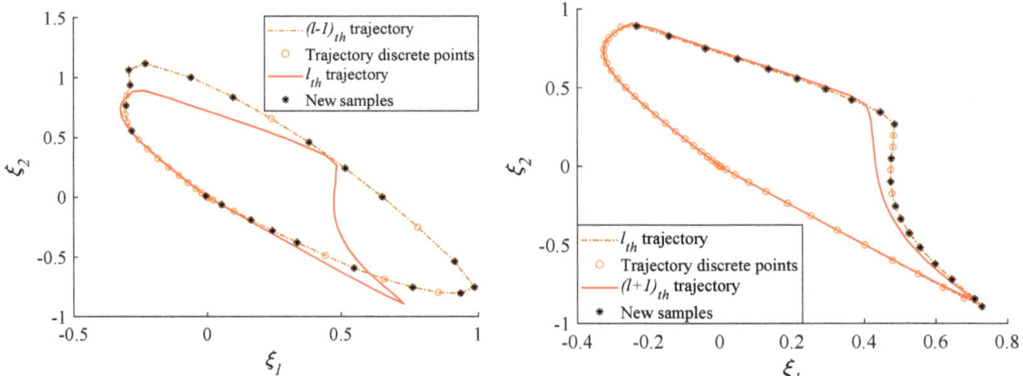

Figure 1. Schematic diagram of SRIRMD sampling strategy.

3.2. Termination Criterion: The State Trajectory Overlap Ratio

The state trajectory overlap ratio, STOR, is designed to intuitively assess the convergence of state trajectories and serve as the termination criterion. The formula for STOR is expressed as follows:

$$A = \prod_{i=1}^{d} \alpha_i \tag{13}$$

where d is dimension of state variables. α_i means the state component trajectory overlap ratio, which reflects the trajectory overlap ratio of the i_{th} state component in two successive iterations. As shown in Figure 2, S^* is the trajectory of the state component ξ_i obtained in the previous iteration, and S^{**} is the trajectory of ξ_i in the current iteration. The α_i of the state component ξ_i can be calculated by the lengths of $\widehat{AB}$ and $\widehat{AC}$, and the specific formula is expressed in Equation (14).

$$\alpha_i = \frac{L_{\widehat{AB}}}{L_{\widehat{AC}}} \tag{14}$$

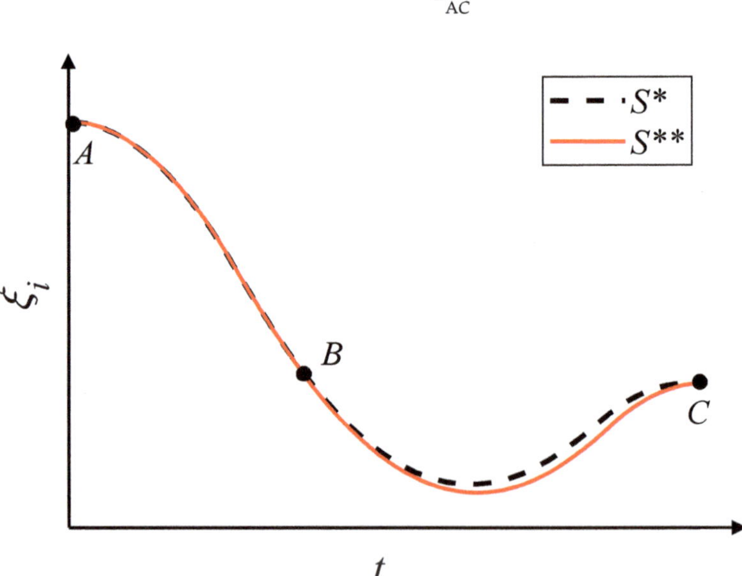

Figure 2. Schematic diagram of the state component trajectory overlap ratio.

Equation (14) denotes the formula for calculating the α_i in the state space. However, the lengths of the trajectories $\overset{\frown}{AB}$ and $\overset{\frown}{AC}$ are not convenient to calculate in the actual computation procedure. To facilitate the calculation, Equation (14) can be mapped from the state space to the time domain since the state trajectories and time points correspond (i.e., each time point corresponds to a specific trajectory value). Hence, Equation (14) is replaced by Equation (15) to compute α_i.

$$\alpha_i = \frac{L_{\overset{\frown}{AB}}}{L_{\overset{\frown}{AC}}} \tag{15}$$

where T_0 and T_1 are represent the overlap and non-overlap periods of trajectories S^* and S^{**} in the time domain T, respectively. T_0 and T_1 can be computed by the following expression.

$$
\begin{aligned}
T_0 &= \left\{ t \;\middle|\; \frac{\left|\dot{\zeta}_i(\mathbf{x}_p^{**}(t),\boldsymbol{\xi}^{**}(t),\mathbf{u}^{**}(t);SM^{**}) - \dot{\zeta}_i(\mathbf{x}_p^{*}(t),\boldsymbol{\xi}^{*}(t),\mathbf{u}^{*}(t);SM^{*})\right|}{\left|\dot{\zeta}_i(\mathbf{x}_p^{**}(t),\boldsymbol{\xi}^{**}(t),\mathbf{u}^{**}(t);SM^{**})\right|} > \beta, t \in T \right\} \\[2mm]
T_1 &= \left\{ t \;\middle|\; \frac{\left|\dot{\zeta}_i(\mathbf{x}_p^{**}(t),\boldsymbol{\xi}^{**}(t),\mathbf{u}^{**}(t);SM^{**}) - \dot{\zeta}_i(\mathbf{x}_p^{*}(t),\boldsymbol{\xi}^{*}(t),\mathbf{u}^{*}(t);SM^{*})\right|}{\left|\dot{\zeta}_i(\mathbf{x}_p^{**}(t),\boldsymbol{\xi}^{**}(t),\mathbf{u}^{**}(t);SM^{**})\right|} \le \beta, t \in T \right\}
\end{aligned}
\tag{16}
$$

where SM^* and SM^{**} are surrogate models of derivative function in the previous and current iterations. β is the allowable deviation factor of the trajectory, which indicates trajectories S^* and S^{**} are also regarded as coincide when their error rate at moment t are not greater than β. It is worth noting that $\beta = 0.01$ in this research. The time domain T is a continuous time series, and it could be uniformly discretized as $T = \left\{ t_0, t_1, \ldots, t_\tau, \ldots, t_f \right\}$ to accelerate computations. Thus, Equation (16) is converted into Equation (17).

$$
\begin{aligned}
T'_0 &= \left\{ t_\tau \;\middle|\; \frac{\left|\dot{\zeta}_i(\mathbf{x}_p^{**}(t),\boldsymbol{\xi}^{**}(t_\tau),\mathbf{u}^{**}(t_\tau);SM^{**}) - \dot{\zeta}_i(\mathbf{x}_p^{*}(t),\boldsymbol{\xi}^{*}(t_\tau),\mathbf{u}^{*}(t_\tau);SM^{*})\right|}{\left|\dot{\zeta}_i(\mathbf{x}_p^{**}(t),\boldsymbol{\xi}^{**}(t_\tau),\mathbf{u}^{**}(t_\tau);SM^{**})\right|} > \beta, \tau = 0,1,2,\ldots,f \right\} \\[2mm]
T'_1 &= \left\{ t_\tau \;\middle|\; \frac{\left|\dot{\zeta}_i(\mathbf{x}_p^{**}(t),\boldsymbol{\xi}^{**}(t_\tau),\mathbf{u}^{**}(t_\tau);SM^{**}) - \dot{\zeta}_i(\mathbf{x}_p^{*}(t),\boldsymbol{\xi}^{*}(t_\tau),\mathbf{u}^{*}(t_\tau);SM^{*})\right|}{\left|\dot{\zeta}_i(\mathbf{x}_p^{**}(t),\boldsymbol{\xi}^{**}(t_\tau),\mathbf{u}^{**}(t_\tau);SM^{**})\right|} \le \beta, \tau = 0,1,2,\ldots,f \right\}
\end{aligned}
\tag{17}
$$

Furthermore, Equation (14) for calculating α_i is transformed into Equation (18).

$$\alpha_i = \frac{n_{T'_1}}{n_{T'_0} + n_{T'_1}} \tag{18}$$

where $n_{T'_0}$ and $n_{T'_1}$ denote the number of elements in the sets T'_0 and T'_1, respectively.

According to the above series of transformations, including mapping and discretization, the calculation of α_i is finally transformed into the statistics of the elements in the sets. Obviously, the denser the time domain T is divided in Equation (17), the more accurate α_i is in Equation (18). At the same time, the following two theorems are derived on the basis of the above definition about A and α_i.

Theorem 1. *The sufficient condition for the convergence of the state trajectory overlap ratio A is that all the state component trajectory overlap ratio α_i converge.*

Proof: From the definitions of A and α_i, it follows that $A \in [0,1], \alpha_i \in [0,1]$. From the perspective of the mathematics, convergences of A and α_i implies that the values of A and α_i converge to 1, i.e.,

$$A \text{ and } \alpha_i \text{ converge} <=> A \to 1, \alpha_i \to 1 \tag{19}$$

i. If the dimension of the state variables $d = 1$, $A = \alpha_1$, the theorem is established.
ii. If the dimension of the state variables $d > 1$, suppose

$$A^k = \prod_{i=1,2,..,k-1,k+1,..,d} \alpha_i \tag{20}$$

When $k = d$,

$$A = A^{d-1} \cdot \alpha_d \tag{21}$$

where $A^{d-1} \in [0,1]$ and $\alpha_d \in [0,1]$. Without considering the specific value of A^{d-1}, only $\alpha_d \to 1$, then A may converge to 1. Conversely, if $\alpha_d \to 1$, then A definitely does not converge to 1 whether or not A^{d-1} converges to 1. Similarly, let k be $d-2, d-3, .., 2$, respectively, so that the sufficient condition for $A \to 1$ is $\alpha_i \to 1, i = 1, 2, .., d$. That means the sufficient condition for the convergence of A is that all α_i converge. $\square$

Theorem 2. *When the state trajectory overlap ratio A converges, every state component trajectory overlap ratio α_i is greater than or equal to A.*

Proof:

i.   If the dimension of the state variables $d = 1$, $A = \alpha_1$, the theorem is established.

ii.   If the dimension of the state variables $d > 1$, Equation (18) can be obtained based on Equations (20) and (21).

$$\alpha_k = \frac{A}{A^k} \tag{22}$$

Suppose A is converged, then A^k is also converged (i.e., $A^k \to 1$), since $A^k \subset A$. Obviously, $\alpha_k \geq A$ can be deduced from Equation (22). Similarly, let k be $1, 2, \ldots, d$, respectively, then $\alpha_i \geq A, i = 1, 2, \ldots, d$ can be proved. That means when A converges, all α_i are greater than or equal to A.

According to the definition of the state trajectory overlap ratio A and the proving procedures of the above two theorems, it could be concluded that taking A as the convergence criterion for the BDCDO solving framework has the following advantages: (a) directly reflects the convergence trend of state trajectory in the iterative solving process, and $A \in [0,1]$, which also quantifies the convergence; and (b) guarantees the convergences of state component trajectories. The state solution of the BDCDO converges only if all the state component trajectories converge. $\square$

3.3. The BDCDO Solving Framework Combined with SRIRMD and STOR

By integrating the SRIRMD sampling strategy and the STOR termination criterion proposed in this work into the BDCDO solving framework, a new BDCDO solving method, named SRIRMD-STOR, is generated as depicted in Figure 3. The input and output of the SRIRMD-STOR method are shown in Table 1, and the specific realization of the SRIRMD-STOR method is listed in Table 2.

Table 1. Input and output of the SRIRMD-STOR method.

Input	The upper and lower bounds of physical design parameters $\mathbf{x}_p$, state variables $\boldsymbol{\xi}$ and control inputs $\mathbf{u}$. The initial guess values $[\mathbf{x}_p^{(0)}, \boldsymbol{\Xi}^{(0)}, \boldsymbol{\Theta}^{(0)}]$ of physical design parameters $\mathbf{x}_p$, state variables $\boldsymbol{\xi}$ and control inputs $\mathbf{u}$. The termination criterion threshold A_0 for the SRIRMD-STOR method. The solving tolerance and max iteration for the DOP solvers [30].
Output	The optimal design point of physical design parameters $\mathbf{x}_p$. The optimal trajectories of state variables $\boldsymbol{\xi}$. The optimal curves of control inputs $\mathbf{u}$.

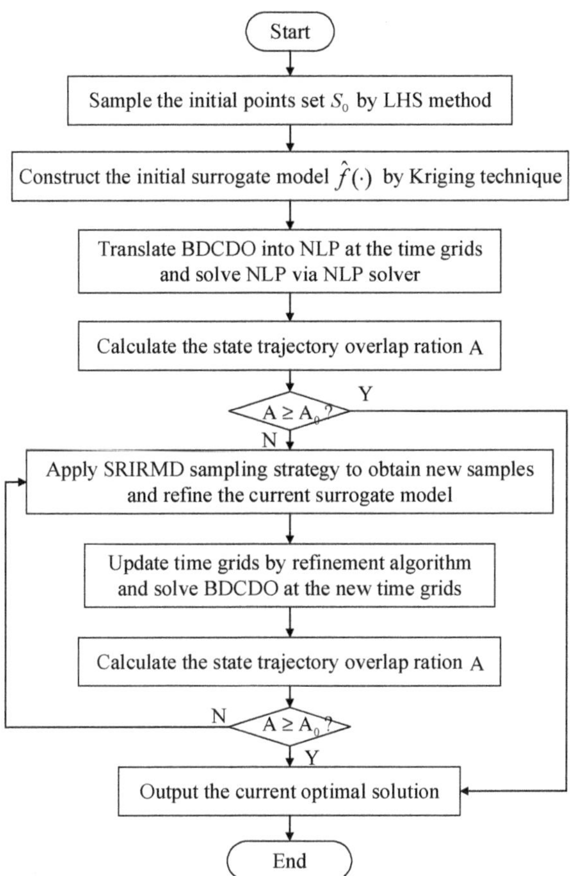

Figure 3. The flowchart of the BDCDO solving framework SRIRMD-STOR.

Table 2. The specific realization of the SRIRMD-STOR method.

The SRIRMD-STOR Method

Step 1: Apply LHS method to sample initial points set S^0 in the design domain consisting of feasible regions of physical design parameters $\mathbf{x}_p$, state variables ξ, and control inputs $\mathbf{u}$.

Step 2: Construct the initial surrogate model $\hat{f}^{(0)}$ of the derivative function by Kriging technique [31] with the initial samples set S^0.

Step 3: Transcribe the BDCDO into the NLP at the time grid nodes via DT, then solve NLP based on the initial guess values of $[\mathbf{x}_p^{(0)}, \Xi^{(0)}, \Theta^{(0)}, \hat{f}^{(0)}]$ and obtain the current optimal plant design parameters, state trajectories, control curves, and performance index $[\mathbf{x}_p^{(1)}, \Xi^{(1)}, \Theta^{(1)}, J^{(1)}]$.

Step 4: Calculate the state component trajectory overlap ratios α_i of all state variables according to the initial guess trajectories and the current optimal trajectories, then calculate the state trajectory overlap ratio A. If $A > A_0$, terminate the solving process; otherwise, go to Step 5.

Step 5: Employ the SRIRMD strategy to select new samples x_{new} from the current DTPs, update the samples set S^1, and rebuild the surrogate model $\hat{f}^{(1)}$.

Step 6: Update the time grid nodes using the grid optimization algorithm and translate the BDCDO into the NLP at the new time grid nodes.

Step 7: Solve NLP based on the current values of plant design parameters; state trajectories and control inputs, and current model $[\mathbf{x}_p^{(l)}, \Xi^{(l)}, \Theta^{(l)}, \hat{f}^{(l)}]$; and acquire the latest optimal plant parameters, state trajectories, control curves, and performance index. Note: l starts from 1.

Step 8: Calculate α_i and A. If $A > A_0$, stop the solving process; otherwise, go to Step 5.

4. Numerical Examples

In this section, two numerical examples are used to verify the feasibility and effectiveness of the BDCDO solving framework combined with the SRIRMD sampling strategy and the STOR termination criterion, also called the SRIRMD-STOR method for short. The first numerical example is a classical multidimensional nonlinear dynamic optimization problem involving six state variables and two control inputs. The second example is a numerical nonlinear dynamic co-design and optimization problem that is sensitive to the accuracy of the grid optimization, i.e., it has high requirements on the number and location of the discrete grid nodes of the optimization problem. To solve those two numerical tests, STOR A is regarded as the termination criterion, and the threshold of A is set to 0.95.

4.1. Example 1: A Mathematical Nonlinear Dynamic Optimization Problem

The mathematical model of the this nonlinear dynamic optimization problem [32] can be described as follows:

$$
\begin{aligned}
\min \quad & J = \int_0^{t_f} [L_2 + I_2 + \tfrac{1}{2}B_1 u_1^2 + \tfrac{1}{2}B_2 u_2^2]dt \\
s.t. \quad & \dot{S} = \Lambda - \tfrac{13}{30000}SI_1 - \tfrac{0.029}{30000}SI_2 - 0.0143S \\
& \dot{T} = 2u_1 L_1 - 0.0143T + (1 - 0.5(1 - u_2))I_1 - \tfrac{13}{30000}TI_1 - \tfrac{0.029}{30000}TI_2 \\
& \dot{L}_1 = \tfrac{13}{30000}SI_1 - 0.6143L_1 - 2u_1 L_1 + 0.4(1 - u_2)I_1 + \tfrac{13}{30000}TI_1 - \tfrac{0.029}{30000}L_1 I_2 \\
& \dot{L}_2 = 0.1(1 - u_2)I_1 - 1.0143L_2 + \tfrac{0.029}{30000}(S + L_1 + T)I_2 \\
& \dot{I}_1 = 0.5L_1 - 1.0143L_1 \\
& \dot{I}_2 = L_2 - 0.0143I_2 \\
& N = S + L_1 + L_2 + I_1 + I_2 + T = 30000
\end{aligned}
\tag{23}
$$

where the state variables $\xi = [S, T, L_1, L_2, I_1, I_2]^T$. The upper and lower bounds of control inputs $\mathbf{u} = [u_1, u_2]^T$ are $\mathbf{u}_U = [0.95, 0.95]^T$ and $\mathbf{u}_L = [0.05, 0.05]^T$. The finial time t_f is set as 5. To solve this DOP based on the mathematical model, the maximum number of iterations of the NLP solver is set to 15 and the solution accuracy is set to 10^{-4} to obtain the exact solution 5152.1. Although the mathematical model provides the explicit expressions of the state equation, it can still be treated as a black-box dynamic optimization problem and solved using the BDCDO solving framework. Hence, in addition to the SRIRMD sampling strategy, the HS [15], TEI [19], and EFDC [20] sampling strategies are also utilized to construct the surrogate models for the derivative functions of the state equation. The termination criterion working with those sampling strategies are the model accuracy at DTPs $\varepsilon < 0.001$ and the successive relative improvement of the objective function $\Delta J < 0.1$, called MASRI. Hence, the BDCDO solving methods combined with those sampling strategies and MASRI are named HS-MASRI, TEI-MASRI, EFDC-MASRI, and SRIRMD-MASRI, respectively. To validate the robustness of these methods, each method is tested ten times. In each test, the initial samples for those methods are the same, the number of initial points $N_0 = 50$, and maximum number of new samples per iteration $\Delta_N = 20$.

The test results of different methods are listed in Table 3, and the comparisons are depicted in Figure 4. *NoS* denotes the sample point size (or number of expensive valuations), and J is the value of the performance index. From Table 1 and Figure 4, it can be observed that the HS-MASRI, TEI-MASRI, EFDC-MASRI, and SRIRMD-MASRI methods require an average of 350, 320, 223, and 170 samples to construct the surrogate models of the derivative functions, respectively. the average performance indexes are 5187.0, 5156.0, 5157.8, and 5152.7. While the SRIRMD-STOR method only needs 145 samples to construct the surrogate models, the average performance index is 5152.9. Compared to HS-MASRI, TEI-MASRI, and EFDC-MASRI, SRIRMD-STOR has the smallest error with the exact value. In SRIRMD-MASRI and SRIRMD-STOR, the sampling strategies are the same, and the termination criterion are different. SRIRMD-MASRI has a little higher solving accuracy than SRIRMD-STOR, while needing many more samples to construct the surrogate models, which indicates that the termination criterion for STOR is more effective than the termination criterion for MASRI by avoiding redundant iterations. As a result, for this numerical example, the BDCDO solving framework combined with SRIRMD and STOR can obtain a more robust and accurate approximate solution with less samples compared to the other methods.

Table 3. The test results of the different methods in Example 1.

Method	HS-MASRI		TEI-MASRI		EFDC-MASRI		SRIRMD-MASRI		SRIRMD-STOR	
Index	NoS	J	NoS	J	NoS	J	NoS	J	NoS	J
	1	350	5161.4	346	5152.3	185	5153.4	153	5152.4	130	5153.1
	2	350	5186.3	240	5157.5	249	5159.7	207	5153.0	170	5153.6
	3	350	5177.1	325	5169.4	230	5153.3	193	5152.8	150	5153.1
	4	350	5166.0	319	5156.4	225	5155.0	183	5152.6	159	5152.6
Test	5	350	5170.8	315	5152.4	238	5165.7	177	5152.8	159	5153.1
	6	350	5178.0	345	5154.3	215	5155.0	184	5152.7	167	5153.0
	7	350	5162.8	346	5155.5	225	5160.7	150	5153.0	130	5153.2
	8	350	5184.7	267	5152.6	231	5157.6	152	5152.3	130	5151.8
	9	350	5224.6	346	5156.3	197	5155.7	145	5152.4	121	5152.6
	10	350	5258.2	346	5153.3	230	5161.9	150	5152.5	130	5153.0

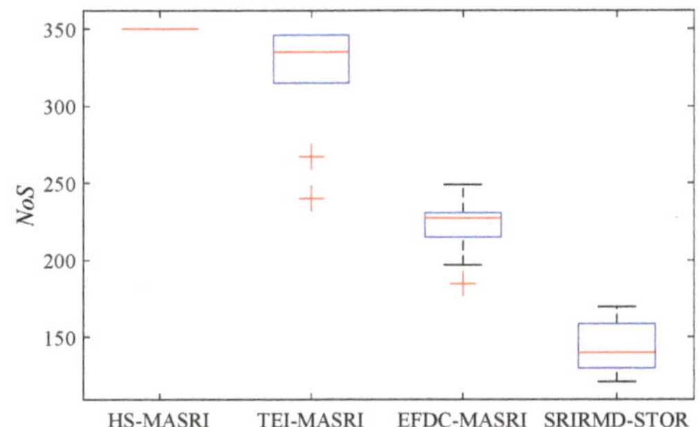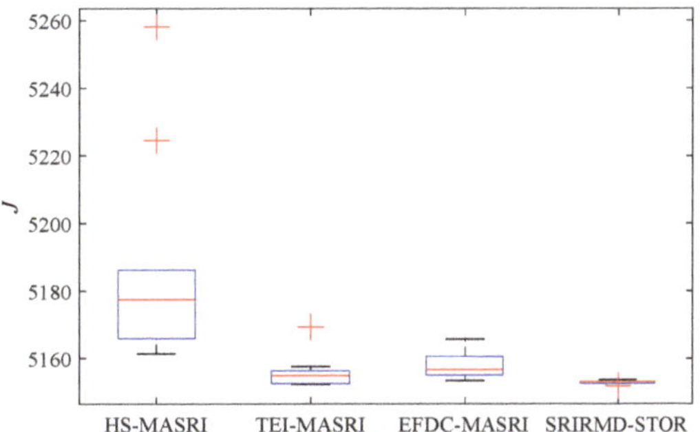

Figure 4. Box-plots of test results of different methods in Example 1.

To visualize the sampling outcomes of the HS-MASRI, TEI-MASRI, EFDC-MASRI, and SRIRMD-STOR methods, the distribution of sample points in different methods and the phase diagrams of optimal trajectories between some state variables are displayed in Figures 5 and 6. The black dots are the initial sample points, the black stars are the new samples obtained via different sampling methods, and the red solid lines are the state trajectories optimized based on the surrogate models. From Figures 5 and 6, it can be observed that the new sample points in the TEI, EFDC, and SRIRMD sampling strategies are located in the vicinity of the state trajectories, except for the HS strategy.

Figure 7 draws the iterative processes of the trajectories of partial state components in the SRIRMD-STOR method. As can be viewed from Figure 7, the trajectories of different state components converge gradually with the iterations.

Figure 8 records the convergence processes of the state component trajectory overlap ratio and the state trajectory overlap ratio in the SRIRMD-STOR method, $\alpha_1, \alpha_2, \alpha_3, \alpha_4, \alpha_5, \alpha_6$, and A are the trajectory overlap ratios of the state components S, T, L_1, L_2, I_1, I_2, and state ξ, respectively. According to Figure 8, the state trajectory overlap ratio A converges to 1 with the convergences of all state components α_i, and $\alpha_i \geq$ A, which verifies Theorem 1 and Theorem 2.

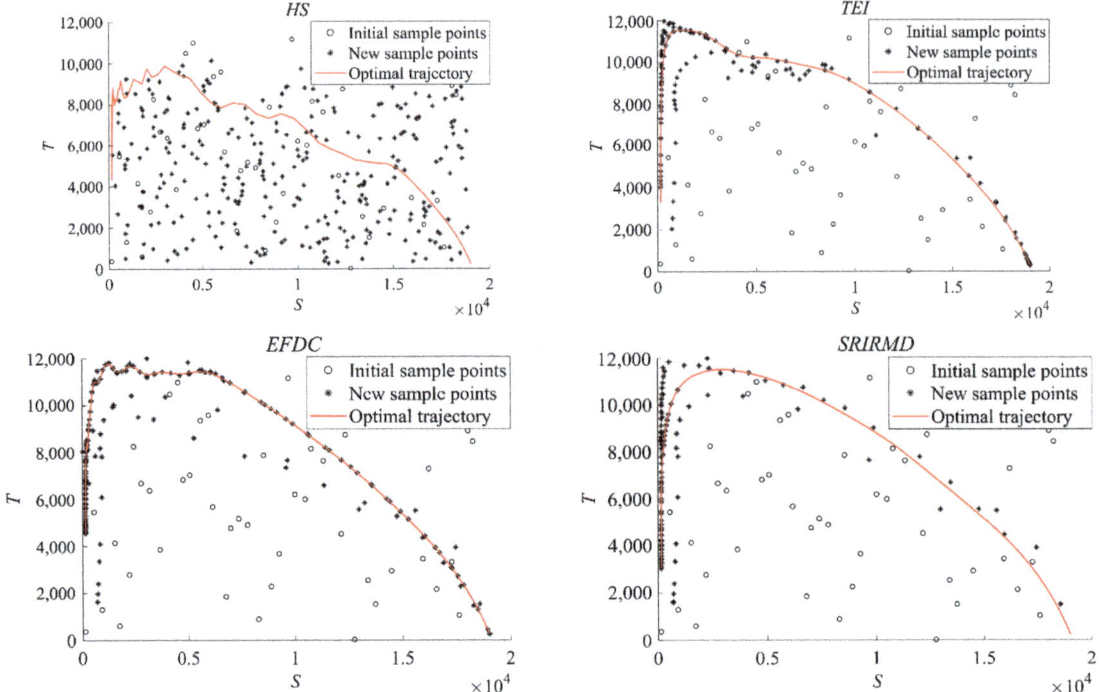

Figure 5. The phase diagrams of optimal trajectories and distribution of samples between state variables S and T.

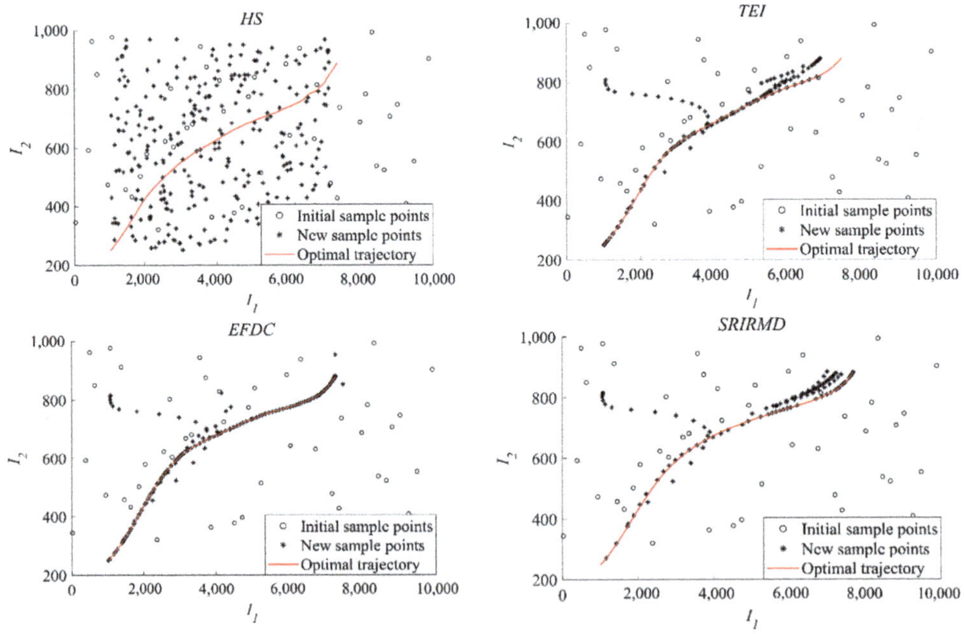

Figure 6. The phase diagrams of optimal trajectories and distribution of samples between state variables I_1 and I_2.

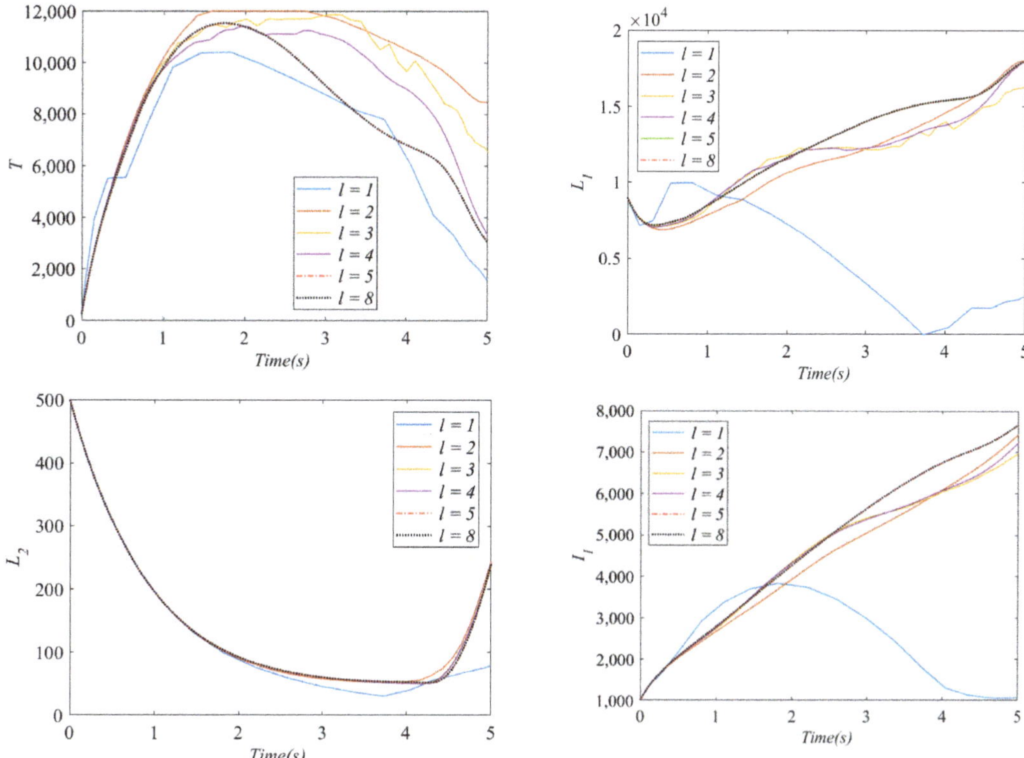

Figure 7. Trajectory iterative processes of state components S, L_1, L_2, and I_1.

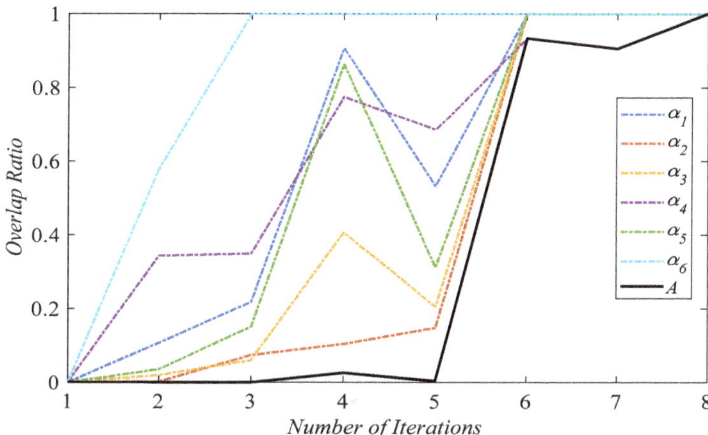

Figure 8. The convergence processes of A and all α_i in the numerical example 1.

Moreover, to better compare the exact solution based on the mathematical model and the approximate solution based on the surrogate model, Figures 9 and 10 show the comparison of the trajectories of the exact and approximate solutions about the state variables and control curves in Example 1, with the dashed lines being the exact solution and the thick solid lines being the approximate solution obtained by the SRIRMD-STOR method. Although the approximate and exact solutions of the control variables do not completely coincide, the trends remain consistent, and the effects on the trajectories of state variables are within acceptable limits.

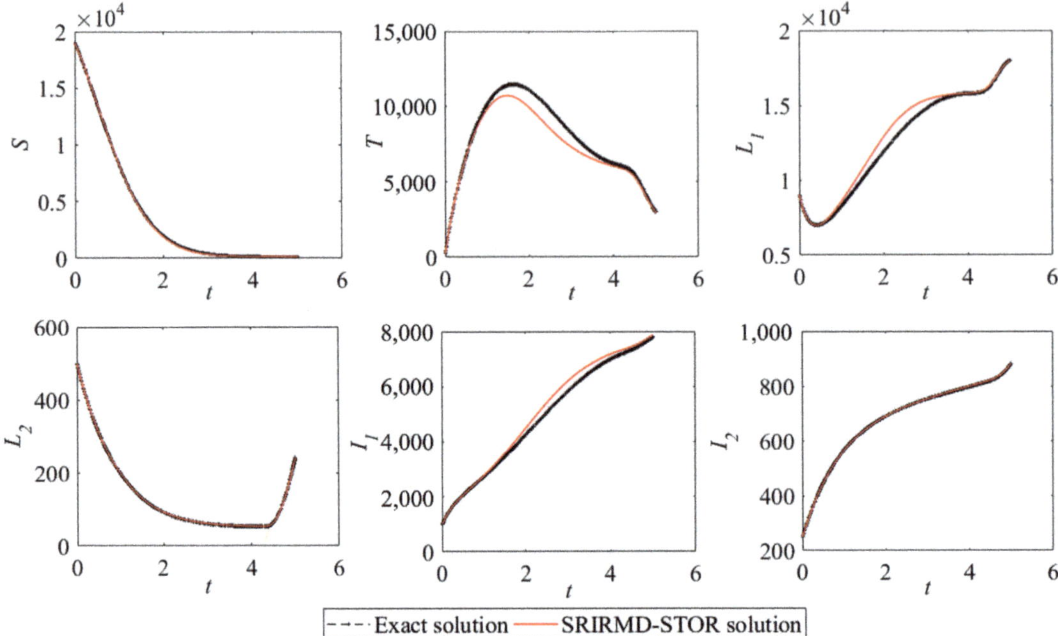

Figure 9. The exact solution and approximate solution of the state variables.

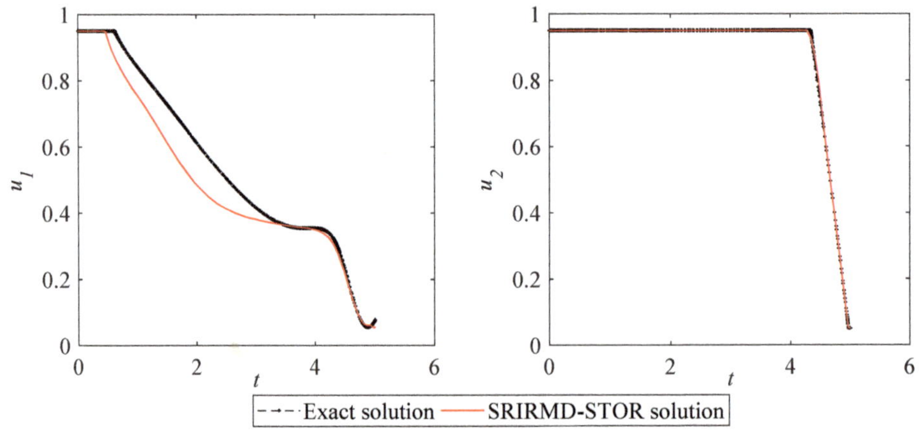

Figure 10. The exact solution and approximate solution of the control variables.

4.2. Example 2: A Mathematical Nonlinear Dynamic Codesign and Optimization Problem

Example 2 is a dynamic co-design and optimization problem with one physical design parameter, one control input, and three state variables, the mathematical model of the problem is as follows

$$
\begin{aligned}
\min_{\mathbf{x}_p, \mathbf{u}(t)} \quad & J = \sin(\mathbf{x}_p) \cdot \cos(\mathbf{x}_p) \cdot t_f \\
s.t. \quad & \dot{x} = v \cdot \sin(u) \\
& \dot{y} = -v \cdot \cos(u) \\
& \dot{v} = 10 \cos(u) \\
& x_p \in [-\pi/2, \pi/2], u \in [-\pi/2, \pi/2], \\
& x \in [50, -50], y \in [0, -50], v \in [0, 6]
\end{aligned}
\tag{24}
$$

where only the objective function contains the plant design parameter $\mathbf{x}_p$. The state variables ξ include $[x, y, v]$, and the initial value and final value of ξ are $\xi(t_0) = [0, 0, 0]$ and $\xi(t_f) = [2, -2, 6]$, respectively. To solve this DOP based on the mathematical model, the maximum number of iterations of the NLP solver is set to 20, the solution accuracy is set to 10^{-6}, the optimal plant design parameter is -0.7854, and the optimal performance index is -50.00. Similar to Example 1, the SRIRMD-STOR, TEI-MASRI, EFDC-MASRI, and SRIRMD-MASRI methods are utilized to solve this example.

The optimal physical design parameters and optimal objective values by different methods are listed in Table 4. As can be observed from Table 2, the approaches based on the surrogate model significantly reduce the number of valuations of the mathematical model and save computational budget. The TEI-MASRI, SRIRMD-MASRI, and SRIRMD-STOR methods obtain the optimal physical parameters and objective values, and the SRIRMD-STOR method performs better in terms of efficiency with the assistant of the termination criterion STOR.

Table 4. The computational cost, optimal plant parameters, and optimal objective values in Example 2.

	Mathematical Model	TEI-MASRI	EFDC-MASRI	SRIRMD-MASRI	SRIRMD-STOR
NoS	1255262	93	55	100	90
X_P	-0.7854	-0.7854	1.5708	-0.7854	-0.7854
J	-50.00	-50.00	0.0000	-50.00	-50.00

To intuitively demonstrate the sampling effect of the SRIRMD sampling strategy, the distribution of sample points and the phase diagram of the optimal trajectory between y and v are drawn in Figure 11. The left figure plots the distribution of all sample points (initial sample points and new sample points), and the right figure displays the positions of new samples, as well as a local zoomed-in view of the left figure near the optimal trajectory. It can be found from Figure 11 that the new sample points in the SRIRMD sampling strategy are all located in the vicinity of the state trajectory.

Figure 12 is the iteration processes of the trajectories of the state components x and v in the SRIRMD-STOR method. As it can be observed in Figure 12, the trajectories of different state components converge gradually with the iterations, and the trajectories of the 12th and 13th iterations tend to coincide. Meanwhile, Figure 13 exhibits the control curves obtained using the SRIRMD-based method.

Figure 14 records the convergence processes of the state component trajectory overlap ratio and the state trajectory overlap ratio in the SRIRMD-STOR method. $\alpha_1, \alpha_2, \alpha_3$ and A are the trajectory overlap ratios of the state components x, y, v, and state ξ, respectively. In light of Figure 14, the state trajectory overlap ratio A converges to 1 with the convergences of all α_i, and $\alpha_i \geq$ A, which verifies Theorem 1 and Theorem 2.

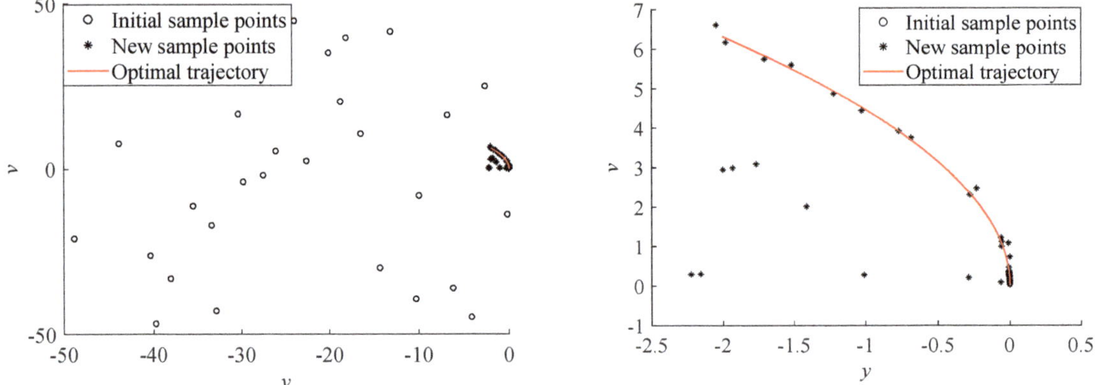

Figure 11. The phase diagrams of the optimal trajectory and distribution of the samples between state variables y and v.

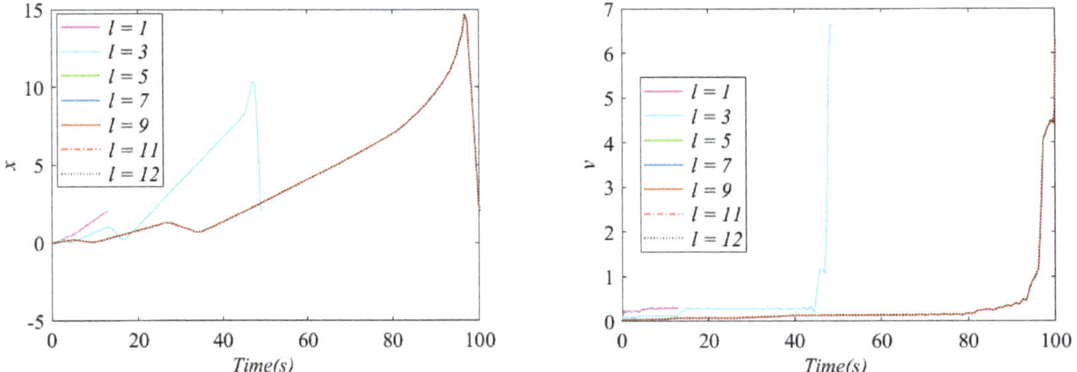

Figure 12. Trajectory iterative processes of state components x and v.

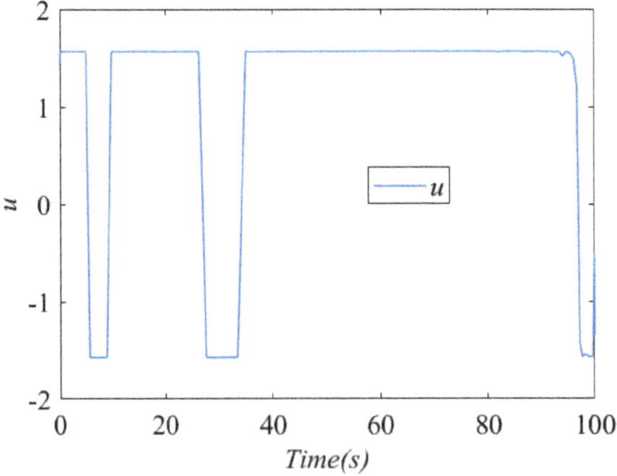

Figure 13. The solution of the control variable u.

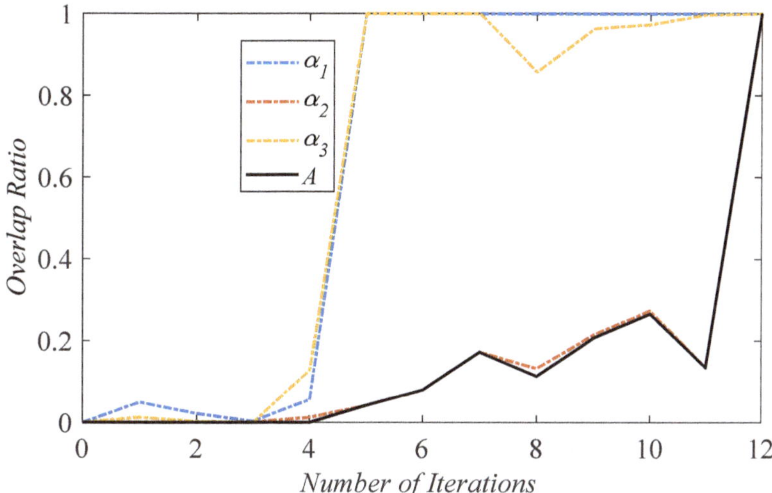

Figure 14. The convergence processes of A and all α_i in the numerical example 2.

5. Engineering Examples

In this section, the SRIRMD-STOR method is applied to optimize the 3-DOF Manutec r3 system and the horizontal axis wind turbine (HAWT) system. Different from the numerical examples, the derivative functions of the state equations are unknown in those dynamic systems, since only the simulation models can be accessed. In addition to the methods proposed in this work, other existing methods are also used to optimize the 3-DOF Manutec r3 system and HAWT system.

5.1. The BDCDO of 3-DOF Manutec r3 System

The industrial robot Manutec r3 [33], as shown in Figure 15, has six links, and only the three degrees of freedom associated with positioning are considered in this research, simplifying the robotic system to a three degrees of freedom (DOF) dynamic system. The goal of the 3-DOF robot co-design and optimization problem is to identify the optimal solution in the design space and state space so that the robot can move from the initial position to the specified position in the minimum time while satisfying the associated state equation constraints, upper and lower bound constraints of plant parameters, and state and control variables. The trajectory optimization formulation of the 3-DOF Manutec r3 system is described as follows:

$$
\begin{aligned}
\min_{\mathbf{x}_p, \mathbf{u}(t)} \quad & J = t_f \\
\text{s.t.} \quad & \dot{\boldsymbol{\xi}}(t) = \mathbf{f}(\mathbf{x}_p, \boldsymbol{\xi}(t), \mathbf{u}(t), t) \\
& \mathbf{x}_p \in [\mathbf{x}_L, \mathbf{x}_U] \\
& \boldsymbol{\xi}(t) \in [\boldsymbol{\xi}_L, \boldsymbol{\xi}_U] \\
& \mathbf{u}(t) \in [\mathbf{u}_L, \mathbf{u}_U]
\end{aligned}
\tag{25}
$$

where the plant design parameters $\mathbf{x}_p$ are the lengths of link 1 and link 2 $[L_1, L_2]$. The state variables $\boldsymbol{\xi}$ consists of the relative angles of rotation $[\alpha, \beta, \gamma]$ and the relative angular velocities $[\dot{\alpha}, \dot{\beta}, \dot{\gamma}]$ between the connecting links, and the control variables $\mathbf{u}$ includes the standardized torque controls $[u_1, u_2, u_3]$. The design intervals of the plant parameters $\mathbf{x}_p$ are $L_1 \in [0.4, 0.5]$ and $L_2 \in [0.9, 1.0]$. The initial value and final value of $\boldsymbol{\xi}$ are $\boldsymbol{\xi}(t_0) = [-2, -2.5, -2, 0, 0, 0]$ and $\boldsymbol{\xi}(t_f) = [2, 2.5, 2, 0, 0, 0]$, and the upper and lower bounds of $\boldsymbol{\xi}$ are $\boldsymbol{\xi}_U = [3, 3, 3, 5, 10, 15]$ and $\boldsymbol{\xi}_L = [-3, -3, -3, -5, -10, -15]$. The control variables are subject to interval constraints $\mathbf{u}_U = [10, 10, 10]$ and $\mathbf{u}_L = [-10, -10, -10]$. To solve this problem, the maximum number of iterations of the NLP solver is set to 20, and the solution accuracy is set to 10^{-6}. In the original dynamic model, the physical design parameters are $\mathbf{x}_p = [0.4500, 0.9500]$, and the optimal solution yields the objective value as 0.9082. As with the above example, in addition to the SRIRMD-STOR method, the TEI-MASRI and EFDC-MASRI methods are also applied to optimize the 3-DOF Manutec r3 system. In the SRIRMD-STOR method, the number of initial points is $N_0 = 25$, and the maximum number of new samples per iteration is $\Delta_N = 20$. It is notable that $\varepsilon < 0.001$ and $\Delta J < 0.0001$ in the termination criterions of the TEI-MASRI and EFDC-MASRI methods.

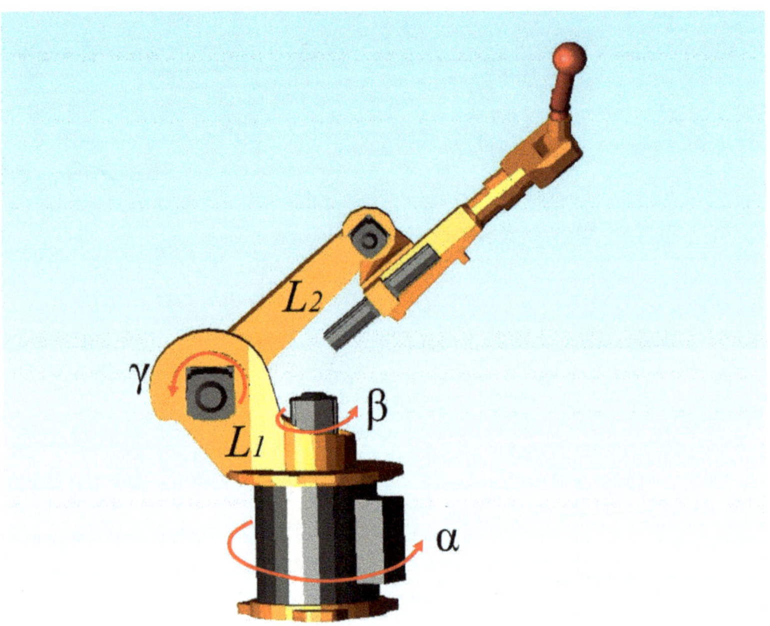

Figure 15. Schematic diagram of a 3-DOF robot.

The optimal physical design parameters and optimal objective values by different methods are presented in Table 5. It can be observed from Table 5 that the surrogate-model-based approaches greatly reduce the number of valuations of the dynamic system and save computational costs compared to the original dynamic-model-based approach. Meanwhile, compared with the original physical design parameters, the optimal physical design parameters obtained by the TEI-MASRI, EFDC-MASRI, SRIRMD-MASRI, and SRIRMD-STOR methods shorten the working time to complete the specified task to a certain extent and improve the efficiency and performance of the robot arm. Among those surrogate model-based methods, the SRIRMD-STOR method obtains the best performance metrics using less samples. Therefore, the BDCDO solving framework combined with SRIRMD and STOR is a better alternative for the co-design and optimization problem of the 3-DOF Manutec r3 system.

Table 5. The computational cost, optimal plant parameters, and optimal objective values in the 3-DOF Manutec r3 system.

	Dynamic Model	TEI-MASRI	EFDC-MASRI	SRIRMD-MASRI	SRIRMD-STOR
NoS	3422	215	256	228	203
$[L_1, L_2]$	[0.4500, 0.9500]	[0.4151, 1.0000]	[0.4121, 0.9339]	[0.4019, 0.9982]	[0.4019, 0.9982]
J	0.9082	0.9067	0.9064	0.9060	0.9060

To graphically demonstrate the sampling outcome of the SRIRMD sampling strategy, the distribution of sample points and the phase diagram of the optimal trajectory between different state variables are shown in Figure 16. The black dots are the initial samples, the black stars are the new samples obtained via SRIRMD, and the red solid lines are the state trajectories optimized based on the surrogate models. As Figure 16 reveals, the new sample points in the SRIRMD sampling strategy are all situated nearby the state trajectories.

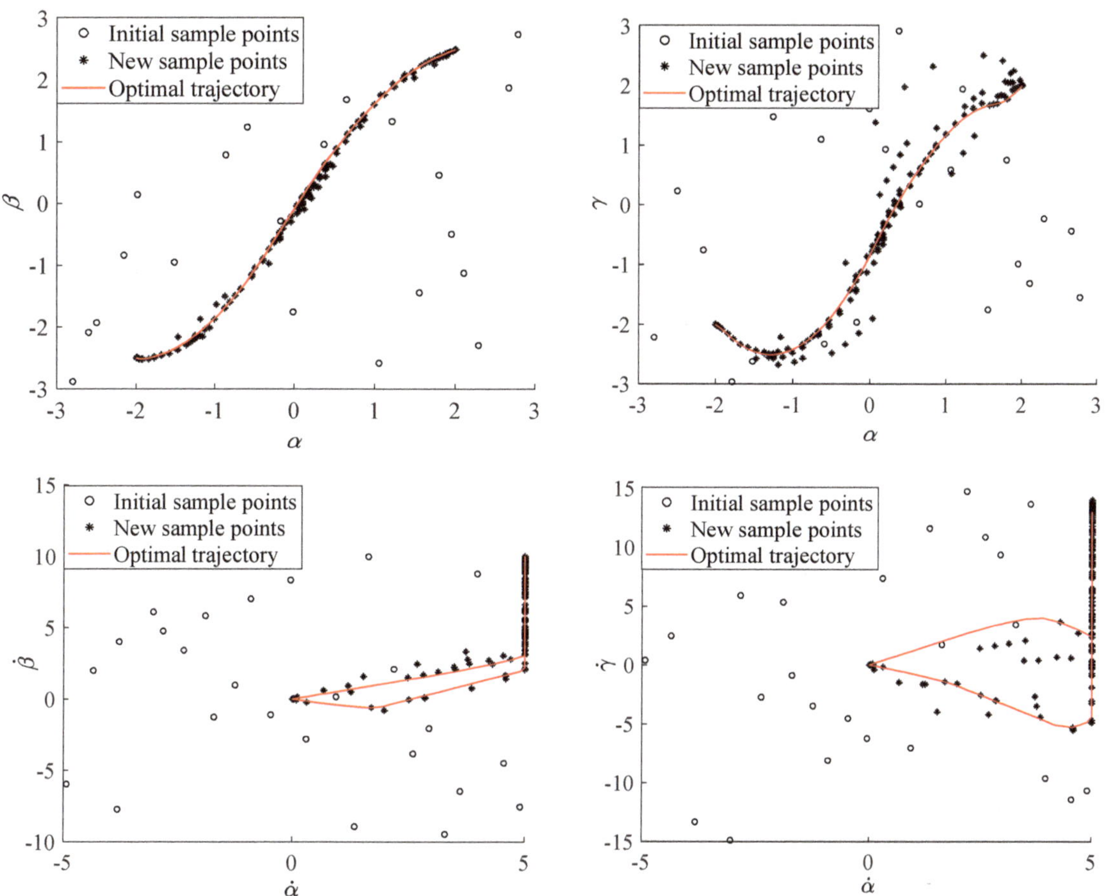

Figure 16. The phase diagrams of the optimal trajectories and distribution of samples between different state variables.

Figure 17 graphs the trajectory iteration processes for the state components $\alpha, \beta, \gamma, \dot{\alpha}, \dot{\beta}$, and $\dot{\gamma}$ in the SRIRMD-STOR method. As visible in Figure 17, the trajectories of the different state components converge gradually as the iterations proceed, and the trajectories of the 17th and 18th iterations tend to coincide. Meanwhile, Figure 18 exhibits the control curves obtained by the SRIRMD method.

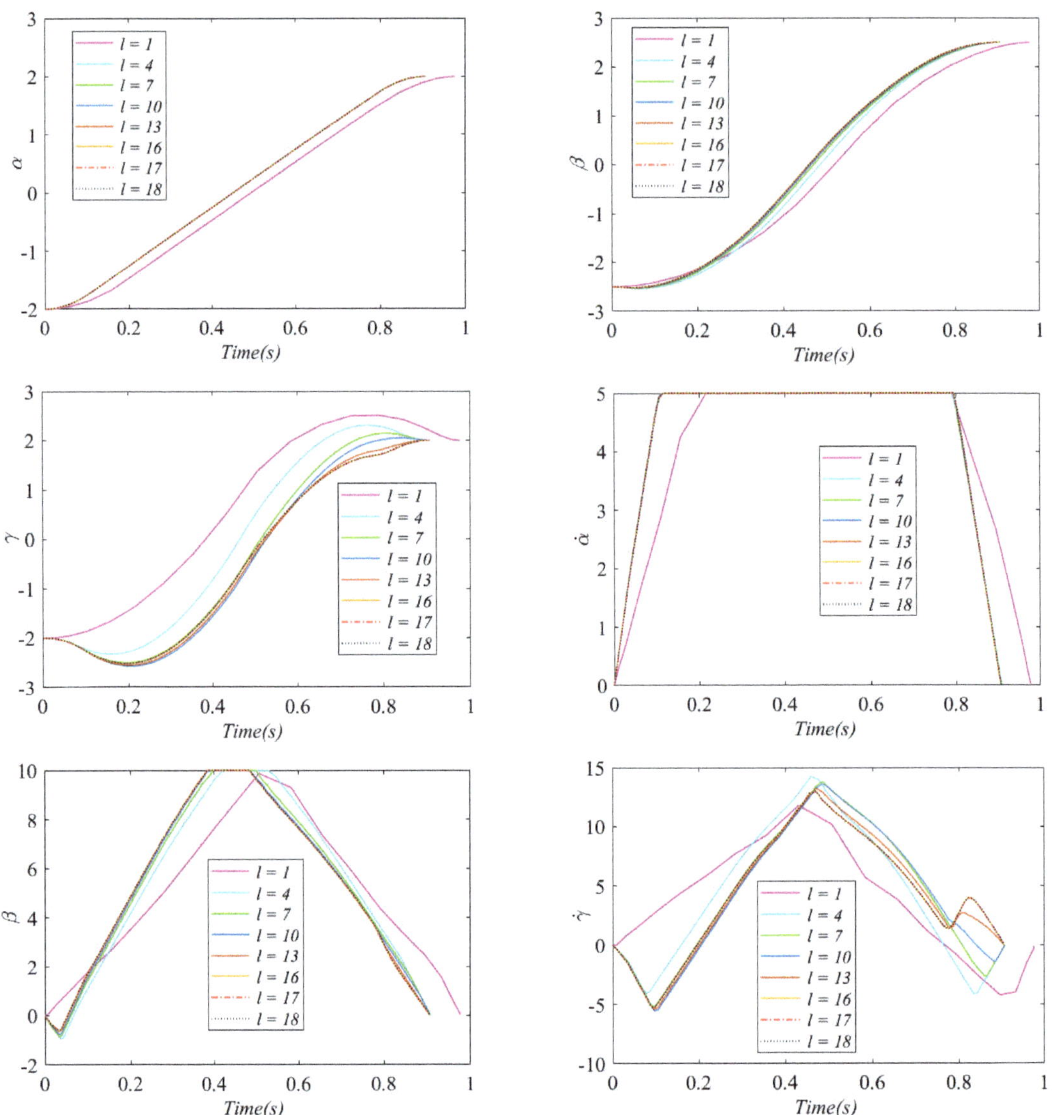

Figure 17. Trajectory iterative processes of the state components $\alpha, \beta, \gamma, \dot{\alpha}, \dot{\beta}$, and $\dot{\gamma}$.

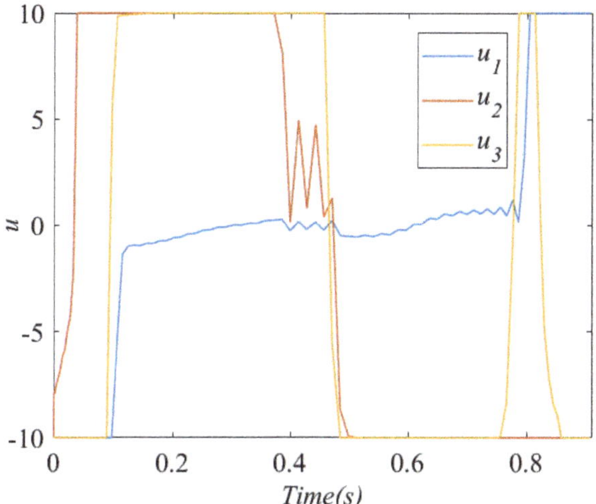

Figure 18. The solution of the control inputs u_1, u_2, u_3.

Figure 19 records the convergence processes of the state component trajectory overlap ratio and the state trajectory overlap ratio in the SRIRMD-STOR method, $\alpha_1, \alpha_2, \alpha_3, \alpha_4, \alpha_5, \alpha_6$, and A are the trajectory overlap ratios of the state components $\alpha, \beta, \gamma, \dot{\alpha}, \dot{\beta}, \dot{\gamma}$, and state ξ, respectively. According to Figure 19, the state trajectory overlap ratio A converges to 1 with the convergences of all α_i, and $\alpha_i \geq$ A, which verifies Theorem 1 and Theorem 2.

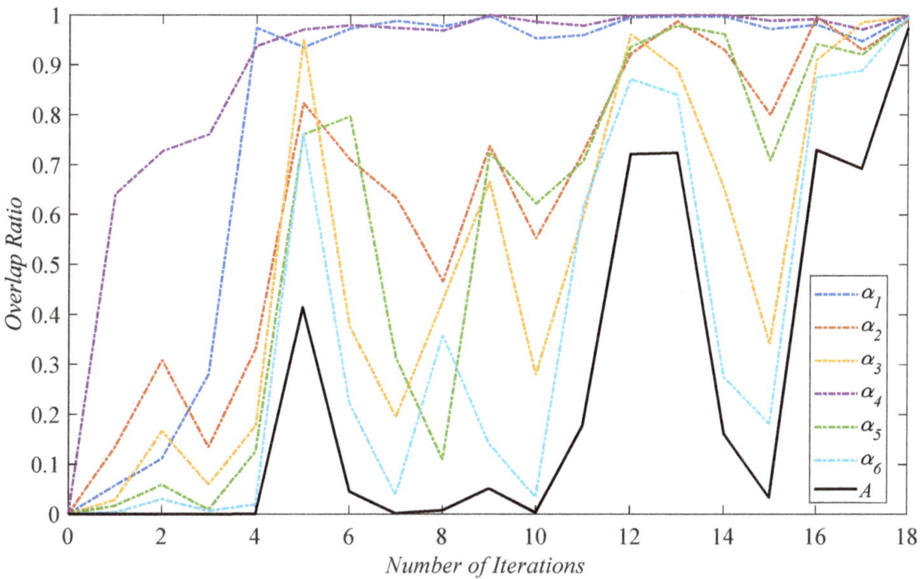

Figure 19. The convergence processes of A and all α_i in the 3-DOF Manutec r3 system.

5.2. The BDCDO of the Horizontal Axis Wind Turbine (HAWT)

The design optimization problem of the HAWT system [4,15,20] is a complex co-design BDOP involving structural parameters and control variables, which can be simulated and estimated by the Advanced Wind Turbine program blade 27 (AWT27) in the Open FAST project. As shown in Figure 20, the structural parameters $\mathbf{x}_p$ in this paper mainly include the hub radius R_h, blade length L_b, and tower height H_t. The control variable **u** is the generator torque G_t. The fore-aft tower-top displacement ζ_1, the side-to-side tower-top displacement ζ_2, the fore-aft tower-top velocity v_1, the side-to-side tower-top velocity v_2, and rotor speed ω are regard as the state variables ξ. The co-design formulation of the HAWT system is expressed as follows:

$$
\begin{aligned}
\min_{\mathbf{x}_p, \mathbf{u}(t)} \quad & J = w_1 m_s(\mathbf{x}_p) + w_2 \int_0^{t_f} (\lambda(t) - \lambda_*(t))^2 dt \\
s.t. \quad & \dot{\xi}(t) = f(\xi(t), \mathbf{x}_p, \mathbf{u}(t), t) \\
& \| \xi_1(t) \|_\infty - \xi_{1\max} \leq 0 \\
& \| \xi_2(t) \|_\infty - \xi_{2\max} \leq 0 \\
& P(V_e) - P_{e\min} \geq 0 \\
& \mathbf{x}_p \in [\mathbf{x}_L, \mathbf{x}_U]
\end{aligned}
\tag{26}
$$

where $m_s(\mathbf{x}_p)$ is the mass of the wind turbine, $\int_0^{t_f} (\lambda(t) - \lambda_*(t))^2 dt$ is the sum of the deviations of the wind blade tip tangential velocity ratio $\lambda(t)$ and the optimal velocity ratio $\lambda_*(t)$ over a period of time, λ is the ratio of leaf tip tangential velocity $\omega \cdot L_b$ to wind speed v, λ_* can be calculated by the power coefficient function, and w_1 and w_2 are the weights of the two terms, respectively. Therefore, the optimization objective of the system is to minimize the sum of the mass and the deviations of speed ratios. What is more, the HAWT system needs to satisfy the structural deflection constraints and $\| \xi_2(t) \|_\infty$. When the wind speed reaches the rated wind speed V_e, the system has to reach the minimum rated power $P_{e\min}$. Since the simulation of the HAWT system involves several disciplines, the RHS function $\dot{\xi}(t) = f(\xi(t), \mathbf{X}_p, \mathbf{u}(t), t)$ of the system is highly nonlinear, and AWT27 takes several seconds to execute a simulation valuation.

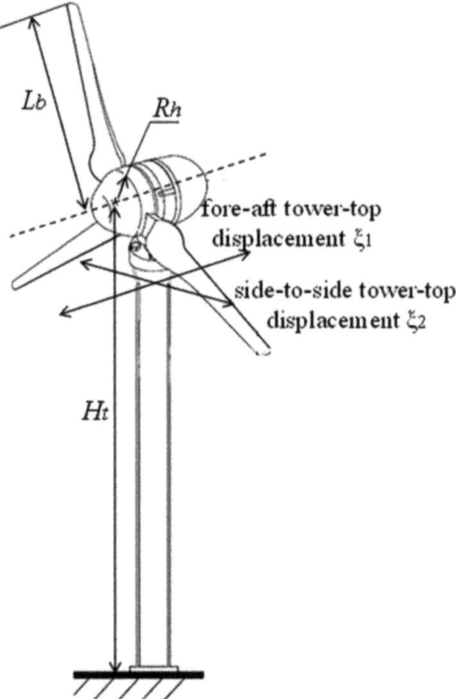

Figure 20. Schematic diagram of the HAWT.

The co-design and optimization problem of HAWT is optimized based on the finite difference technique without using the surrogate model, and the standard optimal objective 805.4801, hub radius $R_h = 1.2000$, blade length $L_b = 13.7330$, and tower height $H_t = 32.3944$ are obtained. Qiao et al. [20] adopted the HS-MASRI, EFDC-MASRI, and TEI-MASRI methods to solve this problem, while the SRIRMD method is used to build the surrogate model of a derivative function in the HAWT system. In the SRIRMD-STOR method, the number of initial points $N_0 = 100$, and maximum number of new samples per iteration $\Delta_N = 10$. The optimization outcomes of those different methods are listed in Table 6. Obviously, the original system-based optimization solution method is costly and necessitates extensive simulation evaluations of AWT27. In contrast, the surrogate model-based optimization methods significantly reduce the number of running valuations of AWT27 and decrease the computational costs. In these model-based optimization solutions, the plant parameters converge to the standard solution $[1.2000, 13.7330, 32.3944]$. Due to the accuracy of the surrogate models, the objective values obtained by various methods are different. Nevertheless, the errors with the standard solution are within the allowed range. More importantly, it is clear that the SRIRMD-STOR method uses the least number of samples in addressing the co-design problem of the HAWT system while it has the higher solution accuracy, improving the solution efficiency and conserving the computational resources.

Table 6. The computational cost, optimal plant parameters, and optimal objective values in the HAWT system.

	Original System	HS-MASRI	EFDC-MASRI	TEI-MASRI	SRIRMD-MASRI	SRIRMD-STOR
NoS	546400	540	291	460	240	210
$[R_h \ L_b \ H_t]$			[1.2000,13.7330,32.3944]			
J	805.4801	806.0783	806.3677	807.1469	805.3558	805.3550
Absolute Error	0	0.5982	0.8876	1.6668	0.1243	0.1251

The wind speed curve input to the HAWT system for a certain time period is displayed in Figure 21. The evolution of the generator torque G_t, the fore-aft tower-top displacement ξ_1, the side-to-side tower-top displacement ξ_2, and the rotor speed ω with this wind speed curve are shown in Figure 22. As can be observed from the figure, in order to optimize the HAWT system, the trend of the control and state variables obtained from the optimization solution is highly consistent with the trend of the wind speed.

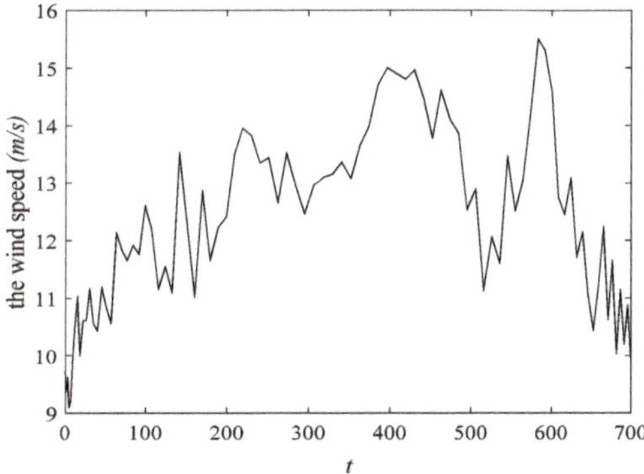

Figure 21. The input of wind speed.

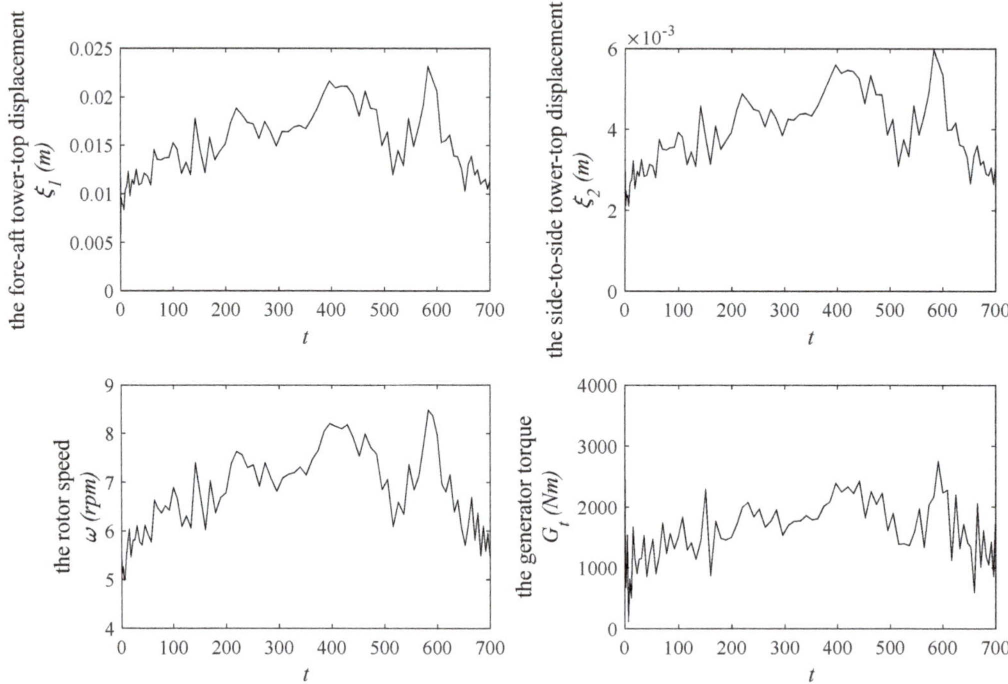

Figure 22. The trends of the state and control variables.

Figure 23 records the convergence processes of the state component trajectory overlap ratio and the state trajectory overlap ratio in the SRIRMD-STOR method, and $\alpha_1, \alpha_2, \alpha_3, \alpha_4, \alpha_5$, and A are the trajectory overlap ratios of the state components $\xi_1, \xi_2, v_1, v_2, \omega$, and state ξ, respectively. According to Figure 23, the state trajectory overlap ratio A converges to 1 with the convergences of all α_i in the 11*th* iteration. $\alpha_i \geq$ A, which verifies Theorems 1 and 2.

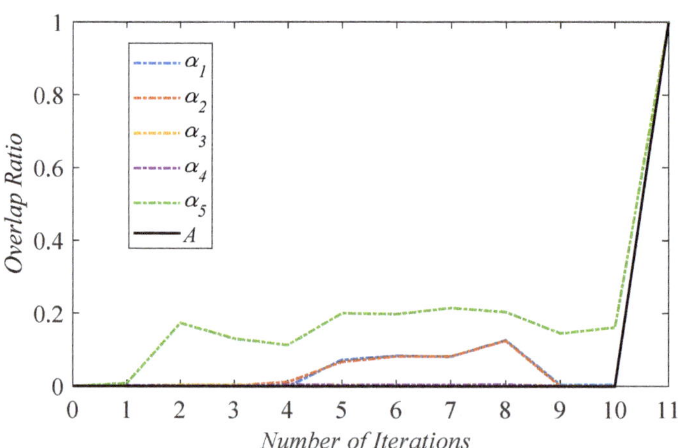

Figure 23. The convergence processes of A and all α_i in the HAWT system.

6. Conclusions

The BDCDO solving framework based on the surrogate models of the derivative functions in the state equation is an effective approach to solve the black-box dynamic co-design and optimization problem. For efficient construction of the surrogate models for the right hand-side functions of the state equation, a novel adaptive sequential sampling strategy, called SRIRMD, was proposed in this work. This strategy refines the surrogate models by selecting suitable sample points from the trajectory discrete points. At the same time, to quantify the convergence and intuitively reflect the convergence trend of the solution during the solving process, a new termination criterion, called the state trajectory overlap ratio (STOR), was also introduced. Finally, the BDCDO solving framework combined with SRIRMD and STOR was utilized to address two numerical optimization problems and two engineering co-design and optimization problems. The numerical examples indicate that the SRIRMD sampling strategy proposed in this work was superior to the existing sampling strategies with respect to both the solution accuracy and robustness. The 3-DOF robot co-design and optimization problem and the horizontal axis wind turbine co-design and optimization problem revealed that the BDCDO solving framework combined with SRIRMD and STOR is a feasible and efficient tool to optimize the black-box dynamic systems. In summary, the proposed sampling strategy and the termination criterion in this research not only improve the efficiency of the BDCDO solving framework but also save the computational budget.

Author Contributions: Methodology, Q.Z. and Y.W.; Software, Q.Z.; Writing—original draft, Q.Z.; and Writing—review and editing, Y.W. and L.L. All authors have read and agreed to the published version of the manuscript.

Funding: This work was supported by the National Key Research and Development Program of China (Grant No. 2018YFB1700905) and National Natural Science Foundation of China (Grant No. 51575205).

Institutional Review Board Statement: Not applicable.

Informed Consent Statement: Not applicable.

Data Availability Statement: Researchers interested in this method can access the code through the corresponding author.

Conflicts of Interest: The authors declare no potential conflict of interest.

References

1. Liu, R.; Mo, Y.; Lu, Y.; Lyu, Y.; Zhang, Y.; Guo, H. Swarm-intelligence optimization method for dynamic optimization problem. *Mathematics* **2022**, *10*, 1803. [CrossRef]
2. Diveev, A.; Sofronova, E.; Zelinka, I. Optimal control problem solution with phase constraints for group of robots by pontryagin maximum principle and evolutionary algorithm. *Mathematics* **2020**, *8*, 2105. [CrossRef]
3. Rodriguez-Gonzalez, P.T.; Rico-Ramirez, V.; Rico-Martinez, R.; Diwekar, U.M. A new approach to solving stochastic optimal control problems. *Mathematics* **2019**, *7*, 1207. [CrossRef]
4. Deshmukh, A.P.; Allison, J.T. Multidisciplinary dynamic optimization of horizontal axis wind turbine design. *Struct. Multidiscip. Optim.* **2016**, *53*, 15–27. [CrossRef]
5. Biegler, L.T. An overview of simultaneous strategies for dynamic optimization. *Chem. Eng. Process.* **2007**, *46*, 1043–1053. [CrossRef]
6. Herber, D.R.; Allison, J.T. Nested and simultaneous solution strategies for general combined plant and control design problems. *J. Mech. Des.* **2018**, *141*, 011402. [CrossRef]
7. Allison, J.T.; Herber, D.R. Multidisciplinary design optimization of dynamic engineering systems. *AIAA J.* **2014**, *52*, 691–710. [CrossRef]
8. Peng, H.J.; Wang, W. Adaptive surrogate model-based fast path planning for spacecraft formation reconfiguration on libration point orbits. *Aerosp. Sci. Technol.* **2016**, *54*, 151–163. [CrossRef]
9. Betts, J.T. *Practical Methods for Optimal Control Using Nonlinear Programming*, 2nd ed.; SIAM Press: Philadelphia, PA, USA, 2010.
10. Eberhard, P.; Dignath, F.; Kübler, L. Parallel evolutionary optimization of multibody systems with application to railway dynamics. *Multibody Syst. Dyn.* **2003**, *9*, 143–164. [CrossRef]
11. Negrellos-Ortiz, A.; Flores-Tlacuahuac, B.; Gutierrez-Limon, M.A. Dynamic optimization of a cryogenic air separation unit using a derivative-free optimization approach. *Comput. Chem. Eng.* **2018**, *109*, 1–8. [CrossRef]
12. Rahmani, R.; Mobayen, S.; Fekih, A.; Ro, J. Robust passivity cascade technique-based control using RBFN approximators for the stabilization of a cart inverted pendulum. *Mathematics* **2021**, *9*, 1229. [CrossRef]
13. Li, Y.; Shen, J.; Cai, Z.; Wu, Y.; Wang, S. A kriging-assisted multi-objective constrained global optimization method for expensive black-box functions. *Mathematics* **2021**, *9*, 149. [CrossRef]

14. Zhang, Q.; Wu, Y.Z.; Lu, L.; Qiao, P. An adaptive Dendrite-HDMR metamodeling technique for high dimensional problems. *J. Mech. Des.* **2022**, *144*, 081701. [CrossRef]

15. Wiangkham, A.; Ariyarit, A.; Aengchuan, P. Prediction of the influence of loading rate and sugarcane leaves concentration on fracture toughness of sugarcane leaves and epoxy composite using artificial intelligence. *Theor. Appl. Fract. Mech.* **2022**, *117*, 103188. [CrossRef]

16. Kudela, J.; Matousek, R. Recent advances and applications of surrogate models for finite element method computations: A review. *Soft Comput.* **2022**. [CrossRef]

17. Deshmukh, A.P.; Allison, J.T. Design of dynamic systems using surrogate models of derivative functions. *J. Mech. Des.* **2017**, *139*, 101402. [CrossRef]

18. Chowdhury, R.; Adhikari, S. Fuzzy parametric uncertainty analysis of linear dynamical systems: A surrogate modeling approach. *Mech. Syst. Signal. Proc.* **2012**, *32*, 5–17. [CrossRef]

19. Wang, Y.; Bortoff, S.A. Co-design of nonlinear control systems with bounded control inputs. In Proceedings of the 11th World Congress on Intelligent Control and Automation, Shenyang, China, 29 June–4 July 2015.

20. Shokry, A.; Espuna, A. Sequential dynamic optimization of complex nonlinear processes based on kriging surrogate models. *Procedia Technol.* **2014**, *15*, 376–387. [CrossRef]

21. Lefebvre, T.; De Belie, F.; Crevecoeur, G. A trajectory-based sampling strategy for sequentially refined metamodel management of metamodel-based dynamic optimization in mechatronics. *Optim. Control. Appl. Methods* **2018**, *39*, 1786–1801. [CrossRef]

22. Qiao, P.; Wu, Y.Z.; Ding, J.W.; Zhang, Q. A new sequential sampling method of surrogate models for design and optimization of dynamic systems. *Mech. Mach. Theory* **2021**, *158*, 104248. [CrossRef]

23. He, Y.P.; McPhee, J. Multidisciplinary design optimization of mechatronic vehicles with active suspensions. *J. Sound Vibr.* **2005**, *283*, 217–241. [CrossRef]

24. Maraniello, S.; Palacios, R. Optimal vibration control and co-design of very flexible actuated structures. *J. Sound Vibr.* **2016**, *377*, 1–21. [CrossRef]

25. Li, M.W.; Peng, H.J. Solutions of nonlinear constrained optimal control problems using quasilinearization and variational pseudospectral methods. *ISA Trans.* **2016**, *62*, 177–192. [CrossRef]

26. Ross, I.M.; Karpenko, M. A review of pseudospectral optimal control: From theory to flight. *Annu. Rev. Control* **2012**, *36*, 182–197. [CrossRef]

27. Liu, X.; Wu, Y.Z.; Wang, B.; Ding, J.W.; Jie, H.X. An adaptive local range sampling method for reliability-based design optimization using support vector machine and Kriging model. *Struct. Multidiscip. Optim.* **2017**, *55*, 2285–2304. [CrossRef]

28. Phiboon, T.; Khankwa, K.; Petcharat, N.; Phoksombat, N.; Kanazaki, M.; Kishi, Y.; Bureerat, S.; Ariyarit, A. Experiment and computation multi-fidelity multi-objective airfoil design optimization of fixed-wing UAV. *J. Mech. Sci. Technol.* **2021**, *35*, 4065–4072. [CrossRef]

29. Liu, H.T.; Ong, Y.S.; Cai, J.F. A survey of adaptive sampling for global metamodeling in support of simulation-based complex engineering design. *Struct. Multidiscip. Optim.* **2017**, *57*, 393–416. [CrossRef]

30. Patterson, M.A.; Rao, A.V. GPOPS-II: A MATLAB software for solving multiple-phase optimal control problems using hp-adaptive gaussian quadrature collocation methods and sparse nonlinear programming. *ACM Trans. Math. Softw.* **2014**, *41*, 1–37. [CrossRef]

31. Lophaven, S.N.; Nielsen, H.B.; Sndergaard, J. *DACE—A MATLAB Kriging Toolbox, Version 2, Informatics and Mathematical Modelling*; Technical University of Denmark: Copenhagen, Denmark, 2002.

32. Jung, E.; Lenhart, S.; Feng, Z. Optimal control of treatments in a two-strain tuberculosis model. *Discret. Contin. Dyn. Syst. Ser. B* **2002**, *2*, 473–482. [CrossRef]

33. Otter, M.; Tuerk, S. *The Dfvlr Models 1 and 2 of the Manutec R3 Robot*; Institut für Dynamik der Flugsysteme Press: Oberpfaffenhofen, Germany, 1988.

Article

Activation Energy Performance through Magnetized Hybrid Fe_3O_4–PP Nanofluids Flow with Impact of the Cluster Interfacial Nanolayer

M. Zubair Akbar Qureshi [1,†], **Qadeer Raza** [1], **Aroosa Ramzan** [1], **M. Faisal** [1], **Bagh Ali** [2], **Nehad Ali Shah** [3,†] and **Wajaree Weera** [4,*]

[1]   Department of Mathematics, Air University, Multan Campus, Multan 49501, Pakistan
[2]   Faculty of Computer Science and Information Technology, Superior University, Lahore 54000, Pakistan
[3]   Department of Mechanical Engineering, Sejong University, Seoul 05006, Korea
[4]   Department of Mathematics, Faculty of Science, Khon Kaen University, Khon Kaen 40002, Thailand
*   Correspondence: wajawe@kku.ac.th
†   These authors contributed equally to this work and are co-first authors.

Abstract: The current work investigated the mass and heat transfer of the MHD hybrid nanofluid flow subject to the impact of activation energy and cluster interfacial nanolayer. The heat transport processes related to the interfacial nanolayer between nanoparticles and base fluids enhanced the base fluid's thermal conductivity. The tiny particles of Fe_3O_4 and PPy were considered due to the extraordinary thermal conductivity which is of remarkable significance in nanotechnology, electronic devices, and modern shaped heat exchangers. Using the similarity approach, the governing higher-order nonlinear coupled partial differential equation was reduced to a system of ordinary differential equations (ODEs). Fe_3O_4–PPy hybrid nanoparticles have a considerable influence on thermal performance, and when compared to non-interfacial nanolayer thermal conductivity, the interfacial nanolayer thermal conductivity model produced substantial findings. The increase in nanolayer thickness from level 1 to level 5 had a significant influence on thermal performance improvement. Further, the heat and mass transfer rate was enhanced with higher input values of interfacial nanolayer thickness.

Keywords: hybrid nanofluid; heat and mass transfer flow; MHD; Fe_3O_4–PPy hybrid nanoparticles; interfacial nanolayer; activation energy

MSC: 00-01; 99-00

Citation: Qureshi, M.Z.A.; Raza, Q.; Ramzan, A.; Faisal, M.; Ali, B.; Shah, N.A.; Weera, W. Activation Energy Performance through Magnetized Hybrid Fe_3O_4–PP Nanofluids Flow with Impact of the Cluster Interfacial Nanolayer. *Mathematics* **2022**, *10*, 3277. https://doi.org/10.3390/math10183277

Academic Editor: Camelia Petrescu

Received: 15 August 2022
Accepted: 3 September 2022
Published: 9 September 2022

Publisher's Note: MDPI stays neutral with regard to jurisdictional claims in published maps and institutional affiliations.

1. Introduction

The activation energy is concomitant with chemical reaction and has a noteworthy role in heat and mass transfer, free convective boundary layer flows in the fields of oil container engineering and geothermal reservoirs. The exploration of thermal transportation in fluid flows is an attractive topic for researchers due to its wide applications. Moreover, thermal stability and instability are in high demand in the current era. Buongiorno et al. [1] proposed the relationship in nanofluids by incorporating Brownian diffusion and thermophoresis. Gurel [2] investigated the melting heat transport of phase change materials subject to the melting boundary condition. The finite volume approach was used to obtain numerical solutions. Dhlamini et al. [3] studied the binary chemical reactions in the mixed convective flow of nanofluids with activation energy. The effects of bioconvection, changing thermal conductivity, and activation energy past an extended sheet were investigated by Chu et al. [4]. Water was regarded as a conventional fluid by Wakif et al. [5] and in this investigation the dynamics of radiative-reactive Walters-b fluid due to mixed convection conveying gyrotactic microorganisms, tiny particles experience haphazard motion, thermo-migration, and Lorentz force. To further explore the precise point of hybrid nanofluid flow, the impact of the magnetic field, heat radiation, and activation energy with a binary chemical reaction was introduced. Sreenivasulu et al. [6] investigated the influence of activation energy on the hybrid nanofluid flow via a flat plate with viscous dissipation and a magnetic field. Ramesh et al. [7] investigated the influence of thermal performance on the usual heat source/sink effect. Chemical reaction and activation energy effects are accounted for in the mass equation. Wasif et al. [8] prepared to extend cavity construction for a broader variety of purposes, beginning with the determination of cavity shape owing to the increase in heat transmission inside that selected cavity for diverse boundary conditions. Kumar et al. [9] investigated the flow of a tangent hyperbolic fluid through a transferring stretched surface. Nonlinear radiation was used to offer warm shipping properties. Activation energy indicated different elements of mass transfer. As a result of an unstable flow over a stretched surface in an incompressible rotating viscous fluid with the appearance of a binary chemical reaction and Arrhenius activation energy, Awad et al. [10] theorized that the spectral relaxation method (SRM) could be employed to evaluate the linked highly nonlinear problem of partial differential equations. Rekha et al. [11] explored the influence of a heat source/sink on nanofluid flow through a cone, wedge, and plate while utilizing a dispersion of aluminum alloys (AA7072 and AA7075) as a base nanoparticles fluid water. The activation energy and porous material are also taken into account in the simulation.

Fe_3O_4–PPy core–shell nanoparticles were created using polymer polypyrrole (PPy), which could be used for cancer combination therapy that is image-guided and controlled remotely after being functionalized with polyethylene glycol. The Fe_3O_4 core, which breaks down slowly in physiological conditions, is used in this system as a magnetically controlled device for cure administration as well as a magnet. Magnetic iron oxide nanoclusters were coated for a light-absorbing near-infrared resonance imaging comparison to create a multifunctional nanocomposite. Due to their remarkable function in separation technology, Fe_3O_4 NPs have been garnering a lot of attention. In addition to having exceptional catalytic and good magnetic characteristics, the nanocomposite developed using the straightforward and easily produced Fe_3O_4 NPs also exhibits good dispensability and biocompatibility [12,13]. Suri et al. [14] studied iron oxide–PPy nanocomposites as gas and moisture sensors. Sun et al. [15] reported nanoparticles of Fe_3O_4–PANI with a very thin PANI covering of the core–shell with badly improved microwave absorption properties. Zhao et al. [16] described a method for making Fe_3O_4/PPy nanocomposites.

Combined mass and heat transfer flows associated with chemical reactions play a crucial function in a wide range of applications, such as transport phenomena, cooling, and heating processes in electronics, binary diffusion systems, absorption reactors, polymer processing, solar energy systems, and the plastics industry. Salmi et al. [17] presented the similarity analysis through the finite element method (FEM) to investigate the non-Fourier behavior of the heat and mass transfer. Roy et al. [18] introduced a binary chemical reaction with an activation energy effect on the heat and mass transfer of a hybrid nanofluid flow over a permeable stretching surface. Oke et al. [19] presented the combined heat and mass transfer effects in the presence of magnetohydrodynamic ternary ethylene glycol-based hybrid nanofluids over a rotating three-dimensional surface with the impact of suction velocity. The unstable MHD convective flow with the heat and mass transfer characteristics for a noncompressible gelatinous electrical system was studied by Babu et al. [20]. The effects of the magnetic field on fluid flow and heat transfer rate have been documented in numerous earlier investigations [21–25]. Sreedevi et al. [26] examined heat and mass transport through a nanofluid. Salmi et al. [27] presented a unique analysis of the combined effects of Hall and ion slip currents, the Darcy–Forchheimer porous medium, and nonuniform magnetic field under the suspension of hybrid nanoparticles with heat and mass transfer aspects. Santhi et al. [28] discussed the unsteady magnetohydrodynamics heat and mass transfer analysis of a hybrid nanofluid flow over a stretching surface with chemical reaction, suction, and slip effects. Raja et al. [29] presented a novel idea of a radiative heat and mass flux 3D hybrid nanofluid, RHF. A Bayesian regularization technique based on backpropagated neural networks (BRT-BNNs) was employed to estimate the solution of the proposed model. Shah et al. [30] investigated the Numerical simulation of a thermally enhanced EMHD flow of a heterogeneous micropolar mixture comprising (60%)-ethylene glycol (EG), (40%)-water (W), and copper oxide nanomaterials (CuO). Bidyasagar et al. [31] analyzed the unsteady laminar flow with heat and mass transfer of an incompressible and hydromagnetic Cu–Al$_2$O$_3$/H$_2$O hybrid nanofluid near a nonlinearly permeable stretching sheet in the presence of nonlinear thermal radiation, viscous–ohmic dissipation, and velocity slip. Further, the impacts of heat generation and absorption, chemical reactions, convective heat, and mass conditions at the boundary were also considered by Farooq et al. [32]. Oke [33] investigated the flow of gold water nanofluids across the revolving upper horizontal surface of a paraboloid of revolution. The development of nanofluids has been groundbreaking in terms of improving fluid thermal and electrical conductivity. A real convective magnetohydrodynamic flow of a Cu–engine oil nanofluid along a vertical plate that has been convectively heated was taken into consideration by Kigio et al. [34].

Cluster interfacial nanolayer is a term that refers to a vast variety of extended quasi-two-dimensional nanoobjects that have unique physical and chemical properties, ranging from liposomes and cell membranes to graphene and layered double hydroxide flakes. Tso et al. [35] examined the effects of the interfacial nanolayer on the efficient thermal conductivity of nanofluids. The suggested model gives an equation to predict the nanolayer thickness for various kinds of nanofluids. On the other hand, in the mathematical model of Murshed et al. [36], a similar issue arises. They picked a ratio of nanolayer thermal conductivity to base fluid thermal conductivity of 1.1–2.5. Acharya et al. [37] examined the hydrothermal variations of radiative nanofluid flow by the influence of nanoparticle diameter and nanolayer. Zhao et al. [38] examined molecular dynamics simulation to investigate the effect of the interfacial nanolayer structure on enhancing the viscosity and thermal conductivity of nanofluids.

Having studied the abovementioned literature, to the best of our knowledge, no study has been conducted on the estimation of heat and mass transfer for hybrid nanofluids flowing across orthogonal porous discs subject to the effects of MHD, activation energy, and cluster interfacial nanolayers on the thermal conductivity model for hybrid nanofluid flows. Motivated by the abovementioned literature's wide scope of hybrid nanoparticles and cluster interfacial nanolayers, we considered studying the present elaborate problem. To enhance the nanoparticles stability, we also considered the activation energy. Using suitable similarity transformation quantities, the governing PDEs were transformed into dimensionless ODEs. To solve the system of ODEs, the Runge–Kutta shooting technique was used to draw numerical and graphical results.

2. Formulation of Governing Equations

The momentum, energy, and concentration equations of the incompressible flow for the two-dimensional velocity field $U = [u(x, y, t), v(x, y, t)]$ of the single-phase model in the presence of chemical reactions, heat source, and activation energy were formulated. In this problem, we assumed a viscous, laminar, incompressible, time-dependent, two-dimensional flow of a hybrid nanofluid containing $Fe_3O_4 - PPy/H_2O$ through a permeable channel of breadth 2a(t). The induced magnetic field was ignored based on the presumption of a low Reynolds number. Further, the thermophysical properties of the base fluid, the single and hybrid nanofluids are expressed in Tables 1 and 2. Both walls of the channel were absorbent and could move above and below with a time-dependent rate (a′(t)). Using these assumptions, the fluid flow-governing equations for conservation of mass, linear momentums, energy, and concentration in vector form are as follows:

$$(\nabla . U = 0), \tag{1}$$

$$\rho_{hnf}\frac{DU}{Dt} + \nabla_p - \nabla . \tau = A \times R \tag{2}$$

$$(\rho c_p)_{hnf}\left(\frac{DT}{Dt}\right) + \nabla . q_c = \beta k_r^2 \left(\frac{T}{T_2}\right)^n \times exp\left(\frac{-E_a}{k^*T}\right)(c - c_2) \tag{3}$$

$$\frac{DC}{Dt} - D\nabla^2.C = -k_r^2\left(\frac{T}{T_2}\right)^n \times exp\left(\frac{-E_a}{k^*T}\right)(c - c_2) \tag{4}$$

where $\frac{D}{Dt} = \frac{\partial}{\partial t} + U.\nabla$, ρ denotes density, t represents time, τ shows the extra shear stress of the fluid, p is pressure, T stands for temperature, C represents concentration, D stands for the diffusion coefficient, $A \times R = \frac{\sigma_e B_0^2}{\rho_{hnf}}U$ signifies magnetic hydrodynamics, E_a denotes activation energy, k^* represents the Boltzmann constant, k_r^2 is the chemical reaction constant, and c_p is the specific heat capacity. The heat flux (q_c) was defined by Fourier's law of conduction, $q_c = -k_{hnf}\nabla T$, and k_{hnf} is the thermal conductivity of a hybrid nanofluid. T_1 denotes the temperature of the lower channel wall and T_2 denotes the temperature of the upper channel wall shown in Figure 1. According to assumptions, the governing Equations (1)–(4) are written as [39]:

$$\frac{\partial u}{\partial x} + \frac{\partial v}{\partial y} = 0 \tag{5}$$

$$\frac{\partial u}{\partial t} + u\frac{\partial u}{\partial x} + v\frac{\partial u}{\partial y} = -\frac{p_x}{\rho_{hnf}} + \nu_{hnf}\left(\frac{\partial^2 u}{\partial x^2} + \frac{\partial^2 u}{\partial y^2}\right) - \frac{\sigma_e B_0^2}{\rho_{hnf}}u \tag{6}$$

$$\frac{\partial v}{\partial t} + u\frac{\partial v}{\partial x} + v\frac{\partial v}{\partial y} = -\frac{p_y}{\rho_{hnf}} + \nu_{hnf}\left(\frac{\partial^2 v}{\partial x^2} + \frac{\partial^2 v}{\partial y^2}\right) \tag{7}$$

$$\frac{\partial T}{\partial t} + u\frac{\partial T}{\partial x} + v\frac{\partial T}{\partial y} = \alpha_{hnf}\left(\frac{\partial^2 T}{\partial y^2}\right) + \frac{1}{(\rho c_p)_{hnf}}\left(\beta k_r^2\left(\frac{T}{T_2}\right)^n * exp\left(\frac{-E_a}{k^*T}\right)(c - c_2)\right) \tag{8}$$

$$\frac{\partial C}{\partial t} + u\frac{\partial C}{\partial x} + v\frac{\partial C}{\partial y} = D\left(\frac{\partial^2 C}{\partial y^2}\right) - k_r^2\left(\frac{T}{T_2}\right)^n * exp\left(\frac{-E_a}{k^*T}\right)(c - c_2) \tag{9}$$

where ρ_{hnf} denotes the density of the hybrid nanofluid and σ_e represents electrical conductivity. The physical model was used in the Cartesian coordinate system (x, y), and the u and v components of velocity were plotted on the *x*- and *y*-axes, respectively. B_0 is the magnetic field strength, α_{hnf} is the coefficient of thermal diffusivity of the hybrid nanofluid, ν_{hnf} is the kinematic viscosity of the hybrid nanofluid, T_1, C_1 and T_2, C_2 represent the temperature and concentration of the lower and upper plates with $T_1 > T_2$ and $C_1 > C_2$. The mathematical expression for the kinematic viscosity of the hybrid nanofluid and the thermal diffusivity of the hybrid nanofluid are given below:

$$\nu_{hnf} = \frac{\mu_{hnf}}{\rho_{hnf}}, \quad \alpha_{hnf} = \frac{k_{hnf}}{(\rho c_p)_{hnf}} \tag{10}$$

where $(\rho c_p)_{hnf}$ is the hybrid nanofluid's specific capacitance and k_{hnf} is the hybrid nanofluid's thermal conductivity. The heat variations inside the fluid flow are minimal, so function T^n may be represented linearly. By excluding higher-order components, T^n may be enlarged using Taylor's series concerning temperature T_2, giving the following approximation:

$$T^n = (1 - n)T_2^n + nT_2^{n-1}T\left(\frac{T}{T_2}\right)^n = (1 - n) + n\frac{T}{T_2} \tag{11}$$

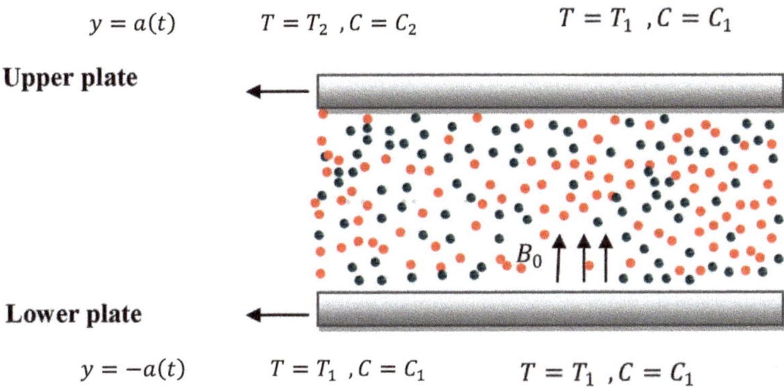

Figure 1. Physical model.

The boundary conditions of the present problem are as follows:

$$y = -a(t),\ u = 0,\ v = -A_1 a'(t),\ T = T_1,\ C = C_1$$
$$y = a(t),\ u = 0,\ v = A_1 a'(t),\ T = T_2,\ C = C_2. \tag{12}$$

The time t derivative is represented by the dash, and A is the wall permeability factor. The suitable similarity transformations are as follows:

$$\eta = \frac{y}{a},\quad u = -\frac{x v_f}{a^2} F_\eta(\eta,t),\quad v = \frac{v_f}{a} F(\eta,t),\ \theta = \frac{T - T_2}{T_1 - T_2},\ \chi = \frac{C - C_2}{C_1 - C_2} \tag{13}$$

In view of Equation (13), the continuity Equation (5) is satisfied, and Equations (6)–(9) can be written as follows:

$$\frac{v_{hnf}}{v_f} F_{\eta\eta\eta\eta} + \alpha\left(3F_{\eta\eta} + \eta F_{\eta\eta\eta}\right) + F_\eta F_{\eta\eta} - \frac{\alpha^2}{v_f} F_{\eta\eta t} - FF_{\eta\eta\eta} - \frac{\rho_f}{\rho_{hnf}} MF_{\eta\eta} = 0, \tag{14}$$

$$\theta_{\eta\eta} + \frac{k_f}{k_{hnf}} Pr\left((1 - \varphi_1 - \varphi_2) + \varphi_1 \frac{(\rho c_p)_{\rho_1}}{(\rho c_p)_{hnf}} + \varphi_2 \frac{(\rho c_p)_{\rho_2}}{(\rho c_p)_{\rho_{hnf}}}\right)(\eta\alpha - F)\theta_\eta - \frac{a^2}{\alpha_{hnf}}\theta_t + \frac{k_f}{k_{hnf}}((1 - (\varphi_1 + \varphi_2))$$
$$+ (\varphi_1)\left(\frac{\rho c_{p_{s1}}}{\rho c_{p_{bf}}}\right) + (\varphi_2)\left(\frac{\rho c_{p_{s2}}}{\rho c_{p_{bf}} s}\right))(1 + (n * \gamma)\theta[\eta])(1 - E + (E * \gamma)\theta[\eta])\chi[\eta] = 0 \tag{15}$$

$$\chi_{\eta\eta} + Sc(\eta\alpha - F)\chi_\eta - \frac{a^2}{D}\chi_t + (Sc * \sigma)(1 + (n * \gamma)\theta[\eta])(1 - E + (E * \gamma)\theta[\eta])\chi[\eta] = 0 \tag{16}$$

Boundary conditions Equation (12):

$$F = -Re f,\,,\,F_\eta = 0,\quad \theta = 1,\ and\ \chi = 1,\ at\ \eta = -1,$$
$$F = Re f,\ ,F_\eta = 0,\quad \theta = 0,\ and\ \chi = 0,\ at\ \eta = 1. \tag{17}$$

The Prandtl number is equal to $Pr = \frac{(\mu c_p)_f}{k_f}$, $\alpha = \frac{a a'(t)}{v_f}$ is the wall expansion ratio, $Re = \frac{A a a'(t)}{v_f}$ is the permeability Reynolds number, $\gamma = \frac{T_1 - T_2}{T_2}$ is the temperature difference parameter, $\sigma = \frac{k_r^2(1 - \gamma)}{a}$ is the dimensionless reaction rate, $M = \frac{\sigma_e B_0^2 a^2}{\mu_f}$ is the magnetic parameter, $E = \frac{E_a}{k^* T}$ is the dimensional activation energy parameter, $Sc = \frac{v_f}{D}$ is the Schmidt number. Finally, we set $F = f Re$ and considered the case following Majdalani et al. [40], where α is a constant, $f = f(\eta)$, $\theta = \theta(\eta)$, and $X(\eta)$, which leads to $\theta_t = 0$, $X_t = 0$, and $f_{\eta\eta t} = 0$; thus, we obtained the following equation:

$$G_1 f_{\eta\eta\eta\eta} + f_{\eta\eta\eta}(\alpha\eta - Re f) + f_{\eta\eta}(3\alpha + Re f_\eta) - G_2 M Re f_{\eta\eta} = 0 \tag{18}$$

$$\theta_{\eta\eta} + G_3 G_4(Pr)((\alpha\eta - Ref)\,\theta_\eta + \frac{k_f}{k_{hnf}}(Pr*\sigma*\lambda)((1+(\gamma*n)\theta[\eta])(1-E+(\gamma*E)\theta[\eta])\chi[\eta] = 0 \qquad (19)$$

$$\chi_{\eta\eta} + Sc(\eta\alpha - Ref)\chi_\eta + (Sc*\sigma)(1+(\gamma*n)\theta[\eta])(1-E+(\gamma*E)\theta[\eta])\chi[\eta] = 0 \qquad (20)$$

and

$$\begin{aligned}
f &= -1\,, & f_\eta &= 0, & \theta &= 1, & \text{and } \chi &= 1, \text{ at } \eta = -1\\
f &= 1, & f_\eta &= 0, & \theta &= 0, & \text{and } \chi &= 0, \text{ at } \eta = 1
\end{aligned} \qquad (21)$$

where $G_1 = \left(\dfrac{1}{(1-(\varphi_1+\varphi_2))^{2.5}\left((1-(\varphi_1+\varphi_2))+(\varphi_1)\left(\frac{\rho_{s1}}{\rho_{bf}}\right)+(\varphi_2)\left(\frac{\rho_{s2}}{\rho_{bf}}\right)\right)} \right), G_2 =$

$\left(\dfrac{1}{\left((1-\varphi_1-\varphi_2)+\varphi_1\left(\frac{\rho_{s1}}{\rho_{bf}}\right)+\varphi_2\left(\frac{\rho_{s2}}{\rho_{bf}}\right)\right)} \right), G_3 = \left((1-(\varphi_1+\varphi_2))+(\varphi_1)\left(\frac{\rho_{cps_1}}{\rho_{cpbf}}\right)+(\varphi_2)\left(\frac{\rho_{cps_2}}{\rho_{cpbf}}\right)\right),$

$G_4 = \left(\dfrac{k_{hnf}}{k_{mbf}}\dfrac{k_{mbf}}{k_f} \right)^{-1}.$

Table 1. Thermophysical features of a hybrid nanofluid and NPs [41].

Physical Properties	H_2O	Fe_3O_4	PPy
$\rho\left(kg\ m^{-3}\right)$	997.0	5180	1.32
$C_p\left(J\ (kg)^{-1}K^{-1}\right)$	4180	670	800
$K\left(Wm^{-1}k^{-1}\right)$	0.6071	9.7	0.24

Table 2. Thermophysical properties of a hybrid nanofluid proposed in [42,43].

For a Nanofluid	For a Hybrid Nanofluid
$\rho_{nf} = (1-\varphi)\rho_f + \varphi\rho_p$	$\rho_{hnf} = \varphi_1\rho_{s1} + \varphi_2\rho_{s2} - (1-\varphi_1-\varphi_2)\rho_{bf}$
$(\rho C_p)_{nf} = (1-\varphi)(\rho C_p)_f + \varphi(\rho C_p)_p$	$\rho c_{phnf} = \varphi_1(\rho C_p)(\rho c_p)_{s1} + \varphi_2(\rho C_p)(\rho c_p)_{s2} + (1-\varphi_1-\varphi_2)(\rho c_p)_{bf}$
$\mu_{nf} = \dfrac{\mu_f}{(1-\varphi)^{2.5}},$	$\mu_{hnf} = \dfrac{\mu_{bf}}{(1-\varphi_1-\varphi_2)^{2.5}}$
$k_{nf} = \dfrac{k_s+(N-1)k_f-(N-1)\varphi(k_{bf}-k_{s1})}{k_s+(N-1)k_f+\varphi(k_f-k_s)}k_f$	$k_{hnf} = \dfrac{k_{s2}+(N-1)k_{mbf}-(N-1)\varphi_{s2}(k_{mbf}-k_{s2})}{k_{s2}+(N-1)k_{mbf}+\varphi_{s2}(k_{mbf}-k_{s2})}k_{mbf}$
$\dfrac{k_{nf}}{kbf} = \dfrac{(k_{p1}-k_{nlr})\varphi_{s1}k_{nlr}(\lambda_2^2-\lambda_1^2+1)+(k_{p1}+k_{nlr})\lambda_2^2(\varphi_{s1}\lambda_1^2(k_{nlr}-k_f)+k_f)}{(\lambda_2^2(k_{p1}+k_{nlr})-(k_{p1}-k_{nlr})\varphi_{s1}(\lambda_2^2+\lambda_1^2-1))k_f}$	where $k_{mbf} = \dfrac{k_{s1}+(N-1)k_{bf}-(N-1)\varphi_{s1}(k_{bf}-k_{s1})}{k_{s1}+(N-1)k_{bf}+\varphi_{s1}(k_{bf}-k_{s1})}k_f$
	$\dfrac{k_{hnfl}}{k_{mbf}} = \dfrac{(k_{p2}-k_{nlr})\varphi_{s2}k_{nlr}(\lambda_2^2-\lambda_1^2+1)+(k_{p2}+k_{nlr})\lambda_2^2(\varphi_{s2}\lambda_1^2(k_{nlr}-k_{bf})+k_{bf})}{(\lambda_2^2(k_{p2}+k_{nlr})-(k_{p2}-k_{nlr})\varphi_{s2}(\lambda_2^2+\lambda_1^2-1))k_{bf}}$
	$\dfrac{k_{mbf}}{kf} = \dfrac{(k_{p1}-k_{nlr})\varphi_{p1}k_{nlr}(\lambda_2^2-\lambda_1^2+1)+(k_{p1}+k_{nlr})\lambda_2^2(\varphi_{p1}\lambda_1^2(k_{nlr}-k_f)+k_f)}{(\lambda_2^2(k_{p1}+k_{nlr})-(k_{p1}-k_{nlr})\varphi_{p1}(\lambda_2^2+\lambda_1^2-1))k_f}$

Variables φ_{s1} and φ_{s2} show volume fraction from the first and second NPs, ρ_f is the base fluid density, ρ_{s1} and ρ_{s2} are the density of the first and second solid NPs, $(\rho C_p)_{s1}$ and $(\rho C_p)_{s2}$ is the thermal capacitance of the first and second solid NPs, the thermal capacitance for the base fluid is represented as $(\rho C_p)_f$, k_{hnfl} is the effective nanolayer thermal conductivity of the hybrid nanofluid, k_f and k_{bf} represent thermal conductivity of the base fluid, $\lambda_1 = 1+\frac{h}{r}$, $\lambda_2 = 1+\frac{h}{2r}$, h is the nanolayer thickness, r is the radius of the particle, k_{s1} and k_{s2} are the thermal conductivities of solid nanoparticles, and k_{nlr} is the thermal conductivity nanolayer.

3. Numerical Procedure

For the determination of the existing flow model, we used the RK shooting technique. The following substitution was required to begin the process:

$$w_1 = f[\eta], \ w_2 = f'[\eta], \ w_3 = f''[\eta], \ w_4 = f'''[\eta], w_5 = \theta[\eta], \ w_6 = \theta'[\eta], w_7 = \chi[\eta], \ w_8 = \chi'[\eta] \tag{22}$$

First, in Equations (18)–(20), the model was changed in the following pattern:

$$f''''[\eta] = \frac{1}{G_1}\left((Ref[\eta] - \alpha\eta)f''[\eta] - (3\alpha + Ref'[\eta])f''[\eta] + G_2 M f''[\eta]\right) \tag{23}$$

$$\theta''[\eta] = -(G_3 G_4 (Pr(\alpha\eta - Ref[\eta])\theta'[\eta] + (Pr * \sigma * \lambda)G_4((1 + (\gamma * n)\theta[\eta])(1 - E + (\gamma * E)\theta[\eta])\chi[\eta]) \tag{24}$$

$$\chi''[\eta] = -(Sc(\eta\alpha - Ref)\chi' + (Sc * \sigma)(1 + (n * \gamma)\theta[\eta])(1 - E + (E * \gamma)\theta[\eta])\chi[\eta]) \tag{25}$$

The following system was obtained by using the substitution contained in Equation (22):

$$\begin{bmatrix} w'_1 \\ w'_2 \\ w'_3 \\ w'_4 \\ w'_5 \\ w'_6 \\ w'_7 \\ w'_8 \end{bmatrix} = \begin{bmatrix} w_2 \\ w_3 \\ w_4 \\ \frac{1}{G_1}((Rew_1 - \alpha\eta)w_4 - (3\alpha + Rew_2)w_3 + G_2 M w_3) \\ w_6 \\ -(G_3 G_4 (Pr(\alpha\eta - Rew_1)w_6 + +(Pr * \sigma * \lambda)G_4((1 + (\gamma * n)w_5)(1 - E + (\gamma * E)w_5)w_7) \\ w_7 \\ -(Sc(\eta\alpha - Rew_1)w_8 + (Sc * \sigma)(1 + (n * \gamma)w_5)(1 - E + (E * \gamma)w_5)w_7) \end{bmatrix} \tag{26}$$

Consequently, the initial condition was as follows:

$$\begin{bmatrix} w'_1 \\ w'_2 \\ w'_3 \\ w'_4 \\ w'_5 \\ w'_6 \\ w'_7 \\ w'_8 \end{bmatrix} = \begin{bmatrix} -1 \\ 0 \\ 1 \\ 0 \\ 1 \\ 0 \\ 1 \\ 0 \end{bmatrix} \tag{27}$$

The above system was solved using mathematics and a suitable initial condition. Here, the accurate Runge–Kutta shooting technique was taken into consideration. The required dimensionless ODEs can easily be tackled with this method. We obtain the initial condition by using the shooting technique in such a way that boundary conditions are satisfied and achieve the desired level of accuracy.

4. Results and Discussion

This section explains the impact of flow on suction/injection permeable Reynolds number R_e, contraction/expansion ratio parameter α, volume friction parameters φ_{s1} and φ_{s2}, magnetic parameter M, nanolayer thickness parameter h, Schmidt number Sc, exothermic/endothermic parameter λ, and dimensionless parameter n on the velocity, temperature, and concentration profiles (Figures 2–6). Figure 2 was plotted to show the effect of M on velocity profile f'. It is shown that with a rising magnetic parameter velocity, the f' component decreased. This is because by enhancing the magnetic value, Lorentz forces are produced, decreasing the axial momentum of fluid particles. We can conclude from this argument that transverse application of the magnetic field normalizes fluid velocity. The effect of E on the mass concentration profile is shown in Figure 3. It is noticed that the mass concentration profile decreased as the augmented value of the dimensionless activation energy parameter increased. The influence of nanolayer thickness on temperature is investigated and recorded in Figure 4. It is observed that the temperature decreased at the lower plate and increased at the upper plate when the value of the nanolayer thickness parameter was increased. Figure 5 depicts the influence of the volume fraction parameter on the temperature profile. It can be seen that the enhancement in volume fraction reduced the temperature in the interval $-1 < \eta < 0$ and increased in the interval $0 < \eta < 1$. Figure 6 shows a comparison graph of effective thermal conductivity and noneffective thermal conductivity, increase in the values of volume fraction φ_{s1} and φ_{s2}; the effective thermal conductivity of hybrid nanofluids has a high heat transfer rate as compared to the non-effusive thermal conductivity of nanofluids. The reason is that noneffective thermal conductivity does not include the influence of the radius of particles and nanolayer thickness. Table 3 represents the variation in shear stress $(f''(-1))$. Physically, shear stress $(f''(-1))$ develops on the boundary of any real fluid flowing over a solid, along with liquids. According to the no-slip requirement, the float velocity has to be identical to the fluid velocity at a few stops from the boundary, even though the float velocity on the boundary has to be zero. The boundary layer is the location that lies between those spots. The shear pressure is inversely correlated with the fluid's stress rate for all Newtonian fluids in laminar float, with viscosity serving as the proportionality constant. At the bottom plate, the heat transfer rate $(\theta'(-1))$ and the mass transfer rate $(X'(-1))$ for the suction and injection instances were calculated. The flow of thermal energy between physical systems is known as heat transfer $(\theta'(-1))$. The rate of heat transfer $(\theta'(-1))$ is determined by the temperatures of the systems and the quality of the intervening medium. The mass transfer $(X'(-1))$ is a physical event that involves the observation of the net movement of generic particles from one point to another. For suction, R_e is less than zero. Suction occurs when inertia is smaller than viscosity. It was noticed that as the value of the expansion/contraction ratio parameter moved from negative to positive, it decreased the shear stress, heat, and mass transfer rate. The enhancement in the heat and mass transfer rates was noticed when the activation energy parameter was increased. It was observed that the heat transfer rate increased with the augmented values of nanolayer thickness. The Prandtl number and nanolayer thickness were opposite to the Nusselt number. The reason is that the Prandtl number is the product of diffusive momentum and the inverse of thermal diffusivity. Increasing the Prandtl number, diffusivity increases together with momentum, while the coefficient of heat flux decreases. The heat transfer rate decreases due to an increase in exothermic and endothermic parameters. It was observed that the mass transfer rate decreased with the augmented values of n. For injection $R_e > 0$ cases, injection occurred when inertia was greater than viscosity. It was observed that the effect of nanolayer thickness h and the Prandtl number had opposite impacts in both suction and injection cases on the heat transfer rate and α, E, λ, φ_{s1}, φ_{s2}, and n had the same impact in both suction and injection cases on shear stress $(f''(-1))$, $(\theta'(-1))$ and mass transfer rate $(X'(-1))$.

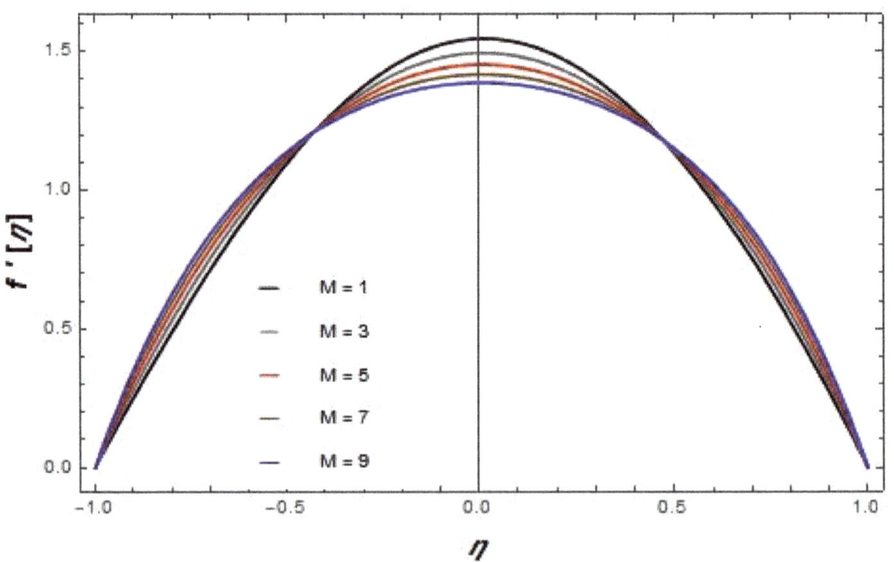

Figure 2. Effect of the magnetic parameter on velocity f'.

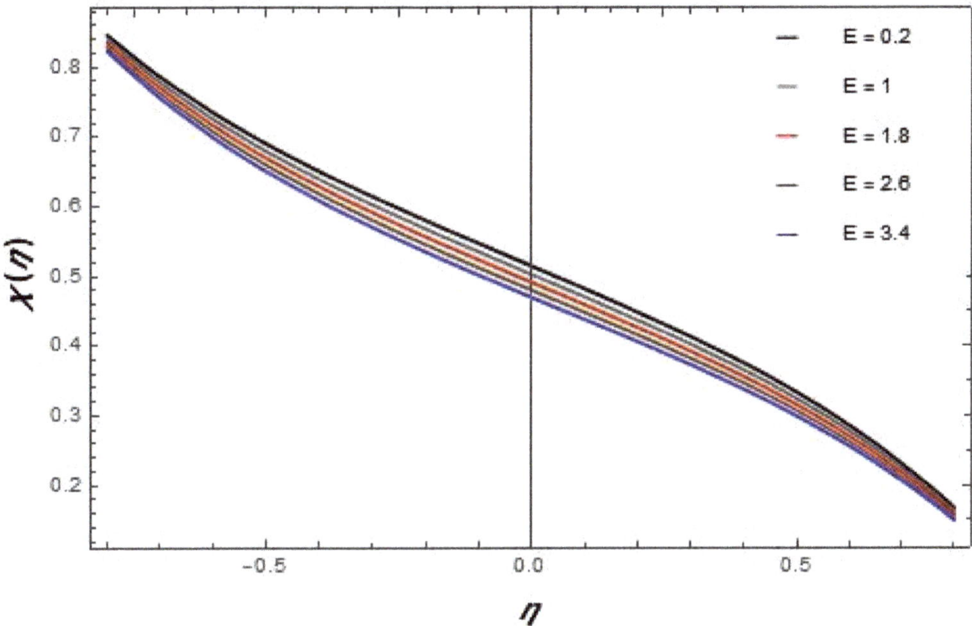

Figure 3. Effect of activation energy on mass concentration.

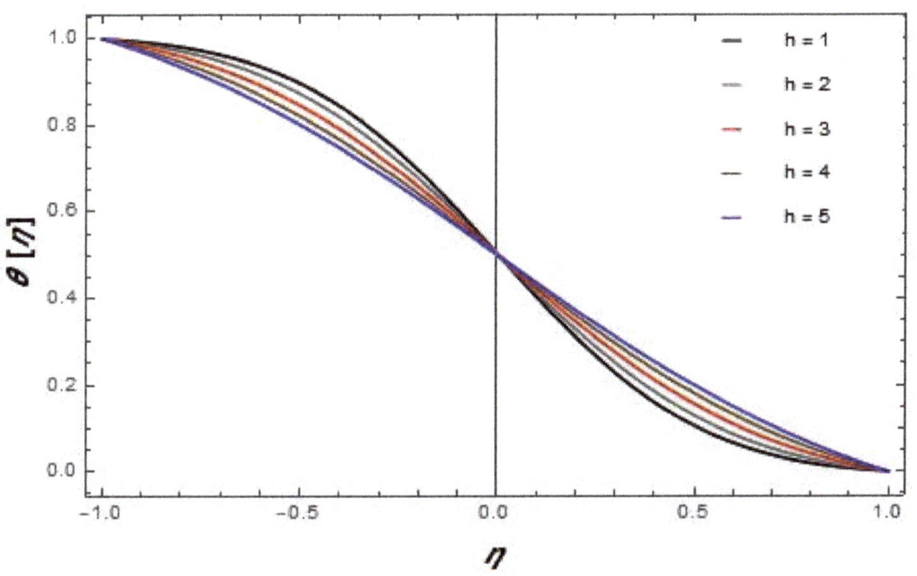

Figure 4. Effect of nanolayer thickness on the temperature profile.

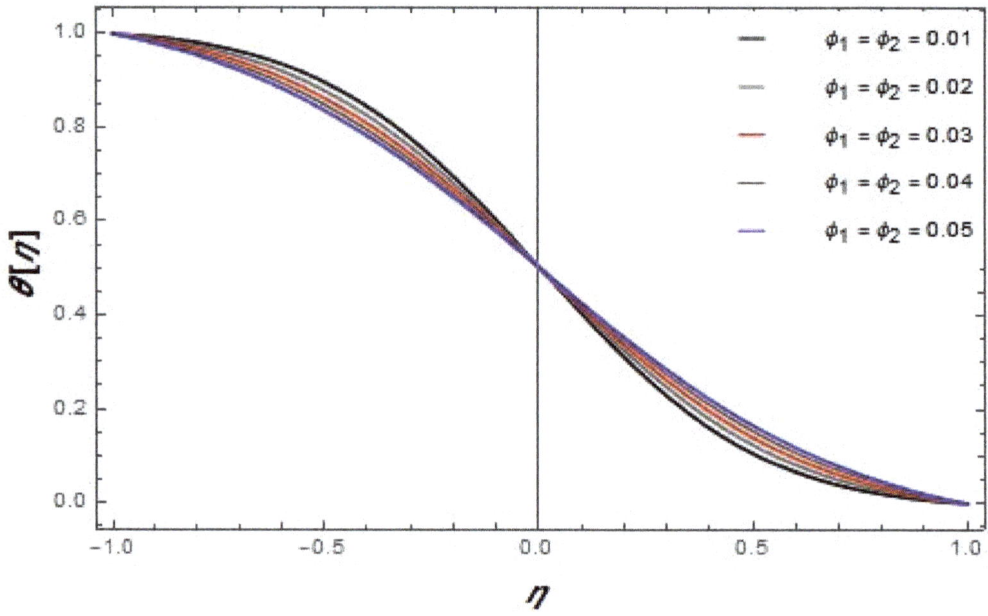

Figure 5. Effect of volume fraction on temperature.

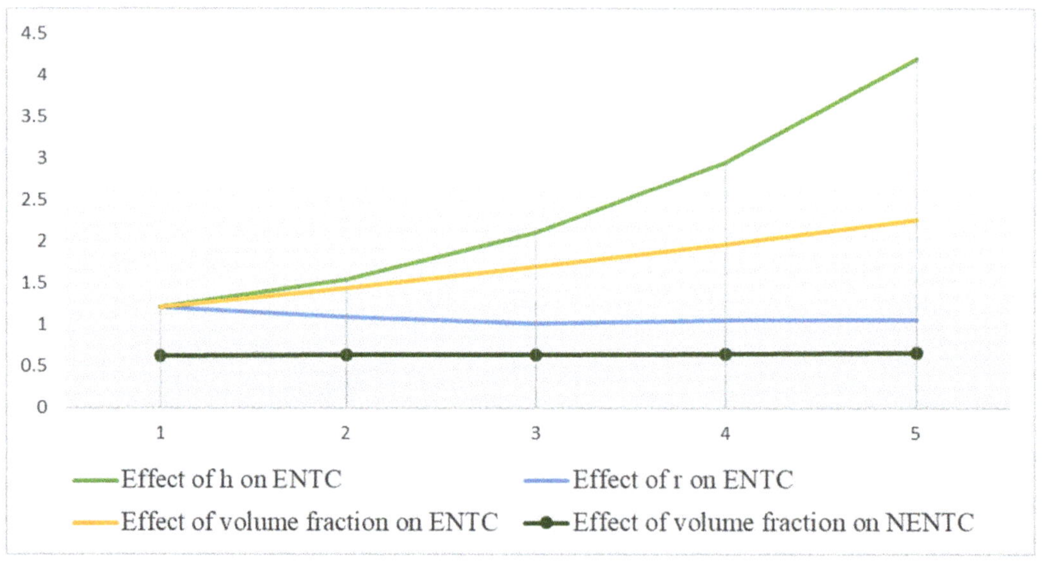

Figure 6. Effect of thermal conductivity and effective thermal conductivity.

Table 3. Variation in shear stress, heat, and mass transfer rate for suction and injection cases at the lower plate.

α	E	h	Pr	λ	n	φ_{p1}	φ_{p2}	$f''(-1)$ for the Suction Case	$\theta'(-1)$ for the Suction Case	$X'(-1)$ for the Suction Case	$f''(-1)$ for the Injection Case	$\theta'(-1)$ for the Injection Case	$X'(-1)$ for the Injection Case
−1.5						0.01	0.01	4.21559	1.80925	0.84674	4.87378	4.40691	1.52166
−1								3.77813	0.94617	0.62276	4.40357	3.20740	1.20431
0								2.94105	0.16084	0.31088	3.49395	1.18698	0.69946
1								2.16279	0.01814	0.14104	2.63460	0.24412	0.36152
1.5								1.79889	0.00558	0.09193	2.22761	0.09233	0.25207
	0.2							2.54393	0.05592	0.21175	3.05725	0.57754	0.50711
	1							2.54393	0.56180	0.22352	3.05725	0.57851	0.55284
	1.8							2.54393	0.05643	0.23519	3.05725	0.57945	0.54940
	2.6							2.54393	0.05667	0.24678	3.05725	0.58037	0.57001
	3.4							2.54393	0.05693	0.25827	3.05726	0.58128	0.59025
		1						2.54393	0.05593	0.21175	3.05725	0.57754	0.50711
		2						2.54393	0.09414	0.21175	3.05725	0.56028	0.50711
		3						2.54393	0.15128	0.21775	3.05725	0.54416	0.50711
		4						2.54393	0.21969	0.21175	3.05725	0.53125	0.50711
		5						2.54393	0.28211	0.21175	3.05725	0.52190	0.50711
			4.5					2.54393	0.1072	0.21176	3.05725	0.55586	0.50716
			5.2					2.54393	0.08231	0.21176	3.0572	0.56589	0.50711
			5.5					2.54393	0.07337	0.21175	3.05725	0.56846	0.50711
			6.1					254393	0.05593	0.21175	305725	0.57754	0.50711
			6.2					2.54393	0.05252	0.21175	3.05725	0.57754	0.50711
				1.2				2.54393	0.05252	0.21175	3.05725	0.56490	0.50711
				1.3				2.54393	0.05138	0.21175	3.05725	0.56489	0.50711
				1.7				2.54393	0.05138	0.21175	3.05725	0.56068	0.50711
				1.9				2.54393	0.05082	0.21175	3.0575	0.55857	0.50711
				2.1				2.54393	0.05025	0.21175	3.05725	0.55646	0.50711
					0.2			2.54393	0.05593	0.21175	3.05725	0.57754	0.50711
					0.3			2.54393	0.05593	0.21161	3.05725	0.57754	0.50694
					0.4			2.54393	0.05592	0.21152	3.05725	0.57757	0.50676
					0.5			2.54393	0.05592	0.21175	3.05725	0.57752	0.50659
					0.6			2.54393	0.05592	0.21175	3.05725	0.57751	0.50643
						0.02		2.05612	0.05014	0.23003	3.14578	0.08917	0.28112
						0.03		1.87661	0.04852	0.22816	2.89971	0.08710	0.25715
						0.04		1.73051	0.04646	0.22648	2.65364	0.08571	0.23846
						0.05		1.55101	0.04462	0.22419	1.30494	0.08325	0.21019
							0.02	1.99860	0.04822	0.22941	2.87560	0.10870	0.25989
							0.03	1.93061	0.04445	0.22871	2.62953	0.09875	0.24845
							0.04	1.88152	0.03947	0.22821	2.38082	0.09650	0.23587
							0.05	1.81351	0.03442	0.22751	1.88343	0.09430	0.22761

5. Conclusions

The impact of the nanolayer on the thermal conductivity of the hybrid nanofluid flow via porous surfaces is presented in this paper. In terms of shear stress, heat transfer rate, and mass transfer rate, numerical and graphical results were achieved.

- Effective nanolayer thermal conductivity indicates better results as compared to non-effective nanolayer thermal conductivity.
- Interfacial nanolayer thickness has a significant effect on the effective thermal conductivity and heat transfer rate of hybrid nanofluids.
- The heat and mass transfer rate increases with the increment in values of the interfacial nanolayer thickness and the activation energy parameter but decreases with the increase in values of particles α, Pr, and λ for the suction case.
- Shear stress is reduced with the increase in volume fraction φ_{p1}, φ_{p2} and the value of α for both cases of suction/injection.
- Mass transfer rate increase with the increment in values of the activation energy parameter.

Author Contributions: Data curation, A.R.; Formal analysis, M.F.; Funding acquisition, W.W.; Methodology, Q.R.; Software, B.A.; Validation, W.W.; Writing—original draft, M.Z.A.Q.; Writing—review & editing, N.A.S.; M.Z.A.Q. and N.A.S. contributed equally to this work and are co-first authors. All authors have read and agreed to the published version of the manuscript.

Funding: This research received funding support from the NSRF via the Program Management Unit for Human Resources & Institutional Development, Research and Innovation, (grant number B05F650018).

Institutional Review Board Statement: Not applicable.

Informed Consent Statement: Not applicable.

Data Availability Statement: The numerical data used to support the findings of this study are included within the article.

Conflicts of Interest: The authors declare no conflict of interest.

Nomenclature

B_0	Uniform magnetic field
C_p	Specific heat capacity
C	Fluid concentration
T_2	Upper plate temperature
T_1	Lower plate temperature
C_2	Upper plate concentration
C_1	Lower plate concentration
K	Dimensionless parameter
M	Magnetic parameter
Pr	Prandtl number
Re	Reynolds number
D	Diffusion coefficient
C_p	Specific heat capacity
K_r	Chemical reaction rate constant
E	Activation energy
σ	Dimensionless reaction rate
h	Nanolayer parameter
γ	Temperature difference parameter
β	Exothermic/endothermic coefficient
ρ_{hnf}	Density for the hybrid nanofluid
K_{bf}	Thermal conductivity for the base fluid
NPs	Nanoparticles
$f''(\eta)$	Shear stress

$\chi'(\eta)$	Mass transfer
μ_{bf}	Viscosity for the base fluid
ν_{hnf}	Kinematic viscosity for the hybrid nanofluid
α	Dimensionless constant
F_η	Dimensionless radial velocity profile
θ_η	Dimensionless temperature profile
σ	Thermal conductivity
V	Kinematic viscosity
μ	Dynamic viscosity
ρ	Density (kg/m^3)
ρc_p	Specific heat capacity
T	Temperature (K)
Sc	Schmidt number
$(\rho c_p)_{hnf}$	Specific heat capacity for the hybrid nanofluid
K_{hnf}	Thermal conductivity for the hybrid nanofluid
p	Pressure
μ_{hnf}	Viscosity for the HNF

References

1. Buongiorno, J.; Venerus, D.C.; Prabhat, N.; McKrell, T.J.; Townsend, J.; Christianson, R.J.; Tolmachev, Y.V.; Keblinski, P.; Hu, L.-W.; Alvarado, J.L.; et al. A benchmark study on the thermal conductivity of nanofluids. *J. Appl. Phys.* **2009**, *106*, 094312. [CrossRef]
2. GÜREL, B. A numerical investigation of the melting heat transfer characteristics of phase change materials in different plate heat exchanger (latent heat thermal energy storage) systems. *Int. J. Heat Mass Transf.* **2020**, *148*, 119117. [CrossRef]
3. Dhlamini, M.; Kameswaran, P.K.; Sibanda, P.; Motsa, S.; Mondal, H. Activation energy and binary chemical reaction effects in mixed convective nanofluid flow with convective boundary conditions. *J. Comput. Des. Eng.* **2018**, *6*, 149–158. [CrossRef]
4. Zhu, C.; Zhu, W.; Xu, L.; Zhou, X. A label-free electrochemical aptasensor based on magnetic biocomposites with Pb2+-dependent DNAzyme for the detection of thrombin. *Anal. Chim. Acta* **2018**, *1047*, 21–27. [CrossRef] [PubMed]
5. Wakif, A.; Animasaun, I.L.; Khan, U.; Shah, N.A.; Thumma, T. Dynamics of radiative-reactive Walters-b fluid due to mixed convection conveying gyrotactic microorganisms, tiny particles experience haphazard motion, thermo-migration, and Lorentz force Phys. *Scripta* **2021**, *96*, 125239. [CrossRef]
6. Sreenivasulu, M.; Vijaya, R.B. Influence of Activation Energy on the Hybrid Nanofluid Flow over a Flat Plate with Quadratic Thermal Radiation: An Irreversibility Analysis. *Int. J. Ambient. Energy* **2022**, 1–29. [CrossRef]
7. Ramesh, G.; Madhukesh, J. Activation energy process in hybrid CNTs and induced magnetic slip flow with heat source/sink. *Chin. J. Phys.* **2021**, *73*, 375–390. [CrossRef]
8. Wasif, M.; Mishal, K.A.; Haque, M.R.; Haque, M.M.; Rahman, F. Investigation of fluid flow and heat transfer for an optimized lid driven cavity shape under the condition of inclined magnetic field. *Energy Eng.* **2021**, *1*, 47–57.
9. Kumar, K.G.; Baslem, A.; Prasannakumara, B.C.; Majdoubi, J.; Rahimi-Gorji, M.; Nadeem, S. Significance of Arrhenius activation energy in flow and heat transfer of tangent hyperbolic fluid with zero mass flux condition. *Microsyst. Technol.* **2020**, *26*, 2517–2526. [CrossRef]
10. Awad, F.G.; Motsa, S.; Khumalo, M. Heat and Mass Transfer in Unsteady Rotating Fluid Flow with Binary Chemical Reaction and Activation Energy. *PLoS ONE* **2014**, *9*, e107622. [CrossRef]
11. Rekha, M.B.; Sarris, I.E.; Madhukesh, J.K.; Raghunatha, K.R.; Prasannakumara, B.C. Activation energy impact on flow of AA7072-AA7075/Water-Based hybrid nanofluid through a cone, wedge and plate. *Micromachines* **2022**, *13*, 302. [CrossRef] [PubMed]
12. Tang, S.; Lan, Q.; Liang, J.; Chen, S.; Liu, C.; Zhao, J.; Cheng, Q.; Cao, Y.-C.; Liu, J. Facile synthesis of Fe$_3$O$_4$ @PPy core-shell magnetic nanoparticles and their enhanced dispersity and acid stability. *Mater. Des.* **2017**, *121*, 47–50. [CrossRef]
13. Rehman, S.U.; Fatima, N.; Ali, B.; Imran, M.; Ali, L.; Shah, N.A.; Chung, J.D. The Casson Dusty Nanofluid: Significance of Darcy–Forchheimer Law, Magnetic Field, and Non-Fourier Heat Flux Model Subject to Stretch Surface. *Mathematics* **2022**, *10*, 2877. [CrossRef]
14. Suri, K.; Annapoorni, S.; Sarkar, A.; Tandon, R. Gas and humidity sensors based on iron oxide–polypyrrole nanocomposites. *Sens. Actuators B Chem.* **2002**, *81*, 277–282. [CrossRef]
15. Sun, Y.; Xiao, F.; Liu, X.; Feng, C.; Jin, C. Preparation and electromagnetic wave absorption properties of core–shell structured Fe3O4–polyaniline nanoparticles. *RSC Adv.* **2013**, *3*, 22554–22559. [CrossRef]
16. Zhao, H.; Huang, M.; Wu, J.; Wang, L.; He, H. Preparation of Fe$_3$O$_4$@PPy magnetic nanoparticles as solid-phase extraction sorbents for preconcentration and separation of phthalic acid esters in water by gas chromatography–mass spectrometry. *J. Chromatogr. B* **2016**, *1011*, 33–44. [CrossRef]
17. Salmi, A.; Madkhali, H.A.; Ali, B.; Nawaz, M.; Alharbi, S.O.; Alqahtani, A. Numerical study of heat and mass transfer enhancement in Prandtl fluid MHD flow using Cattaneo-Christov heat flux theory. *Case Stud. Therm. Eng.* **2022**, *33*, 101949. [CrossRef]

18. Roy, N.C.; Pop, I. Heat and mass transfer of a hybrid nanofluid flow with binary chemical reaction over a permeable shrinking surface. *Chin. J. Phys.* **2021**, *76*, 283–298. [CrossRef]

19. Oke, A.S. Heat and Mass Transfer in 3D MHD Flow of EG-Based Ternary Hybrid Nanofluid Over a Rotating Surface. *Arab. J. Sci. Eng.* **2022**, 1–17. [CrossRef]

20. Babu, B.H.; Rao, P.S.; Varma, S.V.K. Heat and Mass Transfer on Unsteady Magnetohydrodynamics (MHD) Convective Flow of Casson Hybrid Nanofluid Over a Permeable Media with Ramped Wall Temperature. *J. Nanofluids* **2022**, *11*, 552–562. [CrossRef]

21. Kakaç, S.; Pramuanjaroenkij, A. Review of convective heat transfer enhancement with nanofluids. *Int. J. Heat Mass Transf.* **2009**, *52*, 3187–3196. [CrossRef]

22. Demir, H.; Dalkilic, A.; Kürekci, N.; Duangthongsuk, W.; Wongwises, S. Numerical investigation on the single phase forced convection heat transfer characteristics of TiO_2 nanofluids in a double-tube counter flow heat exchanger. *Int. Commun. Heat Mass Transf.* **2011**, *38*, 218–228. [CrossRef]

23. Fetecau, C.; Shah, N.A.; Vieru, d. General Solutions for Hydromagnetic Free Convection Flow over an Infinite Plate with Newtonian Heating, Mass Diffusion and Chemical Reaction. *Commun. Theor. Phys.* **2017**, *68*, 768–782.

24. Ashraf, M.Z.; Rehman, S.U.; Farid, S.; Hussein, A.K.; Ali, B.; Shah, N.A.; Weera, W. Insight into Significance of Bioconvection on MHD Tangent Hyperbolic Nanofluid Flow of Irregular Thickness across a Slender Elastic Surface. *Mathematics* **2022**, *10*, 2592. [CrossRef]

25. Lou, Q.; Ali, B.; Rehman, S.U.; Habib, D.; Abdal, S.; Shah, N.A.; Chung, J.D. Micropolar Dusty Fluid: Coriolis Force Effects on Dynamics of MHD Rotating Fluid When Lorentz Force Is Significant. *Mathematics* **2022**, *10*, 2630. [CrossRef]

26. Sreedevi, P.; Reddy, P.S. Impact of Convective Boundary Condition on Heat and Mass Transfer of Nanofluid Flow Over a Thin Needle Filled with Carbon Nanotubes. *J. Nanofluids* **2020**, *9*, 282–292. [CrossRef]

27. Salmi, A.; Madkhali, H.A.; Nawaz, M.; Alharbi, S.O.; Alqahtani, A. Numerical study on non-Fourier heat and mass transfer in partially ionized MHD Williamson hybrid nanofluid. *Int. Commun. Heat Mass Transf.* **2022**, *133*, 105967. [CrossRef]

28. Santhi, M.; Rao, K.V.S.; Reddy, P.S.; Sreedevi, P. Heat and mass transfer characteristics of radiative hybrid nanofluid flow over a stretching sheet with chemical reaction. *Heat Transf.* **2020**, *50*, 2929–2949. [CrossRef]

29. Raja, M.A.Z.; Shoaib, M.; Khan, Z.; Zuhra, S.; Saleel, C.A.; Nisar, K.S.; Islam, S.; Khan, I. Supervised neural networks learning algorithm for three dimensional hybrid nanofluid flow with radiative heat and mass fluxes. *Ain Shams Eng. J.* **2021**, *13*, 101573. [CrossRef]

30. Shah, N.A.; Wakif, A.; El-Zahar, E.R.; Ahmad, S.; Yook, S.-J. Numerical simulation of a thermally enhanced EMHD flow of a heterogeneous micropolar mixture comprising (60%)-ethylene glycol (EG), (40%)-water (W), and copper oxide nanomaterials (CuO). *Case Stud. Therm. Eng.* **2022**, *35*, 102046.

31. Kumbhakar, B.; Nandi, S.; Chamkha, A.J. Unsteady hybrid nanofluid flow over a convectively heated cylinder with inclined magnetic field and viscous dissipation: A multiple regression analysis. *Chin. J. Phys.* **2022**, *79*, 38–56.

32. Farooq, U.; Lu, D.; Munir, S.; Ramzan, M.; Suleman, M.; Hussain, S. MHD flow of Maxwell fluid with nanomaterials due to an exponentially stretching surface. *Sci. Rep.* **2019**, *9*, 7312. [CrossRef] [PubMed]

33. Oke, A.S. Combined effects of Coriolis force and nanoparticle properties on the dynamics of gold–water nanofluid across nonuniform surface. *Z. Angew. Math. Mech.* **2022**, e202100113. [CrossRef]

34. Kigio, J.K.; Nduku, M.W.; Samuel, O.A. Analysis of Volume Fraction and Convective Heat Transfer on MHD Casson Nanofluid over a Vertical Plate. *Fluid Mech.* **2021**, *7*, 1–8. [CrossRef]

35. Tso, C.; Fu, S.; Chao, C.Y. A semi-analytical model for the thermal conductivity of nanofluids and determination of the nanolayer thickness. *Int. J. Heat Mass Transf.* **2014**, *70*, 202–214. [CrossRef]

36. Murshed, S.; Leong, K.; Yang, C. Thermophysical and electrokinetic properties of nanofluids—A critical review. *Appl. Therm. Eng.* **2008**, *28*, 2109–2125. [CrossRef]

37. Acharya, N.; Mabood, F.; Shahzad, S.; Badruddin, I. Hydrothermal variations of radiative nanofluid flow by the influence of nanoparticles diameter and nanolayer. *Int. Commun. Heat Mass Transf.* **2021**, *130*, 105781. [CrossRef]

38. Zhao, C.; Tao, Y.; Yu, Y. Molecular dynamics simulation of thermal and phonon transport characteristics of nanocomposite phase change material. *J. Mol. Liq.* **2021**, *329*, 115448. [CrossRef]

39. Ahmad, S.; Farooq, M.; Mir, N.A.; Anjum, A.; Javed, M. Magneto-hydrodynamic flow of squeezed fluid with binary chemical reaction and activation energy. *J. Cent. South Univ.* **2019**, *26*, 1362–1373. [CrossRef]

40. Majdalani, J.; Zhou, C.; Dawson, C.A. Two-dimensional viscous flow between slowly expanding or contracting walls with weak permeability. *J. Biomech.* **2002**, *35*, 1399–1403. [CrossRef]

41. Saba, F.; Ahmed, N.; Khan, U.; Waheed, A.; Rafiq, M.; Mohyud-Din, S.T. Thermophysical Analysis of Water Based ($Cu–Al_2O_3$) Hybrid Nanofluid in an Asymmetric Channel with Dilating/Squeezing Walls Considering Different Shapes of Nanoparticles. *Appl. Sci.* **2018**, *8*, 1549. [CrossRef]

42. Murshed, S.M.S.; Leong, K.; Yang, C. Investigations of thermal conductivity and viscosity of nanofluids. *Int. J. Therm. Sci.* **2008**, *47*, 560–568. [CrossRef]

43. Raza, Q.; Qureshi, M.Z.A.; Khan, B.A.; Kadhim Hussein, A.; Ali, B.; Shah, N.A.; Chung, J.D. Insight into Dynamic of Mono and Hybrid Nanofluids Subject to Binary Chemical Reaction, Activation Energy, and Magnetic Field through the Porous Surfaces. *Mathematics* **2022**, *10*, 3013. [CrossRef]

Article

Power-Law Nanofluid Flow over a Stretchable Surface Due to Gyrotactic Microorganisms

Hossam A. Nabwey [1,2,*], Waqar A. Khan [3], A. M. Rashad [4], Fazal Mabood [5] and Taha Salah [6]

[1] Department of Mathematics, College of Science and Humanities in Al-Kharj, Prince Sattam Bin Abdulaziz University, Al-Kharj 11942, Saudi Arabia
[2] Department of Basic Engineering Science, Faculty of Engineering, Menoufia University, Shebin El-Kom 32511, Egypt
[3] Department of Mechanical Engineering, College of Engineering, Prince Mohammad Bin Fahd University, Al Khobar 31952, Saudi Arabia
[4] Department of Mathematics, Faculty of Science, Aswan University, Aswan 81528, Egypt
[5] Department of Information Technology, Fanshawe College London, London, ON N5Y 5R6, Canada
[6] Basic and Applied Sciences Department, College of Engineering and Technology, Arab Academy for Science & Technology and Maritime Transport (AASTMT), Aswan Branch 81528, Egypt
* Correspondence: eng_hossam21@yahoo.com or h.mohamed@psau.edu.sa

Abstract: This study aims to learn more about how the flow of a power-law nanofluid's mixed bio-convective stagnation point flow approaching a stretchable surface behaves with the presence of a passively controlled boundary condition. The governing equations incorporate the motile bacterium and nanoparticles, and the current model includes Brownian motion and thermophoresis effects. The governing equations are transformed into ordinary differential equations, which are then numerically solved using the Runge–KuttaFehlberg (RKF) with the shooting technique. The controlling parameters are chosen as follows: the velocity ratio parameter, ε, is taken between 0.1 and 1.5; the mixed convection parameter, λ, is considered in the range 0–3; the buoyancy ratio parameter is considered in the range between 0.1 and 4; the bio-convection parameter, Rb, is taken in the range 0–1; nanofluid parameters are taken in the range 0.1–0.7; the bioconvection Schmidt number is considered in the range 0.1–3; the Prandtl number is taken between 1–4; and the Schmidt number is taken between 1 and 3. The Nusselt number, skin friction, and nanoparticle volume fraction profiles are shown graphically to observe the impact of several parameters under consideration. Both the Schmidt number and the Brownian motion parameter are shown to significantly increase the Sherwood number. Thermophoresis, however, has been proven to lower the Sherwood number. Furthermore, the bioconvection constant and Peclet number both help to slow down the rate of mass transfer. The presented theoretical investigation has a considerable role in engineering, where nanofluid flow is applied to organize a bioconvection process to develop power generation and mechanical energy. One of the more essential features of bioconvection is the aggregation of nanoparticles with motile microorganisms requested to augment the stability, heat, and mass transmission.

Keywords: Brownian; motion; nanofluids; thermophoresis; bio-convection; power-law fluid

MSC: 76D05; 76D10; 80A10; 80A19

Citation: Nabwey, H.A.; Khan, W.A.; Rashad, A.M.; Mabood, F.; Salah, T. Power-Law Nanofluid Flow over a Stretchable Surface Due to Gyrotactic Microorganisms. *Mathematics* 2022, 10, 3285. https://doi.org/10.3390/math10183285

Academic Editors: Camelia Petrescu and Valeriu David

Received: 24 July 2022
Accepted: 7 September 2022
Published: 9 September 2022

Publisher's Note: MDPI stays neutral with regard to jurisdictional claims in published maps and institutional affiliations.

1. Introduction

The importance of nanofluids has been increasing with time, and investigators intend to study the behavior of nanofluids subjected to heat transfer systems. Nanofluids and their implications in the industrial sector have grown more because of their homogeneous nature in thermal conductivity and rudimentary heat transfer. Typical fluids such as propylene glycol, water, and ethylene glycol, among others, have poor heat transfer properties. Nanofluid, a homogenous solid–liquid mixture, is applied to enhance the thermal conductivity of the base fluid. Choi [1] and Das et al. [2] exposed the most remarkable characteristic of nanofluids: thermal conductivity is dependent on temperature. Nanofluids are extensively used in energy and biomedical applications (nano-drug delivery, cancer therapeutics, and nano cryosurgery) [3–5]. Buongiorno [6] examined the effect of convective transport in nanofluid by observing the heat transfer properties of the Brownian motion and thermophoresis. Numerous studies are presented in the literature to demonstrate the uses of nanofluid in various fields [7–10].

The study of heat relocation in power-law (non-Newtonian) fluids has received significant attention because of its application in different branches of modern technologies, industries, and engineering like polymer-thickened oils, liquid crystals, polymeric suspensions, and physiological fluid mechanics. Furthermore, instances showing a diversity of non-Newtonian characteristics contain biological fluids, pharmaceutical formulations, toiletries, synthetic lubricants, cosmetics, paints, and foodstuffs (see Irvine and Karni [11]). Various models have been reported to analyze the non-Newtonian attitude toward fluids. Among these patterns, which are famous for following the empirical Ostwald–de Waele model, in which the shear stress varies according to a power function of the strain rate, gained much acceptance. The theoretical analysis of power-law fluid was first scrutinized by Schowalter [12] and Acrivos et al. [13]. Rashad et al. [14] examined the power-law nanofluid flow across a vertical cone in a porous medium. Later on, several studies were analyzed by many investigators [5,15–17].

Bioconvection occurs as the natural microbe swims upwards. Thus, the microorganism is denser than the base fluids. Because there are so many microbes on the upper surface of the foundation, it becomes weak. As a result, the bacteria decrease and promote bioconvection, and the microbes' return to swimming strengthens the process. This bacterial emigration into the water raises the temperature and mass transfer in the environment. Because of medical advancements, microscopic kinds have significantly contributed to the improvement in human life. Microorganisms are essential for life and it cannot exist without them. Decreasing the length of the cavities and the cell resistance enables the construction of continuum numerical patterns. It is often approved that the nanoparticles of concentration distribution are massive relative to the cell pivot. Bioconvection occurs as combined nanofluids are addressed using heat and mass conversion. Platt [18] further proposed the concept of bioconvection, which characterizes the micro-structural flow brought on by gradation density, in addition to motile gyro-tacticmicro-organisms. The first study of the bioconvection of gyro-tactic motile bacteria, including nanoparticles, was conducted by Kuznetsov and Avramenko [19]. Kuznetsov [20] presented key discoveries of nanofluidbioconvection in a horizontal porous layer, including both nanoparticles and gyro-tactic motile bacteria. Khan and coworkers [7,21–24] investigated the free convection of non-Newtonian nanofluid numerically down a vertical plate in a porous media. They considered that the medium contains gyrotactic microorganisms and that the temperature, nanoparticle concentration, and motile microbe density are all controlled in the plate.

The local Nusselt, Sherwood, and density numbers are found to be strongly influenced by nanofluid and bioconvection parameters. Additionally, they provided a mathematical model to examine the flow of a water-based nanofluid containing gyrotactic microorganisms around a truncated cone with a convective boundary condition at the surface. It has been discovered that, as a surface grows rougher, the densities of the mobile microorganisms, Sherwood number, Nusselt number, and skin friction all increase. Nabwey and collaborators [8–10] investigated the flow of a nanofluid containing gyrotactic bacteria over an isothermal cone surface in the presence of viscous dissipation and Joule heating. Consideration was given to the combined effects of a transverse magnetic field and Navier slip in the flow. They also considered mixed bioconvective flow on a vertical wedge in a Darcy porous media filled with a nanofluid that contains both nanoparticles and gyrotactic bacteria. To combine energy and concentration equations with passively controlled boundary conditions, the effects of thermophoresis and Brownian motion are considered. They found that the buoyancy ratio and magnetic field parameters increase the local skin friction coefficient, Nusselt number, Sherwood number, and local density of the motile microorganism's number. Ishak et al. [25] analyzed the flow of a two-dimensional stagnation point of an incompressible viscous fluid near a steady mixed convection boundary layer flow across a stretching vertical sheet in its plane. For an aiding flow, they demonstrated that both the skin friction coefficient and the local Nusselt number increase with the buoyancy ratio; however, when the Prandtl number increases, only the local Nusselt number increases and the skin friction coefficient decreases.

However, the current study intends to close the knowledge gap regarding the mixed bioconvective stagnation point flow of a power-law nanofluid towards a stretchable surface. The nanofluid flow will be mathematically modeled using Buongiorno's two-component, including the Brownian movement and thermophoresis aspects. Moreover, modeling of the motile microorganism and nanoparticles is addressed in the governing equations.

2. Governing Equations

The present study considers the mixed bioconvection flow of a non-Newtonian power-law nanofluid having motile microorganisms and obeying the Ostwald–de Waele model [18] near the stagnation point at a heated stretchable vertical surface coinciding with the plane y = 0. The flow is confined to the region y > 0, where x and y are the cartesian coordinates. The model suggested by Buongiorno is utilized for the nanofluid attitude in which the influence of thermophoresis and Brownian movement is taken into consideration. The stretchable surface is maintained at a constant temperature Tw along with the constant density of motile microorganisms N_w. The ambient temperature, concentration, and motile microorganisms are symbolized as T∞, C∞, and N∞, respectively. It is considered that the stretching velocity is given by Uw(x) = cx and the velocity of external flow in the neighborhood of the stagnation point at x = y = 0 is given by U∞(x) = ax, where a and c are positive constants. Although, in the past, this reality is eliminated, in a practical situation, there is no nanoparticle flux on the boundaries, and the values of the nanofluid fraction C adapt to the concentration distribution. This means that we consider passively controlled boundary conditions as proposed by Kuznetsov and Nield [26].

Under the above-mentioned assumptions, the physical description of the problem under consideration in Figure 1 with Boussinesq approximations can be expressed as follows [8,24]:

$$\frac{\partial u}{\partial x} + \frac{\partial v}{\partial y} = 0 \tag{1}$$

$$u\frac{\partial u}{\partial x} + v\frac{\partial u}{\partial y} = U_\infty \frac{dU_\infty}{dx} + \frac{1}{\rho_f}\frac{\partial \tau_{xy}}{\partial y} + \frac{1}{\rho_f}\left[\begin{array}{c}(1 - C_\infty)g\beta(T - T_\infty) \\ -(\rho_p - \rho_f)g(C - C_\infty) \\ -(\rho_m - \rho_f)g\gamma(N - N_\infty)\end{array}\right] \tag{2}$$

$$u\frac{\partial T}{\partial x} + v\frac{\partial T}{\partial y} = \alpha\frac{\partial^2 T}{\partial y^2} + \tau\left[D_B\frac{\partial C}{\partial y}\frac{\partial T}{\partial y} + \frac{D_T}{T_\infty}\left(\frac{\partial T}{\partial y}\right)^2\right] \tag{3}$$

$$u\frac{\partial C}{\partial x} + v\frac{\partial C}{\partial y} = D_B\frac{\partial^2 C}{\partial y^2} + \frac{D_T}{T_\infty}\frac{\partial^2 T}{\partial y^2} \tag{4}$$

$$u\frac{\partial N}{\partial x} + v\frac{\partial N}{\partial y} + \frac{bWc}{C_\infty}\left[\frac{\partial}{\partial y}\left(N\frac{\partial C}{\partial y}\right)\right] = D_m\frac{\partial^2 N}{\partial y^2} \tag{5}$$

The boundary conditions can be set in the following form [14]:

$$u = U_w(x), v = 0, T = T_w, D_B\frac{\partial C}{\partial y} + \frac{D_T}{T_\infty}\frac{\partial T}{\partial y} = 0, N = N_w \text{ at } y = 0 \tag{6a}$$

$$u = U_\infty(x), T = T_\infty, C = C_\infty, N = N_\infty \text{ as } y \to \infty \tag{6b}$$

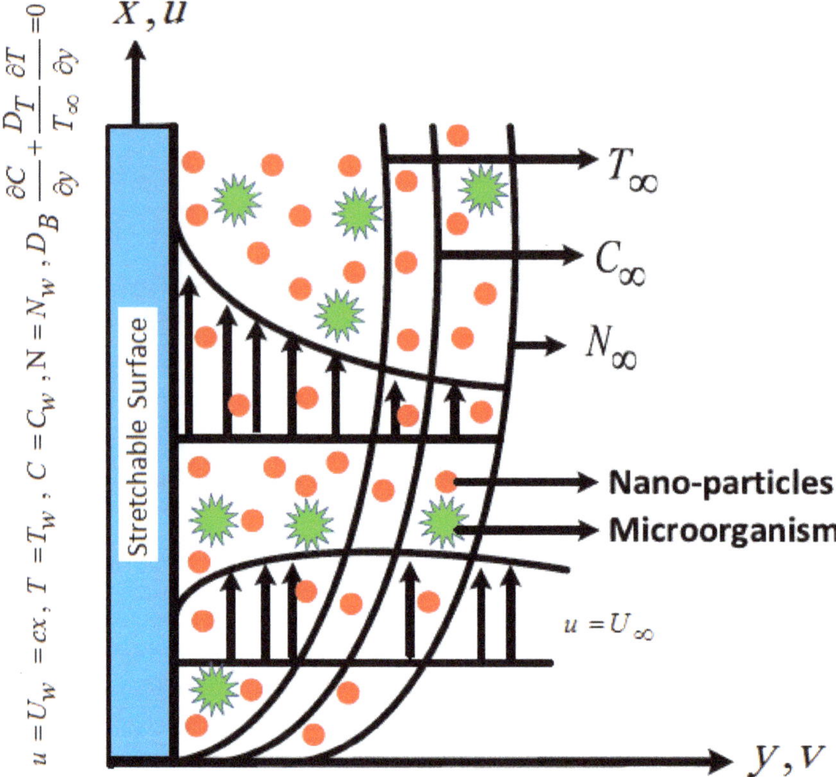

Figure 1. Schematic functionality of the flow.

In the present problem, we have $\partial u/\partial y > 0$ when $a/c > 1$ (the ratio of free stream velocity and stretching velocity), which gives the shear stress where $\tau_{xy} = K(\partial u/\partial y)^{n}$. Here, K is the consistency coefficient and n is the power-law fluid. It is noted that, when $n = 1$, the fluid is Newtonian; when $n < 1$, the fluid is called pseudoplastic power-law fluid; and when $n > 1$, it is called dilatants power-law fluid.

Here (u, v) are the velocity components, along with the (x, y) directions. Here, T, C, and N are the fluid temperature, concentration, and density of motile microorganisms, respectively, and g is the gravitational acceleration. Wc denotes the maximum cell swimming speed, α stands for thermal diffusivity, β is the coefficient of thermal expansion, γ represents the average volume of a microorganism, ρ_f represents the density of the fluid, ρ_p denotes the density of the particles, ρ_m is the density of the microorganism, $\tau = (\rho c)_p/(\rho c)_f$ is the nanofluid heat capacity ratio, $(\rho c)_f$ is the heat capacity of the base fluid and $(\rho c)_p$ is the effective heat capacity of the nanoparticle material, Dn stands for diffusivity of the microorganisms, D_B represents the Brownian diffusion coefficient, and D_T stands for the thermophoretic diffusion coefficient of the microorganisms.

It is observed that the continuity equation is automatically determined by specifying the upgraded stream function, such that $u = (\partial\psi/\partial y)$, $v = -(\partial\psi/\partial x)$, and exhibits the following non-dimensional variables:

$$\theta = \frac{T - T_\infty}{T_w - T_\infty}, \phi = \frac{C - C_\infty}{C_\infty}, \chi = \frac{N - N_\infty}{N_w - N_\infty},$$

$$\psi = \left(\frac{K/\rho_f}{c^{1-2n}}\right)^{1/(n+1)} x^{2n/(n+1)} F(\eta), \ \eta = y\left(\frac{c^{2-n}}{K/\rho_f}\right)^{1/(n+1)} x^{(1-n)/(1+n)}$$

$$(7)$$

Equations (1)–(5) take the following non-dimensional form [8,9]:

$$nF''^{(n-1)}F''' + \frac{2n}{1+n}FF'' - F'^2 + \varepsilon^2 + \lambda\theta - Nr\phi - Rb\,\chi = 0 \tag{8}$$

$$\theta'' + \Pr\left(\frac{2n}{1+n}F\theta' + Nb\theta'\phi' + Nt\theta'^2\right) = 0 \tag{9}$$

$$\phi'' + Sc\frac{2n}{n+1}F\phi' + \frac{Nt}{Nb}\theta'' = 0 \tag{10}$$

$$\chi'' + Sb\frac{2n}{1+n}F\chi' - Pe\big(\phi\chi' + (\chi+\sigma)\phi''\big) = 0 \tag{11}$$

$$F'(0) = 1,\, F(0) = 0,\, \theta(0) = 1,\, Nb\phi'(0) + Nt\theta'(0) = 0,\, \chi(0) = 1 \tag{12a}$$

$$F'(\infty) = \varepsilon,\, \theta(\infty) = 0,\, \phi(\infty) = 0,\, \chi(\infty) = 0 \tag{12b}$$

where the prime denotes differentiation with respect to η and $\lambda = \frac{Gr_x}{Re_x^2}$ is the dimensionless mixed convection parameter, $Nr = \frac{(\rho_p - \rho_f)C_\infty}{\rho_f\beta(T_w - T_\infty)(1-C_\infty)}$ stands for the buoyancy ratio parameter, $Gr_x = \frac{(1-C_\infty)\rho_f g\beta(T_w - T_\infty)}{(K/\rho_f)^2}$ is the local Grashof number, $Re_x = \frac{(cx)^{2-n}x^n}{K/\rho_f}$ is the local Reynolds number, $Nb = \frac{\tau D_B C_\infty}{cx^2 Re_x^{-2/(n+1)}}$ is the Brownian motion parameter, $Nt = \frac{\tau D_T(T_w - T_\infty)}{T_\infty cx^2 Re_x^{-2/(n+1)}}$ is the thermophoresis parameter, $\Pr = \frac{cx^2}{\alpha}Re_x^{-2/(n+1)}$ is the Prandtl number and $Sc = \frac{cx^2}{D_B}Re_x^{-2/(n+1)}$ is the Schmidt number, $Rb = \frac{(N_w - N_\infty)\gamma(\rho_m - \rho_f)}{\rho_f\beta(T_w - T_\infty)(1-C_\infty)}$ is the bioconvection Rayleigh number, and $\varepsilon = a/c$ stands for the ratio of the velocity parameter. $Sb = \frac{cx^2 Re_x^{\frac{-2}{1+n}}}{D_m}$ denotes the bioconvection Schmidt number, $\sigma = \frac{N_\infty}{N_w - N_\infty}$ is the bioconvection constant, and $Pe = \frac{bWc}{D_m}$ represents the bioconvection Peclet number.

Various engineering quantities of interest like local skin friction C_f, the local Nusselt number N_{ux}, and the local density of the motile microorganisms' number N_{nx} are explored for the present nanofluid flow model. These quantities are defined as follows:

$$C_f = \frac{2\tau_w}{(cx)^2\rho_f};\ Nu_x = \frac{q_w x}{k_f(T_w - T_\infty)};\ Nn_x = \frac{q_n x}{D_n(T_w - T_\infty)} \tag{13}$$

For more clarification, the expressions of the shear stress τ_w, wall flux q_w (i.e., heat flux), and q_n (i.e., motile microorganisms density flux) are given as follows:

$$\tau_w = K\left(\frac{\partial u}{\partial y}\right)_{y=0};\ q_w = -k_f\left(\frac{\partial T}{\partial y}\right)_{y=0};\ q_n = -D_n\left(\frac{\partial N}{\partial y}\right)_{y=0} \tag{14}$$

By invoking the transformations of Equation (8), Equations (15) and (16) are reduced as follows:

$$\frac{1}{2}C_f Re_x^{1/(1+n)} = (F''(0))^n;\ Nu_x Re_x^{-1/(1+n)} = -\theta'(0);\ Nn_x Re_x^{-1/(1+n)} = -\chi'(0) \tag{15}$$

3. Numerical Solution and Code Validation

Using MAPLE 22, Equations (8)–(11) subject to boundary conditions (12) were solved numerically. In order to solve boundary value issues numerically, this software, by default, employs a four-fifths order Runge–Kutta–Fehlberg approach. Its reliability and precision have been repeatedly demonstrated in numerous heat transfer articles. The unity coefficient of the term was changed to a continuation $(101 - 100\lambda)$, or $(10 - 9\lambda)$ was used in the dsolve command in order to speed convergence for all values of the governing parameters selected for this investigation. Without making this adjustment, MAPLE produces results that do not conform to the asymptotic values, but produces results that have a sharp angle at which the axis intersects. The numerical solution to challenging ODE boundary value problems in Maple's help section contains more details on resolving the convergence challenges. Using a value of 8 for the similarity variable $\eta_{\max}$, the asymptotic boundary conditions from Equation (12a,b) were substituted as follows.

$$F'(8) = \varepsilon, \theta(8) = 0, \phi(8) = 0, \chi(8) = 0 \tag{16}$$

The selection of $\eta_{\max} = 8$ guaranteed that all numerical solutions appropriately approximated the asymptotic values. This is a crucial feature that is frequently missed in the literature on boundary layer fluxes.

To authenticate the model's validity, we have compared the skin friction values for several values ε in Tables 1–3, while Table 4 compares the heat transfer values with the existing literature. It exhibits good agreement for various parameters, indicating that our numerical solution is valid.

Table 1. Comparison of numerical values of $F''(0)$ at $\lambda = 0$, $n = 1$.

ε	Ishak et al. [10]	Khan and Rashad [25]	Present Results
0.1	−0.9694	−0.96939	−0.969386154
0.2	−0.9181	−0.91811	−0.918107089
0.5	−0.6673	−0.66726	−0.667263673
2	2.0175	2.017503	2.0175028007
3	4.7294	4.729282	11.751990603

Table 2. Comparison of $F''(0)$ for various values of Pr at $n = 1$ and $\lambda = Nr = 0$.

Pr	Wang [23]	Gorla and Sidawi [24]	Khan and Pop [8]	Present Results
0.07	0.0656	0.0656	0.0663	0.0659
0.2	0.1691	0.1691	0.1691	0.1690
0.7	0.4539	0.5349	0.4539	0.4539
2.0	0.9113	0.9113	0.9113	0.9113
7.0	1.8954	1.8905	1.8954	1.8954
20.0	3.3539	3.3539	3.3539	3.3539
70.0	6.4622	6.4622	6.4621	6.4622

Table 3. Comparison of $F''(0)$ for various values of n and a/c at $n = 1$ and $\lambda = Nr = 0$.

n	Mahapatra et al. [27]	Present Results	Mahapatra et al. [27]	Present Results
	$\varepsilon = 1.1$		$\varepsilon = 1.5$	
0.4	0.1035	0.1043	1.2019	1.2020
0.6	0.1193	0.1238	0.1691	1.0170
0.8	0.1407	0.14210	0.9434	0.9431
1.0	0.1643	0.16412	0.9095	0.9089
1.2	0.1888	0.18871	0.8937	0.8932
1.5	0.2257	0.22504	0.8853	0.8840

Table 4. Comparison of numerical values of $-\theta'(0)$ at $\lambda = \varepsilon = Nb = Nt = 0$, $n = 1$.

Pr	Khan et al. [28]	Present Results
0.7	0.4539	0.45445
2	0.9113	−0.91135
7	1.8954	−1.89540
20	3.3539	−3.35391

4. Results and Discussion

In this study, the mixed bioconvective stagnation-point flow of a power-law nanofluid over a stretchy sheet was computationally studied using the Runge–Kutta–Fehlberg method of the seventh order (RKF7) in conjunction with the shooting method. The influence of gyrotactic microorganisms at the surface is taken into account. Figure 2a shows the effects of the bioconvection Rayleigh number and buoyancy parameter on the dimensionless velocity, with all other parameters held constant. We notice that the dimensionless velocity increases significantly in the vicinity of the surface and then drops to the boundary layer edge with the Rayleigh number Rb. The dimensionless velocity overshoots at the region of the surface owing to the existence of buoyant forces. The Rayleigh number increases the buoyancy forces because of bioconvection, increasing the dimensionless velocity. The effects of mixed convection and velocity ratio parameters on the dimensionless velocity are presented in Figure 2b. The convergence rate depends upon the velocity ratio parameter. As the velocity ratio increases, the convergence rate increases. Within the hydrodynamic boundary layer, the mixed convection parameter also plays an important role. When the mixed convection parameter is increased, the dimensionless velocity increases.

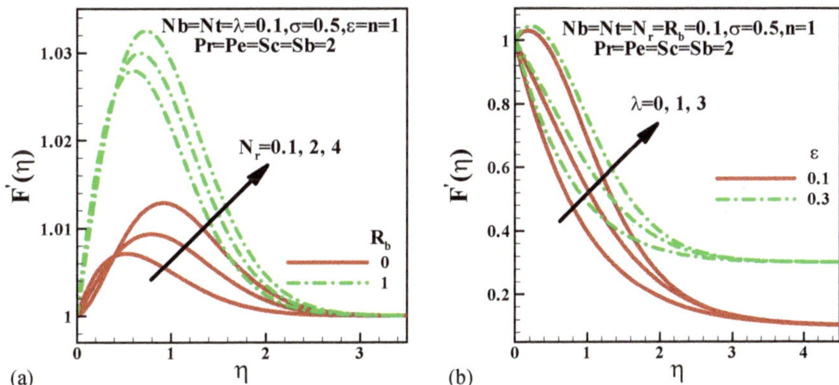

Figure 2. Variation of dimensionless velocity with (**a**) the buoyancy ratio parameter and bioconvection Rayleigh number and (**b**) the dimensionless mixed convection parameter and velocity ratio parameter.

The impacts of nanofluid parameters Nb and Nt are explained in Figure 3a. The Brownian motion parameter Nb keeps particles moving in a fluid. This keeps particles from settling, resulting in colloidal solutions that are more stable. It helps in enhancing the dimensionless velocity within the boundary layer. On the other side, the thermophoresis parameter generates a force due to temperature difference. Nanoparticles are transported towards the lower temperature zone by this force.

Consequently, the dimensionless velocity increases inside the boundary layer. In heat transfer, the bioconvection Schmidt number is equivalent to the Prandtl number. With a Schmidt number of one, momentum and mass transfer by diffusion are alike, and the velocity and concentration boundary layers are almost identical. An increasing bioconvection Schmidt number reduces the dimensionless velocity and hence the hydrodynamic boundary layer thickness, as shown in Figure 3b.

The effects of the thermophoresis parameter on the dimensionless temperature are presented in Figure 4 for several fluids. Thermophoresis is more important in a mixed convection process, where the flow is generated by the buoyancy force caused by a temperature differential. The nanoparticles move in the direction of a temperature drop, and decreasing the bulk density improves the heat transfer process. It is worth noting that nanoparticles transport thermal energy from high-temperature areas to lower-temperature areas. As a result, the thickness of the thermal boundary layer thickens as the thermophoresis parameter Nt increases. This fact is explained in Figure 4. The Prandtl number determines the thickness of the thermal boundary layer. As the Prandtl number increases, the momentum diffusivity dominates the behavior and, as a result, the thickness of the thermal boundary layer decreases.

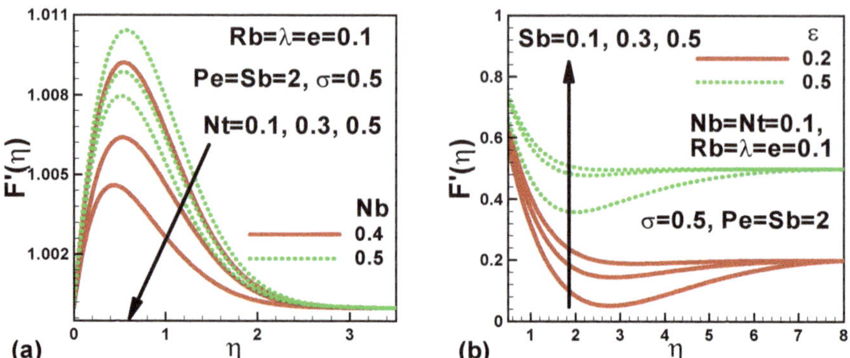

Figure 3. Variation of dimensionless velocity with (**a**) nanofluid parameters and (**b**) bioconvection Schmidt number.

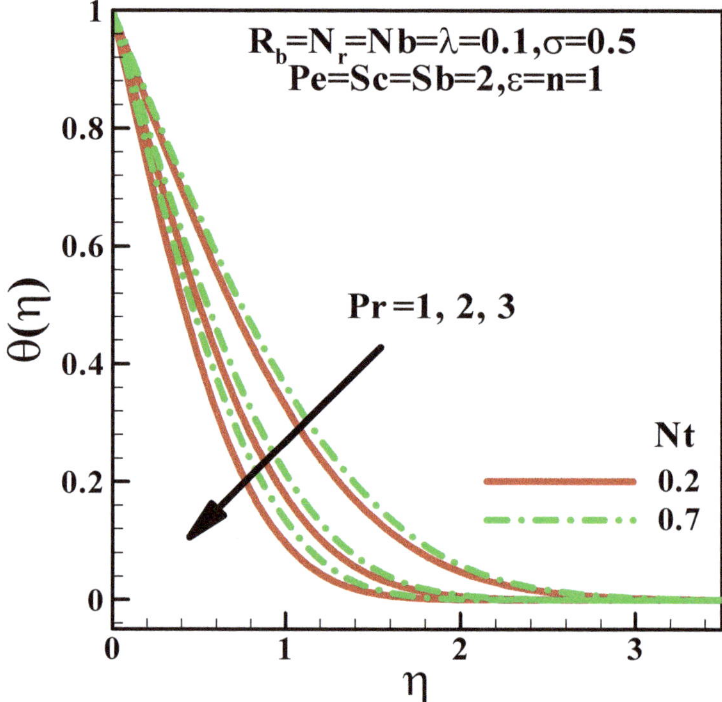

Figure 4. Variation in dimensionless temperature with the thermophoresis parameter for different fluids.

Figure 5a demonstrates the influence of nanofluid parameters on the dimensionless concentration at different thermophoresis parameters $Nt = 0.4$ and $Nt = 0.5$. The thermophoresis and Brownian processes cause the nanoparticle distribution to become non-uniform throughout the domain, as shown in Figure 5a. When the particle concentration is low and the Rayleigh number is low, the distribution of nanoparticles is more uniform.

Nanoparticle concentration rises when Nt increases because the thermophoresis parameter represents the movement of particles due to the temperature gradient.

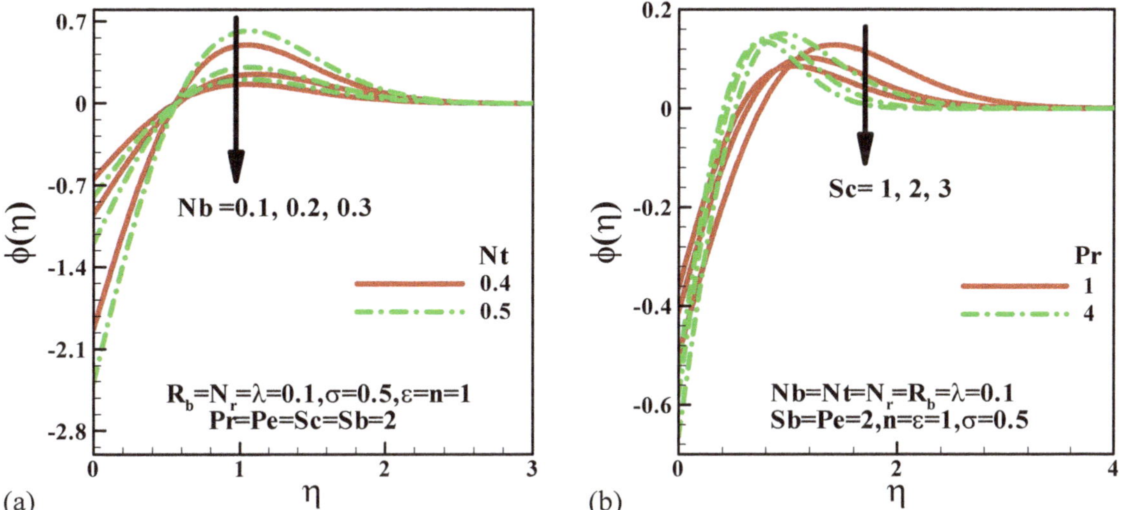

Figure 5. Variation in the dimensionless nanofluid concentration with (**a**) nanofluid parameters and (**b**) Schmidt number for different fluids.

Figure 5b depicts the influence of the Schmidt number Sc on the dimensionless concentration for several fluids. The dimensionless concentration overshoots near the surface and drops to zero, as observed. The reason is that the dimensionless velocity rises towards the surface before falling to zero. It is worth noting that, in the surface region, the dimensionless concentration rises with the Schmidt number. This is because the mass diffusivity diminishes, resulting in a lower concentration of nanoparticles. As a result, the concentration boundary layer thickness decreases as the Schmidt number Sc distance from the cone surface increases and increases as the Schmidt number Nt decreases. However, in the passively controlled model, it is assumed that there is no nanoparticle flux at the plate and that its particle fraction value adjusts accordingly. Thus, the passively controlled nanofluid model [26] can be used in practical applications. A numerical survey is then performed for all four profiles embodying the velocity, temperature, nanoparticle volumetric fraction, and density of motile microorganisms.

The effects of the bioconvection Schmidt number for different values of Peclet number are presented in Figure 6a. The large values of the Peclet number suggest an advectively dominated distribution, while a smaller value indicates a dispersed flow. As the Peclet number increases, the boundary layer thickness of motile microorganisms increases. Conversely, the bioconvection Schmidt number tends to suppress the boundary layer thickness. It is observed that the dimensionless motile microorganism density decreases with the bioconvection Schmidt number, but increases with the Peclet number. This can be attributed to the substantial decrease in mass diffusivity, which generates a lower concentration. Figure 6b illustrates the influence of the bioconvection constant for different values of the Brownian motion parameter. Nanoparticles are not self-propelled in a nanofluid. Brownian motion and the thermophoresis effect cause them to move. Motile microorganisms are mixed with a dilute suspension of nanoparticles to increase mass transfer and microscale mixing, as well as nanofluid stability in the flow. For this reason, the Brownian motion parameter tends to decrease the dimensionless microorganisms while the bioconvection constant tends to increase the microorganism's density.

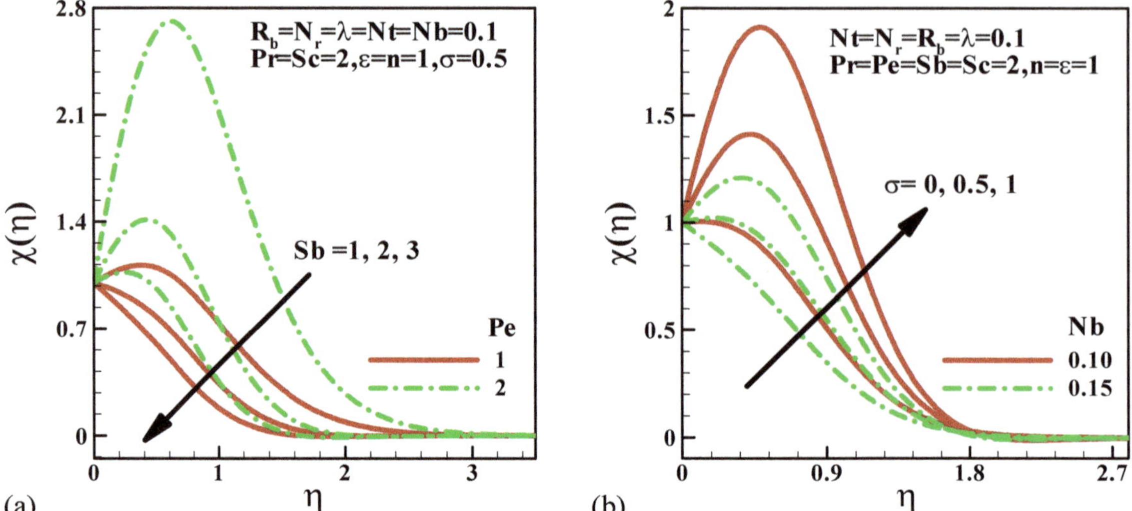

Figure 6. Variation of dimensionless motile micro-organism density with (**a**) the bioconvection Schmidt number with different Peclet numbers and (**b**) the bioconvection constant and Brownian motion parameter.

For several values of the bioconvection Rayleigh number and dimensionless mixed convection parameter, the variation in skin friction with the buoyancy ratio parameter is shown in Figure 7a. The skin friction is observed to rise with the bioconvection Rayleigh number and dimensionless mixed convection parameter, but decreases slightly with the buoyancy parameter. The skin friction is exceptionally high in the absence of the buoyancy effect and subsequently tends to decrease along with the buoyancy parameter. However, compared with buoyancy force convection, increasing the bioconvection Rayleigh number and dimensionless mixed convection parameter enhanced the convection heat. These results are anticipated; in the interim, heat is produced as a result of increased skin friction, resulting in the formation of a layer of hot fluid close to the surface. It is interesting to note that, as long as skin friction values are positive, we can see that drag force is imparted to the surface via the fluid. Figure 7b explains the effects of nanofluid parameters on the dimensionless heat transfer for different fluids. It is important to note that the Nusselt number decreases with both nanofluid parameters, but increases with the Prandtl number. It is commonly known that the Nusselt number represents the ratio of convective to conductive heat transfer; as a result, with more significant Nusselt numbers, heat convection predominates and the Nusselt number decreases as Nb and Nt increase.

The ratio of momentum diffusivity to mass diffusivity is known as the Schmidt number. In heat transmission, this is like the Prandtl number. When there is simultaneous momentum and mass transmission, this is used to characterize flows. The Sherwood number measures the efficacy of mass transfer at the surface. The variation in the Sherwood number with the Schmidt number is depicted in Figure 8a for different values of the thermophoresis parameter and Brownian number. It is perceived that the Sherwood number increases significantly with the Schmidt number and Brownian motion parameter. However, the thermophoresis parameter tends to reduce the Sherwood number.

The variation in the dimensionless local density number of the motile microorganisms with bioconvection parameters is depicted in Figure 8b. The motile microorganism mass transfer rate is significantly increased when the bioconvection Schmidt number increases. The bioconvection Peclet number and bioconvection constant reduce the rate of motile microorganism mass transfer. This is because Pe is directly related to Wc (maximum cell swimming speed) and inversely proportional to D_m (the diffusivity of microorganisms). As a result, larger Pe values diminish microorganism speed and reduce microorganism diffusivity. This will result in lower microorganism concentrations in the border layer and a higher rate of motile micro-organism mass transfer.

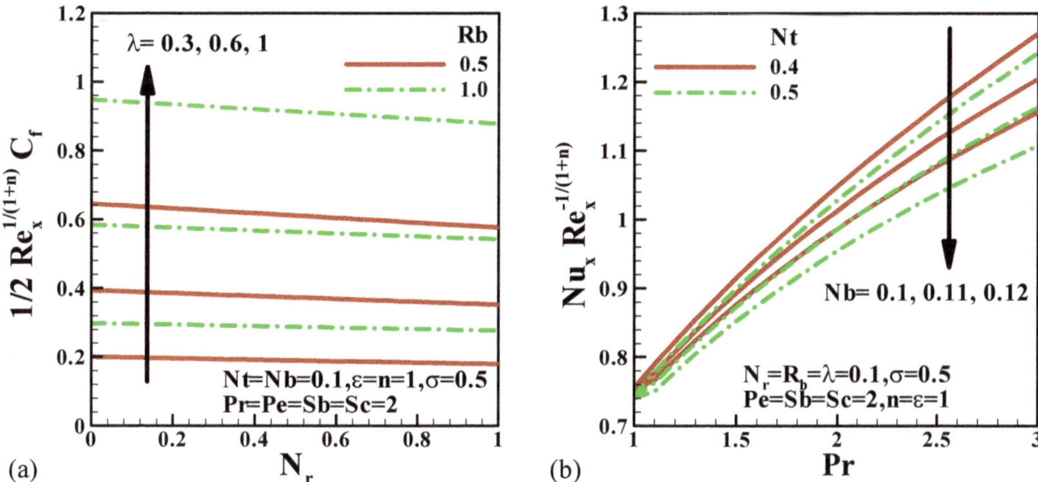

Figure 7. Variation in skin friction with (**a**) buoyancy ratio parameters for different values of bioconvection Rayleigh number and dimensionless mixed convection parameter and (**b**) variation in the Nusselt number with the Prandtl number for different values of nanofluid parameters.

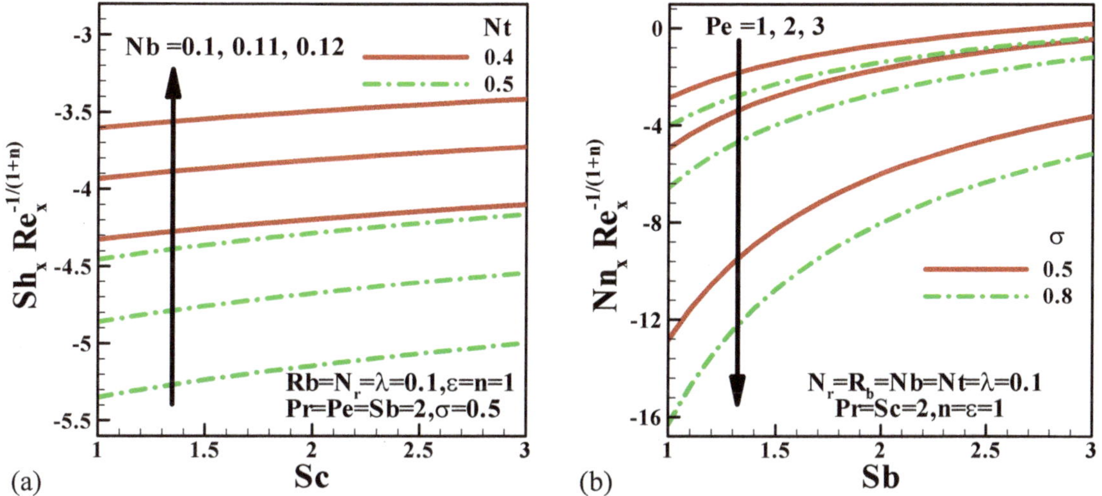

Figure 8. (**a**) Variation in the Sherwood number with the Schmidt number for different nanofluid parameters and (**b**) variation in the density number of the motile microorganisms.

5. Conclusions

The mixed bioconvective flow of water-based nanofluid containing micro-organisms is investigated numerically using a Runge-Kutta–Fehlberg method of the seventh order (RKF7) coupled with a shooting method. The effects of bioconvection and nanofluid parameters on the dimensionless variables and quantities of interest are investigated numerically. The results are presented graphically and are compared with the existing data.

In the RKF7 method, the following are the primary conclusions that can be deduced from the study:

- Besides the bioconvection Schmidt number, all other parameters enhance the dimensionless velocity inside the boundary layer.
- Thermal boundary layer thickness decreases with the increasing Prandtl number.
- The nanofluid parameters generate non-uniform nanoparticle distribution throughout the domain.
- Dimensionless motile microbe density decreases as the bio-convection Schmidt number rises, but rises when the Peclet number falls.
- Skin friction is slightly reduced by the buoyancy parameter, but is slightly increased by the dimensionless mixed convection parameter and the bioconvection Rayleigh number.
- Nanofluid parameters reduce the Nusselt number, while the Prandtl number enhances it.
- Schmidt number and Brownian motion parameter both significantly boost the Sherwood number. Thermophoresis, on the other hand, tends to lower the Sherwood number.
- The bioconvection Peclet number and bioconvection constant contribute to slowing down the rate of mass transfer in motile microorganisms.

Author Contributions: All authors contributed equally. All authors have read and agreed to the published version of the manuscript.

Funding: This research received no external funding.

Data Availability Statement: Data are available upon request.

Conflicts of Interest: The authors declare no conflict of interest.

Nomenclature

a and c	positive constants
C	concentration
C_f	local skin-friction coefficient
Dn	diffusivity of the microorganisms
D_B	Brownian diffusion coefficient
D_T	thermophoretic diffusion coefficient of the microorganisms
F'	dimensionless velocity
g	gravitational acceleration
Gr_x	local Grashof number
Sb	bioconvection Schmidt number
Sc	Schmidt number
K	consistency coefficient
k_f	thermal conductivity
N	density of motile microorganisms
n	power-law fluid
Nb	Brownian motion number
Nr	buoyancy ratio parameter
Nt	thermophoresis number
Nu_x	Nusselt number
Nn_x	density number
Pe	bioconvectionPéclet number
Pr	Prandtl number
q	wall heat flux
Rb	bioconvection Rayleigh number
Re_x	local Reynolds number
T	temperature
u and v	dimensionless velocity component in the x-direction

$U_w(x)$	stretching velocity
$U_\infty(x)$	free stream velocity
w_c	maximum cell swimming speed
x	streamwise coordinate
y	transverse coordinate
Greek Symbols	
α	thermal diffusivity
β	coefficient of thermal expansion
γ	average volume of a microorganism
σ	bioconvection constant
η	pseudo-similarity variable
θ	dimensionless temperature
φ	nanoparticle volume fraction
ψ	non-dimensional stream function
λ	mixed convection parameter
ε	ratio of velocity parameter
χ	dimensionless density of motile microorganisms
μ	dynamic viscosity
ν	kinematic viscosity
ρ_f	density of the fluid
$\rho_{f\infty}$	density of the base fluid
ρ_p	density of the particles
$\rho_{m\infty}$	density of the microorganism
$(\rho c)_f$	heat capacity of the fluid
$(\rho c)_p$	effective heat capacity of the nanoparticle material
ρ	density
Subscripts	
w	condition at the wall
∞	condition at infinity

References

1. Choi, S.U.S. Enhancing thermal conductivity of fluids with nanoparticles. In Proceedings of the 1995 ASME International Mechanical Engineering Congress and Exposition, San Francisco, CA, USA, 12–17 November 1995; pp. 99–105.
2. Das, K.; Putra, N.; Thiesen, P.; Roetzel, W. Temperature dependence of thermal conductivity enhancement for nanofluid. *J. Heat Transf.* **2003**, *125*, 567–574. [CrossRef]
3. Gorla, R.S.R.; El-Kabeir, S.M.M.; Rashad, A.M. Heat transfer in the boundary layer on a stretching circular cylinder in a nanofluid. *J. Thermophys. Heat Transf.* **2011**, *25*, 183–186. [CrossRef]
4. Chamkha, A.J.; Rashad, A.M. Natural convection from a vertical permeable cone in nanofluid saturated porous media for uniform heat and nanoparticles volume fraction fluxes. *Int. J. Numer. Methods Heat Fluid Flow* **2012**, *22*, 1073–1085. [CrossRef]
5. Chamkha, A.J.; Rashad, M.; Gorla, R.S.R. Non-Similar Solutions for Mixed Convection along with a Wedge Embedded in a Porous Medium Saturated by a Non-Newtonian Nanofluid: Natural Convection Dominated Regime. *Int. J. Numer. Methods Heat Fluid Flow* **2014**, *24*, 1471–1786. [CrossRef]
6. Buongiorno, J. Convective transport in nanofluids. *ASME J. Heat Transf.* **2006**, *128*, 240–250. [CrossRef]
7. Khan, W.A.; Rashad, A.M.; Abdou, M.M.M.; Tlili, I. Natural Bioconvection Flow of A Nanofluid Containing Gyrotactic Microorganisms About A Truncated Cone. *Eur. J. Mech./B Fluids* **2019**, *75*, 133–142. [CrossRef]
8. Chamkha, A.J.; Nabwey, H.A.; Abdelrahman, Z.M.A.; Rashad, A.M. Mixed Bioconvective Flow Over a Wedge in Porous Media Drenched with a Nanofluid. *J. Nanofluids* **2020**, *9*, 24–35. [CrossRef]
9. Nabwey, H.A.; El-Kabeir, S.M.M.; Rashad, A.M.; Abdou, M.M.M. Viscous Dissipation and Joule Heating Effects on MHD Bioconvection Flow of a Nanofluid Containing Gyrotactic Microorganisms over a Vertical Isothermal Cone. *J. Nanofluids* **2020**, *9*, 242–255. [CrossRef]
10. Nabwey, H.A.; El-Kabeir, S.M.M.; Rashad, A.M.; Abdou, M.M.M. Gyrotactic Microorganisms Mixed Convection Flow of Nanofluid over a Vertically Surfaced Saturated Porous Media. *Alex. Eng. J.* **2021**, *61*, 1804–1822. [CrossRef]
11. Irvine, T.F.; Karni, J. Non-Newtonian fluid flow and heat transfer. In *Handbook of Single-Phase Convective Heat Transfer*; Kakac, S., Shah, R.K., Aung, W., Eds.; Wiley: New York, NY, USA, 1987; pp. 20.1–20.57.
12. Schowalter, W.R. The application of boundary-layer theory to power-law pseudoplastic fluids: Similar solutions. *AICHE J.* **1960**, *6*, 24–28. [CrossRef]
13. Acrivos, A.; Shah, M.J.; Petersen, E.E. Momentum and heat transfer in laminar boundary layer flows of non-Newtonian fluids past external surfaces. *AICHE J.* **1960**, *6*, 312–318. [CrossRef]

14. Rashad, A.M.; EL-Hakiem, M.A.; Abdou, M.M.M. Natural convection boundary layer of a non-Newtonian fluid about a permeable vertical cone embedded in a porous medium saturated with a nanofluid. *Comput. Math. Appl.* **2011**, *62*, 3140–3151. [CrossRef]
15. Rashad, A.M.; Chamkha, A.J.; Abdou, M.M.M. Mixed Convection Flow Of Non-Newtonian Fluid From Vertical Surface Saturated In A Porous Medium Filled with A Nanofluid. *J. Appl. Fluid Mech.* **2013**, *6*, 301–309.
16. Chamkha, A.J.; Abbasbandy, S.; Rashad, A.M. Non-Darcy Natural Convection Flow of a Non-Newtonian Nanofluid over a Cone Saturated in a Porous Medium with Uniform Heat and Volume Fraction Fluxes. *Int. J. Numer. Methods Heat Fluid Flow* **2015**, *25*, 422–437. [CrossRef]
17. Nabwey, H.A.; Boumazgour, M.; Rashad, A.M. Group Method Analysis Of Mixed Convection Stagnation-Point Flow of Non-Newtonian Nanofluid over a Vertical Stretching Surface. *Indian J. Phys.* **2017**, *91*, 731–742. [CrossRef]
18. Platt, J.R. Bioconvection Patterns in Cultures of Free-Swimming Organisms. *Science* **1961**, *133*, 1766–1767. [CrossRef]
19. Kuznetsov, A.V.; Avramenko, A.A. Effect of small particles on the stability of bioconvection in a suspension of gyrotactic microorganisms in a layer of finite depth. *Int. Commun. Heat Mass Transf.* **2004**, *31*, 1–10. [CrossRef]
20. Kuznetsov, A.V. The onset of nanofluidbioconvection in a suspension containing both nanoparticles and gyrotactic microorganisms. *Int. Commun. Heat Mass Transf.* **2010**, *37*, 1421–1425. [CrossRef]
21. Waqas, H.; Khan, S.U.; Hassan, M.; Bhatti, M.M.; Imran, M. Analysis of the bioconvection flow of modified second-grade nanofluid containing gyrotactic microorganisms and nanoparticles. *J. Mol. Liq.* **2019**, *291*, 111231. [CrossRef]
22. Khan, W.A.; Uddin, M.J.; Ismail, A.I. Free convection of non-Newtonian nanofluids in porous media with gyrotactic microorganisms. *Transp. Porous Media* **2013**, *97*, 241–252. [CrossRef]
23. Khan, W.A.; Rashad, A.M. Combined effects of radiation and chemical reaction on heat and mass transfer by MHD stagnation-point flow of a Micropolar fluid towards a stretching surface. *J. Niger. Math. Soc.* **2017**, *36*, 219–238.
24. Beg, O.A.; Uddin, M.J.; Khan, W.A. Bioconvective Non-Newtonian Nanofluid Transport in Porous Media Containing Micro-Organisms in a Moving Free Stream. *J. Mech. Med. Biol.* **2015**, *15*, 5. [CrossRef]
25. Ishak, A.; Nazar, R.; Pop, I. Mixed convection boundary layers in the stagnation point flow toward a stretching vertical sheet. *Meccanica* **2006**, *41*, 509–518. [CrossRef]
26. Kuznetsov, A.V.; Nield, D.A. Natural convective boundary-layer flow of a nanofluid past a vertical plate: A revised model. *Int. J. Therm. Sci.* **2014**, *77*, 126–129. [CrossRef]
27. Mahapatra, T.R.; Nandy, S.K.; Gupta, A.S. Magnetohydrodynamic stagnation-point flow of a power-law fluid towards a stretching surface. *Int. J. Non-Linear Mech.* **2009**, *44*, 123–128. [CrossRef]
28. Khan, M.; Malik, R.; Munir, A.; Khan, W.A. Flow and heat transfer to Siskonanofluid over a nonlinear stretching sheet. *PLoS ONE* **2015**, *10*, e0125683.

Article

Prediction and Optimization of Pile Bearing Capacity Considering Effects of Time

Mohammadreza Khanmohammadi [1], Danial Jahed Armaghani [2,*] and Mohanad Muayad Sabri Sabri [3]

[1] Department of Civil Engineering, Isfahan University of Technology, Isfahan 8415683111, Iran
[2] School of Civil and Environmental Engineering, University of Technology Sydney, Ultimo, NSW 2007, Australia
[3] Peter the Great St. Petersburg Polytechnic University, 195251 St. Petersburg, Russia
* Correspondence: danial.jahedarmaghani@uts.edu.au

Abstract: Prediction of pile bearing capacity has been considered an unsolved problem for years. This study presents a practical solution for the preparation and maximization of pile bearing capacity, considering the effects of time after the end of pile driving. The prediction phase proposes an intelligent equation using a genetic programming (GP) model. Thus, pile geometry, soil properties, initial pile capacity, and time after the end of driving were considered predictors to predict pile bearing capacity. The developed GP equation provided an acceptable level of accuracy in estimating pile bearing capacity. In the optimization phase, the developed GP equation was used as input in two powerful optimization algorithms, namely, the artificial bee colony (ABC) and the grey wolf optimization (GWO), in order to obtain the highest bearing capacity of the pile, which corresponds to the optimum values for input parameters. Among these two algorithms, GWO obtained a higher value for pile capacity compared to the ABC algorithm. The introduced models and their modeling procedure in this study can be used to predict the ultimate capacity of piles in such projects.

Keywords: pile bearing capacity; genetic programming; artificial bee colony; gray wolf optimization; optimization purposes

MSC: 68Txx

Citation: Khanmohammadi, M.; Armaghani, D.J.; Sabri Sabri, M.M. Prediction and Optimization of Pile Bearing Capacity Considering Effects of Time. *Mathematics* **2022**, *10*, 3563. https://doi.org/10.3390/math10193563

Academic Editors: Camelia Petrescu and Valeriu David

Received: 16 July 2022
Accepted: 13 September 2022
Published: 29 September 2022

Publisher's Note: MDPI stays neutral with regard to jurisdictional claims in published maps and institutional affiliations.

1. Introduction

Pile foundations are structural elements that are mainly used when the surface soil is weak and there is an urgent need to transfer the structural load to the further layers of the soil, or when soil settlement is an essential concern in the designing process. In terms of the pile's role in load transmission, calculating the precise ultimate bearing capacity of pile foundations is an important topic for geotechnical engineers. Besides this, some scholars have indicated that pile bearing capacity can be considered as a time-dependent parameter, exhibiting an increasing trend after a specific period [1–3]. Pile setup is a geotechnical phenomenon referring to a time-dependent increase in the ultimate bearing capacity of pile foundations. It is assumed that pile setup occurs due to the dissipation of the excess pore water pressure (EPWP) generated as a result of pile installation [4].

Furthermore, it is widely accepted that this phenomenon develops by incorporating three main stages, including the non-uniform dissipation of EPWP, the uniform dissipation of EPWP, and aging [5]. Results of different studies indicate that setup considerably affects the side resistance, while when it comes to the tip resistance, it has exhibited less change or a decrease owing to relaxation [1,6–10]. Predicting the time-dependent bearing capacity of pile foundations has always been an interesting topic for researchers. Moreover, considering the pile setup, the design process of piles can be more economical.

Many studies have been presented in which analytical or numerical models were developed to forecast the pile setup [11–13]. One of the most well-known investigations in this area is a study conducted by Skov and Denver [14] to find an equation to estimate the pile setup. The setup equation was revised using different geotechnical properties to achieve this goal. Finally, a semi-empirical equation was proposed by them introducing a practical variable called setup parameter (A). This pioneering study was a starting point for other researchers. For example, Haque and Abu-Farsakh [6] published a paper in which the application of a nonlinear multivariable regression model in the prediction of pile setup was investigated. Although the studies conducted using this group of techniques were able to create an effective equation, pile setup is a complex issue considering the complicated soil–pile interaction. Therefore, analytical methods and regression analysis do not seem to be powerful enough for prediction purposes [15].

In recent years, several studies have presented the successful usage of intelligent algorithms to simulate complex problems in civil and geotechnical engineering [16–29]. Several scholars have highlighted the applicability of these techniques in predicting pile-related issues, e.g., pile capacity, settlement, lateral deflection [30–33]. In a study conducted by Lee and Lee [34], the application of artificial neural networks (ANNs) in the prediction of pile bearing capacity was investigated. The results of the model and in situ pile load tests were utilized to verify the developed model. Finally, it was concluded that the error back-propagation neural network used in this study had good performance since the maximum error in the prediction process did not exceed 25%. Shahin [35] utilized intelligent computing to model the axial capacity of pile foundations. For this purpose, an ANN technique was employed to predict the axial capacity of driven piles and drilled shafts using a total of 174 data points. Furthermore, a comparison was made between CPT-based methods and the ANN to evaluate their performances in the prediction area. The results indicated that ANN with a correlation coefficient of 0.85 and 0.97 for driven and drilled shaft validation datasets showed acceptable performance. Samui [36] investigated the application of the support vector machine as a powerful machine learning technique to estimate the pile bearing capacity. Three inputs, including penetration depth ratio, mean normal stress, and the number of bowls, were considered for this aim. Eventually, using evaluation criteria such as coefficient of correlation, the developed model predicted the pile bearing capacity with sufficient accuracy. In another study, Momeni et al. [37] used the results from 50 dynamic load tests to predict the bearing capacity of piles using an ANN-based predictive model optimized with a genetic algorithm. The final data indicated that the developed model, with a correlation coefficient of 0.99, successfully predicted the target very close to its actual value.

Other studies tried to improve the performance of the base intelligent models using optimization algorithms. For instance, Dehghanbanadaki et al. [38] used the gray wolf optimization (GWO) algorithm to enhance the performance of the adaptive neuro-fuzzy inference system (ANFIS) for estimating the ultimate bearing capacity of single driven piles. The results showed that the actual values of pile bearing capacity had been successfully estimated using the GWO-ANFIS model, and their results improved upon the ANFIS model. In another study implemented by Armaghani et al. [33], a combination of ANFIS and group data handling methods optimized with a competitive imperialism algorithm (ICA) was utilized to forecast the pile bearing capacity. Based on the data and the evaluation criteria, the proposed model could be considered a powerful technique regarding pile foundations' design process.

Previous works did not include a time component in their input parameters, and their input parameters were mostly pile geometry-related. However, this study includes a separate input directly related to time, which is the main difference between this study and those published previously. Another contribution in this study is related to the optimization phase. An intelligent equation has been developed to predict pile capacity using the genetic programming (GP) technique. Then, the proposed GP equation is used in two optimization techniques, namely artificial bee colony (ABC) and GWO to maximize pile capacity. A database containing information about 256 data samples has been considered to achieve these goals. The models mentioned above and their results are discussed and compared to introduce a new procedure for predicting pile capacity.

The rest of this paper is organized as follows:

Section 2 describes the methodology background of the used models in predicting and optimizing pile capacity. Section 3 gives the needed information regarding the database used for modeling. Section 4 discusses the process of prediction models to develop a GP model and its evaluation. The optimization process regarding two algorithms, i.e., ABC and GWO, is given in Section 5. Section 6 discusses both the prediction and optimization phases. Sections 7 and 8 describe limitations, future works, and concluding remarks of this study.

2. Methodology Background

2.1. Genetic Programming

Genetic programming (GP) is an evolutionary computing algorithm [39], which simulates natural selection and biological evolution and automatically generates the best computer program based on the problem in the search space [40]. In GP, the individual represents the candidate's solution to the problem. In the process of evolution, GP evaluates individual fitness, simulates the survival principle of survival of the fittest, and guides the population to carry out genetic operations (replication, crossover, and mutation) to renew the population. The goal of the GP algorithm is to gradually make some individuals in the population have better performance through several generations of evolution.

Figure 1 shows the flow chart to develop GP. First, a predetermined number of individuals are created as an initial population by randomly combining different elements of the function set and terminator set according to the program structure. Fitness values are then given to every individual. The fitness value reflects the ability of the individual to solve problems where the higher the value, the better the individual's performance. After that, individuals are selected based on fitness values, and those with higher fitness are more likely to be selected. Genetic evolution of selected individuals is used to generate the next generation's population. Individuals in the new population are repeatedly evaluated, selected, replicated, crossed, and mutated to complete genetic evolution. This stops when the maximum number of evolutions is reached or a certain condition is met. The best solution to the problem is the individual with the best fitness value.

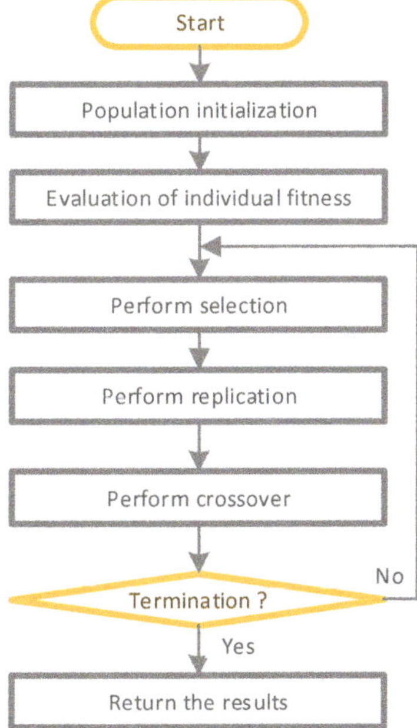

Figure 1. The flowchart of GP.

2.2. Gray Wolf Optimization

Gray wolf optimization (GWO) is a swarm-based optimization algorithm inspired by the predation behavior of wolves [41]. Compared with other traditional intelligent swarm algorithms, GWO has the advantages of fewer parameters, easy implementation, great convergence speed, and global search ability, so it has been widely used in many fields [42]. Through observation, it is found that wolves hunt mainly in three parts: first tracking, chasing, and approaching prey; then surrounding and harassing prey from all directions until it stops moving; and finally, attacking the prey. Figure 2 shows the process of GWO, a is based on a linear decrease iteration convergence factor, and A is the value in the interval $[-2a, 2a]$, by setting the $|a| < 1$ or > 1 to implement the prey. C can be arbitrarily set in the interval $[0,2]$, indicating the weight of prey affected by the position of the gray wolf. α, β and δ represent the potential superior solution of the optimization objective, where α is the optimal solution, β is the suboptimal solution, and δ is the third optimal solution.

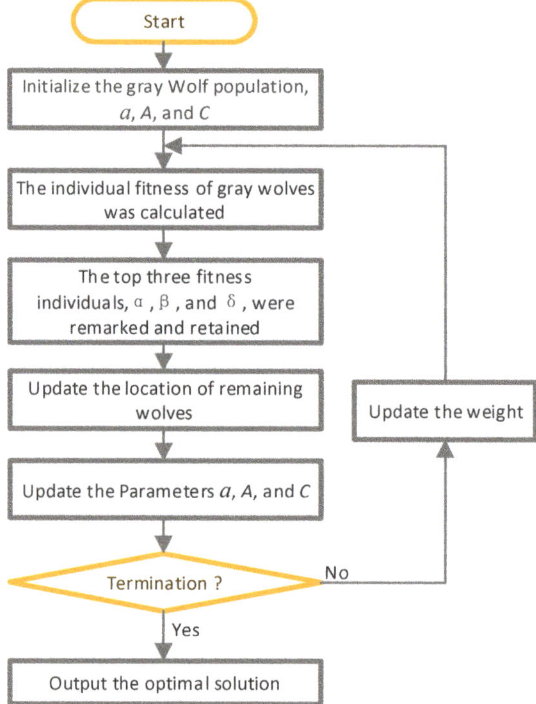

Figure 2. The process of GWO.

2.3. Artificial Bee Colony

An artificial bee colony (ABC) is an intelligent optimization model that mimics the honey harvesting operation of bees [43]. Food supplies, hired bees, and non-hired bees are the three components of the system [44]. Three kinds of artificial bees are used in the ABC algorithm: lead bees, scouts, and followers. The lead and scout bees seek the optimum solution sequentially, while the scout bees watch to see whether they fall into the local optimal. A random search for alternative food sources occurs if they fall within the local ideal. As the mass of nectar in a food source corresponds to a solution's mass, each food source represents one potential answer. The ABC may locate the best food source or the best solution via a cyclic search. The ABC flowchart is shown in Figure 3.

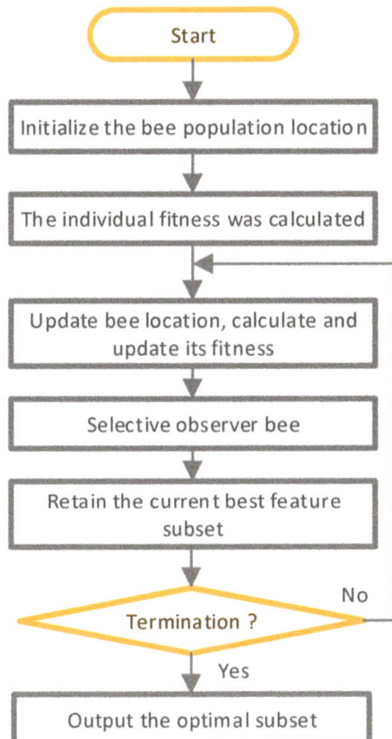

Figure 3. The process of ABC.

3. Database Establishment

3.1. Case Study and Input Parameters

Mahshahr in Khuzestan Province, near the Persian Gulf, located in southwest Iran, was selected for developing petrochemical industries over the past three decades. Different types of precast piles were constructed in various projects built or under construction in this area. The original soil of this region was clay to silty clay with an average plasticity index range of 8 to 20 and SPT counts (2 to 15) down to at least 30 m. In order to determine the pile bearing capacity precisely and to optimize the required pile embedment depths, various "test piles" were driven at different points on the sites. Pile Dynamics Analyzer (PDA) equipment was used to perform a dynamic load test (DLT) on all test piles at End-of-Driving (EOD) and Beginning-of-Restrike (BOR) conditions. The DLT program was performed in three phases to verify the variations in the pile capacities with time. The first phase of the DLT was carried out simultaneously as driving the test piles (EOD time). The next phase of tests was performed at different times after the initial driving of piles. In addition, some axial static load tests (SLTs) were carried out, loading the piles to their ultimate capacities. Test results show that a significant "soil setup" has occurred.

A database containing information about 256 data samples was utilized to develop the pile bearing capacity models. There are five independent variables to predict the target variable: pile setup. Independent variables cover a range of information about pile and soil properties i.e., pile diameter (PD, m), length of pile (LOP, m), initial bearing capacity (IC, kPa), time after EOD (T, days), and undrained shear strength (Su, kPa). The dependent variable in this database is the ultimate capacity (UC) of the pile (kPa) measured through the site and other mentioned parameters.

3.2. Statistical Information on the Data

Five relevant factors, including LOP, PD, IC, Su, and T, were measured to build a database for developing the intelligent model to forecast UC. The database is composed of 256 datasets. Statistical analysis was applied to analyze the collected database. Figure 4 presents the boxplots of input and output variables. The box plots are not symmetrical, the database is not a normal distribution, and many data points exceed the upper and lower tentacles of the boxplots. Because the data distribution is unknown, these outliers cannot be eliminated. As shown in Figure 5, Pearson correlation coefficients in Equation (1) between any two variables are calculated [45], and the deeper the color, the stronger the positive correlation, whereas the lighter the color, the stronger the negative correlation. It can be seen that UC has a negative correlation with LOP and PD in five input variables.

$$r = \frac{\sum_{i=1}^{n}\left(X_i - \overline{X}\right)\left(Y_i - \overline{Y}\right)}{\sqrt{\sum_{i=1}^{n}\left(X_i - \overline{X}\right)^2}\sqrt{\sum_{i=1}^{n}\left(Y_i - \overline{Y}\right)^2}} \tag{1}$$

where X_i and Y_i are variables, $\overline{X}$ and $\overline{Y}$ are their mean values, and n is the total number of data points.

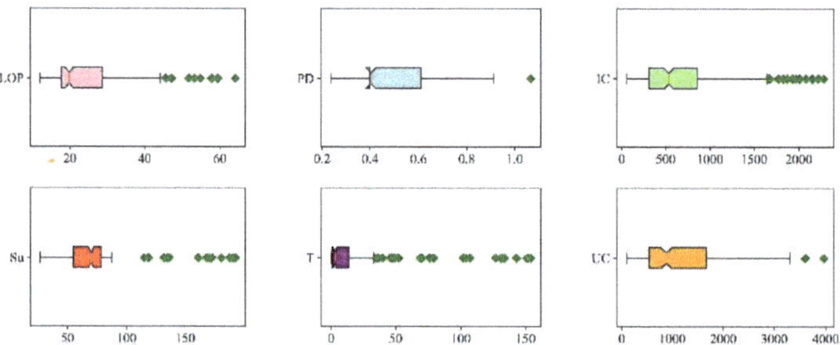

Figure 4. Six input parameters and their box plots.

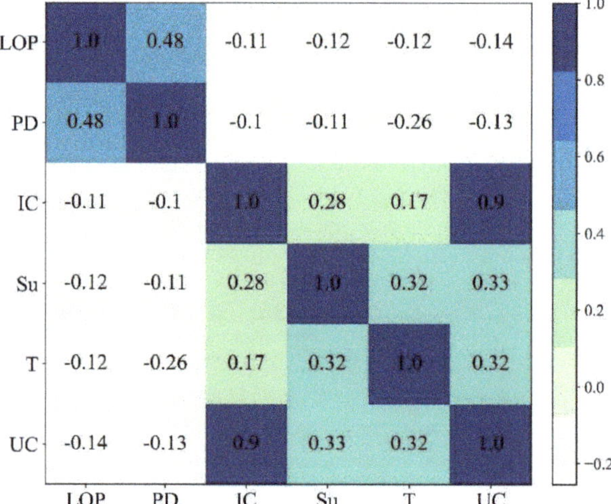

Figure 5. The heatmap of inputs and their correlations.

4. Prediction of Pile Capacity

4.1. GP Modeling Procedure

In this study, UC correlates with LOP, PD, IC, Su, and T; therefore, UC $= f$ (LOP, IC, PD, Su, and T). GP was implemented to find a function for predicting UC to explore the relationship between UC and the other five input parameters. In this way, an intelligent equation that is easy to implement can be established for predicting pile capacity. The steps to generating the UC prediction formula by GP are as follows:

(1) A training set and a testing set were created by randomly dividing the database. Then, 80 percent of the database (204 datasets) was dedicated to the training set, while the remaining 20 percent was devoted to testing (52 datasets). The initial population is randomly generated from the database and function sets. The function sets include $+$, $-$, $\times$, $\div$, $\sqrt{\ }$, sin, cos, and tan.

(2) The testing set is adapted to fit the prediction equation. After the genetic operation, i.e., selection, crossover, and variation, the preliminary prediction formula is obtained [46].

(3) The fitness function of the population is defined, and it is employed to evaluate the fitness of each formula in the population. Root mean square error (RMSE) as the fitness function was used in this study. The fitness value is calculated according to Equation (2), where M means the number of training or testing sets, and UC' represents the predicted value of the formula generated by GP.

$$\text{RMSE} = \sqrt{\frac{1}{M} \sum_{i=1}^{M} (\text{UC} - \text{UC}')^2} \tag{2}$$

(4) Repeat steps (2–3) until the training time reaches the termination rule.

(5) At the end of GP, the final optimal formula is evaluated from the goodness of fit coefficient R^2 between the predicted UC obtained by the formula and the real UC. R^2 is calculated according to Equation (3).

$$R^2 = 1 - \frac{\sum_{i=1}^{M} (\text{UC} - \hat{\text{UC}})^2}{\sum_{i=1}^{M} (\text{UC} - \text{UC})^2} \tag{3}$$

where $\hat{\text{UC}}$ represents mean values of the UC.

4.2. Results

The number of iterations is set to 4000, and Figure 6 exhibits the convergence of fitness values during iterations. When the iteration reaches 2000, the fitness value does not descend. Accordingly, the result returned at the end of the iteration is considered the optimal solution. Figure 7 presents the tree structure of optimal results. The tree structure can be simplified to Equation (4). Equation (4) is the final equation developed by GP to estimate the *UC*.

$$\begin{aligned} \text{UC} = IC + 2T + (IC + Su(\sin(\sqrt{(LOP + Su)}) \\ + \sin(LOP + Su)) + 3T - 2\sin(PD - T) + \sin(\sin(LOP) \\ + \cos(\sin(tanPD - T))) \end{aligned} \tag{4}$$

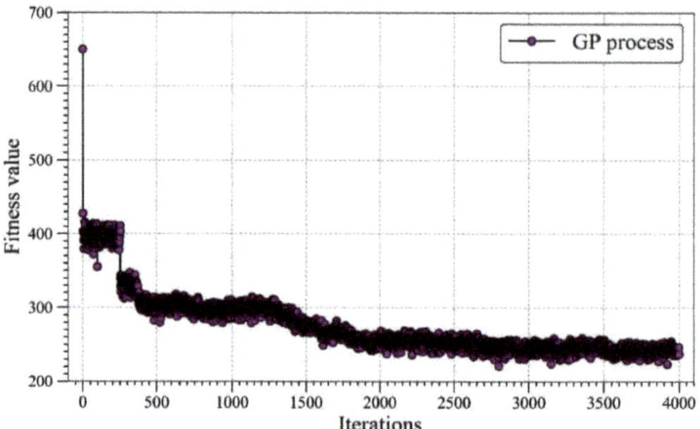

Figure 6. The value of fitness function during iterations.

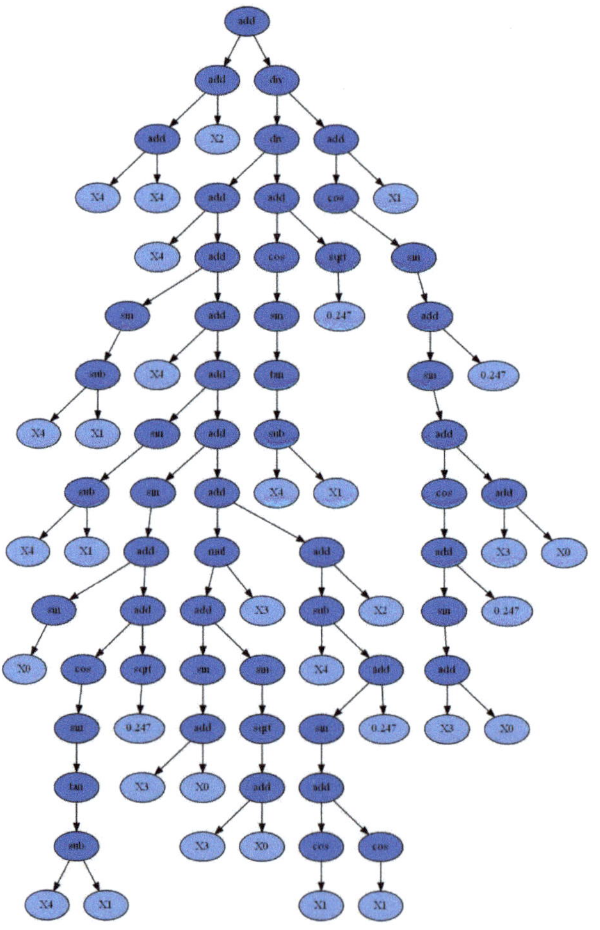

Figure 7. Tree structure representation of optimal results (X0 = LOP; X1 = PD; X2 = IC; X3 = Su; X4 = T).

For evaluating the performance of the developed equation, R^2, RMSE, mean absolute error (MAE), variance account for (VAF), and A-20 index were introduced to evaluate the performance of Equation (4) in training and testing sets [46–49]. Equations (5)–(7) display the calculation equations for MAE, VAF, and A-20 index, respectively. When the MAE gets closer to 0, the model has better accuracy. When the VAF reaches 100, the predicted UC is perfectly equated to the actual. When the predicted UC is equal to the actual UC, the A-20 index is 1.

$$MAE = \frac{1}{M} \sum_{i=1}^{M} |UC - UC'| \tag{5}$$

$$VAF = [1 - \frac{var(UC - UC')}{var(UC)}] U \times 100 \tag{6}$$

$$A - 20 = \frac{m20}{M} \tag{7}$$

where $var(\cdot)$ means the variance, and $m20$ is the number of samples with a ratio of the predicted value to the actual value in the range (0.8–1.2).

Figure 8 shows the predicted results and five regression indicators in training and testing tests. When the predicted UC equals the true UC, the corresponding point falls on the red line in the figure. The points falling between the two purple dotted lines indicate that the ratio of the predicted UC to the real UC is between 0.8 and 1.2. The A-20 index indicates that some of the predicted values are different from the actual values.

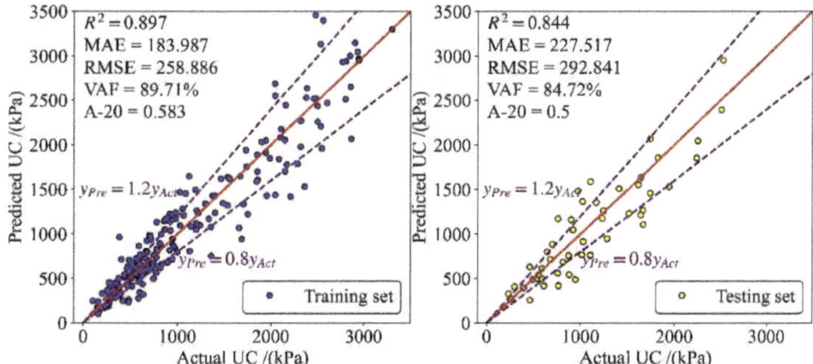

Figure 8. The performance of equation developed by GP in training and testing sets.

5. Optimizing Pile Capacity Using Metaheuristic Algorithms

5.1. Gray Wolf Optimization

In the last section, the performance of the developed equation is evaluated. Some optimization techniques have been introduced to maximize Equation (4) to improve the UC. GWO was implemented to find the maximum UC. To perform GWO, an open-source *Python* library, *Mealpy,* was applied [50]. The main parameters of GWO used the default parameters in Mealpy. To see more about how to implement GWO in *Python*, the reference [50] used in this study is useful.

Before optimization modeling, the range of parameters needs to be determined. As shown in Table 1, the input range of five parameters was selected as the optimization range. The maximum UC is found in the range. The swarm is set to 50, 100, 150, and 250 [22]. Figure 9 shows the fitness variation during GWO. When the swarm is 50, the found UC is the maximum. When LOP is 38.59, PD is 0.247, IC is 2273, Su is 157.46, T is 153.18, the maximum UC is 6098.488.

Table 1. The input parameters range.

Parameters	Range
LOP	12.009–64.008
PD	0.236–1.067
IC	57.3–2276
Su	26.97–191.52
T	0.008–154

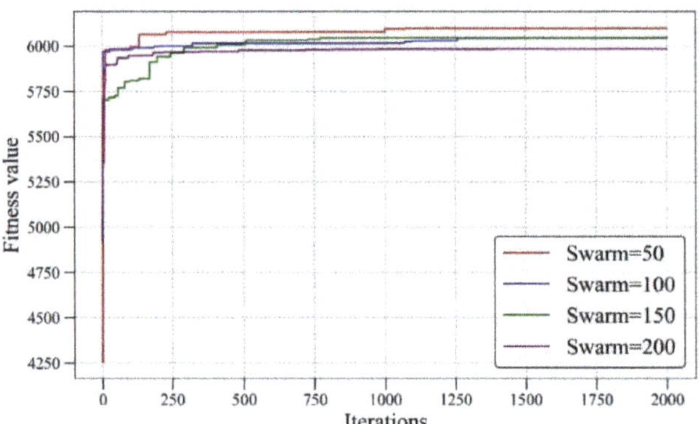

Figure 9. The fitness variation in GWO.

5.2. Artificial Bee Colony Algorithm

ABC was also implemented to compare optimization techniques to find the maximum UC in Equation (4). The default parameters suggested in Mealpy [50] were also considered in this study to construct an ABC optimization model. The optimization range used the parameters range in Table 1. The swarm is set to 50, 100, 150, and 250. Figure 10 shows the fitness variation during the process of ABC. When the swarm is set to 100, 150, and 200, the found UC is the maximum. When LOP is 38.47, PD is 0.240, IC is 2276, Su is 157.46, and T is 170.16, the maximum UC is 6043.64. It is apparent that GWO performs better than ABC in finding the maximum UC.

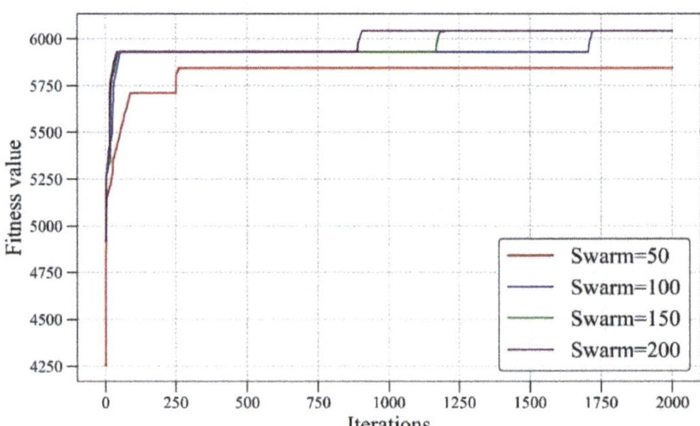

Figure 10. The fitness variation in ABC.

6. Discussion

GP was adopted to develop the equation for predicting the UC, and the developed equation received R^2 of 0.897 in the training set and R^2 of 0.844 in the testing set. Five regressions revealed that the developed equation can better forecast the UC than previous methods. To analyze the strength of GP for predicting UC, some other widely used machine learning models were also developed to build intelligent models for predicting UC. These widely used models include random forest (RF), gradient boosting machine (GBM), adaptive boosting machine (AdaBoost), ANN, support vector machine (SVM), k-nearest neighbor (KNN), and decision tree (DT). These models were developed according to the default parameters in Scikit-learn [51].

These models were developed using the training set, and the testing set was used to evaluate their performance. An easy way to compare the results of several modeling approaches is to use a Taylor diagram. The Taylor diagram cleverly combines the correlation coefficient, the centered RMSE, and the standard deviation into a polar diagram as a result of these inputs. A cosine connection [52] may be seen in Equation (8) between the correlation coefficient, the center RMSE, and the standard deviation.

$$E'^2 = \sigma_p{}^2 + \sigma_a{}^2 - 2\sigma_p\sigma_a R \tag{8}$$

In Equation (8), E' is the centered RMSE between measured and predicted parameters, $\sigma_p{}^2$ is the variance of predicted parameters, $\sigma_a{}^2$ is the variance of measured parameters, and R is the correlation coefficient between measured and predicted parameters.

The Taylor diagrams for the training and testing sets are shown in Figures 11 and 12, respectively. The closer the model is to the reference point, the smaller the centered RMSE of the model, the higher the correlation coefficient between the prediction results and the actual results, and the better performance of the model. According to this graph, a model's performance improves as it gets closer to its associated "Reference" point. It can be found that GP has outstanding performance during the training and testing stages.

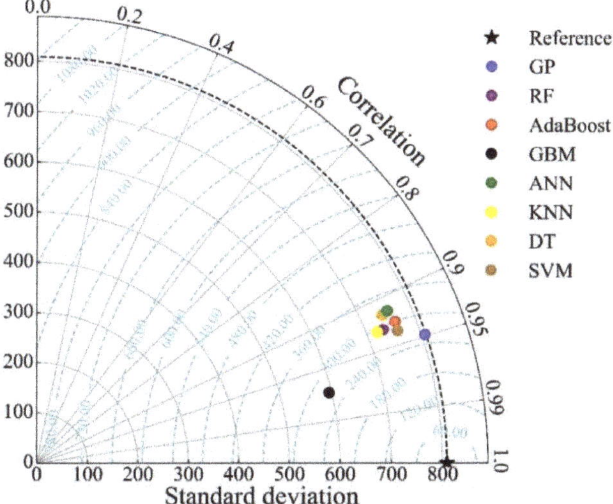

Figure 11. Taylor diagram of training set (RF: random forest, ANN: artificial neural network, DT: decision tree, SVM: support vector machine, KNN: k-nearest neighbors, GBM: gradient boosting machine, AdaBoost: adaptive boosting machine).

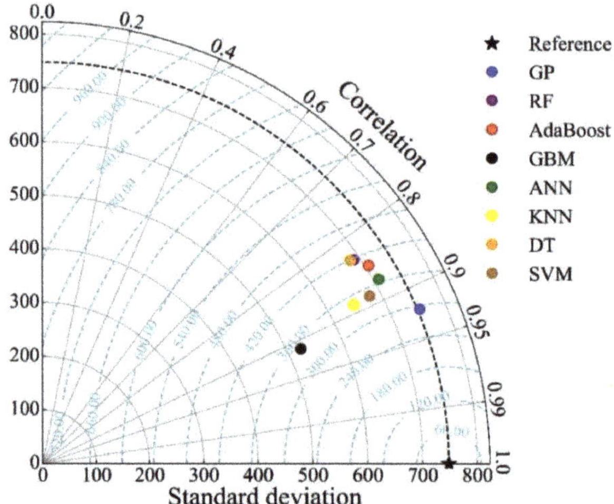

Figure 12. Taylor diagram of the test set (RF: random forest, ANN: artificial neural network, DT: decision tree, SVM: support vector machine, KNN: k-nearest neighbors, GBM: gradient boosting machine, AdaBoost: adaptive boosting machine).

Additionally, GWO and ABC were implemented to find the maximum UC. Table 2 shows the optimized parameters. The GWO performs better than ABC. The maximum UC found by GWO is 6089.488, which is an increase of 54% compared to the maximum UC in this database. The maximum UC found by ABC is 6043.64, which is an increase of 52.6% compared to the maximum UC in this database. It is apparent that using the optimized parameters can improve UC.

Table 2. Optimized values of input parameters for the maximum UC.

Parameter	Actual Value	Optimized Value	
		GWO	ABC
LOP	24.0	38.59	38.47
PD	0.457	0.247	0.240
IC	1642.7	2273	2276
Su	172.0	157.46	157.46
T	6.0	153.18	170.16
Maximum UC	3960.0	6098.488	6043.64

7. Limitations and Future Works

According to the previous research on this subject, it is essential to consider that other variables may have a profound impact on the prediction process of pile setup, such as coefficient of consolidation, or over consolidation ratio, which have not been considered in this study due to the lack of appropriate data sets. In addition, to make these types of studies more informative for civil engineers, previous empirical equations or developed theories in the area of pile capacity can be considered and used in the portion of data preparation. In this way, a civil engineer or a geotechnical engineer has enough knowledge regarding data preparation. A combination of these theories together with AI models makes these types of studies different and more applicable than an application of AI methodologies. The proposed techniques in both the prediction and optimization phases of this study were constructed based on the entire database described in Section 3 and are valid in the range of this database. The results may be different if out-of-range inputs are used.

8. Conclusions

A different view regarding the common pile capacity studies was considered in this study. To evaluate the effect of the soil setup on the pile bearing capacity over time, an intelligent equation using a GP model was proposed. To develop the prediction models, a comprehensive database obtained from some geotechnical projects carried out in Mahshahr, Iran, was used. In addition, a new section, namely optimization, has been proposed for maximizing the bearing capacity. The following conclusions and remarks can be drawn from this study:

- The proposed GP equation is easy to implement and is of interest to civil and geotechnical engineers. An intelligent equation proposed by GP showed an acceptable level of accuracy in predicting pile capacity. Results with R^2 values of 0.897 in the training stage and 0.844 in the testing stage indicate that this GP model is capable enough to be implemented for predicting pile capacity.
- In the optimization phase, two powerful algorithms, namely GWO and ABC, were applied to maximize pile capacity. Obtaining the highest capacity of the pile is considered the ultimate objective of such projects. Although both algorithms are powerful in maximizing pile capacity, GWO performed better. Increase percentages of 52.6 and 54 were obtained by ABC and GWO, respectively, in their pile capacity results.
- For the best optimization algorithm (i.e., GWO), values of 38.59 m, 0.247 m, 2273 kPa, 157.46 kPa, 153.18 days, and 6098.488 kPa were obtained for LOP, PD, IC, Su, T, and UC, respectively. The proposed models and obtained results of this study can be used in designing pile capacity before implementing relevant projects.

Author Contributions: M.K.: conceptualization, methodology, investigation, writing—original draft preparation, writing—review and editing. D.J.A.: conceptualization, methodology, investigation, formal analysis, writing—original draft preparation, writing—review and editing, supervision. M.M.S.S.: writing—original draft preparation, writing—review and editing, supervision, funding acquisition. All authors have read and agreed to the published version of the manuscript.

Funding: The research is partially funded by the Ministry of Science and Higher Education of the Russian Federation under the strategic academic leadership program 'Priority 2030' (Agreement 075-15-2021-1333 dated 30 September 2021).

Data Availability Statement: Data is available upon request.

Conflicts of Interest: The authors declare no conflict of interest.

References

1. Titi, H.H.; Wije Wathugala, G. Numerical procedure for predicting pile capacity—Setup/freeze. *Transp. Res. Rec.* **1999**, *1663*, 25–32. [CrossRef]
2. Roy, M.; Blanchet, R.; Tavenas, F.; Rochelle, P. La Behaviour of a sensitive clay during pile driving. *Can. Geotech. J.* **1981**, *18*, 67–85. [CrossRef]
3. Fakharian, K.; Khanmohammadi, M. Comparison of pile bearing capacity from CPT and dynamic load tests in clay considering soil setup. In *Frontiers in Offshore Geotechnics III*; CRC Press: Boca Raton, FL, USA, 2015; pp. 539–544.
4. Khanmohammadi, M.; Fakharian, K. Evaluation of performance of piled-raft foundations on soft clay: A case study. *Geomech. Eng.* **2018**, *14*, 43–50.
5. Komurka, V.E.; Wagner, A.B.; Edil, T.B. *Estimating Soil/Pile Set-Up*; Wisconsin Highway Research Program: Madison, WI, USA, 2003.
6. Abu-Farsakh, M.Y.; Haque, M.N. Estimation and Incorporation of Pile Setup into LRFD Design Methodology. In Proceedings of the Transportation Research Board 97th Annual Meeting, Washington, DC, USA, 7–11 January 2018.
7. Abu-Farsakh, M.Y.; Haque, M.N.; Tavera, E.; Zhang, Z. Evaluation of pile setup from osterberg cell load tests and its cost–benefit analysis. *Transp. Res. Rec.* **2017**, *2656*, 61–70. [CrossRef]
8. Haque, M.N.; Steward, E.J. Evaluation of pile setup phenomenon for driven piles in Alabama. In *Geo-Congress 2020: Foundations, Soil Improvement, and Erosion*; American Society of Civil Engineers: Reston, VA, USA, 2020; pp. 200–208.
9. Lanyi-Bennett, S.A.; Deng, L. Effects of inter-helix spacing and short-term soil setup on the behaviour of axially loaded helical piles in cohesive soil. *Soils Found.* **2019**, *59*, 337–350. [CrossRef]
10. Khanmohammadi, M.; Fakharian, K. Numerical modelling of pile installation and set-up effects on pile shaft capacity. *Int. J. Geotech. Eng.* **2017**, *13*, 484–498. [CrossRef]

11. Fakharian, K.; Khanmohammadi, M. Effect of OCR and Pile Diameter on Load Movement Response of Piles Embedded in Clay over Time. *Int. J. Geomech.* **2022**, *22*, 04022091. [CrossRef]

12. Bogard, J.D.; Matlock, H. Application of model pile tests to axial pile design. In Proceedings of the Offshore Technology Conference, Houston, TX, USA, 7–10 May 1990.

13. Yan, W.M.; Yuen, K. V Prediction of pile set-up in clays and sands. In *IOP Conference Series: Materials Science and Engineering*; IOP Publishing: Bristol, UK, 2010; Volume 10, p. 12104.

14. Skov, R.; Denver, H. Time-dependence of bearing capacity of piles. In Proceedings of the Third International Conference on the Application of Stress-Wave Theory to Piles, Ottawa, ON, Canada, 25–27 May 1988; pp. 25–27.

15. Gardner, M.W.; Dorling, S.R. Artificial neural networks (the multilayer perceptron)—A review of applications in the atmospheric sciences. *Atmos. Environ.* **1998**, *32*, 2627–2636. [CrossRef]

16. Parsajoo, M.; Armaghani, D.J.; Mohammed, A.S.; Khari, M.; Jahandari, S. Tensile strength prediction of rock material using non-destructive tests: A comparative intelligent study. *Transp. Geotech.* **2021**, *31*, 100652. [CrossRef]

17. Hasanipanah, M.; Monjezi, M.; Shahnazar, A.; Armaghani, D.J.; Farazmand, A. Feasibility of indirect determination of blast induced ground vibration based on support vector machine. *Measurement* **2015**, *75*, 289–297. [CrossRef]

18. Li, D.; Liu, Z.; Armaghani, D.J.; Xiao, P.; Zhou, J. Novel Ensemble Tree Solution for Rockburst Prediction Using Deep Forest. *Mathematics* **2022**, *10*, 787. [CrossRef]

19. Koopialipoor, M.; Asteris, P.G.; Mohammed, A.S.; Alexakis, D.E.; Mamou, A.; Armaghani, D.J. Introducing stacking machine learning approaches for the prediction of rock deformation. *Transp. Geotech.* **2022**, *34*, 100756. [CrossRef]

20. De-Prado-Gil, J.; Zaid, O.; Palencia, C.; Martínez-García, R. Prediction of Splitting Tensile Strength of Self-Compacting Recycled Aggregate Concrete Using Novel Deep Learning Methods. *Mathematics* **2022**, *10*, 2245. [CrossRef]

21. Barkhordari, M.; Armaghani, D.; Asteris, P. Structural Damage Identification Using Ensemble Deep Convolutional Neural Network Models. *Comput. Model. Eng. Sci.* **2022**, *134*, 2. [CrossRef]

22. Zhou, J.; Qiu, Y.; Khandelwal, M.; Zhu, S.; Zhang, X. Developing a hybrid model of Jaya algorithm-based extreme gradient boosting machine to estimate blast-induced ground vibrations. *Int. J. Rock Mech. Min. Sci.* **2021**, *145*, 104856. [CrossRef]

23. Zhou, J.; Li, X.; Mitri, H.S. Classification of rockburst in underground projects: Comparison of ten supervised learning methods. *J. Comput. Civ. Eng.* **2016**, *30*, 4016003. [CrossRef]

24. Zhou, J.; Chen, C.; Wang, M.; Khandelwal, M. Proposing a novel comprehensive evaluation model for the coal burst liability in underground coal mines considering uncertainty factors. *Int. J. Min. Sci. Technol.* **2021**, *31*, 799–812. [CrossRef]

25. Zhou, J.; Shen, X.; Qiu, Y.; Li, E.; Rao, D.; Shi, X. Improving the efficiency of microseismic source locating using a heuristic algorithm-based virtual field optimization method. *Geomech. Geophys. Geo-Energy Geo-Resour.* **2021**, *7*, 89. [CrossRef]

26. Liu, Z.; Armaghani, D.J.; Fakharian, P.; Li, D.; Ulrikh, D.V.; Orekhova, N.N.; Khedher, K.M. Rock Strength Estimation Using Several Tree-Based ML Techniques. *Comput. Model. Eng. Sci.* **2022**, *133*, 3. [CrossRef]

27. Yang, H.; Wang, Z.; Song, K. A new hybrid grey wolf optimizer-feature weighted-multiple kernel-support vector regression technique to predict TBM performance. *Eng. Comput.* **2020**, *38*, 2469–2485. [CrossRef]

28. Yang, H.; Song, K.; Zhou, J. Automated Recognition Model of Geomechanical Information Based on Operational Data of Tunneling Boring Machines. *Rock Mech. Rock Eng.* **2022**, *55*, 1499–1516. [CrossRef]

29. Kardani, N.; Bardhan, A.; Samui, P.; Nazem, M.; Asteris, P.G.; Zhou, A. Predicting the thermal conductivity of soils using integrated approach of ANN and PSO with adaptive and time-varying acceleration coefficients. *Int. J. Therm. Sci.* **2022**, *173*, 107427. [CrossRef]

30. Baziar, M.H.; Saeedi Azizkandi, A.; Kashkooli, A. Prediction of pile settlement based on cone penetration test results: An ANN approach. *KSCE J. Civ. Eng.* **2015**, *19*, 98–106. [CrossRef]

31. Alkroosh, I.; Nikraz, H. Predicting pile dynamic capacity via application of an evolutionary algorithm. *Soils Found.* **2014**, *54*, 233–242. [CrossRef]

32. Khari, M.; Armaghani, D.J.; Dehghanbanadaki, A. Prediction of Lateral Deflection of Small-Scale Piles Using Hybrid PSO–ANN Model. *Arab. J. Sci. Eng.* **2020**, *45*, 3499–3509. [CrossRef]

33. Armaghani, D.J.; Harandizadeh, H.; Momeni, E.; Maizir, H.; Zhou, J. An optimized system of GMDH-ANFIS predictive model by ICA for estimating pile bearing capacity. *Artif. Intell. Rev.* **2021**, *55*, 2313–2350. [CrossRef]

34. Lee, I.-M.; Lee, J.-H. Prediction of pile bearing capacity using artificial neural networks. *Comput. Geotech.* **1996**, *18*, 189–200. [CrossRef]

35. Shahin, M.A. Intelligent computing for modeling axial capacity of pile foundations. *Can. Geotech. J.* **2010**, *47*, 230–243. [CrossRef]

36. Samui, P. Prediction of pile bearing capacity using support vector machine. *Int. J. Geotech. Eng.* **2011**, *5*, 95–102. [CrossRef]

37. Momeni, E.; Nazir, R.; Armaghani, D.J.; Maizir, H. Prediction of pile bearing capacity using a hybrid genetic algorithm-based ANN. *Measurement* **2014**, *57*, 122–131. [CrossRef]

38. Dehghanbanadaki, A.; Khari, M.; Amiri, S.T.; Armaghani, D.J. Estimation of ultimate bearing capacity of driven piles in c-φ soil using MLP-GWO and ANFIS-GWO models: A comparative study. *Soft Comput.* **2021**, *25*, 4103–4119. [CrossRef]

39. Koza, J.R.; Poli, R. Genetic programming. In *Search Methodologies*; Springer: Berlin/Heidelberg, Germany, 2005; pp. 127–164.

40. Koza, J.R.; Koza, J.R. *Genetic Programming: On the Programming of Computers by Means of Natural Selection*; MIT Press: Cambridge, MA, USA, 1992; Volume 1, ISBN 0262111705.

41. Mirjalili, S.; Mirjalili, S.M.; Lewis, A. Grey wolf optimizer. *Adv. Eng. Softw.* **2014**, *69*, 46–61. [CrossRef]

42. Faris, H.; Aljarah, I.; Al-Betar, M.A.; Mirjalili, S. Grey wolf optimizer: A review of recent variants and applications. *Neural Comput. Appl.* **2018**, *30*, 413–435. [CrossRef]
43. Karaboga, D. *An Idea Based on Honey Bee Swarm for Numerical Optimization*; Technical Report-tr06; Erciyes University, Engineering Faculty, Computer Engineering Department: Kayseri, Turkey, 2005.
44. Karaboga, D. Artificial bee colony algorithm. *Scholarpedia* **2010**, *5*, 6915. [CrossRef]
45. Schober, P.; Boer, C.; Schwarte, L.A. Correlation coefficients: Appropriate use and interpretation. *Anesth. Analg.* **2018**, *126*, 1763–1768. [CrossRef]
46. Armaghani, D.J.; Asteris, P.G. A comparative study of ANN and ANFIS models for the prediction of cement-based mortar materials compressive strength. *Neural Comput. Appl.* **2020**, *33*, 4501–4532. [CrossRef]
47. Zeng, J.; Asteris, P.G.; Mamou, A.P.; Mohammed, A.S.; Golias, E.A.; Armaghani, D.J.; Faizi, K.; Hasanipanah, M. The Effectiveness of Ensemble-Neural Network Techniques to Predict Peak Uplift Resistance of Buried Pipes in Reinforced Sand. *Appl. Sci.* **2021**, *11*, 908. [CrossRef]
48. Mahmood, W.; Mohammed, A.S.; Asteris, P.G.; Kurda, R.; Armaghani, D.J. Modeling Flexural and Compressive Strengths Behaviour of Cement-Grouted Sands Modified with Water Reducer Polymer. *Appl. Sci.* **2022**, *12*, 1016. [CrossRef]
49. Murlidhar, B.R.; Nguyen, H.; Rostami, J.; Bui, X.; Armaghani, D.J.; Ragam, P.; Mohamad, E.T. Prediction of flyrock distance induced by mine blasting using a novel Harris Hawks optimization-based multi-layer perceptron neural network. *J. Rock Mech. Geotech. Eng.* **2021**, *13*, 1413–1427. [CrossRef]
50. Van Thieu, N. *A collection of the State-of-the-Art Meta-Heuristics Algorithms in Python: Mealpy*; Zenodo: Genève, Switzerland, 2020.
51. Pedregosa, F.; Varoquaux, G.; Gramfort, A.; Michel, V.; Thirion, B.; Grisel, O.; Blondel, M.; Prettenhofer, P.; Weiss, R.; Dubourg, V. Scikit-learn: Machine learning in Python. *J. Mach. Learn. Res.* **2011**, *12*, 2825–2830.
52. Taylor, K.E. *Taylor Diagram Primer*; PCMDI: Livermore, CA, USA, 2005.

Article

Analysis and Performance Evaluation of a Novel Adjustable Speed Drive with a Homopolar-Type Rotor

Songlin Guo [1], Zhengkang Yi [1], Pan Liu [2], Guoshuai Wang [2], Houchuan Lai [2], Kexun Yu [1] and Xianfei Xie [1,*]

[1] State Key Laboratory of Advanced Electromagnetic Engineering and Technology, Huazhong University of Science and Technology, Wuhan 430074, China
[2] Southwest Institute of Technical Physics, Chengdu 610041, China
* Correspondence: xiexianfei@hust.edu.cn

Abstract: The use of a magnetic adjustable speed drive is a popular choice in industrial settings due to its efficient operation, vibration isolation, low maintenance, and overload protection. Most conventional magnetic adjustable speed drives use various forms of the permanent magnets (PMs). Due to the PMs, this type of machine has continuous free-wheeling losses in the form of hysteresis and induced eddy currents. In recent years, the homopolar-type rotor has been widely used in high-speed machines, superconducting machines, and in the application of flywheel energy storage. This study proposes a new application of the homopolar-type rotor. A novel adjustable speed drive with a homopolar-type rotor (HTR-ASD), which has obvious advantages (no brush, no permanent magnet, and no mechanical flux regulation device), is designed and analyzed in this study. Its speed and torque can be adjusted only by adjusting the excitation current. Firstly, in this study, the structure, operation principles, and flux-modulated mechanism of the HTR-ASD are studied. The homopolar-type rotor has a special three-dimensional magnetic circuit structure with the same pole. The 3D-FEM is usually used to calculate its parameters, which is time consuming. In this study, an analytical method is developed to solve this issue. To analytically calculate the torque characteristics, the air gap magnetic flux density, and the winding inductance parameter, the equivalent circuit and the air gap permeance are researched to simplify the analysis. Then, the key parameters of the HTR-ASD are calculated. Finally, the performance of the HTR-ASD is comparatively studied using the analytical method and finite element method, and a comparison of the results is carried out. The comparison indicates that the analytical method is in good agreement with simulation results, and that it is very helpful for designing homopolar-type rotor machines. According to the analysis, the proposed adjustable speed drive displays a great performance in relation to the operating characteristics of a flexible mechanical speed drive.

Keywords: homopolar-type rotor; magnetic adjustable speed drive; analytical analysis; operating characteristics

MSC: 00A06

Citation: Guo, S.; Yi, Z.; Liu, P.; Wang, G.; Lai, H.; Yu, K.; Xie, X. Analysis and Performance Evaluation of a Novel Adjustable Speed Drive with a Homopolar-Type Rotor. *Mathematics* **2022**, *10*, 3712. https://doi.org/10.3390/math10193712

Academic Editors: Camelia Petrescu and Valeriu David

Received: 15 September 2022
Accepted: 9 October 2022
Published: 10 October 2022

Publisher's Note: MDPI stays neutral with regard to jurisdictional claims in published maps and institutional affiliations.

1. Introduction

Mechanical coupling adopts a rigid structure, which is simple, reliable and low cost. However, it requires a high alignment accuracy between the power input end and load end during installation. Meanwhile, it cannot isolate harmful vibrations and has no overload protection function [1]. That means the use of a solid medium to transmit power cannot solve the inherent problems of harmful vibration isolation and overload protection at the input and output ends. Figure 1 shows a damaged rotating shaft and bearing due to shafting vibration.

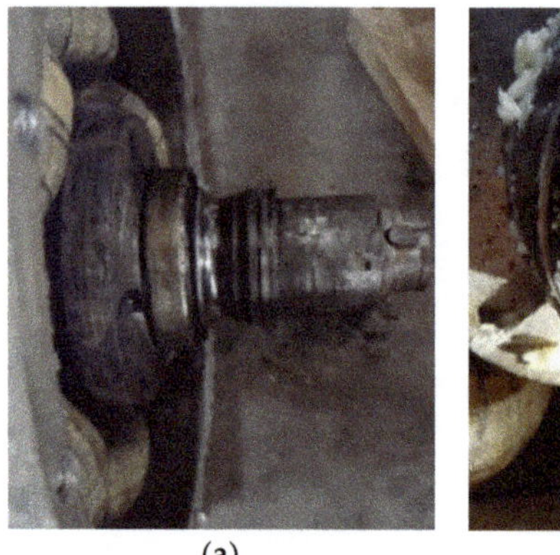

(a)   (b)

Figure 1. A damaged rotating shaft and bearing due to shafting vibration. (**a**) The damaged rotating shaft. (**b**) The damaged bearing.

Compared with mechanical coupling, magnetic adjustable speed drives have attracted a great deal of attention. As the electromagnetic field is used as the power transmission medium, the transmission link has no direct mechanical contact, leading to complete isolation between the power drive end and the load end, which perfectly solves many problems such as the isolation of harmful vibrations, overload protection, motor safety starting with loads, etc. [2–4].

At present, most of the existing magnetic adjustable speed drives contain permanent magnets, and speed adjustment is mainly achieved through the non-rotary mechanical speed regulation structure to adjust the air gap length [5,6]. For permanent magnet adjustable speed drives, because they contain permanent magnets, this type of machine has continuous free-wheeling losses in the form of hysteresis and induced eddy currents, which may lead to high-temperature loss of excitation and vibration loss of excitation. Additionally, because they contain a mechanical speed regulation structure, this also increases the complexity and reduces the reliability of the system.

The homopolar-type rotor is very simple and robust, and has been widely used in high-speed ac machines [7]. In some conditions, it can have a similar performance to the typically used PM machines [8]. For this reason, researchers have paid much attention to this type of machine. The authors of [9] use a bearingless ac homopolar alternator for a flywheel energy storage system, which avoids significant mechanical friction, increases the motor efficiency and increases the operational lifespan. The authors of [10] use a novel permanent magnet homopolar inductor machine with a mechanical flux modulator for a flywheel energy storage system. The authors of [11] use this type of rotor for a bearingless motor, which can be driven up to an ultrahigh speed of 100,000 r/min. The authors of [12] use a homopolar motor in a mining truck with a carrying capacity of 90 tons.

In addition to the above application, this study proposes a new application of the homopolar-type rotor that could be used to regulate the speed of the load, named the homopolar-type rotor adjustable speed drive (HTR-ASD). It usually contains a homopolar-type rotor, a squirrel-cage rotor and a non-rotary shell with an excitation winding. This machine has no brush, no permanent magnet, and no mechanical flux regulation device. At the same time, the rotating parts of the device are composed of a solid homopolar-type rotor and a simple squirrel cage structure, making it fit for high-speed or high-temperature occasions [13,14]. Its magnetic excitation is produced by a dc current in a stationary field with the winding fixed to the shell. In the regulation process, the speed and torque can be adjusted only by adjusting the amplitude of excitation current. This current can be completely turned off during idling times to eliminate magnetic losses.

The performance of the adjustable speed drive may be studied by either numerical or analytical approaches [2]. The former, such as the finite element method (FEM), albeit precise, are time consuming. To simplify the analysis of magnetic adjustable speed drives, some researchers use an analytical method. The analytical methods mainly include the field analysis analytical model and the magnetic equivalent circuit (MEC) model. The field analysis analytical model is based on Maxwell's equations and boundary conditions. The MEC is a simple analytical calculation method [15,16]. In recent years, it has been applied in the design of eddy current couplings [17] and retarders [18,19]. The authors of [20] use an analytical method to calculate the torque characteristics of a novel hybrid superconducting magnetic coupling with axial flux. The authors of [21,22] attempt to simplify the actual 3D geometric model as a 2D model for research, aiming to increase the efficient of the preliminary design. However, most of the analyses are for the PM adjustable speed drive and are not suitable for the adjustable speed drive proposed in this study.

The homopolar-type rotor has a three-dimensional magnetic circuit structure with the same pole and the 3D-FEM is often used for its analysis [23]. The use of the 3D-FEM enables an accurate result to be obtained; however, this method is time consuming. Therefore, the 3D-FEM is usually used for the final performance check. To conveniently obtain an effective no-load air gap flux density, a simplified 2D equivalent analysis model of the homopolar machine is proposed by [24]. Through this method, the no-load effective air gap flux density can be calculated. However, whether this method is applicable to the load condition of this machine is not stated. To calculate the load condition of this type of machine, the authors of [25] adopted a 2D simplified analysis method for a PM homopolar inductor machine. However, this model is for PM homopolar machines and is not suitable for electric excitation machines. Aiming to simplify the calculation of a 3D magnetic circuit for this type of machine, some researchers have used MEC [26,27]. As for the parameter calculations, the authors of [27] use the rotor shape function to speed up the calculation and analysis process. However, the authors of [27] ignore the difference between the rotor shape and the air gap permeance, so the corresponding conclusion is not accurate enough.

In this study, an analytical examination of the homopolar-type rotor is performed, which is found to be effective in the preliminary design stages and analysis of electric machines. To analyze the speed regulation characteristics, the equivalent circuit of the HTR-ASD is obtained and the torque of this machine is calculated by using it. The air gap permeance function is analyzed, which is used not only for analyzing the air gap magnetic field parameters, but also for calculating the winging parameters. The air gap permeance function in this study is directly related to the rotor shape, which means that it is much more accurate than in [27]. By using the analytical method proposed in this study, researchers can quickly obtain the primary scheme of the machine and evaluate its performance [28–30].

The remainder of this paper is organized as follows. In Section 2, the operation principle and the flux-modulated mechanism of the HTR-ASD are analyzed in detail. The equivalent circuit of the HTR-ASD is studied and the torque of the HTR-ASD is calculated in Section 3. Then, the analytical method is proposed and key parameters of the HTR-ASD are calculated. In Section 4, an HTR-ASD prototype is designed and the performances of the HTR-ASD are comparatively studied by the analytical method and the finite element method. The comparison of the results shows the accuracy of the analytical method, indicating that the proposed adjustable speed drive can be applied successfully.

2. Structure and Operation Principles

2.1. Structure

A three-dimensional view of the proposed HTR-ASD is shown in Figure 2. It is composed of a homopolar-type rotor, a squirrel-cage rotor and a non-rotary shell with an excitation winding. The squirrel-cage core is formed by laminated silicon steel sheets and embedded with a squirrel cage whose middle part is composed of non-ferromagnetic material. The homopolar-type rotor is fabricated with high-strength solid steel. The shell and the excitation winding are the non-rotary parts of the machine.

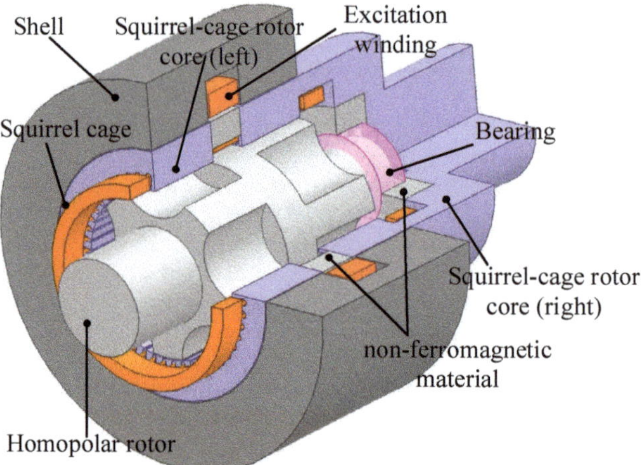

Figure 2. Three-dimensional simplified view of an HTR-ASD.

As Figure 3 shows, the homopolar-type rotor is connected to the prime motor and the squirrel-cage rotor is connected to the load. When the HTR-ASD is working, the torque transmitted by the HTR-ASD is determined by the slip of the homopolar-type rotor and the squirrel-cage rotor, which can be expressed by:

$$s = \frac{n_{HTR} - n_{SCR}}{n_{HTR}} \tag{1}$$

where n_{HTR} is the speed of the homopolar-type rotor and n_{SCR} is the speed of the squirrel-cage rotor. Therefore, when the load torque is certain, the slip can be changed by adjusting the dc excitation current, so that the speed can be adjusted.

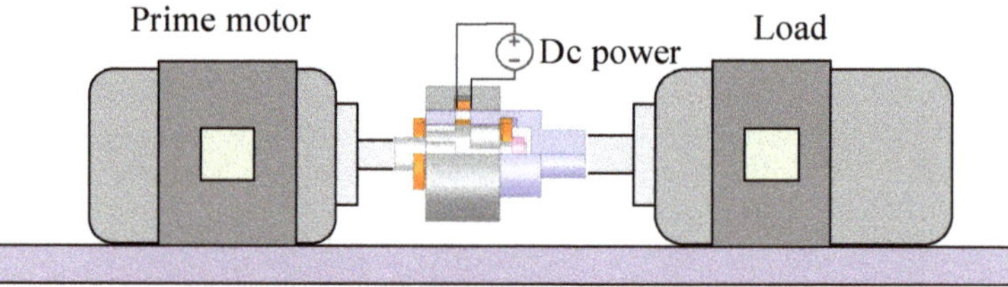

Figure 3. The working platform of the HTR-ASD.

2.2. Operation Principle

The excitation winding provides the flux for the HTR-ASD. The flux is closed through the shell, the air gap between the shell and the squirrel-cage rotor, the squirrel-cage rotor core, the air gap between the squirrel-cage and the HTR, and the HTR, as shown in Figure 4. Additionally, Figure 5 shows that the ac component of air gap flux density is generated due to the different air gap permeances corresponding to the rotor teeth and slots. When the HTR rotates, a synchronous rotating magnetic field is generated in space. The alternating component of the magnetic field generates a corresponding current in the squirrel-cage rotor. The current interacts with the rotating magnetic field in the air gap to generate electromagnetic torque.

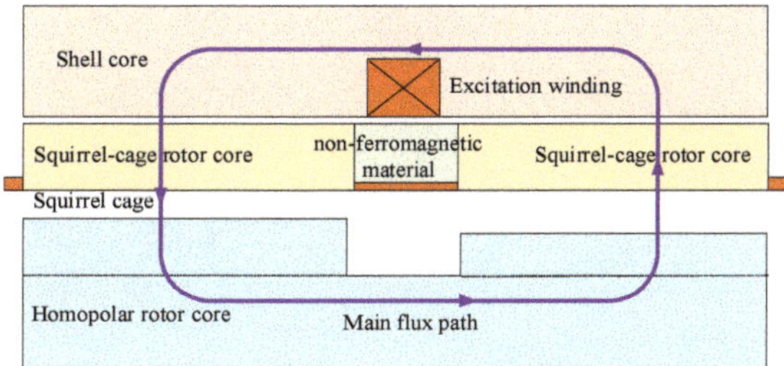

Figure 4. The main flux path in no-load operation.

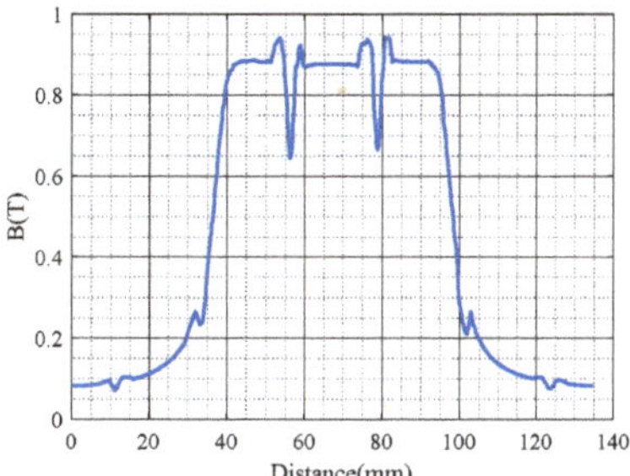

Figure 5. Air gap flux density distributions at different positions of the HTR-ASD.

3. The Equivalent Circuit for Analysis and the Analytical Calculation of Key Parameters

3.1. The Equivalent Circuit for Analysis and the Calculation of Output Torque

Although the winding structure of the squirrel-cage rotor is a squirrel cage type, the winding can still be converted into equivalent three-phase winding to simplify the analysis. Therefore, the equation of the HTR-ASD in the rotor d-q frame can be expressed as:

$$
\begin{bmatrix} u_{sd} \\ u_{sq} \\ u_f \end{bmatrix} = p \begin{bmatrix} L_{sd} & 0 & M_{af} \\ 0 & L_{sq} & 0 \\ \frac{3}{2}M_{af} & 0 & L_f \end{bmatrix} \begin{bmatrix} i_{sd} \\ i_{sq} \\ i_f \end{bmatrix} + \begin{bmatrix} r_s & 0 & 0 \\ 0 & r_s & 0 \\ 0 & 0 & r_f \end{bmatrix} \begin{bmatrix} i_{sd} \\ i_{sq} \\ i_f \end{bmatrix} + \begin{bmatrix} -\omega\psi_{sq} \\ \omega\psi_{sd} \\ 0 \end{bmatrix} \tag{2}
$$

where $\omega = \omega_{HTR} - \omega_{SCR}$. ω_{HTR} is the angular velocity of the homopolar-type rotor, and ω_{SCR} is the angular velocity of the squirrel-cage rotor.

To obtain the equivalent circuit, the excitation winding is converted to the squirrel-cage rotor side. The flux linkage equation can be expressed as:

$$
\begin{bmatrix} \psi_{sd} \\ \psi'_f \end{bmatrix} = \begin{bmatrix} L_{sd} & L_{md} \\ L_{md} & L'_f \end{bmatrix} \begin{bmatrix} i_{sd} \\ i'_f \end{bmatrix} \tag{3}
$$

where $i'_f = \frac{2}{3}i_f M_{af}/L_{md}$.

As the squirrel cage is short circuited, there is $u_{sd} = u_{sq} = 0$. Therefore, the equivalent circuit is as shown in Figure 6.

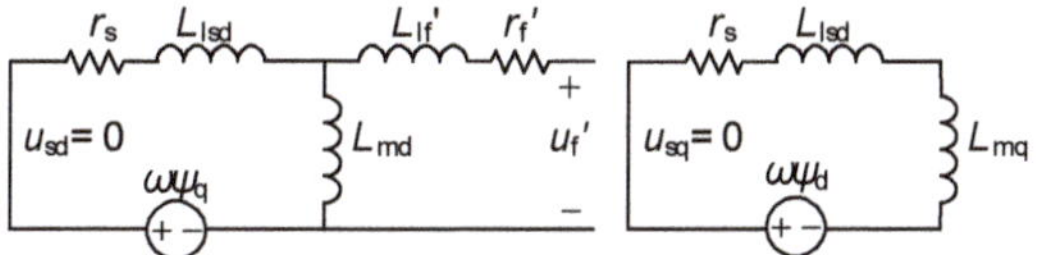

Figure 6. The equivalent circuit of HTR-ASD.

When HTR-ASD operates in steady state, there is:

$$\begin{cases} I_{sq}= -\dfrac{\omega\psi_{sd}}{r_s} \\ I_{sd} = \dfrac{\omega\psi_{sq}}{r_s} \end{cases} \tag{4}$$

The electromagnetic torque can be expressed as:

$$T_{em}= 1.5p\left(\psi_{sd}I_{sq} - \psi_{sq}I_{sd}\right)= -1.5p\frac{r_s}{\omega}\left(I_{sq}^2+I_{sd}^2\right) \tag{5}$$

Combined with Equations (3) and (4), I_{sd} can be expressed as:

$$I_{sd} = \frac{\omega^2 L_{sq}L_{md}i'_f}{r_s^2+\omega^2 L_{sq}L_{sd}} \tag{6}$$

The steady-state salient ratio ρ is defined as:

$$\rho = \frac{L_{sq}}{L_{sd}} \tag{7}$$

Combined with Equations (4)–(7), T_{em} can be expressed as:

$$T_{em}= -1.5pr_s i'^2_f\frac{\omega L_{md}^2\left(r_s^2+\rho^2\omega^2 L_{sd}^2\right)}{\left(r_s^2+\rho\omega^2 L_{sd}^2\right)^2} \tag{8}$$

When $\rho = 1$, T_{em} can be expressed as:

$$T_{em}= -\frac{2}{3}pr_s i^2_f\frac{M_{af}^2}{\frac{r_s^2}{\omega}+\omega L_{sd}^2} \tag{9}$$

From Equations (7)–(9), it can be seen the torque of the HTR-ASD is related to the excitation current and slip speed. When the excitation current is constant, its torque characteristics are similar to an asynchronous motor. When the load torque is constant, the speed can be adjusted by changing the excitation current. Generally, the difference between L_{sq} and L_{sd} is not too large, and Equation (9) can be used to reflect the torque of the HTR-ASD for simplifying the calculations.

3.2. Calculation of Air Gap Magnetic Field Parameters

Strictly speaking, because the homopolar-type rotor has a special three-dimensional magnetic circuit structure with the same pole, it is necessary to develop a 3D-FEM to accurately calculate its parameters. Nevertheless, since this method requires huge computation time, it is usually used for the final performance check of the design and is not suitable for analytical research and calculations.

To simplify the calculation, the air gap performance function can be considered. The authors of [27] use the rotor shape function to represent the air gap performance function. However, according to the hypothesis of the equal magnetic potential plane, the air gap magnetic field is perpendicular to the rotor surface. Figure 7a shows the axial view of the HTR-ASD, and Figure 7b shows the no-load magnetic density distribution within one rotor tooth pitch. Obviously, the air gap magnetic density waveform is very different from the rotor slot shape.

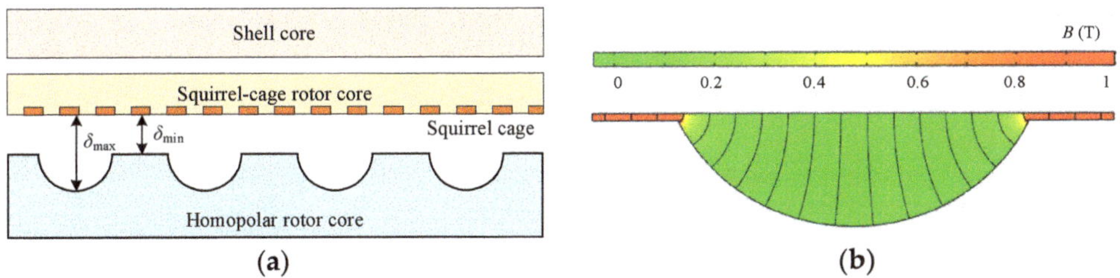

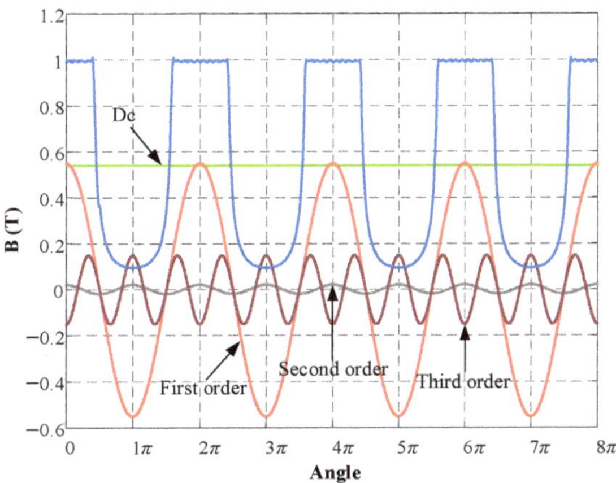

Figure 7. The axial view of the HTR-ASD and no-load magnetic density distribution within one rotor tooth pitch. (**a**) The axial view of the HTR-ASD. (**b**) No-load magnetic density distribution within one rotor tooth pitch.

Before analyzing the composite magnetic flux density, it is necessary to analyze the waveform of single-side air gap magnetic flux density. Figure 8 shows the air gap permeance waveform and its components. To calculate different slot shapes, the per-unit values of the air gap performance function λ_n^* are adopted. $\lambda^*(\theta)$ is multiplied by the reference value Λ_B to obtain the actual value, in which the reference value of specific permeability can be expressed by:

$$\Lambda_B = \mu_0 / (k_\delta \delta_{min}) \tag{10}$$

where μ_0 and k_δ denote the vacuum permeability and Carter's coefficient of slotting, respectively.

Figure 8. Air gap rate permeance waveform and each component.

The definition of the per-unit air gap permeance function is:

$$\lambda^*{}_\delta(\theta) = \frac{B(\theta)}{\Lambda_B F_\delta} = \sum_{n=0}^{\infty} \lambda_n \cos n\theta \tag{11}$$

where F_δ is the magnetomotive force (MMF) of the air gap.

The air gap magnetic density on both sides during no-load excitation can be expressed as:

$$\begin{cases} B_{dcl} = F_{F\delta} \sum_{n=0}^{\infty} \lambda_n \cos n\theta \\ B_{dcr} = F_{F\delta} \sum_{n=0}^{\infty} (-1)^{n+1} \lambda_n \cos n\theta \end{cases} \tag{12}$$

The per-unit value of the dc air gap permeance function can be expressed as:

$$\lambda_{dc}^{*}(\theta) = \frac{B_{dcl}+B_{dcr}}{F_{F\delta}\Lambda_{B}} = 2\sum_{n=0}^{\infty(odd)} \lambda_{n}\cos n\theta \tag{13}$$

The amplitudes of armature winding MMF on the d-axis and q-axis can be expressed as:

$$\begin{cases} F_{ad} = F_{1m}\cos\theta_{1} \\ F_{aq} = F_{1m}\sin\theta_{1} \end{cases} \tag{14}$$

The d-axis and q-axis components of air gap magnetic density on the left and right sides caused by armature reaction can be expressed as:

$$\begin{cases} B_{dl} = k_{dm}F_{1m}\cos\theta_{1}\sum_{n=0}^{\infty}\lambda_{n}\cos n\theta \\ B_{dr} = k_{dm}F_{1m}\cos\theta_{1}\sum_{n=0}^{\infty}(-1)^{n+1}\lambda_{n}\cos n\theta \end{cases} \tag{15}$$

$$\begin{cases} B_{ql} = k_{qm}F_{1m}\sin\theta_{1}\sum_{n=0}^{\infty}\lambda_{n}\cos n\theta \\ B_{qr} = k_{qm}F_{1m}\sin\theta_{1}\sum_{n=0}^{\infty}(-1)\lambda_{n}\cos n\theta \end{cases} \tag{16}$$

where k_{dm} and k_{qm} represent the proportion of air gap MMF in parallel d-axis and q-axis magnetic circuits on both sides.

The per unit values of the d-axis and q-axis air gap permeance functions can be expressed as:

$$\lambda_{d}^{*}(\theta) = \frac{B_{dl}+B_{dr}}{k_{dm}F_{1m}\Lambda_{B}} = (2\lambda_{0}+\lambda_{2})\cos\theta + \sum_{n=3}^{\infty(odd)}(\lambda_{n-1}+\lambda_{n+1})\cos n\theta \tag{17}$$

$$\lambda_{q}^{*}(\theta) = \frac{B_{ql}+B_{qr}}{k_{qm}F_{1m}\Lambda_{B}} = (2\lambda_{0}-\lambda_{2})\sin\theta + \sum_{n=3}^{\infty(odd)}(\lambda_{n-1}-\lambda_{n+1})\sin n\theta \tag{18}$$

Therefore, $\lambda_{dc}^{*}(\theta)$, $\lambda_{d}^{*}(\theta)$, and $\lambda_{q}^{*}(\theta)$ can be regarded as a bridge between the rotor shape and the machine parameters. When the rotor shape is determined, their values can be obtained from a look-up table [31]. After that, they can be used to analytically calculate the air gap magnetic flux density and the winding inductance parameter.

3.3. Calculation of Excitation Winding Parameters

Another parameter to be calculated is the excitation time constant, which is closely related to the resistance and inductance of the excitation winding. Figure 9 shows the excitation window and its size, which is used for the assembly of excitation windings.

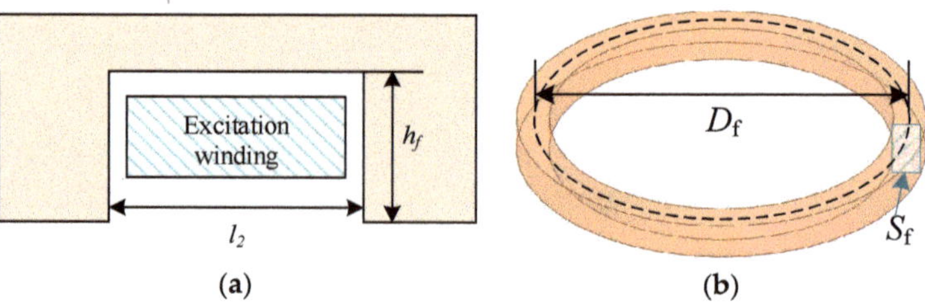

Figure 9. Excitation window and excitation winding. (**a**) Excitation window and its size. (**b**) Excitation winding.

The resistance of the excitation winding can be expressed as:

$$r_f = \frac{\rho_{Cu} N_f \pi D_f}{S_{cf}} \tag{19}$$

where ρ_{Cu} is the conductivity of copper, N_f is the turn of excitation winding, D_f is the excitation coil diameter and S_{cf} is the cross-sectional area of the excitation coil.

Under the excitation current alone, the magnetic density of a one-sided air gap between the HTR and the squirrel-cage rotor can be expressed as:

$$B_{dcl}(\theta) = \frac{N_f I_f}{2} k_m \sum_{n=0}^{\infty} \lambda_n \cos n\theta \tag{20}$$

Therefore, the average air gap flux density at one side of the machine can be expressed as:

$$B_{av} = \frac{1}{2\pi} \int_0^{2\pi} B_{dcl}(\theta) d\theta = \frac{N_f I_f}{2} k_m \lambda_{dc0}^* \Lambda_B \tag{21}$$

The main flux linkage of excitation winding is:

$$\psi_{ff} = N_f B_{av} S_\delta = I_f N_f^2 \pi R_H (l_1 + 2\delta) k_m \lambda_{dc0}^* \Lambda_B \tag{22}$$

where S_δ represents the total area of a one-sided air gap between HTR and the squirrel-cage rotor, R_H is the radius of the HTR, and l_1 is the single length of the HTR.

The main inductance of the excitation winding is:

$$L_{ff} = \frac{\psi_{ff}}{I_f} = N_f^2 \pi R_H (l_1 + 2\delta) k_m \lambda_{dc0}^* \Lambda_B \tag{23}$$

Moreover, (23) shows that the main self-inductance of the excitation winding only contains the dc component, because in the same pole magnetic field structure, the self-inductance parameters of the excitation winding are determined by the overall magnetic circuit state and have nothing to do with the details of the air gap flux density waveform.

The excitation time constant can be expressed by:

$$t_f = \frac{L_{ff}}{r_f} = \frac{N_f \pi R_H (l_1 + 2\delta) k_m \lambda_{dc0}^* \Lambda_B}{\rho_{Cu} \pi D_f} S_{cf} \tag{24}$$

In the design of an HTR-ASD, the excitation winding time constant t_f is expected to be as small as possible. On the one hand, it can reduce the excitation establishment time and improve the system mobility. On the other hand, it can make it easier to adjust the flux linkage of the excitation winding in the process of speed regulation, in order to strengthen the dynamic response ability of the system in the process of speed regulation.

3.4. Calculation of Armature Winding Parameters

By using $\lambda_d^*(\theta)$ and $\lambda_q^*(\theta)$, the armature winding parameters can be easily obtained. L_{md} and L_{mq} can be expressed as:

$$L_{md} = \frac{2m\mu_0 D_i(l + 2\delta) k_{dm}}{\delta k_\delta \pi} \left(\frac{NK_{N1}}{p}\right)^2 \lambda_{d1}^*(\theta) \tag{25}$$

$$L_{mq} = \frac{2m\mu_0 D_i(l + 2\delta) k_{qm}}{\delta k_\delta \pi} \left(\frac{NK_{N1}}{p}\right)^2 \lambda_{q1}^*(\theta) \tag{26}$$

where D_i is the inner diameter of the squirrel-cage rotor and l is the length of a single side core. $\lambda_{d1}^*(\theta)$ and $\lambda_{q1}^*(\theta)$ are the fundamental components of $\lambda_d^*(\theta)$ and $\lambda_q^*(\theta)$.

The steady-state salient ratio ρ can be expressed as:

$$\rho = \frac{L_{la}+L_{sq}}{L_{la}+L_{sd}} \tag{27}$$

According to Equations (11) and (12), under no-load excitation, the composite magnetic density of armature winding cutting can be expressed as:

$$B_{\mathrm{dc}}(\theta) = \frac{N_f I_f}{2} k_m \lambda_{\mathrm{dc}}^*(\theta) \Lambda_B \tag{28}$$

Therefore, the fundamental component of mutual inductance between excitation winding and armature winding can be expressed as:

$$M_{af} = \frac{\mu_0 D_i (l+2\delta)\lambda_1^*}{\delta k_\delta}\frac{N K_{N1}}{p} N_f \tag{29}$$

From the calculations of the above parameters, it can be clearly seen that by using $\lambda_{dc}^*(\theta)$, $\lambda_d^*(\theta)$, and $\lambda_q^*(\theta)$, the design flow becomes more efficient. As for the calculation of leaked inductance, it is the same as that of a conventional machine. Furthermore, because the winding in the conductor rotor core is a squirrel cage type, the end ring parameters need to be considered [32].

3.5. Magnetic Circuit Calculation

To consider the influence of different position saturation on the calculation of the inductance parameters, the magnetic circuit of the HTR-ASD needs to be calculated. Considering that the surfaces of each part of the HTR-ASD are equimagnetic potential surfaces, the calculation can be simplified using Carter's coefficient. Figure 10 shows the calculation model of the homopolar-type rotor obtained by Carter's factor.

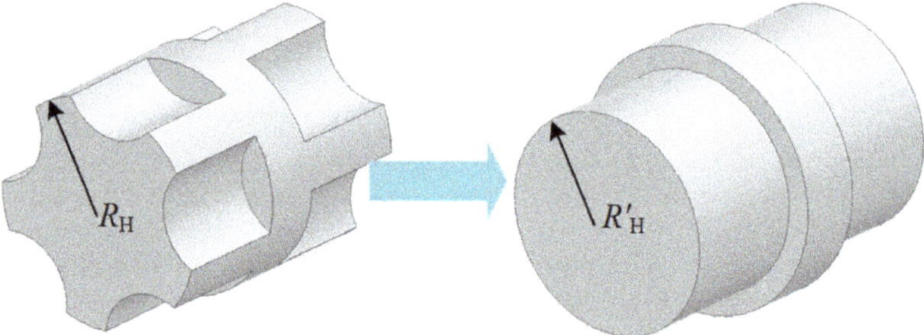

Figure 10. The key parameters and magnetic equivalent circuit of the HTR-ASD.

Figure 11a shows the key parameters of the machine and Figure 11b shows the MEC of the calculation. $\delta\prime_1$ can be written as:

$$\delta\prime_1 = \delta_{\min} k_{\delta HTR} k_{\delta SCR} \tag{30}$$

where $k_{\delta HTR}$ and $k_{\delta SCR}$ are the Carter coefficients of the homopolar-type rotor and the squirrel-cage rotor.

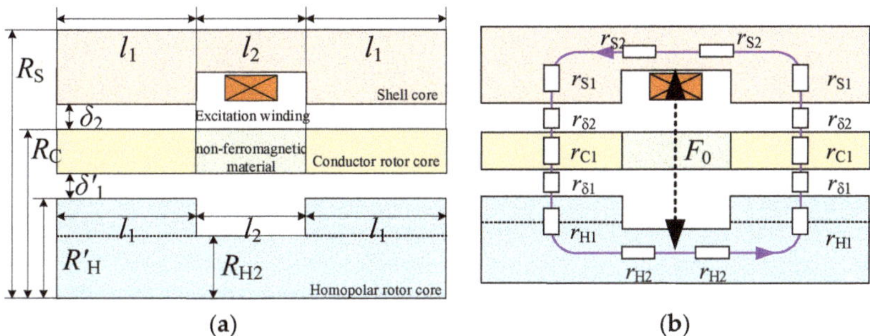

Figure 11. The key parameters and magnetic equivalent circuit of the HTR-ASD. (**a**) The key parameters of the machine. (**b**) The MEC of the calculation.

Therefore, the reluctances can be expressed as:

$$
\begin{cases}
r_{S1} = \dfrac{ln(R_S/(R_C+\delta_2))}{2\mu_S\pi l_1} \\[2mm]
r_{S2} = \dfrac{l_2}{2\mu_S\pi\left(R_S-R_C-\delta_2-h_f\right)^2} \\[2mm]
r_{\delta 2} = \dfrac{ln(1+\delta_2/R_C)}{2\mu_0\pi l_1} \\[2mm]
r_{\delta 1} = \dfrac{ln\left(1+\delta_1'/R_H'\right)}{2\mu_0\pi l_1} \\[2mm]
r_{C1} = \dfrac{ln\left(1+\delta_1'/R_H'\right)}{2\mu_C\pi l_1} \\[2mm]
r_{H1} = \dfrac{ln\left(R_H'/R_{H2}\right)}{2\mu_H\pi l_1} \\[2mm]
r_{H2} = \dfrac{l_2}{2\mu_H\pi R_{H2}^2}
\end{cases}
\tag{31}
$$

The use of a MEC can simplify the calculation of a 3D magnetic circuit and speed up the calculation and analysis processes. At the same time, the air gap magnetic density can be determined by $\lambda_{dc}^*(\theta)$ after calculating the no-load magnetic circuit.

3.6. Summary of the Analysis and Design Method of the HTR-ASD

The above analysis can be summarized as follows:

(1) When the torque and speed requirements are determined, the key parameters of an HTR-ASD can be obtained using the equivalent circuit and expression (9).

(2) When the key parameters, like L_{sq} and L_{sd}, are determined, the rotor shape and the winding parameters can be determined by $\lambda_{dc}^*(\theta)$, $\lambda_d^*(\theta)$, $\lambda_q^*(\theta)$, and expressions (25) and (26).

(3) To consider the influence of different position saturation on the calculation of inductance parameters, a MEC can be used. By using expression (31), the influence of different position saturation on the calculation of inductance parameters can be taken into consideration.

(4) As for the dynamic characteristics of the HTR-ASD, the s-function simulation model can be established based on expressions (2) and (3).

4. Performance Analysis

4.1. Prototype Design and FEM Analysis

To verify the accuracy of the above analysis and study the characteristics of the machine, a prototype is designed and its parameters are illustrated in Table 1.

Table 1. The parameters of the HTR-ASD.

Parameter	Value	Unit
Pole-pair numbers of the HTR	5	-
The slot numbers of the squirrel-cage rotor	48	-
Air gap length between the squirrel cage and the HTR	1	mm
Air gap length between the squirrel cage and the shell	1	mm
The diameter of the HTR	120	mm
The inner diameter of the shell	182	mm
The length of the shaft	30	mm
Total length	150	mm
The turns of excitation winding	400	-

A 3D finite element model was established to calculate the electromagnetic parameters. Figure 12 shows the 3D-FEM model and the mesh of the rotor finite element model. Figure 13 shows the no-load magnetic field distribution of the axial and radial views at an excitation current of 6A.

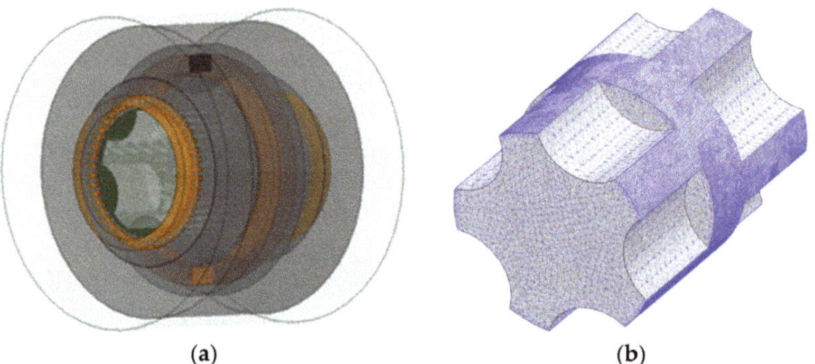

(a)   (b)

Figure 12. Three-dimensional FEM of the HTR-ASD. (**a**) The FEM model of the HTR-ASD. (**b**) Mesh of the rotor finite element model.

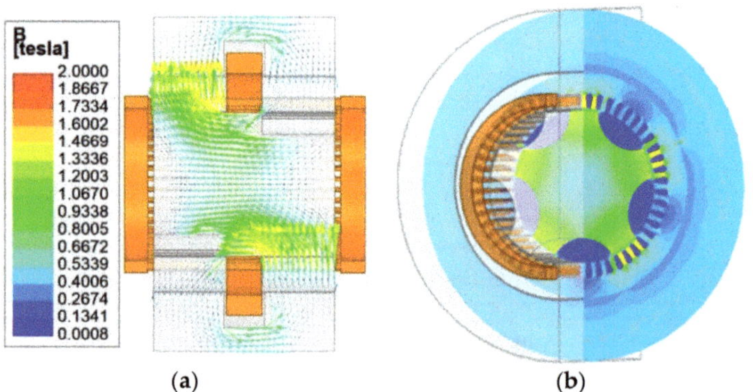

(a)   (b)

Figure 13. No-load magnetic field distribution of the axial and radial views. (**a**) The no-load magnetic field distribution of the axial view. (**b**) The no-load magnetic field distribution of the radial view.

Figure 14 shows a comparison between the analytical calculations and the simulation of no-load air gap flux density distribution. This shows that the proposed air gap permeance function and the MEC model of the HTR-ASD are accurate and can be used to calculate the magnetic field of the machine. Figure 15 shows the air gap flux density distribution at different slip speeds and an excitation current of 6A. Additionally, Figure 16 shows the squirrel-cage current density distribution at different slip speeds and an excitation current of 6A.

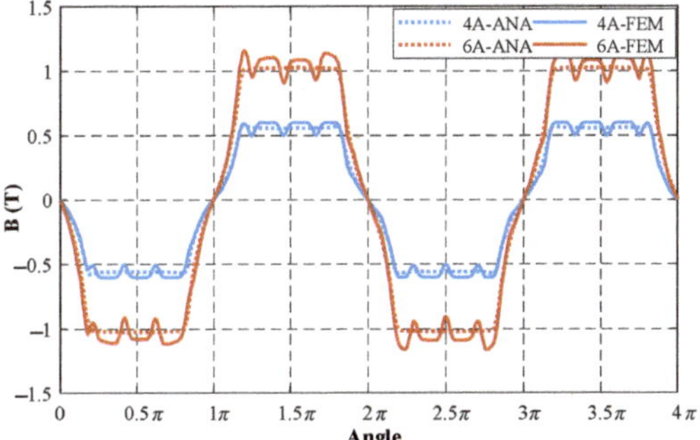

Figure 14. No-load magnetic field distribution of the axial and radial views.

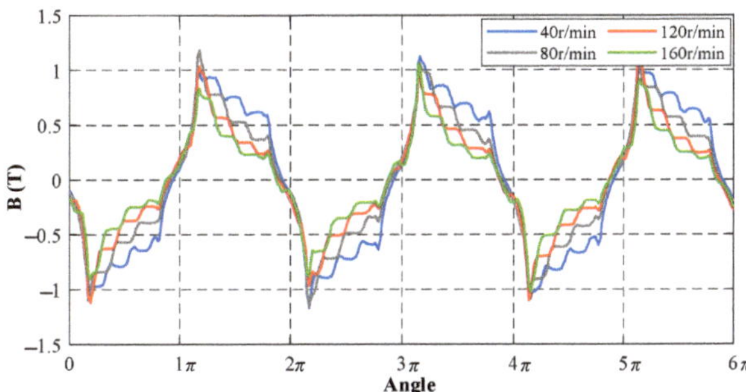

Figure 15. Air-gap flux density distribution under different slip speed at 6A excitation current.

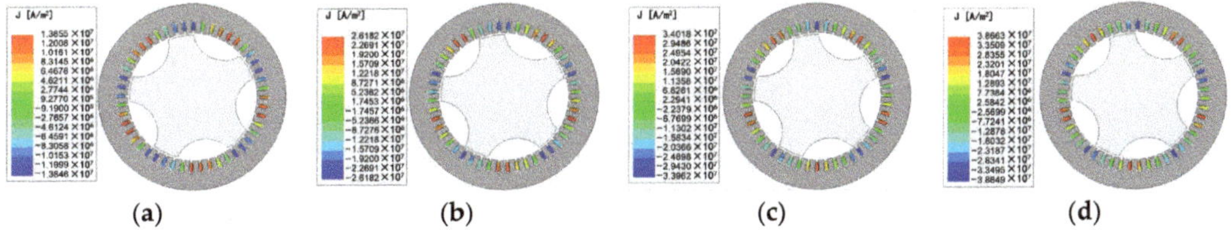

Figure 16. Current density distribution under different slip speeds and an excitation current of 6A. (**a**) Slip speed = 40 r/min; (**b**) slip speed = 80 r/min; (**c**) slip speed = 120 r/min; (**d**) slip speed = 160 r/min.

4.2. Speed Regulation Characteristics

Figure 17 shows the output torque of the HTR-ASD under different slip speeds and excitation currents. From Figure 17, it can be clearly seen that the speed and torque of the HTR-ASD can be easily adjusted by changing the excitation current. Additionally, the output torque is proportional to the square of the current, which is similar to the characteristics of the voltage regulated speed control of an asynchronous motor. Through a comparison between the analytical calculations and simulations, the accuracy of the analytical analysis in this study is verified. Figure 18 shows the operating characteristics at different prime mover speeds. When the speed of the prime mover changes, its characteristics are like those of the variable frequency speed regulation of an asynchronous motor.

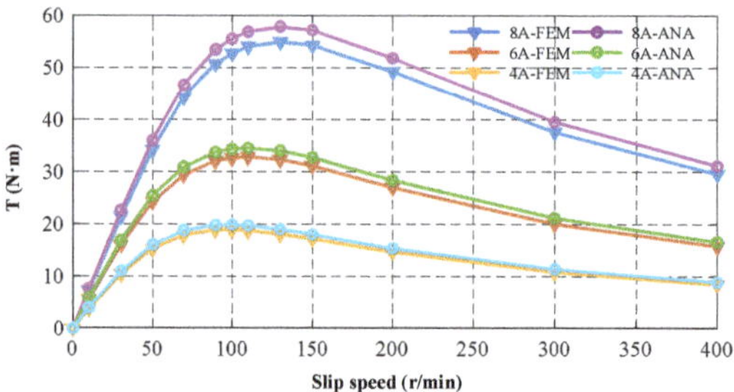

Figure 17. The output torque of HTR-ASD under different slip speed and excitation currents.

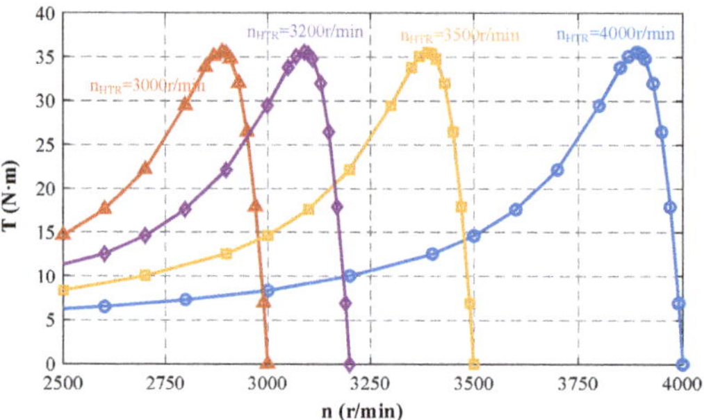

Figure 18. The mechanical properties of the HTR-ASD.

When the inductance parameters of the machine are calculated, the transient torque response of the HTR-ASD can be obtained by the s-function simulation model, which is much quicker than the FEM. Figure 19 shows the transient torque response of the HTR-ASD calculated by the two methods under different slip speeds and an excitation current of 6A. As can be seen from Figure 19, the results of the two methods are basically consistent. Furthermore, the higher the slip speed, the longer the response time because of the larger current.

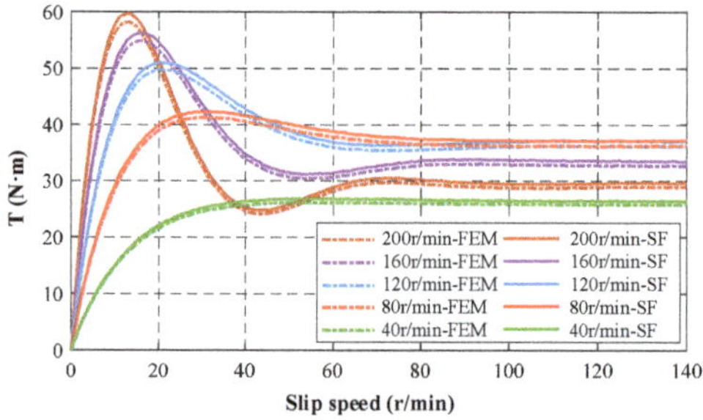

Figure 19. Transient torque response of the HTR-ASD under different slip speeds and an excitation current of 6A.

5. Conclusions

In this study, a new type of adjustable speed drive, named the HTR-ASD, is proposed. Its unilateral air gap magnetic field is unipolar, while its synthetic air gap magnetic field is bipolar. The HTR-ASD has an absence of brushes, permanent magnets, and mechanical flux regulation devices, leading to an obvious advantage of high reliability. The speed and torque can be adjusted only by adjusting the excitation current with dc power. Meanwhile, the rotating parts of the device are composed of a solid homopolar-type rotor and simple squirrel-cage structure. This simple and robust structure makes it more suitable for working in harsh environments. In order to calculate its steady and dynamic characteristics, the equation and equivalent circuit of the HTR-ASD are analyzed in a rotor d-q frame. Additionally, the air gap permeance functions are developed to simplify the analysis of the air gap magnetic density and the calculation of the parameters, which may make the design flow more efficient. Finally, a protype is designed and simulated by the FEM, and analytical analyses are carried out to verify and evaluate the HTR-ASD's performance. The comparison between the FEM and the analytical analyses are developed, and the results show great agreement in relation to accuracy. In addition, the results of the operating characteristics indicate that this machine is very suitable for use as an adjustable speed drive.

Author Contributions: Conceptualization, S.G. and K.Y.; methodology, Z.Y.; software, P.L., H.L., and G.W.; validation, S.G. and X.X.; formal analysis, S.G. and Z.Y.; investigation, K.Y.; resources, K.Y. and P.L.; data curation, Z.Y. and X.X.; writing—original draft preparation, S.G. and X.X.; writing—review and editing, S.G. and X.X.; visualization, X.X.; supervision, X.X.; project administration, X.X.; funding acquisition, P.L., H.L. and G.W. All authors have read and agreed to the published version of the manuscript.

Funding: This work was supported by the National Natural Science Foundation of China (52007072), the National Natural Science Foundation of China (51821005) and the interdisciplinary program of Wuhan National High Magnetic Field Center (WHMFC 202110).

Data Availability Statement: Not applicable.

Conflicts of Interest: The authors declare no conflict of interest.

References

1. Dai, X.; Liang, Q.H.; Cao, J.Y.; Long, Y.J.; Mo, J.Q.; Wang, S. Analytical Modeling of Axial-Flux Permanent Magnet Eddy Current Couplings with a Slotted Conductor Topology. *IEEE Trans. Magn.* **2017**, *52*, 1–15. [CrossRef]
2. Mohammadi, S.; Mirsalim, M.; Vaez-Zadeh, S.; Talebi, H.A. Analytical Modeling and Analysis of Axial-Flux Interior Permanent-Magnet Couplers. *IEEE Trans. Ind. Electron.* **2014**, *61*, 5940–5947. [CrossRef]
3. Erasmus, A.S.; Kamper, M.J. Computationally Efficient Analysis of Double PM-Rotor Radial-Flux Eddy Current Couplers. *IEEE Trans. Ind. Applicat.* **2017**, *53*, 3519–3527. [CrossRef]
4. Aydin, M.; Huang, S.; Lipo, T.A. Design, analysis, and control of a hybrid field-controlled axial-flux permanent-magnet motor. *IEEE Trans. Ind. Electron.* **2010**, *57*, 78–87. [CrossRef]
5. Mohammadi, S.; Kirtley, J.; Azari, M.N. Modelling of axial-flux eddy-current couplers. *IET Electr. Power Appl.* **2020**, *14*, 1238–1246. [CrossRef]
6. Li, Y.; Lin, H.; Tao, Q.; Lu, X.; Yang, H.; Fang, S.; Wang, H. Analytical analysis of an adjustable-speed permanent magnet eddy-current coupling with a non-rotary mechanical flux adjuster. *IEEE Trans. Magn.* **2019**, *55*, 1–5. [CrossRef]
7. Tsao, P.; Senesky, M.; Sanders, S.R. An integrated flywheel energy storage system with homopolar inductor motor/generator and high-frequency drive. *IEEE Trans. Ind. Applicat.* **2003**, *39*, 1710–1725. [CrossRef]
8. Severson, E.; Nilssen, R.; Undeland, T.; Mohan, N. Outer-rotor ac homopolar motors for flywheel energy storage. In Proceedings of the 7th IET International Conference on Power Electronics, Machines and Drives, Manchester, UK, 8–10 April 2014; pp. 1–6.
9. Severson, E.; Nilssen, R.; Undeland, T.; Mohan, N. Dual-Purpose No-Voltage Winding Design for the Bearingless AC Homopolar and Consequent Pole Motors. *IEEE Trans. Ind. Appl.* **2015**, *51*, 2884–2895. [CrossRef]
10. Yang, J.T.; Li, Q.; Huang, S.D.; Ye, C.Y.; Liu, P.; Ma, B.; Wang, L. Design and Analysis of a Novel Permanent Magnet Homopolar Inductor Machine with Mechanical Flux Modulator for Flywheel Energy Storage System. *IEEE Trans. Ind. Electron.* **2022**, *69*, 7744–7755. [CrossRef]
11. Asama, J.; Chiba, A. Performance Evaluation of a Homopolar Bearingless Motor for Ultrahigh Speed Applications. *IEEE Trans. Ind. Appl.* **2021**, *57*, 6913–6920. [CrossRef]
12. Dmitrievskii, V.; Prakht, V.; Anuchin, A.; Kazakbaev, V. Traction Synchronous Homopolar Motor: Simplified Computation Technique and Experimental Validation. *IEEE Access* **2020**, *8*, 185112–185120. [CrossRef]
13. Kalsi, S.; Hamilton, K.; Buckley, R.G.; Badcock, R.A. Superconducting AC Homopolar Machines for High-Speed Applications. *Energies* **2019**, *12*, 86. [CrossRef]
14. Dmitrievskii, V.; Prakht, V.; Kazakbaev, V.; Anuchin, A. Comparison of Interior Permanent Magnet and Synchronous Homopolar Motors for a Mining Dump Truck Traction Drive Operated in Wide Constant Power Speed Range. *Mathematics* **2022**, *10*, 1581. [CrossRef]
15. Aberoomand, V.; Mirsalim, M.; Fesharakifard, R. Design optimization of double-sided permanent-magnet axial eddy-current couplers for use in dynamic applications. *IEEE Trans. Energy Convers.* **2019**, *34*, 909–920. [CrossRef]

16. Li, Z.; Wang, D.Z.; Zheng, D. Accurate Prediction and Analysis of Electromagnetic Fields and Forces in Flux-Focusing Eddy Current Coupling With Double Slotted Conductor Rotors. *IEEE Access* **2018**, *6*, 37685–37699. [CrossRef]
17. Dong, K.; Yu, H.T.; Hu, M.Q.; Liu, J.; Huang, L.; Zhou, J.H. Study of axial-flux-type superconducting eddy-current couplings. *IEEE Trans. Appl. Supercond.* **2017**, *27*, 1–5. [CrossRef]
18. Le, Y.Z.; Liu, Y.P.; Li, D.S. Performance analysis and optimization of liquid-cooled and flywheel-type eddy current retarder. *IEEE Trans. Magn.* **2019**, *55*, 1–5.
19. Guo, W.G.; Li, D.S.; Ye, L.Z. A model of magnetic field and braking torque in liquid-cooled permanent-magnet retarder accounting for the skin effect on permeability. *IEEE Trans. Veh. Technol.* **2019**, *68*, 10618–10626. [CrossRef]
20. Telezing, B.; Yang, C.J.; Ombolo, P.; Peng, Z.Z.; Tai, J.X.; Zhu, L. Torque Characteristics Analysis of a Novel Hybrid Superconducting Magnetic Coupling With Axial-Flux Using a Magnetic Equivalent Circuit Model. *IEEE Access* **2022**, *10*, 45594–45604. [CrossRef]
21. Wang, J.; Zhu, J. A simple method for performance prediction of permanent magnet eddy current couplings using a new magnetic equivalent circuit model. *IEEE Trans. Ind. Electron.* **2018**, *65*, 2487–2495. [CrossRef]
22. Guo, B.Z.; Li, D.S.; Shi, J.R.; Gao, Z.W. A Performance Prediction Model for Permanent Magnet Eddy-Current Couplings Based on the Air-Gap Magnetic Field Distribution. *IEEE Trans. Magn.* **2022**, *58*, 1–9. [CrossRef]
23. Ye, C.Y.; Yang, J.T.; Xiong, F.; Zhu, Z.Q. Relationship between Homopolar Inductor Machine and Wound-Field Synchronous Machine. *IEEE Trans. Ind. Electron.* **2020**, *67*, 919–930. [CrossRef]
24. Yang, J.T.; Ye, C.; Xu, W.; Liang, X.; Li, W. Investigation of a Two-Dimensional Analytical Model of the Homopolar Inductor Alternator. *IEEE Trans. Appl. Supercond.* **2018**, *28*, 1–5. [CrossRef]
25. Yang, J.T.; Li, Q.; Feng, Y.J.; Liu, P.; Huang, S.D.; Wang, L. Simulation and Experimental Analysis of a Mechanical Flux Modulated Permanent Magnet Homopolar Inductor Machine. *IEEE Trans. Transport. Electrif.* **2022**, *8*, 2629–2639. [CrossRef]
26. Severson, E.; Nilssen, R.; Undeland, T.; Mohan, N. Magnetic Equivalent Circuit Modeling of the AC Homopolar Machine for Flywheel Energy Storage. *IEEE Trans. Energy Convers.* **2015**, *30*, 1670–1678. [CrossRef]
27. Yang, J.T.; Ye, C.Y.; Huang, S.D.; Li, Y.; Xiong, F.; Zhou, Y.; Xu, W. Analysis of the Electromagnetic Performance of Homopolar Inductor Machine Through Nonlinear Magnetic Equivalent Circuit and Air-Gap Permeance Function. *IEEE Trans. Ind. Appl.* **2020**, *56*, 267–276. [CrossRef]
28. Lubin, T.; Rezzoug, A. Steady-State and Transient Performance of Axial-Field Eddy-Current Coupling. *IEEE Trans. Ind. Electron.* **2015**, *62*, 2287–2296. [CrossRef]
29. Jin, Y.X.; Kou, B.Q.; Li, L.Y. Improved Analytical Modeling of an Axial Flux Double-Sided Eddy-Current Brake with Slotted Conductor Disk. *IEEE Trans. Ind. Electron.* **2022**, *69*, 13277–13286. [CrossRef]
30. Yang, C.J.; Peng, Z.Z.; Tai, J.X.; Zhu, L.; Telezing, B.J.K.; Ombolo, P.D. Torque Characteristics Analysis of Slotted-Type Eddy-Current Couplings Using a New Magnetic Equivalent Circuit Model. *IEEE Trans. Magn.* **2020**, *56*, 1–8. [CrossRef]
31. Lou, Z.X.; He, Y.G.; Cheng, Y.; Ye, C.Y.; Yu, K.X. Analytical calculation of d- and q-axis synchronous reactances of homopolar inductor alternator. In Proceedings of the 2014 17th International Symposium on Electromagnetic Launch Technology, La Jolla, CA, USA, 7–11 July 2014; pp. 1–8.
32. Li, Y.B.; Lin, H.Y.; Yang, H. A Novel Squirrel-Cage Rotor Permanent Magnet Adjustable Speed Drive with a Non-Rotary Mechanical Flux Adjuster. *IEEE Trans. Energy Convers.* **2021**, *36*, 1036–1044. [CrossRef]

 *mathematics*

Article

Inspection Interval Optimization for Aircraft Composite Tail Wing Structure Using Numerical-Analysis-Based Approach

Salman Khalid [1], Hee-Seong Kim [2], Heung Soo Kim [1,*] and Joo-Ho Choi [2]

[1] Department of Mechanical, Robotics and Energy Engineering, Dongguk University-Seoul, 30 Pil-dong 1 Gil, Jung-gu, Seoul 04620, Korea
[2] Department of Aerospace & Mechanical Engineering, Korea Aerospace University, Gyeonggi-do, Goyang-si 10540, Korea
* Correspondence: heungsoo@dgu.edu; Tel.: +82-2-2260-8577; Fax: +82-2-2263-9379

Abstract: Recently, there has been a tremendous increase in the use of fiber-reinforced composite (FRCP) in the aviation and aerospace industries due to its superior properties of high strength, stiffness, and low weight. The most important feature of implementing composite materials in aviation is their behavior under dynamic loads and resistance to fatigue. To predict the life of composite structures and optimize the inspection interval, it is essential to predict the damage behavior of composites. In this study, a model of fatigue delamination damage of composite specimens was first constructed using a finite element analysis (FEA)-based approach. The FEA modeling was verified through comparison with experimental specimen data, and the verified FEA model was applied to the composite material aircraft tail wing structure. In this case, a Monte Carlo simulation (MCS) was performed by building a response surface model while considering the uncertainty of the mechanical parameters. Through this process, the risk as a function of flight time could be quantitatively evaluated, and the inspection interval was optimized by selecting the combination with the lowest number of repeated inspections that met the permitted risk criteria.

Keywords: fiber-reinforced composites; finite element analysis; delamination; inspection interval; aircraft tail wing structure

MSC: 65-04

Citation: Khalid, S.; Kim, H.-S.; Kim, H.S.; Choi, J.-H. Inspection Interval Optimization for Aircraft Composite Tail Wing Structure Using Numerical-Analysis-Based Approach. *Mathematics* **2022**, *10*, 3836. https://doi.org/10.3390/math10203836

Academic Editors: Camelia Petrescu and Valeriu David

Received: 20 September 2022
Accepted: 14 October 2022
Published: 17 October 2022

Publisher's Note: MDPI stays neutral with regard to jurisdictional claims in published maps and institutional affiliations.

1. Introduction

To ensure the safe and continuous operation of aircraft, maintenance is a key activity [1]. Efficient maintenance can save high maintenance costs and can increase the service life of aircraft structures. Recently, the development of the structural health monitoring approach (condition-based maintenance) has enabled maintenance engineers to more frequently monitor the health condition of aircraft structures [2]. For this purpose, additional sensors are embedded in structures to provide health information, thus making condition-based maintenance more expensive than scheduled maintenance. Therefore, the practice of scheduled maintenance remains more dominant than condition-based maintenance. The main challenge in scheduled maintenance is the determination of efficient inspection intervals to reduce maintenance costs and maintain high safety standards [3].

The proportion of FRCPs in aircraft structures is increasing every year as the technical limitations of composite materials are gradually resolved [4]. FRCPs offer high stiffness, high strength-to-weight ratio, and excellent fatigue performance, making them suitable for the manufacturing of complex aircraft composite structures. Aircraft industries, such as Boeing 787 and Airbus A380, are using composite materials for their primary structures, such as the fuselage skin and wing spars [5]. Unlike metals, these composites suffer from complex damage mechanisms because of their anisotropic properties. Among these, fatigue delamination and debonding damage are the major causes of failure in composites [6–8].

During aircraft flight, fatigue load continuously occurs, thus making the structures more susceptible to fatigue delamination damage [9]. Therefore, for the accurate prediction of the life span of composite structures, it is important to predict the fatigue delamination damage.

The commonly applied maintenance method in the aviation industry is the maintenance steering group 3 (MSG-3) [10], which aids in determining the inspection interval of aircraft structures. However, MSG-3 has the disadvantage of being heavily dependent on engineering experience, while the functional/structural detail evaluation of various new composite aircraft structures is limited. Therefore, the use of MSG-3 is inadequate for direct application to composite structures. Furthermore, it is difficult to maintain structural uniformity in composites because of the inaccuracies of the manufacturing process and the random variation in properties in composites. Therefore it is challenging to predict the failure of composite materials using the traditional deterministic approaches [11]. The usage of deterministic approaches results in the underutilization of the composite material. To utilize the material to its full capacity without compromising its structural safety, the uncertainties in the composite material should be considered for its realistic design, which is not possible in deterministic analysis. Probabilistic analysis offers a solution of incorporating the uncertainties in the design variables to compute the inherent risk in a structure subjected to service loading conditions. Therefore probabilistic approaches [12–14] have received considerable attention when it comes to addressing the uncertainty in design and maintenance.

Recently, Dinis et al. [15] proposed a probabilistic-design-based approach for aircraft maintenance and repair. The approach employed the usage of a Bayesian network to cope with the uncertainty in both scheduled and unscheduled maintenance. A real dataset based on 372 aircraft industrial maintenance projects was used. Similarly, Chen et al. developed an approach for the optimization of inspection intervals for composite structures for dent and delamination damage. The idea was to quantify the structural residual strength and maintenance cost for the different inspection intervals. The proposed approach was implemented on an aircraft wing. A historical dataset from the Chinese aircraft industry was used to develop the proposed approach. A POD curve created using general visual inspection (GVI) and detailed inspection (DET) data was selected as a method of damage detection. The probability of detecting damage according to dent damage was calculated using a Monte Carlo simulation. From these simulation results, a procedure for calculating the optimal inspection cycle that considered the structural reliability and maintenance cost was presented. However, the main limitation of this approach was that it was based on the actual repair data after the damage was confirmed. The approach did not consider the cause and progression of the delamination and dent damage.

Similarly, Dinggiang et al. [11] developed an optimized inspection interval approach by considering dent and delamination damage. The study used the maintenance records of 12 aircraft over 10 years of operation time. Impact damage was considered the main cause of damage, and the average expected number of impacts per year was calculated by comparing the maintenance history of such impact damage and the service life of the aircraft. The failure probability of the structure was calculated by simulating the residual strength and damage growth of the structure according to the impact damage that occurred during the service life operation. This study also utilized the actual maintenance data. The limitations of this approach were the limited damage data and that it was difficult to obtain the damage maintenance data from the aircraft industry. Further, the obtained data included the information after the damage occurred, and lacked information on the damage progression and the accurate cause of the damage. To overcome the data availability problem and the lack of progressive damage knowledge, an FEA-based approach can be used. Gianella et al. [16] developed a probabilistic framework for fatigue reliability assessment by considering multi-source uncertainties. The sensitivity of each input variable was obtained, and the influence of the variable on the life prediction was derived. The above-presented literature approaches are all based on real aircraft maintenance and damage data. However, the main limitation of the approaches available in the literature is the availability of real aircraft maintenance data to develop structural health monitoring approaches for the prediction of the fatigue life of the composite structures. The acquisition of the real damage data requires the embedding of additional sensors on the skin of aircraft structures, thus making the maintenance strategies more expensive. Therefore, to overcome the unavailability of the real-life operating data problem, this study proposed a methodology that uses the FEA-based model for the generation of fatigue damage growth curves and further implements this approach for the risk assessment and optimization of the inspection interval of the KT-100 aircraft tail wing structure. To the authors' best knowledge, no such study can be found in the literature that utilized a finite-element-analysis-based approach for the inspection interval optimization of aircraft composite structures.

In this study, a novel FEA-based approach was proposed for the inspection interval optimization of an aircraft composite tail wing structure. First, the FEA-based fatigue delamination model was constructed for the composite specimen and was verified through comparison with experimental data. The verified FEA model was extended to the composite aircraft tail wing structure of a KT-100 aircraft (Korea Aerospace Industries, Ltd., KAI). In this case, a Monte Carlo simulation was performed by building a response surface model that considered the uncertainty of the mechanical parameters. Through this process, the risk according to each flight time could be quantitatively evaluated, and the inspection interval was optimized by selecting the combination with the lowest number of repeated inspections within the conditions that met the permitted risk criteria.

2. Proposed Finite-Element-Analysis-Based Inspection Interval Optimization Approach

Figure 1 shows the proposed FEA-based inspection interval optimization approach. The developed methodology consisted of the following five phases:

Phase 1. The geometry, fatigue-loading spectrum data, and skin-debonding damage case scenario of the KT-100 aircraft tail wing structure were obtained from KAI.

Phase 2. A fatigue delamination damage model was developed for a simple composite specimen and extended to the full-scale aircraft tail wing geometry.

Phase 3. The uncertainty of mechanical parameters was included, and the design of experiments was created based on Latin hypercube sampling (LHS) scenarios.

Phase 4. A Monte Carlo simulation was performed by building a response surface model.

Phase 5. Risk assessment and inspection interval optimization of the tail wing structure were undertaken.

2.1. Development of the Finite Element Model

Modern aircraft structures, such as the wings and fuselage, utilize FRCPs. The composite laminates are highly susceptible to delamination, which is considered one of the major damage mechanisms in composites among all other types of damage. The delamination propagation can occur under the fatigue loading, thus causing stiffness and gradual strength degradation and leading to catastrophic failure of composite structures. Therefore, the characterization of the fatigue delamination resistance in composite materials is necessary for their damage tolerance design and reliability assessment. In aircraft composite structures, stringers are joined to the skin via adhesive bonding. During the flight, cyclic fatigue causes separation between the skin and stringer, which may result in delamination failure. Therefore, it is important to predict fatigue delamination initiation and propagation so that these composite panels do not fail prematurely. To enhance the fatigue life and reliability of composite structures, several researchers have investigated the delamination growth in composites under fatigue loading. A variety of models are proposed in the literature for the prediction of fatigue delamination growth at the coupon level. However, the prediction of fatigue delamination in complex geometries, such as aircraft wing structures, is still an open issue. The most popular approach for the characterization of fatigue crack growth is Paris' law [17–19]. Paris' law relates the fatigue crack growth rate to the stress intensity factor and energy release rate. Equation (1) shows the basic form of Paris' law [20]:

$$dA/dN = Cf(G)^m \tag{1}$$

where C and m represent the fitting parameters and $f(G)$ is a function of the energy release rate (G). In metals, the stress intensity factor variation (ΔK) is usually adopted for fatigue crack growth. On the other hand, in composite laminated structures, the energy release rate (ΔG) variation seems to provide a better description of experimental results, as shown in Equation (2):

$$\frac{dA}{dN} = C(\Delta G)^m = C(G_{max} - G_{min}) \tag{2}$$

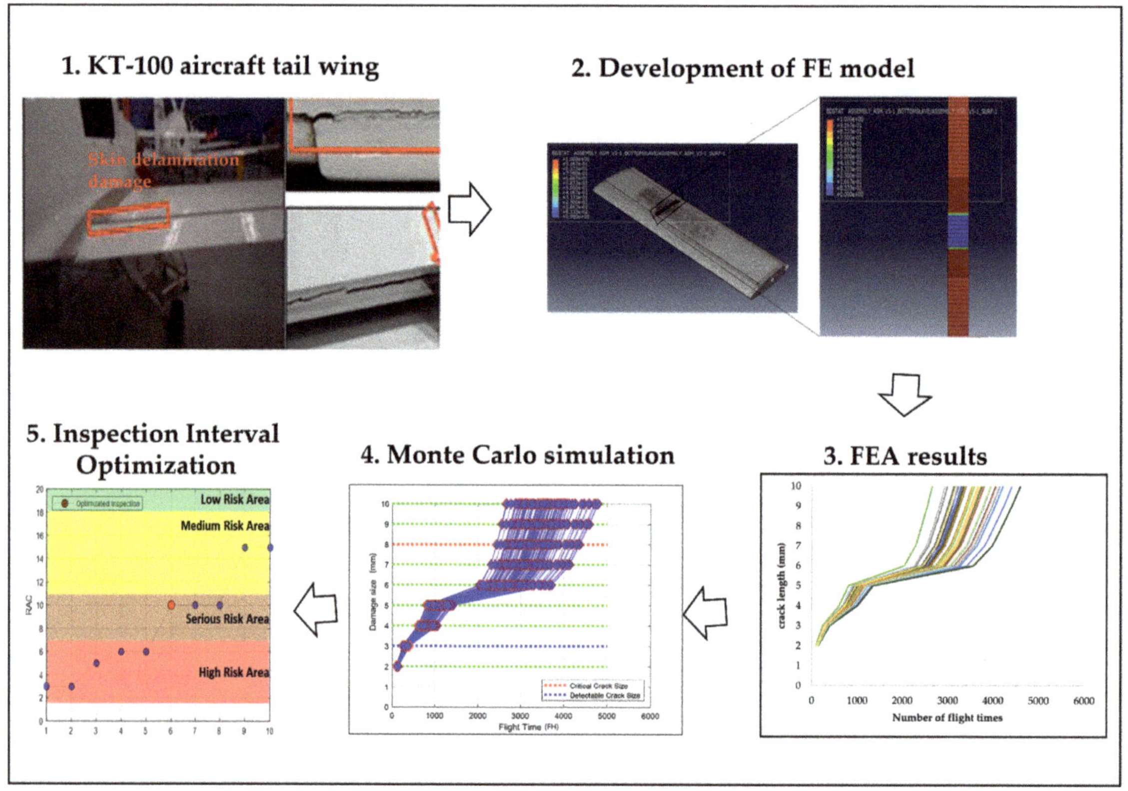

Figure 1. Schematic of the proposed FE-based inspection interval optimization approach.

The FE model implemented in this study and included in the FE code ABAQUS [21] was built on Equation (2) to estimate the fatigue crack growth rate.

In a numerical model, delamination is usually modeled using a damage mechanics or fracture mechanics approach in combination with Paris' law. Different approaches are found in the literature in the context of damage mechanics. Among these, the cohesive zone modeling approach [22–24] received considerable attention for delamination modeling. This approach provides good results in combination with Paris' law for simple geometries and test specimens. However, this approach is not suitable for complex geometries. On the other hand, the virtual crack closure technique (VCCT) [9,25] derived from fracture mechanics is found built into several commercial FE codes. This approach is suitable for implementation in complex geometries and can simulate fatigue delamination growth in combination with Paris' law. The fatigue crack growth in an ABAQUS simulation employs VCCT criteria to compute the energy release rate. The crack propagation starts when the criterion based on Equation (3) is satisfied:

$$f = \frac{N}{c_1 \Delta G^{c2}} \geq G_{max} > G_{th} \tag{3}$$

where N is the current cycle number and c_1 and c_2 are fitting parameters that are experimentally determined. Once the onset criterion is satisfied, the fatigue delamination growth rate is governed by Paris' law, which is shown in Equation (4):

$$\frac{dA}{dN} = c_3 (\Delta G)^{c_4} \tag{4}$$

where c_3 and c_4 are fitting parameters.

The fatigue delamination finite element was first implemented for the double cantilever beam (DCB) composite specimen. The results of the numerical model were compared with the benchmark experimental study [23,26]. The composite specimen had a length of 254 mm and a width of 25 mm. The thickness of each arm was 3 mm. The initial delamination was induced in the specimen with a length of 51 mm and was located in the center of the plies, as shown in Figure 2. The specimen consisted of a T300/1076 carbon fiber epoxy composite with 24 unidirectional plies.

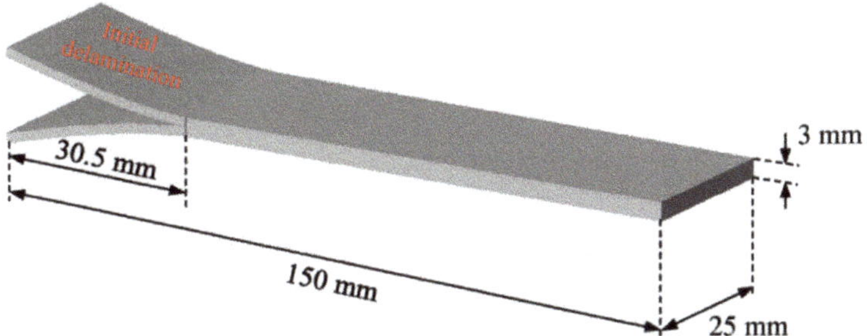

Figure 2. DCB specimen geometry with initial delamination.

The material properties used in the numerical model were taken from [26] and are shown in Table 1.

Table 1. Material properties and fatigue parameters of T300/1076 graphite epoxy.

Parameters	Notations	Value
Elastic modulus in direction 1	E1	139,400 MPa
Elastic modulus in directions 2 and 3	E2 = E3	10,160 MPa
Shear modulus in directions 12 and 13	G12 = G13	4600 MPa
Shear modulus in direction 23	G23	3540 MPa
Poisson's ratio in direction 12 and 13	ν12	0.3
Poisson's ratio in direction 23	ν23	0.436
Fracture toughness in direction 1	G_{IC}	0.17 kJ/m^2
Fracture toughness in direction 2	G_{iiC}	0.49 kJ/m^2
Lower fatigue crack growth threshold	r_1	0.67
Upper fatigue crack growth threshold	r_2	0.067

Continuum shell elements (SC8R) were used for the modeling of the DCB specimen. A single element is used throughout the thickness of each arm. The refined mesh was used in the damage propagation zone and the remaining region consisted of a coarse mesh. First, the load–displacement curve was computed for quasi-static loading. The simulation curve was computed and compared with the experimental benchmark case study result, as shown in Figure 3. The numerical model showed a linear response and a good correlation was found, both in terms of the initial stiffness and peak load between the numerical model results and the experimental benchmark case study.

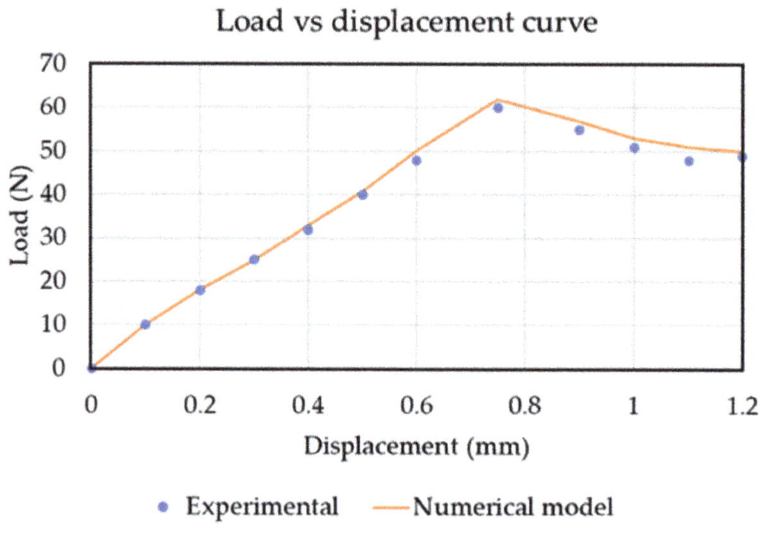

Figure 3. Load vs. displacement curve of the DCB specimen [26].

For the fatigue crack propagation analysis, the triangular load cycle as applied in the experimental benchmark case study [23,26] was applied as a fatigue loading cycle. As expected, the delamination length increased rapidly at the start of the loading cycles. The delamination stopped propagating at around 3.7 million cycles. The numerical results computed in ABAQUS showed good agreement with the experimental benchmark results, as shown in Figure 4.

Once the fatigue delamination crack propagation model was established, the model was extended from the composite specimen to the KT-100 aircraft tail wing structure. The tail wing is located behind the main lifting surface of the aircraft and provides stability and control. The design of the KT-100 horizontal stabilizer consists of upper and lower skins. The upper and lower skins of the sandwich structure act as a spur structure. The upper and lower skins are bonded and tightened to make a box-shaped structure. Three ribs exist inside the box structure. Skin debonding from the rib is the most critical damage that can occur in an aircraft tail wing structure. Figure 5 shows skin-debonding damage. Therefore, in this study, skin/rib-debonding damage was modeled using the fatigue progressive damage model.

The geometry of the tail wing was provided by the Korean Airforce and imported from the 3D model in ABAQUS. To simplify the model, bolts and rivets were not considered in the geometry. Initial delamination of 32 mm was introduced between the middle rib and upper skin, as shown in Figure 6a. To avoid the loss of computational power, shell elements (S4R) were used to model the tail wing structure with 49,209 total elements. The mesh was kept refined in the crack propagation region and coarse in the remaining regions, as shown in Figure 6b.

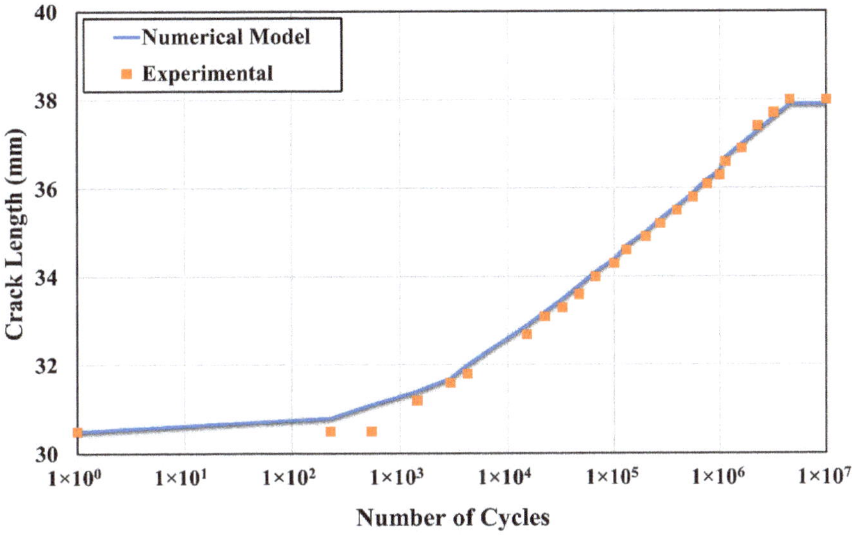

Figure 4. Comparison of the numerical and experimental fatigue delamination propagation curve [23,26].

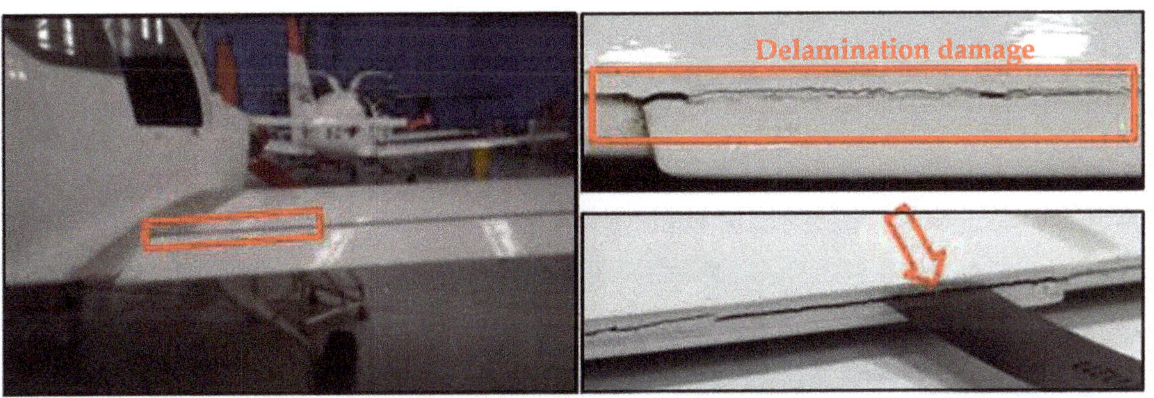

Figure 5. Skin-debonding damage in aircraft tail wing structure.

(a) Initial delamination

(b) Mesh configuration

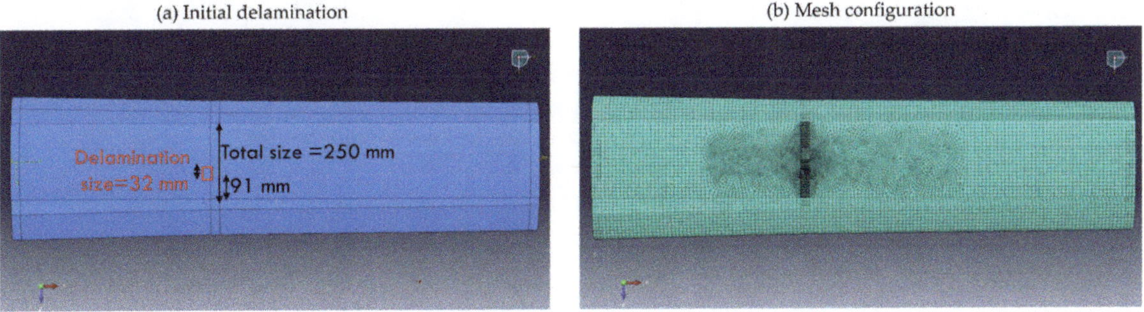

Figure 6. (**a**) Geometry of a tail wing with initial delamination and (**b**) the mesh configuration of the model.

The loads and boundary conditions are used as in an actual flight scenario. One side of the wing was kept fixed, and the shear forces were applied at the other end with the flight loading spectrum as a fatigue cycle provided by the Korean Airforce. Figure 7 shows the flight operating loading spectrum with a normalized amplitude.

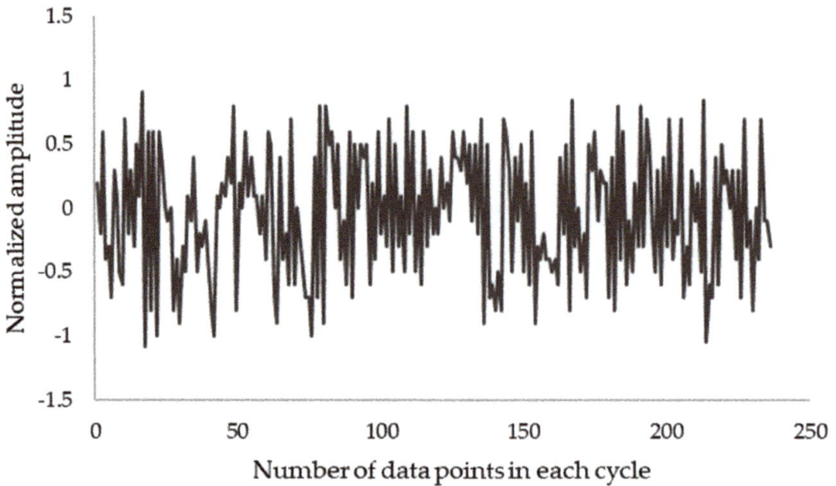

Figure 7. Flight loading spectrum for each fatigue cycle.

The bond stat plot (crack propagation plot) output in ABAQUS represents the fatigue crack propagation. The blue color represents the unbonded region, while the red color represents the bonded region. Figure 8 represents the BDSTAT plot for the tail wing structure. The BDSTAT plot was computed between the upper skin and the middle rib of the composite structure.

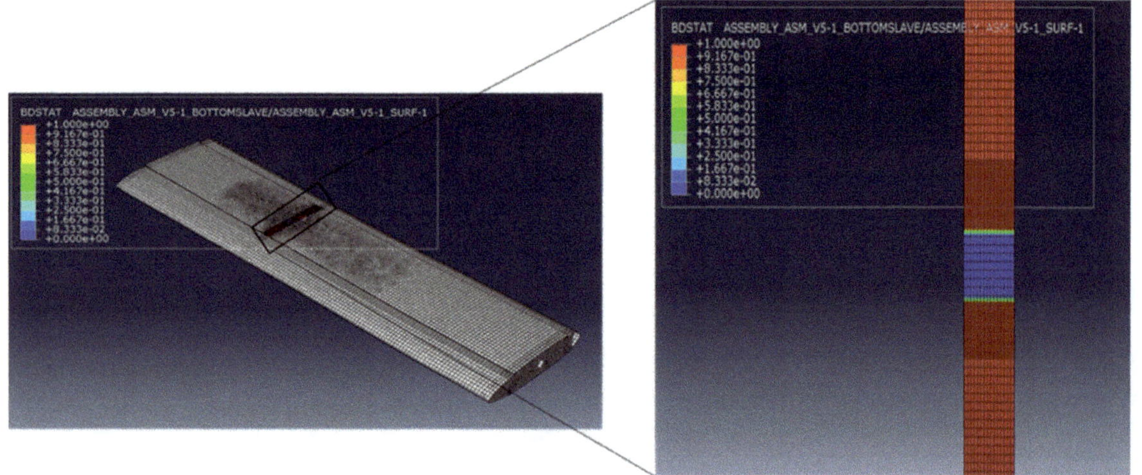

Figure 8. BDSTAT plot representing the cracked region between the upper skin and the middle.

Different case simulations were carried out for the different values of the applied loading scenarios by using the flight operating load spectrum. The simulation was run for 8000 flight hours (FHs), and the crack propagation plots are analyzed. The first case scenario represented the actual loading condition with the magnitude of shear forces. The other three case scenarios were simulated to observe the fatigue crack propagation. Table 2 shows the case simulation scenarios.

Table 2. Case simulation scenarios.

Case Simulation	Applied Shear Force Magnitude	Load Increase (%)
Case 1	1.849 KN	-
Case 2	2.2 KN	18.9%
Case 3	2.6 KN	40.6%
Case 4	3.0 KN	62.2%
Case 5	3.7 KN	100%

The first case simulation consisted of the applied load of 1.849 KN (actual flight loading scenario) for the applied operating load spectrum. The simulation was carried out for 8000 FHs, and it was observed that the crack did not propagate. As the case represents a real loading scenario, it is customary that the crack propagation was slow, and it took more than 8000 FHs to propagate the crack. As the applied load was increased, the crack propagation region increased, as shown in Figure 9. Therefore, it was concluded that to observe the crack propagation, the applied loading must be increased to more than the real flight loading scenario.

Figure 9. Crack propagation plot for the different applied loading conditions.

Figure 10a shows the fatigue cracks propagation plot measured as a function of the number of cycles for case simulation 5. The cracks started to propagate around 153 flight times, and increase rapidly until 1436 FHs. From the 14,336 cycles over 3692 FHs, the crack propagation occurred linearly with a low crack propagation rate, while after 4692 cycles, the crack propagation increased rapidly up to 4783 cycles until it reached the defined crack threshold length of 10 mm. The graph trend of the current model results was compared with the crack propagation curve in the literature [27] for a composite. It was found that compared with the composite crack propagation trend in the literature, the current numerical model showed a similar trend of crack propagation.

(a) Numerical model   (b) Literature model

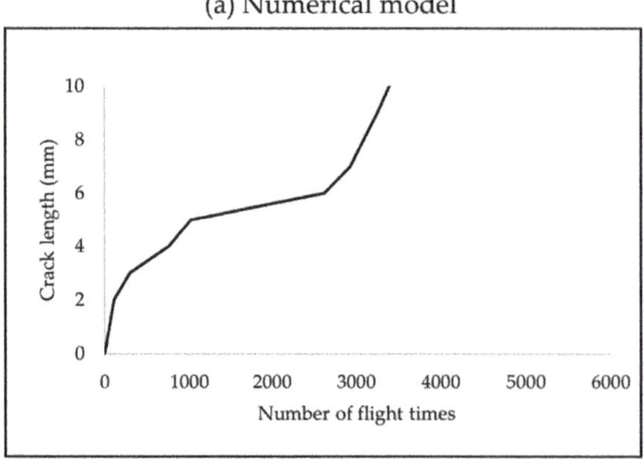
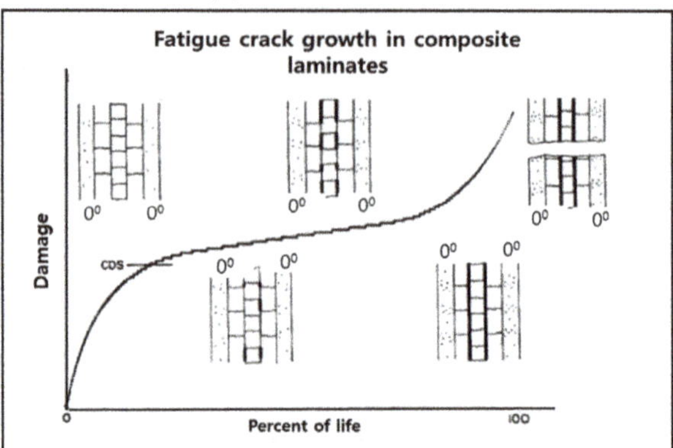

Figure 10. (**a**) Crack propagation plot of the current numerical model and (**b**) a comparison with the literature trend of the composite fatigue crack propagation curve [27].

2.2. Sensitivity Analysis and Design of Experiments (DOE)

FRCPs subjected to cyclic loading are most likely to fail with fatigue delamination crack growth. Many factors can affect the fatigue delamination growth, such as the constituent material parameters, geometry, and environmental conditions. However, the most common practice is to check the effect of mechanical parameters on the fatigue delamination behavior of composite laminates. For this purpose, sensitivity analysis [28] was undertaken to assess the sensitivity of crack growth to uncertain mechanical parameters. Sensitivity analysis can be used as a tool to understand how uncertain inputs can affect a model's performance. Sensitivity analysis is a systematic assessment method that is generally performed to assess the impact of individual input uncertain parameters on the model output response. It is an essential part of every risk assessment analysis that seeks to learn things such as how the model outputs change with the change in inputs and how it affects the model output decisions. The sensitivity analysis enhances the overall confidence in the risk assessment. Further, it improves the prediction of the model by studying the model response to the change in input variables and by analyzing the interaction between the variables. The knowledge of these sensitive parameters can help to better comprehend the fatigue delamination behavior and can pinpoint the direction of an optimal composite design. In this study, the effect of varying the mechanical properties was studied to examine the fatigue delamination behavior. Table 1 shows that a total of eight mechanical properties and two fatigue parameters were considered to examine the effect of fatigue delamination behavior. The parameters were varied by +2% of the mean value, and the model output fatigue delamination growth was computed. It was observed that E1 and G23 showed the most sensitive behavior compared with the other parameters. Figure 11 shows the relative error plot.

After pinpointing the most sensitive mechanical inputs, the design of experiments (DOE) was carried out by using Latin hypercube sampling (LHS) [29]. For the generation of DOE scenarios, input factors should be defined. In the case of fatigue crack propagation in the tail wing structure, two input factors (E1 and G23) were chosen. The error variation of +2% was kept for random sampling for the generation of thirty DOE samples, as shown in Table A1 of Appendix A. Figure 12 shows the fatigue crack propagation curves combined into a single plot. It was observed that for a crack delamination length threshold of 10 mm, the number of flight times range from approximately 2500 to 4600.

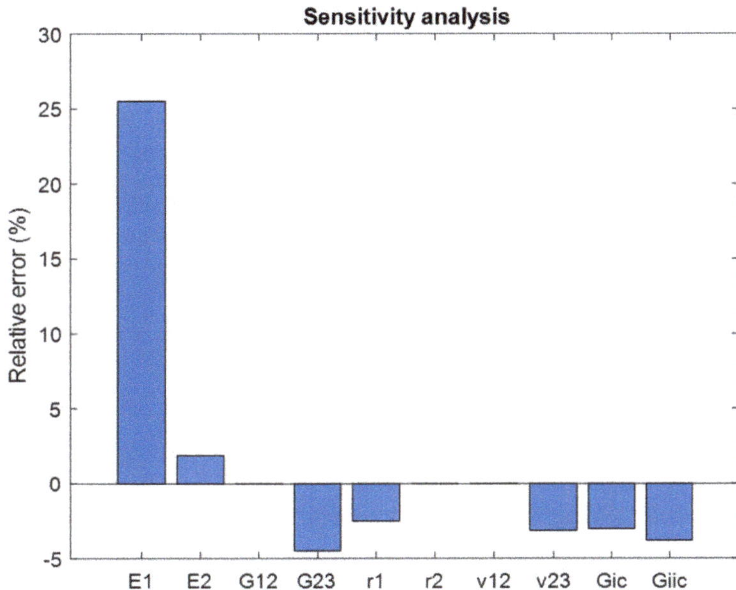

Figure 11. Sensitivity analysis plot representing the relative error of each parameter with respect to the exact simulation parameters fatigue behavior.

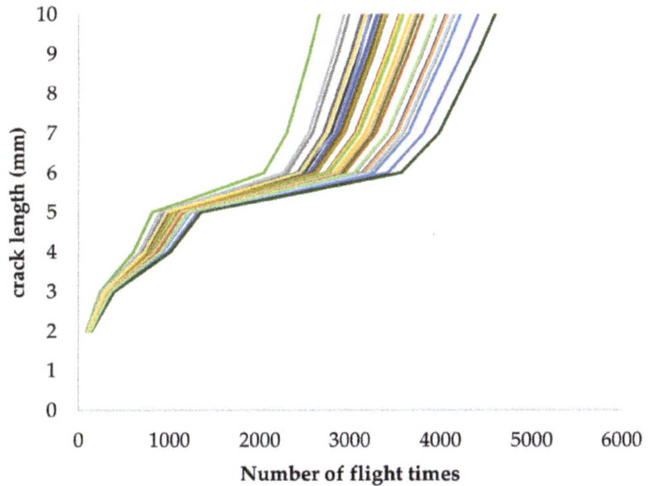

Figure 12. Fatigue delamination behavior of DOE data generation scenarios.

3. Risk Assessment and Inspection Interval Optimization

This section provides the results of the risk assessment and optimization of inspection interval for a composite aircraft tail wing structure. In the first stage of risk assessment, it is highly desirable to develop an efficient response surface that requires fewer FE executions. The composite crack propagation curve response surface was generated for both the sensitive parameters for the damage range of 2 to 10 mm. Thirty samples generated from the LHS were used for the generation of a total of nine response surfaces, as shown in Figure 13a. The average value of the mean square error (R^2) of the nine response surfaces was 0.9987, with a minimum R^2 value of 0.9962. It was confirmed that the response surface model satisfied the minimum standard value of $R^2 \geq 0.990$ set in this study. The present study dealt with the reliability evaluation of the structure using an efficient adaptive response-surface-based MCS technique. The analysis should consider all the uncertainties required for accurate damage growth modeling and risk assessment. For this purpose, damage growth simulation was performed using an MCS. The crack propagation curves using response surface modeling were accurately simulated compared with FE simulations, as represented in Figure 13b.

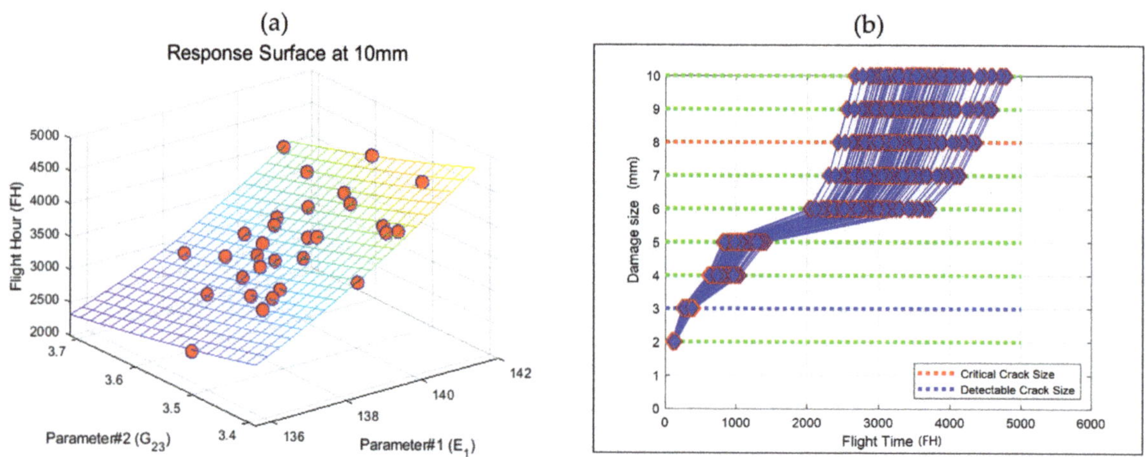

Figure 13. (**a**) Response surface generation using Latin hypercube sampling design and (**b**) the simulation response surface based on FEA simulations.

After the development of the response surface, we estimated the single flight probability of failure (SFPOF) assuming the structure was non-repairable. For the FRCPs, nondestructive inspection (NDI) was insufficient to detect the cracks that can propagate to complete failure of the structure. Therefore, it is essential to minimize the risk by computing the minimum inspection cycle. For this purpose, SFPOF was proposed in 1980 to assess the risk of aircraft failure [30]. It provides the probability of failure during one flight. To evaluate the risk, the criteria may vary depending on the operating environment conditions. The US Department of Defense proposed that a structural risk assessment should be performed on a component-by-component basis, and defined the limits on $SFPOF$ of between 10^{-7} and 10^{-5} for each component. According to the suggested range, if $SFPOF > 10^{-5}$, the component is unacceptable for operation. For $10^{-5} > SFPOF > 10^{-7}$, the structure requires repair and modification to ensure long-term operation. For $SFPOF < 10^{-7}$, the structure is safe for long-term operation. In this study, $SFPOF$ defined the amount of damage reached in the component with respect to the total number of simulations, as shown in Equation (5):

$$SFPOF = P(a \geq a_{critical}) = \frac{N_{critical}}{N_{simulation}} \tag{5}$$

where $N_{critical}$ is the number of simulations exceeding the critical damage size and $N_{simulation}$ is the total number of simulations.

In this study, $SFPOF$ was computed at 3000 FHs. At 3000 FHs, the damage distribution is calculated. The probability was computed for the scenario that the damage was greater than the critical crack size, which was 8 mm. Using the above process, the SFPOF was calculated for the total number of FH, as shown in Figure 14.

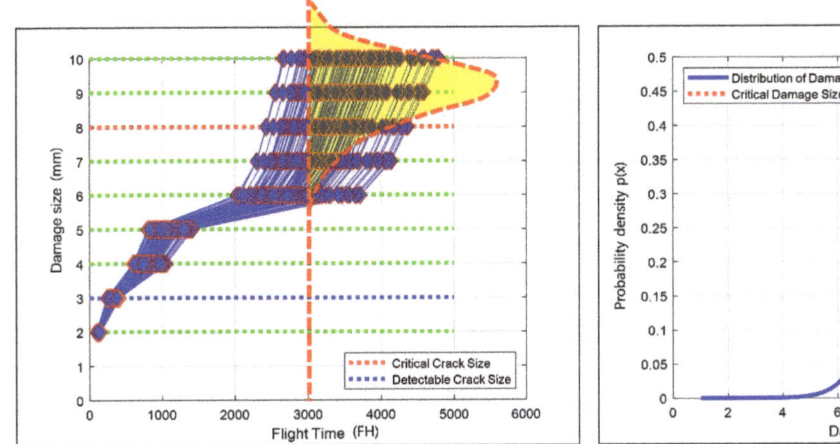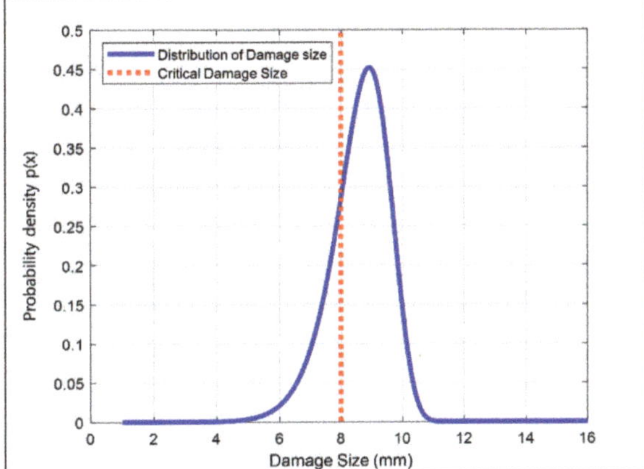

Figure 14. Single flight probability of failure calculation at 3000 FHs.

For a critical component, such as an aircraft tail wing, the common practice is to perform multiple inspections. The reason for repeated inspections is that the inspections are never perfect. There is always the possibility of misclassification. Therefore, repeated inspections are likely to reduce the inspection cost. For the determination of an optimal inspection plan, an optimal number of repeated inspections is needed. The time between repeated inspections can be computed using the following equation:

$$T_{repeat} = \frac{T_{design} - T_{inital}}{N_{Inspection} + 1} \qquad (6)$$

where T_{inital} is the initial inspection cycle, T_{design} is the operating life, and $N_{Inspection}$ is the number of repeated inspections. In this study, the service life of the tail wing structure considered was 3000 FHs, with the first inspection cycle at 200 FHs. Figure 15 shows the calculation of repeat inspection cycles with respect to the number of repeated inspections.

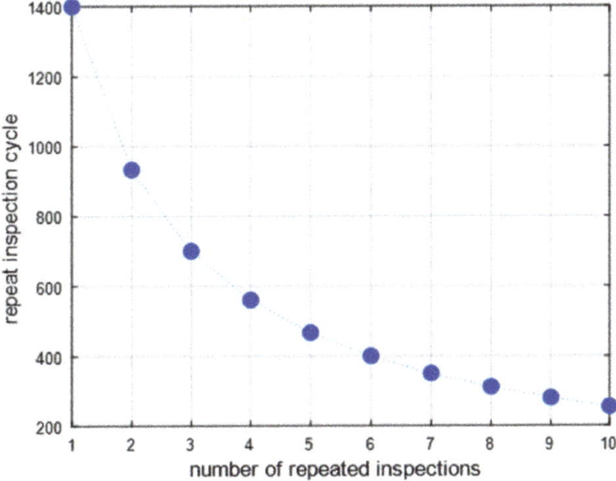

Figure 15. Number of repeated inspections with respect to the number of inspection plans.

The criteria for determining the optimal inspection cycle in this study was based on the US Airforce standard of risk assessment matrix [31]. In the event of an accident, the severity level is divided into four levels based on the type of result, component damage, etc. The Risk Assessment Code, or Hazard Risk Index, is a risk level that is calculated by combining the severity and probability of occurrence, as shown in Table 3. A high risk constitutes the first−fifth level range. The serious risk of component failure falls in the sixth–ninth level range, the medium risk falls in the 10th–17th level, whereas the low risk is in the 18th−20th level range.

Table 3. US Airforce airworthiness risk assessment matrix [31].

USAF Airworthiness Risk Assessment Matrix			Severity Category			
Probability Level	Probability per FH or Sortie	Freq per 100 K FH or 100 K Sorties	Catastrophic (1)	Critical (2)	Marginal (3)	Negligible (4)
Frequent (A)	$10^{-3} \leq Prob$	$100 \leq Freq$	1	3	7	13
Probable (B)	$10^{-4} \leq Prob < 10^{-3}$	$10 \leq Freq < 100$	2	5	9	16
Occasional (C)	$10^{-5} \leq Prob < 10^{-4}$	$1 \leq Freq < 10$	4	6	11	18
Remote (D)	$10^{-6} \leq Prob < 10^{-5}$	$0.1 \leq Freq < 1$	8	10	14	19
Improbable (E)	$0 < Prob < 10^{-6}$	$0 \leq Freq < 0.1$	12	15	17	20
Eliminated (F)	$Prob = 0$	$Freq = 0$	Eliminated			

The overall process implemented in this study for determining the optimal inspection interval is divided into three steps, as shown in Figure 16:

Step #1. Determination of the severity category

In the event of an accident caused by a defined major failure mode, the severity level was determined after predicting the consequences.

Step #2. Calculation of the probability of failure (probability level)

The probability of failure was calculated by computing the SFPOF for each flight time.

Step #3. Risk assessment code

Steps #1 and #2 were combined to calculate the risk. If the calculated risk was less than the target level, step #2 was repeated after modifying the inspection cycle combination.

In the case example of an aircraft tail wing, the first step was computed by assuming the severity level to be critical. In the second step, the assumed operating life was 3000 flight times. After setting it equal to a critical value, the SFPOF was calculated for each FH until the end of the operating life, and the maximum SFPOF was set as the reference value. The RAC from the maximum probability of failure and severity level was calculated. If the target risk level was a medium risk: RAC 10−17, then the combination of the least number of repeated inspections among the combinations of inspection cycles that satisfied RAC 10−17 is selected. In this example, the optimal inspection cycle was calculated when the number of repeated inspections was six and fell within the medium risk level, as shown in Figure 17.

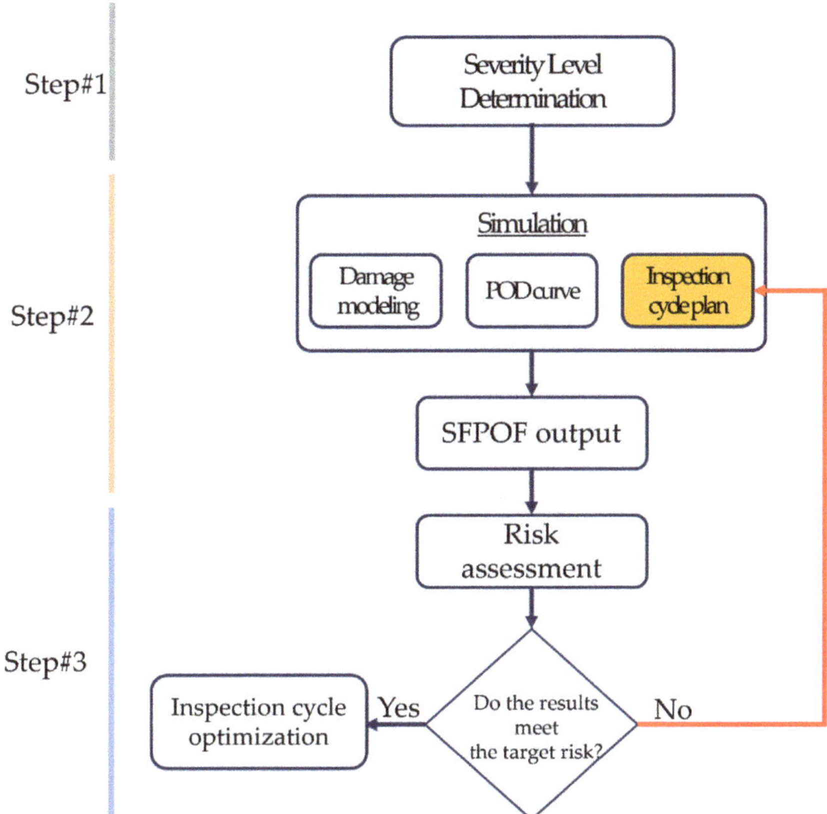

Figure 16. Process of determining the optimal inspection cycle.

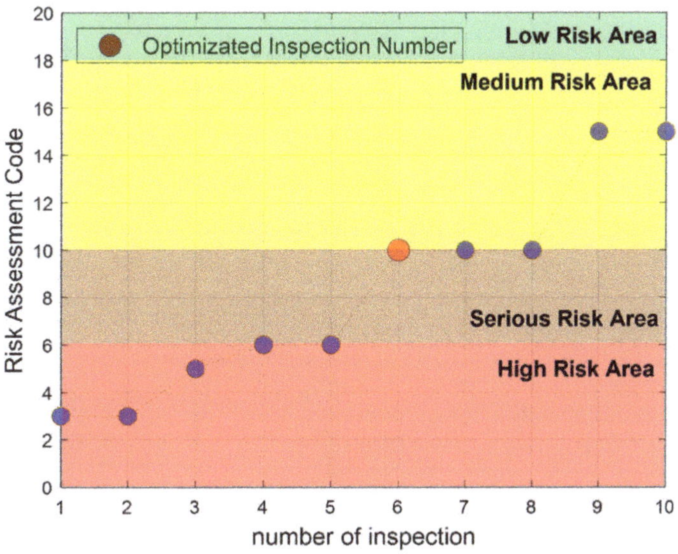

Figure 17. Selection of optimized inspection from the RAC-vs.-severity-level curve.

4. Conclusions

This study provided the risk assessment and optimization of the inspection interval of a composite aircraft tail wing structure. Composite structures are more prone to fatigue delamination damage and such damages can ultimately lead to the catastrophic failure of the complete aircraft composite structures, such as aircraft tail wings. Therefore, different aircraft maintenance strategies were proposed for the accurate prediction of the fatigue life of composite structures. However, the main limitation of the approaches available in the literature is the availability of real aircraft maintenance data to develop structural health monitoring approaches for the prediction of the fatigue life of the composite structures. The acquisition of the real damage data requires the embedding of additional sensors on the skin of aircraft structures, thus making the maintenance strategies more expensive. Therefore, to overcome the unavailability of real-life operating data, the study proposed the methodology of using the FEA-based model for the generation of fatigue damage growth curves and further implemented this approach for the risk assessment and optimization of the inspection interval of the KT-100 aircraft tail wing structure. The overall methodology of the proposed study and the concluding remarks are summarized as follows:

- The FEA model based on VCCT and Paris' law was implemented and compared with a real experimental curve. The fatigue damage model was extended to a full aircraft tail wing geometry and the fatigue delamination growth curve was computed.
- A sensitivity analysis was undertaken to check the effect of mechanical parameters on the fatigue delamination growth curve; E1 and G23 were found to be the most sensitive parameters. The Latin hypercube sampling technique was used for the DOE data generation scenarios, where 30 scenarios were generated. Based on LHS, an efficient response surface was generated. A damage growth simulation was performed using an MCS.
- In the end, a probabilistic risk analysis method was proposed based on the risk matrix of the US military specification, and the risk was analyzed based on the severity and frequency of structural failure. In future research, based on the process of determining the optimal inspection cycle, we will consider both the risk and the cost associated with the inspection.

Author Contributions: Conceptualization, H.S.K. (Heung Soo Kim) and J.-H.C.; methodology, S.K. and H.-S.K. (Hee-Seong Kim); software, S.K. and H.-S.K. (Hee-Seong Kim); formal analysis, S.K.; resources, H.S.K. (Heung Soo Kim) and J.-H.C.; writing—original draft preparation, S.K.; writing—review and editing, S.K., H.S.K. (Heung Soo Kim), J.-H.C. and H.-S.K. (Hee-Seong Kim); supervision, H.S.K. (Heung Soo Kim) and J.-H.C. All authors have read and agreed to the published version of the manuscript.

Funding: This research was supported under the project "Research and Development of Composite Internal Defect Risk Assessment Method" by the Aero Technology Research Institute and supported by the National Research Foundation of Korea (NRF) grant funded by the Korean government (MSIT) (no. 2020R1A2C1006613) and BK−21 four.

Conflicts of Interest: The authors declare that they have no conflict of interest.

Appendix A

Table A1. Latin hypercube sampling scenarios with E1 and G23 as input factors.

Scenario Number (#)	E1 (MPa)	G23 (MPa)	Scenario #	E1 (MPa)	G23 (MPa)
1	139.7615909	3.438312739	16	138.6539501	3.506192126
2	141.3938702	3.56605425	17	138.7957379	3.587573885
3	138.0581118	3.678908272	18	139.5075777	3.609318242
4	139.1752097	3.532368614	19	137.7304732	3.486625586
5	138.4700897	3.575752631	20	139.9177379	3.581053108

Table A1. *Cont.*

Scenario Number (#)	E1 (MPa)	G23 (MPa)	Scenario #	E1 (MPa)	G23 (MPa)
6	135.5688385	3.501017317	21	137.4000267	3.51591805
7	140.1825004	3.523911518	22	138.4367088	3.542198006
8	139.3109788	3.600841752	23	139.6792856	3.406417978
9	137.4727095	3.482559356	24	138.2926045	3.385928254
10	138.9296798	3.628621725	25	137.8217986	3.558572124
11	138.1894966	3.551958713	26	139.2390456	3.520360535
12	140.9149363	3.445628384	27	137.1665889	3.57807592
13	136.9461698	3.465241411	28	138.2448875	3.616984057
14	140.4141209	3.550065463	29	139.615228	3.423103266
15	140.7574458	3.638565444	30	141.2357918	3.711960967

References

1. Manco, P.; Caterino, M.; Macchiaroli, R.; Rinaldi, M.; Fera, M. *Aircraft Maintenance: Structural Health Monitoring Influence on Costs and Practices*; Wiley: Hoboken, NJ, USA, 2021; Volume 396, p. 2000302.
2. Wild, G.; Pollock, L.; Abdelwahab, A.K.; Murray, J. The Need for Aerospace Structural Health Monitoring: A Review of Aircraft Fatigue Accidents. *Int. J. Progn. Health Manag.* **2021**, *12*. [CrossRef]
3. Temucin, T.; Tuzkaya, G.; Vayvay, O. Aircraft Maintenance Routing Problem–A Literature Survey. *Promet-Traffic Transp.* **2021**, *33*, 491–503. [CrossRef]
4. Healey, R.; Wang, J.; Chiu, W.K.; Chowdhury, N.M.; Baker, A.; Wallbrink, C. A Review on Aircraft Spectra Simplification Techniques for Composite Structures. *Compos. Part C Open Access* **2021**, *5*, 100131. [CrossRef]
5. Das, M.; Sahu, S.; Parhi, D. Composite Materials and Their Damage Detection Using AI Techniques for Aerospace Application: A Brief Review. *Mater. Today Proc.* **2021**, *44*, 955–960. [CrossRef]
6. Khalid, S.; Lee, J.; Kim, H.S. Series Solution-Based Approach for the Interlaminar Stress Analysis of Smart Composites under Thermo-Electro-Mechanical Loading. *Mathematics* **2022**, *10*, 268. [CrossRef]
7. Khalid, S.; Kim, H.S. Recent Studies on Stress Function-Based Approaches for the Free Edge Stress Analysis of Smart Composite Laminates: A Brief Review. *Multiscale Sci. Eng.* **2022**, *4*, 73–78. [CrossRef]
8. Khalid, S.; Kim, H.S. Progressive Damage Modeling of Inter and Intra Laminar Damages in Open Hole Tensile Composite Laminates. *JCOSEIK* **2019**, *32*, 233–240. [CrossRef]
9. Teimouri, F.; Heidari-Rarani, M.; Aboutalebi, F.H. An XFEM-VCCT Coupled Approach for Modeling Mode I Fatigue Delamination in Composite Laminates under High Cycle Loading. *Eng. Fract. Mech.* **2021**, *249*, 107760. [CrossRef]
10. Ahmadi, A.; Söderholm, P.; Kumar, U. On Aircraft Scheduled Maintenance Program Development. *J. Qual. Maint. Eng.* **2010**, *3*, 229–255. [CrossRef]
11. Jing, C.; Dingqiang, D. Inspection Interval Optimization for Aircraft Composite Structures with Dent and Delamination Damage. *J. Syst. Eng. Electron.* **2021**, *32*, 252–260. [CrossRef]
12. Ushakov, A.; Stewart, A.; Mishulin, I.; Pankov, A. *Probabilistic Design of Damage Tolerant Composite Aircraft Structures*; Federal Aviation Administration, Office of Aviation Research: Washington, DC, USA, 2002.
13. Kan, H.-P.; Kane, D. *Probabilistic Certification of Integrally Bonded Composite Structures—An Assessment*; American Institute of Aeronautics and Astronautics: Denver, CO, USA, 2002; p. 1388.
14. Lin, K.Y.; Styuart, A.V. Probabilistic Approach to Damage Tolerance Design of Aircraft Composite Structures. *J. Aircr.* **2007**, *44*, 1309–1317. [CrossRef]
15. Dinis, D.; Barbosa-Póvoa, A.; Teixeira, Â.P. Valuing Data in Aircraft Maintenance through Big Data Analytics: A Probabilistic Approach for Capacity Planning Using Bayesian Networks. *Comput. Ind. Eng.* **2019**, *128*, 920–936. [CrossRef]
16. Giannella, V. Uncertainty Quantification in Fatigue Crack-Growth Predictions. *Int. J. Fract.* **2022**, *235*, 179–195. [CrossRef]
17. Zhu, M.; Gorbatikh, L.; Lomov, S.V. An Incremental-Onset Model for Fatigue Delamination Propagation in Composite Laminates. *Compos. Sci. Technol.* **2020**, *200*, 108394. [CrossRef]
18. Zhou, S.; Li, Y.; Fu, K.; Wu, X. Progressive Fatigue Damage Modelling of Fibre-Reinforced Composite Based on Fatigue Master Curves. *Thin-Walled Struct.* **2021**, *158*, 107173. [CrossRef]
19. Dávila, C. From SN to the Paris Law with a New Mixed-Mode Cohesive Fatigue Model for Delamination in Composites. *Theor. Appl. Fract. Mech.* **2020**, *106*, 102499. [CrossRef]
20. Raimondo, A.; Doesburg, S.; Bisagni, C. Numerical Study of Quasi-Static and Fatigue Delamination Growth in a Post-Buckled Composite Stiffened Panel. *Compos. Part B Eng.* **2020**, *182*, 107589. [CrossRef]
21. *Abaqus Analysis User's Manual-Abaqus Version 6.14*; Simulia: Johnston, RI, USA.

22. Rozylo, P. Experimental-Numerical Study into the Stability and Failure of Compressed Thin-Walled Composite Profiles Using Progressive Failure Analysis and Cohesive Zone Model. *Compos. Struct.* **2021**, *257*, 113303. [CrossRef]
23. Chen, S.; Mitsume, N.; Bui, T.Q.; Gao, W.; Yamada, T.; Zang, M.; Yoshimura, S. Development of Two Intrinsic Cohesive Zone Models for Progressive Interfacial Cracking of Laminated Composites with Matching and Non-Matching Cohesive Elements. *Compos. Struct.* **2019**, *229*, 111406. [CrossRef]
24. Liang, Y.-J.; Dávila, C.G.; Iarve, E.V. A Reduced-Input Cohesive Zone Model with Regularized Extended Finite Element Method for Fatigue Analysis of Laminated Composites in Abaqus. *Compos. Struct.* **2021**, *275*, 114494. [CrossRef]
25. Heidari-Rarani, M.; Sayedain, M. Finite Element Modeling Strategies for 2D and 3D Delamination Propagation in Composite DCB Specimens Using VCCT, CZM and XFEM Approaches. *Theor. Appl. Fract. Mech.* **2019**, *103*, 102246. [CrossRef]
26. *NASA/TM-2008-215123*; An Approach to Assess Delamination Propagation Simulation Capabilities in Commercial Finite Element Codes. National Aeronautics and Space Administration: Hampton, VA, USA, 2008.
27. Munagala, P. Fatigue Life Prediction of GFRP Composite Material at Coupon and Component Level. Master's Thesis, West Virginia University Libraries, Morgantown, WV, USA, 2005.
28. Chamis, C.C. Probabilistic Simulation of Multi-Scale Composite Behavior. *Theor. Appl. Fract. Mech.* **2004**, *41*, 51–61. [CrossRef]
29. Matala, A. *Sample Size Requirement for Monte Carlo Simulations Using Latin Hypercube Sampling*; Helsinki University of Technology: Espoo, Finland, 2008; Volume 25.
30. Domyancic, L.; McFarland, J.M.; Cardinal, J.W. Review of Methods for Calculating Single Flight Probability of Failure. In Proceedings of the AIAA Scitech 2021 Forum, Virtual Event, 11–15 & 19–21 January 2021; p. 1490.
31. Altowairqi, M.M. *Evaluation of RSAF Airworthiness and Applicability*; Air Force Institute of Technology Wright-Patterson: Wright-Patterson AFB, OH, USA, 2018.

Article

Exploration of Multiple Transfer Phenomena within Viscous Fluid Flows over a Curved Stretching Sheet in the Co-Existence of Gyrotactic Micro-Organisms and Tiny Particles

Pachiyappan Ragupathi [1,†], N. Ameer Ahammad [2], Abderrahim Wakif [3], Nehad Ali Shah [4,†] and Yongseok Jeon [5,*]

[1] Department of Mathematics, Sri Ramakrishna Mission Vidyalaya College of Arts and Science, Coimbatore 641020, India
[2] Department of Mathematics, Faculty of Science, University of Tabuk, P.O. Box 741, Tabuk 71491, Saudi Arabia
[3] Laboratory of Mechanics, Faculty of Sciences Aïn Chock, Hassan II University of Casablanca, Casablanca 20000, Morocco
[4] Department of Mechanical Engineering, Sejong University, Seoul 05006, Korea
[5] Interdisciplinary Major of Maritime AI Convergence, Department of Mechanical Engineering, Korea Maritime & Ocean University, Busan 49112, Korea
* Correspondence: ysjeon@kmou.ac.kr
† These authors contributed equally to this work and are co-first authors.

Citation: Ragupathi, P.; Ahammad, N.A.; Wakif, A.; Shah, N.A.; Jeon, Y. Exploration of Multiple Transfer Phenomena within Viscous Fluid Flows over a Curved Stretching Sheet in the Co-Existence of Gyrotactic Micro-Organisms and Tiny Particles. *Mathematics* 2022, 10, 4133. https://doi.org/10.3390/math10214133

Academic Editors: Camelia Petrescu, Valeriu David and Efstratios Tzirtzilakis

Received: 16 September 2022
Accepted: 2 November 2022
Published: 5 November 2022

Abstract: In the present study, the magnetohydrodynamics (MHD) bio-convective flow and heat transfer of nanofluid, due to the swimming of the gyrotactic micro-organisms over a curved stretched sheet, is examined. In addition, thermophoresis and Brownian motion behaviors are also investigated by assuming slip conditions at the boundary. A non-linear system of partial differential equations (PDEs) is reduced to a system of ordinary differential equations (ODEs). For convergent solutions, the obtained ODE system is solved by the use of the BVP4C routine integrated MATLAB package. In addition, the impacts of different influential parameters on motile micro-organisms, temperature, velocity, and concentration profiles are deliberated. The velocity field is observed to be reduced when the slip parameter increases. As the main results, it is demonstrated that the distribution of motile microorganisms against the curvature parameter decreases significantly. Similarly, it is found that the nanofluid parameters (i.e., Brownian motion and thermophoresis parameters) and the Peclet number reduce the motile micro-organisms' number. On the other hand, it is evidenced that the motile micro-organisms' distribution can be improved with an increase in bio-convective Schmidt number.

Keywords: bio-convection; gyrotactic micro-organisms; curved stretching sheet; slip condition; thermophoresis; Brownian diffusion

MSC: 76D05; 82D80

1. Introduction

It is well known that magnetohydrodynamics (MHD) is a concept common to both Physics and Mathematics that deals with the study of the interactions of magnetic fields in conducting fluids. The involvement of magnetic fields results in forces that in turn affect the fluid. The structure and intensity of the magnetic fields themselves are therefore possibly altered. The relative performance of the advective movements in the fluid is a key question for a certain conducting fluid experiencing a diffusive impact induced by the resistivity. It also has several application areas such as aerodynamics, life sciences, polymer or fiberglass, cooling systems, exchangers, metallurgy, etc. Hady et al. [1] examined the MHD flow of nanofluid-having gyrotactic micro-organisms with viscous dissipation effects. Pal and Mondal [2] investigated the nanofluid MHD flow with gyrotactic micro-organisms including thermal radiation effects. Yasmin et al. [3] discussed MHD micropolar fluid flows due to a curved stretching sheet. Nagaraja and Gireesha [4] addressed the MHD flow of Casson fluid. Additionally, the exponential heat generation and chemical reaction effects were also investigated. Few attempts on the topic can be mentioned in the studies [5–8].

Bio-convection results from to the upward-swimming of an average number of micro-organisms that are heavier than water. The swimming micro-organisms are collected at the upper water surface. When the collected layer of micro-organisms becomes thicker and thicker, the surface becomes unstable. As a result, a large portion of the gathering falls deeper into the water. This process is repeated by the micro-organisms, and eventually results in bio-convection. Kessler [9] was the person who first noticed and studied the gyrotaxis of microbes. Recently, it has been discovered that several significant phenomena are dependent on the gyrotaxis of microorganisms. These physical phenomena include accumulation at free water surfaces [10], turbulent channel flows in photobioreactors [11], the formation of a thin phytoplankton layer brought on by gyrotactic trapping [12], and microscale patches of motile phytoplankton [13]. Alharbi et al. [14] scrutinized the bio-convection caused by gyrotactic micro-organisms present in the magnetic hybrid nanofluid. This study attempted to support the Targeted Drug Delivery (TDD) system. Modal and Pal [15] inspected the influence of variable viscosity in the bio-convection of micro-organisms present in the nanofluid. Bio-convection in the existence of the Marangoni thermo-solutal effect was considered by Kairi et al. [16]. Khan and Nadeem [17] studied the bio-convection of Maxwell nanofluid. The notion of variability in the thermal conductivity model to analyze the bio-convective Williamson nanofluid was looked over by Abdelmalek et al. [18]. Similarly, numerous investigations on the bio-convection of micro-organisms have been addressed by researchers [19–24].

Due to its various applications in the area of research and production, boundary layer flow over-stretching surfaces is an attractive topic for researchers (Wang [25], Noghrehabadi et al. [26], Rauf et al. [27]). Flows generated by fiber spinning, injection molding, glass molding, spray coating, and pulling of rinsed wires, paper, rubber, glass-fiber, polymer sheet production, etc., are some of the useful applications. As an extension of the stretching surface, the current work is connected with the fluid flow through a curved stretching surface grabbing the attention of numerous researchers. Hayat et al. [28] studied the entropy optimization of CNTs (Carbon Nano Tubes) over a curved stretching sheet. Similarly, Raza et al. [29] examined the entropy optimization of Carreau fluid over a curved stretching sheet. A non-Fourier heat flux model was taken up by Madhukesh et al. [30] to investigate the hybrid nanofluid flow. Darcy-Forchheimer flows of CNTs driven by a curved stretching sheet were considered by Gireesha et al. [31]. Stagnation point flow, involving MHD and Joule heating, was demonstrated by Zhang et al. [32]. The latest developments concerning curved stretching sheets are mentioned in Refs [33–38].

The distribution and swimming properties of gyrotactic microorganisms, in a variety of flows, including horizontal shear flow [11], density stratified flow [39], steady vertical flow [12,40], free surface flow [9], Poiseuille flow [9], as well as the flow past a single vertical circular cylinder [41], have all been the subject of extensive research. The findings demonstrate that gravitational torque and the viscous torque, caused by flow shear in a fluid flowing with non-zero vorticity, have an impact on the swimming of gyrotactic phytoplankton species. Although they are crucial for the prediction of the corresponding concentration distribution, the nanofluid flow behavior relating to the swimming characteristics of gyrotactic microorganisms is currently poorly understood, particularly when Brownian diffusion and thermophoresis are combined.

Ultimately, the goal of this research is to investigate the MHD bio-convective heat transfer caused by gyrotactic micro-organism swimming within the nanofluid past a curved stretched sheet. Using the BVP4c integrated MATLAB package, the solutions to the non-linear system of ODEs are solved. Differences in motile microorganisms, temperature, velocity, and concentration profiles are explained in terms of various influencing parameters, via graphs and tables. The manuscript is prepared in such a way that: Section 2 presents the problem formulation. The numerical scheme's validation is explained in

Section 3. Section 4 contains comments on the collected results, while Section 5 has a list of significant observations.

2. Problem Formulation

Consider a two-dimensional MHD nanofluid flow conveying nano-sized particles and gyrotactic micro-organisms across a curved surface of radius R, as seen in Figure 1. Indeed, the curved sheet is stretched linearly along the $s-$direction with a variable velocity $U_w = as$, in which a velocity slip condition U_{slip} is imposed at the fluid-solid interface, where a is a positive constant. In addition, a uniform magnetic flux density B_0 is applied radially on the developed electrically conducting nanofluid flow.

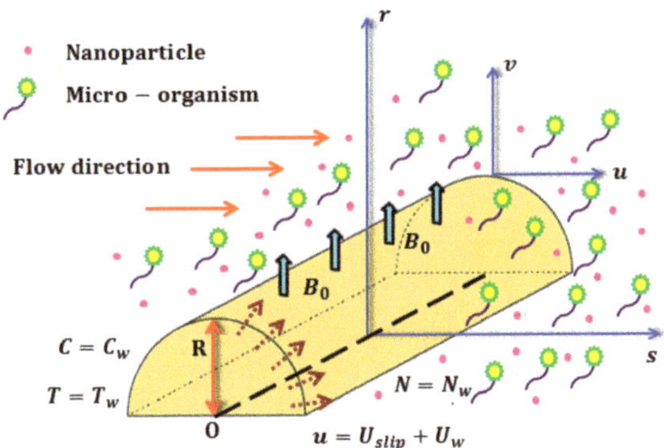

Figure 1. Flow configuration.

The following physical suppositions are adopted:

- The present bio-convective flow is related to a dilute non-homogeneous mixture.
- The studied mixture behaves as an electrically conducting Newtonian media.
- The constituents of the nanofluidic medium are in thermal equilibrium.
- The present MHD non-homogeneous flow is developed in the laminar regime.
- The main governing equations are derived accordingly based on the boundary layer approximations by combining a known non-homogeneous nanofluid model with the conservation equation of gyrotactic micro-organisms.
- As long as the classical formulation of Buongiorno's approach [42] is adopted as a suitable model to describe the present non-homogeneous nanofluid flow, the thermo-physical expressions of the nanofluid (i.e., density, viscosity, heat capacitance, thermal conductivity, and electrical conductivity) should not be mentioned, because they are included implicitly in the control flow parameters. Therefore, the effects of nanoparticles' shape and initial volume fraction can be excluded from this investigation.
- In most practical studies, the nanoparticles are prepared in a spherical form.
- Joule heating, Hall current effect, magnetic induction phenomenon, and viscous dissipation are ignored in this investigation as physical constraints.

Based on the aforementioned assumptions, the governing conservation equations are written in the steady state as follows [37]:

$$\frac{\partial v}{\partial r} + \left(\frac{1}{r+R}\right)v + \left(\frac{R}{r+R}\right)\frac{\partial u}{\partial s} = 0, \tag{1}$$

$$\left(\frac{1}{r+R}\right)u^2 = -\frac{1}{\rho}\frac{\partial p}{\partial r}, \tag{2}$$

$$v\frac{\partial u}{\partial r} + \left(\frac{R}{r+R}\right)u \quad \frac{\partial u}{\partial s} + \left(\frac{1}{r+R}\right)uv$$
$$= -\frac{1}{\rho}\left(\frac{R}{r+R}\right)\frac{\partial p}{\partial s} + v\left[\frac{\partial^2 u}{\partial r^2} + \left(\frac{1}{r+R}\right)\frac{\partial u}{\partial r} - \left(\frac{1}{r+R}\right)^2 u\right] \tag{3}$$
$$- \frac{\sigma}{\rho}B_0^2\, u,$$

$$v\frac{\partial T}{\partial r} + \left(\frac{R}{r+R}\right)u\frac{\partial T}{\partial s} = \frac{k}{(\rho C_P)}\left[\left(\frac{1}{r+R}\right)\frac{\partial T}{\partial r} + \frac{\partial^2 T}{\partial r^2}\right] + \tau\left[D_B\frac{\partial C}{\partial r}\frac{\partial T}{\partial r} + \frac{D_T}{T_\infty}\left(\frac{\partial T}{\partial r}\right)^2\right], \tag{4}$$

$$v\frac{\partial C}{\partial r} + \left(\frac{R}{r+R}\right)u\frac{\partial C}{\partial s} = D_B\left[\left(\frac{1}{r+R}\right)\frac{\partial C}{\partial r} + \frac{\partial^2 C}{\partial r^2}\right] + \frac{D_T}{T_\infty}\left[\left(\frac{1}{r+R}\right)\frac{\partial T}{\partial r} + \frac{\partial^2 T}{\partial r^2}\right], \tag{5}$$

$$v\frac{\partial N}{\partial r} + \left(\frac{R}{r+R}\right)u\frac{\partial N}{\partial s} = D_m\left[\left(\frac{1}{r+R}\right)\frac{\partial N}{\partial r} + \frac{\partial^2 N}{\partial r^2}\right] - \frac{bW_c}{C_w - C_\infty}\frac{\partial}{\partial r}\left(N\frac{\partial C}{\partial r}\right), \tag{6}$$

where the symbols u and v denote the $s-$ and $r-$velocity components. p means the pressure, σ is the nanofluid electrical conductivity. (ρC_P) reflects the nanofluid heat capacitance. D_T represents the thermophoresis coefficient. T, T_w and T_∞ designate the nanofluid temperature, the wall temperature, and the ambient temperature, respectively. D_B refers to the coefficient of Brownian diffusion. C, C_w and C_∞ indicate the nanofluid concentration (i.e., nanoparticles' volume fraction), the wall concentration, and the ambient concentration, respectively. D_m signifies the coefficient of motile micro-organisms' diffusion. N, N_w and N_∞ stand for the motile micro-organisms' concentration, the motile micro-organisms' concentration at the wall, and the motile micro-organisms' concentration at the ambient region, respectively. b symbolizes the chemotaxis constant. W_c marks the maximum cell speed.

For the flow problem the appropriate boundary conditions are:

$$\left\{\begin{array}{l} u = U_{slip} + U_w,\ v = 0,\quad T = T_w,\ C = C_w,\ N = N_w\ \text{at}\ r = 0, \\ u \to 0,\ \frac{\partial u}{\partial r} \to 0,\ T \to T_\infty,\ C = C_\infty,\ N = N_w\ \text{as}\ r \to \infty \end{array}\right\} \tag{7}$$

Here the velocity slip is given by:

$$U_{slip} = \beta\left(\frac{\partial u}{\partial r} - \frac{u}{r+R}\right), \tag{8}$$

where β denotes the slip length. $\beta = 0$ denotes the no-slip boundary condition. The following new variables are defined to simplify the flow equations:

$$\left\{\begin{array}{l} \frac{\eta}{r} = \sqrt{\frac{a}{v}},\ F' = \frac{u}{U_w},\ F = -\frac{(r+R)}{R\sqrt{av}}v\ ,\ \theta = \frac{T-T_\infty}{T_w-T_\infty}, \\ \phi = \frac{C-C_\infty}{C_w-C_\infty},\ \chi = \frac{N-N_\infty}{N_w-N_\infty},\ P = \frac{p}{\rho U_w^2} \end{array}\right\}. \tag{9}$$

Using Equation (9), Equations (1)–(6) takes the following non-dimensional form as follows:

$$P' - \frac{F'^2}{(\eta + A)} = 0, \tag{10}$$

$$F''' + \frac{F''}{(\eta + A)} - \frac{F'}{(\eta + A)^2} + \frac{AFF''}{(\eta + A)} + \frac{AFF'}{(\eta + A)^2} - \frac{AF'^2}{(\eta + A)} - \frac{2AP}{(\eta + A)} - MF' = 0, \tag{11}$$

$$\theta'' + \frac{\theta'}{(\eta + A)} + \frac{\Pr AF\theta'}{(\eta + A)} + \Pr Nt\ \theta'^2 + \Pr Nb\ \theta'\phi' = 0, \tag{12}$$

$$\phi'' + \frac{\phi'}{(\eta + A)} + \frac{Sc AF\phi'}{(\eta + A)} + \frac{Nt}{Nb}\left[\theta'' + \frac{\theta'}{(\eta + A)}\right] = 0, \tag{13}$$

$$\chi'' + \frac{\chi'}{(\eta + A)} + \frac{Sb AF\chi'}{(\eta + A)} + Pb\left[\chi'\phi' + (\tau_0 + \chi)\phi''\right] = 0 \tag{14}$$

The related boundary conditions in the non-dimensional form are given by:

$$\left\{ \begin{array}{c} F = 0, \ F' = 1 + \beta_1\left(F'' - \frac{1}{A}F'\right), \ \theta = \phi = \chi = 1 \ \text{at} \ \eta = 0, \\ F' = F'' = \theta = \phi = \chi = 0 \ \text{ as } \ \eta \to \infty \end{array} \right\}. \tag{15}$$

The parameters in non-dimensional forms are represented in Table 1 below:

Table 1. Non-dimensional parameters and their related expressions.

Parameters	Expressions	Parameters	Expressions
$M = \frac{\sigma B_0^2}{\rho a}$	Magnetic parameter	$Nb = \frac{\tau D_B(C_w - C_\infty)}{v}$	Brownian motion parameter
$A = \sqrt{\frac{a}{v}}R$	Curvature parameter	$Sc = \frac{v}{D_B}$	Schmidt number
$\beta_1 = \beta\sqrt{\frac{a}{v}}$	Slip parameter	$Sb = \frac{v}{D_m}$	Bio-convective Schmidt number
$Pr = \frac{v(\rho C_P)}{k}$	Prandtl Number	$Pb = \frac{bW_c}{D_m}$	Bio-convective Peclet number
$Nt = \frac{\tau D_T(T_w - T_\infty)}{v T_\infty}$	Thermophoresis parameter	$\tau_0 = \frac{N_\infty}{N_w - N_\infty}$	Dimensionless bio-convective factor
$Re_s = \frac{U_w s}{v}$	Reynolds number	$\tau = \frac{(\rho C_P)_{np}}{(\rho C_P)}$	Dimensionless thermal factor

The physical quantities of interest are represented as follows:

$$C_f = \frac{\tau_{rs}}{\rho U_w^2}, \ \text{where} \ \tau_w = \mu\left(\frac{\partial u}{\partial r} - \frac{u}{r+R}\right)_{r=0}, \tag{16}$$

$$Nu_s = \frac{s q_w}{k(T_w - T_\infty)}, \ \text{where} \ q_w = -k\left(\frac{\partial T}{\partial r}\right)_{r=0}, \tag{17}$$

$$Sh_s = \frac{s q_j}{D_B(C_w - C_\infty)}, \ \text{where} \ q_j = -D_B\left(\frac{\partial C}{\partial r}\right)_{r=0}, \tag{18}$$

$$Mn_s = \frac{s q_m}{D_m(N_w - N_\infty)}, \ \text{where} \ q_m = -D_m\left(\frac{\partial N}{\partial r}\right)_{r=0}, \tag{19}$$

where τ_w represents the surface shear stress. q_w denotes the wall heat flux. q_j designates the wall mass flux. q_m stands for the wall motile micro-organisms' flux. The non-dimensional forms of Equations (16)–(19) are given as:

$$C_f Re_s^{\frac{1}{2}} = F''(0) - \frac{F'(0)}{A}, \tag{20}$$

$$Nu_s Re_s^{-\frac{1}{2}} = -\theta'(0), \tag{21}$$

$$Sh_s Re_s^{-\frac{1}{2}} = -\phi'(0), \tag{22}$$

$$Mn_s Re_s^{-\frac{1}{2}} = -\chi'(0). \tag{23}$$

3. Validation

To validate the methodology used in the present study, we compare the obtained results for different values of the slip parameter (β_1) with those of Wang [24], Noghrehabadi et al. [25], Sahoo and Do [26] and Abbas et al. [37], by assuming that $M = 0$ and $A = 1000$. When the curvature parameter A tends towards the infinity value, the curved stretching surface is assumed to be a flat stretching surface. Thus, by fixing $A = 1000$, the results are found to be in good agreement. The current results are shown in Table 2, which provides a basis for comparison with Wang [24], Noghrehabadi et al. [25], Sahoo and Do [26], and Abbas et al. [37].

Table 2. Comparison of $C_f Re_s^{\frac{1}{2}}$ for various values of β_1, when $M = 0$ and $A = 1000$.

β_1	[24]	[25]	[26]	[37]	**Present Results**
0.0	−1.0	−1.0002	−1.0011	−1.0000	−1.00068
0.1	-	−0.8720	−0.8714	−0.8720	−0.87262
0.2	-	−0.7763	−0.7749	−0.7763	−0.77682
0.3	−0.701	−0.7015	−0.6997	−0.7015	−0.70193
0.5	-	−0.5911	−0.5891	−0.5911	−0.59149
1.0	−0.430	−0.4301	−0.4284	−0.4301	−0.43034
2.0	−0.284	−0.2839	−0.2828	−0.2839	−0.28407
3.0	-	−0.2140	−0.2133	−0.2140	−0.21412
5.0	−0.145	−0.1448	−0.1444	−0.1448	−0.14487
10.0	-	−0.0812	−0.0810	−0.0812	−0.08125
20.0	−0.0438	−0.0437	−0.0437	−0.0437	−0.04379

4. Results and Discussion

The MATLAB software is used herein, through the so-called BVP4C routine, to solve the coupled set of nonlinear ODEs given by Equations (10)–(14) and their accompanying boundary conditions. To achieve mathematical results, we have utilized the following values for various non-dimensional parameters: $M = 0.5$, $A = 0.5$, $\beta_1 = 1.0$, $Pr = 4.0$, $Nt = 0.2$, $Nb = 0.3$, $Sc = 6.0$, $Sb = 6.0$, $Pb = 0.1$, $\tau_0 = 1$. With the exception of the modified parameters displayed in the figures, these are maintained as constant. We have discussed the influence of various parameters, such as magnetic parameter (M), curvature parameter (A), slip parameter (β_1), thermophoresis parameter (Nt), Prandtl number (Pr), Brownian motion parameter (Nb), bio-convection Schmidt number (Sb), Schmidt number (Sc), bio-convection Peclet number (Pb). Some of these were examined based on the local motile micro-organisms' number. Table 3 summarizes the values for the physical quantities of interest given in Equations (20)–(23).

Table 3. Numerical values of $C_f Re_s^{\frac{1}{2}}$, $Nu_s Re_s^{-\frac{1}{2}}$, $Sh_s Re_s^{-\frac{1}{2}}$, and $Mn_s Re_s^{-\frac{1}{2}}$.

Parameters	**Values**	$C_f Re_s^{\frac{1}{2}}$	$Nu_s Re_s^{-\frac{1}{2}}$	$Sh_s Re_s^{-\frac{1}{2}}$	$Mn_s Re_s^{-\frac{1}{2}}$
M	0.5	−0.685157	0.341839	1.173836	0.867494
	1.0	−0.737808	0.247285	0.899088	0.583058
	1.5	−0.761642	0.203697	0.790827	0.433161
A	1.0	−0.643659	0.312729	1.078490	0.876261
	1.5	−0.612839	0.31028	1.076535	0.903080
	2.0	−0.592397	0.310773	1.081319	0.922313
β_1	1.0	−0.685157	0.341839	1.173836	0.867494
	1.5	−0.510308	0.284749	0.992354	0.696359
	2.0	−0.406574	0.245495	0.880211	0.574382
Pr	3.0	−0.685157	0.353240	1.160884	0.870119
	4.0	−0.685157	0.341839	1.173836	0.867494
	5.0	−0.685157	0.320823	1.192109	0.863649
Nb	0.2	−0.685156	0.446899	1.079823	0.888697
	0.3	−0.685157	0.341839	1.173836	0.867494
	0.4	−0.685157	0.258463	1.211724	0.858719
Nt	0.2	−0.685157	0.341839	1.173836	0.867494
	0.3	−0.685157	0.299689	1.172226	0.869968
	0.4	−0.685157	0.264082	1.179707	0.870639

Table 3. *Cont.*

Parameters	Values	$C_f Re_s^{\frac{1}{2}}$	$Nu_s Re_s^{-\frac{1}{2}}$	$Sh_s Re_s^{-\frac{1}{2}}$	$Mn_s Re_s^{-\frac{1}{2}}$
	5.0	−0.685156	0.360332	1.033888	0.898135
Sc	5.5	−0.685157	0.350414	1.106071	0.882278
	6.0	−0.685157	0.341839	1.173836	0.867494
	5.0	−0.685157	0.341839	1.173836	0.730776
Sb	5.5	−0.685157	0.341839	1.173836	0.801320
	6.0	−0.685157	0.341839	1.173836	0.867494
	0.2	−0.685157	0.341838	1.173835	0.507114
Pb	0.4	−0.685157	0.341838	1.173834	−0.246490
	0.6	−0.685157	0.341838	1.173834	−1.053887

4.1. Curvature Parameter Effects

Figure 2 demonstrates a deteriorating impression of velocity $F'(\eta)$ when A becomes larger. Physically, the increasing curvature of the sheet significantly increases the resistance of the flow which slows down the velocity. The same figure shows a similar decreasing pattern for temperature $\theta(\eta)$; as the resistance towards fluid flow is larger for the improving curvature parameter, the concentration of the fluid also improves, which slows the temperature evolution. Figure 3 shows how the nanofluid concentration $\phi(\eta)$ and the concentration of motile micro-organisms $\chi(\eta)$ behave as the radius of curvature, A, increases. As this parameter is increased, the CBL and MMBL are seen to decrease, which is also reflected in the reduction of concentration $\phi(\eta)$ and concentration of motile micro-organisms $\chi(\eta)$.

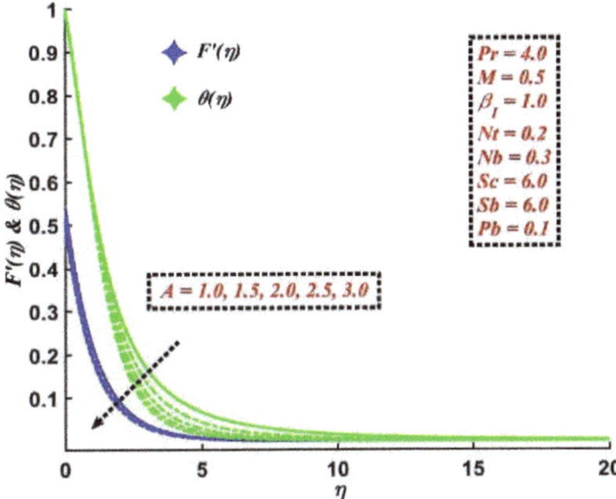

Figure 2. Influence of the curvature parameter on $F'(\eta)$ and $\theta(\eta)$.

4.2. Magnetic Parameter Effects

The effect of the magnetic parameter M on the dimensionless velocity, temperature, concentration, and concentration of motile micro-organisms' fields are shown in Figures 4 and 5. The magnetic parameter is the proportion of electromagnetic force to inertial force; thus, when M increases, the velocity field decreases. Due to the presence of a magnetic field, the Lorentz forces are considered to be in hydro-magnetic flow. As M increases, the strength of the induced magnetic forces increases, with a drop in the velocity field. In addition, the temperature field increases with increasing M at any point on the BL. This is because when a magnetic field is applied to a flow area, it produces a Lorentz force, which acts as a retarding force, causing the temperature of the fluid inside the BL to rise, as seen in Figure 4. Furthermore, the sheet's surface temperature may be controlled by varying the strength of the applied magnetic field, which also helps in improving the $\phi(\eta)$ and $\chi(\eta)$, as can be seen in Figure 5.

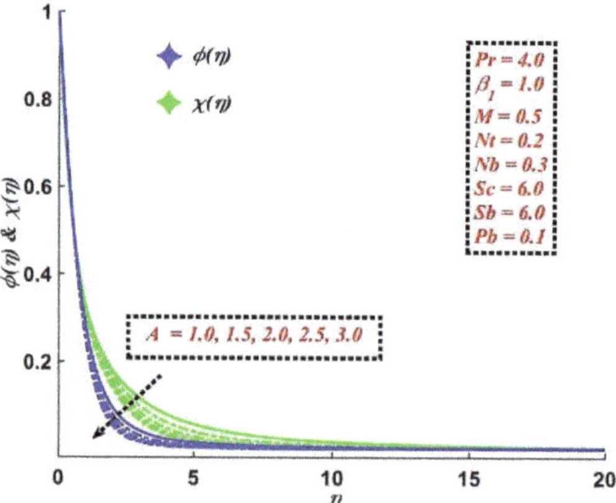

Figure 3. Influence of the curvature parameter on $\phi(\eta)$ and $\chi(\eta)$.

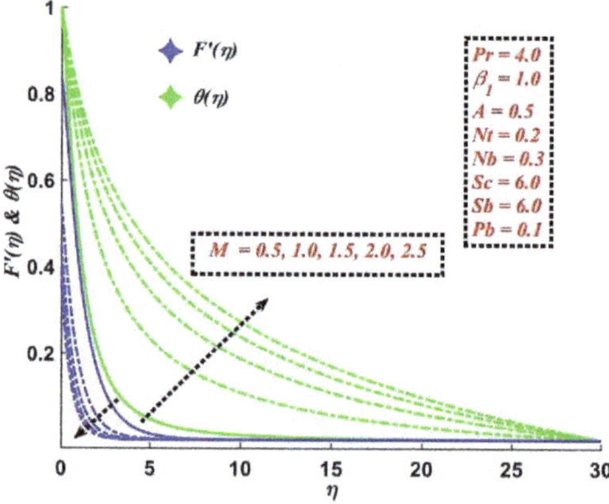

Figure 4. Influence of the magnetic parameter on $F'(\eta)$ and $\theta(\eta)$.

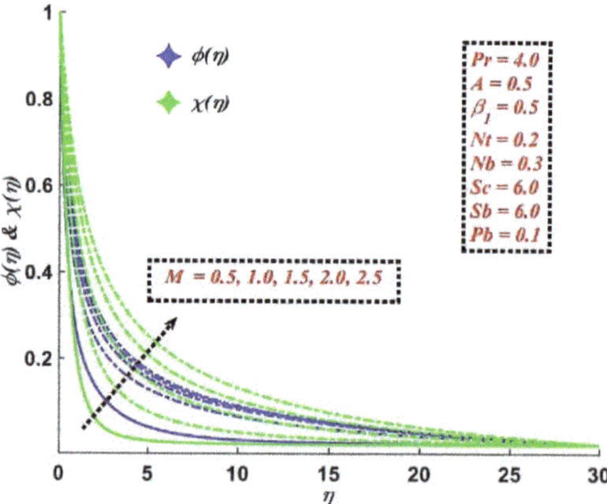

Figure 5. Influence of the magnetic parameter on $\phi(\eta)$ and $\chi(\eta)$.

4.3. Slip Parameter Effects

Figure 6 shows the velocity and temperature fields for varying values of β_1. The velocity decreases as the slip parameter increases, while the temperature increases. This is because when the slip condition occurs, the stretching sheet's velocity differs from the flow near the sheet's velocity. The fluid does not receive a majority of the stretching velocity. As a result, the velocity profile is reduced. In contrast, when β_1 is increased, subsequently, the rate of heat transmission from the surface to the ambient fluid is significantly reduced. Thus, the temperature field improves. The same effects are observed for concentration and concentration motile micro-organisms' profiles in Figure 7. Increases in the slip parameter induce surface friction, which generates a frictional force that causes the particles moving through the fluid to slow down. As a result, the distributions of the nanofluid concentration and the concentration of motile micro-organisms are amplified.

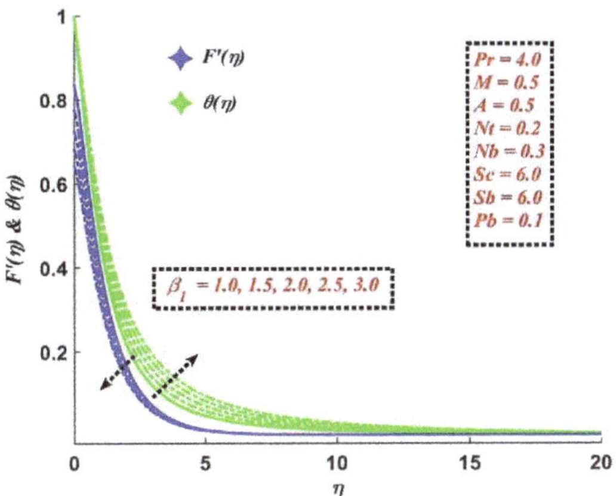

Figure 6. Influence of the slip parameter on $F'(\eta)$ and $\theta(\eta)$.

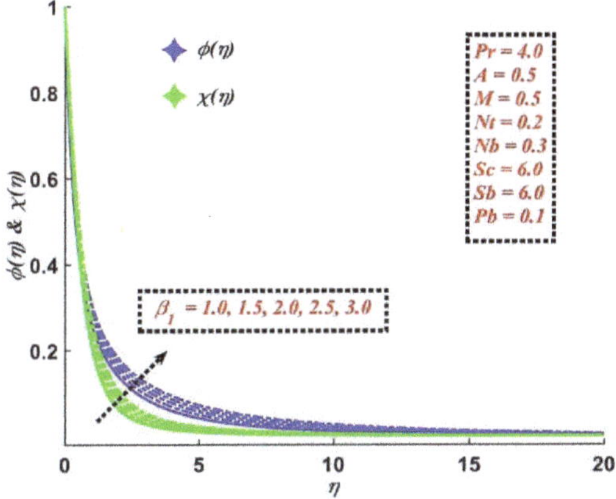

Figure 7. Influence of the slip parameter on $\phi(\eta)$ and $\chi(\eta)$.

4.4. Prandtl Number Effects

Figure 8 shows how different values of the Prandtl number, Pr, affect the temperature and concentration distribution. As can be seen in Figure 8, increasing the Pr lowers the temperature and concentration. Pr is calculated by the amount of momentum to thermal diffusion. As the Pr rises, thermal and mass diffusion decreases, resulting in a smaller TBL and CBL, as it turned out to reduce $\theta(\eta)$ and $\phi(\eta)$.

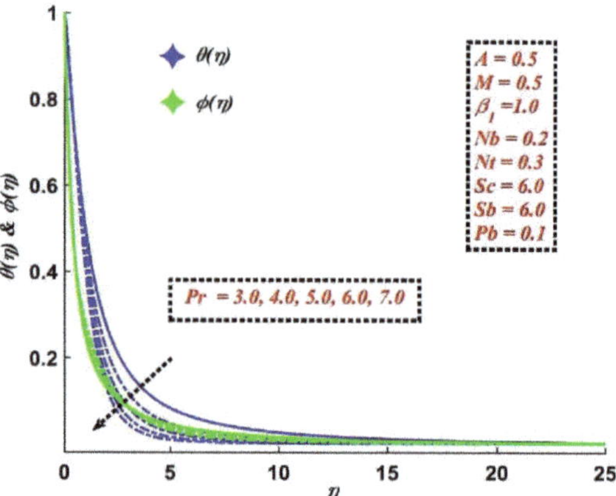

Figure 8. Influence of the Prandtl number on $\theta(\eta)$ and $\phi(\eta)$.

4.5. Thermophoresis and Brownian Motion Parameter Effects

From Figure 9, we can see the behavior of Nt on $\theta(\eta)$ and $\phi(\eta)$. As is evident in the figure, $\theta(\eta)$ and $\phi(\eta)$ are both increased for Nt. Logically, Nt determines the intensity of the TBL and CBL. When Nt rises, the particles begin to move faster, leading to increased kinetic energy within the flow domain; this leads to a rise in $\theta(\eta)$ and TBL thickness. Similarly, a marginal change in Nt causes $\phi(\eta)$ to significantly enhance.

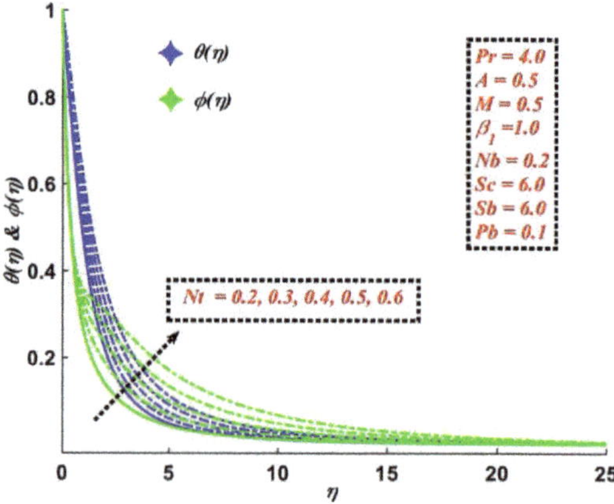

Figure 9. Influence of the thermophoresis parameter on $\theta(\eta)$ and $\phi(\eta)$.

The change in the Nt causes the fluid particles to move quickly, releasing surplus thermal energy and causing a rise in CBL thickness. As a result, $\phi(\eta)$, demonstrated in Figure 10, shows a significant increase. The temperature gradient is significantly affected by the Brownian motion parameter Nb. When Nb grows, it produces an increase in $\theta(\eta)$, which promotes the TBL thickness. Upgrading Nb causes faster fluid particle movement, and, as a result, a rise in $\theta(\eta)$ and TBL thickness is noted, as can be seen in Figure 10. As mentioned earlier, speeding up the particle movement diminishes the concentration gradient; the particles begin to migrate quickly from regions of greater to lower concentration when the mobility of the fluid particles upsurges, with an upsurge in Nb. Thus, an increase in Nb causes a drop in $\phi(\eta)$, as shown in Figure 10.

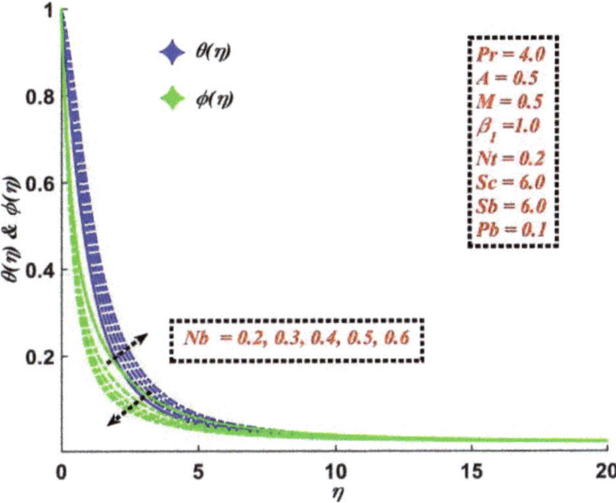

Figure 10. Influence of the Brownian motion parameter on $\theta(\eta)$ and $\phi(\eta)$.

4.6. Schmidt and Peclet Number Effects

The Schmidt number Sc has a considerable influence on the mass distribution as it increases. Such influence on $\phi(\eta)$ and $\chi(\eta)$ is depicted in Figures 11 and 12. The Schmidt number describes the mass momentum transition. It is a physical number that is calculated as the proportion of kinematic viscosity to mass diffusivity in the flow regime, where mass and momentum diffusion circulation mechanisms occur simultaneously. From Figures 11 and 12, it is clear that increasing the Schmidt and bio-convection Schmidt numbers reduces the mass and the micro-organism diffusion and, as a result, $\phi(\eta)$ and $\chi(\eta)$ are decreased.

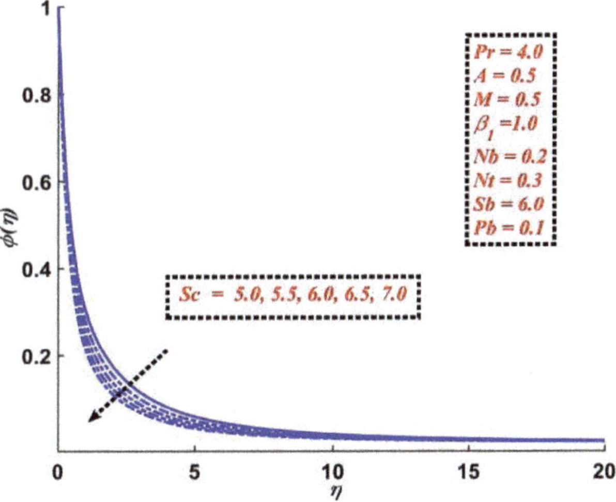

Figure 11. Influence of the Schmidt number on $\phi(\eta)$.

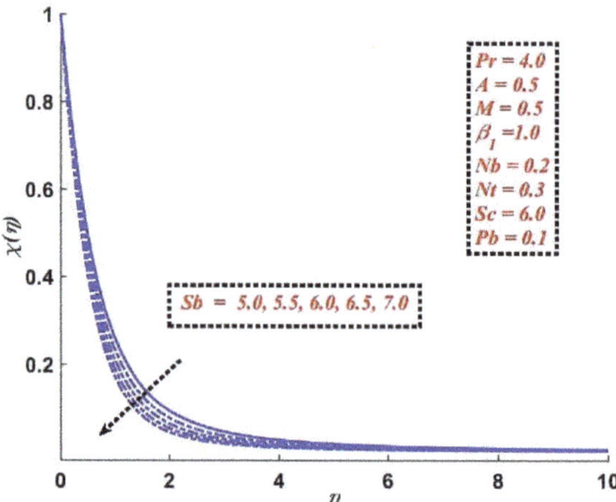

Figure 12. Influence of the bio-convection Schmidt number on $\chi(\eta)$.

Figure 13 demonstrates the effect of Pb on $\chi(\eta)$. The increment in Pb enhances $\chi(\eta)$. By using values greater than one and less than one, the estimated Peclet number establishes whether diffusion or convection is the dominant mode of mass movement. Diffusion is a process in which molecules move down a concentration gradient in a net flux. Despite convection being far faster than diffusion, diffusion is the most efficient mode of transport for very small volumes, such as in microfluidic systems. It is noticeable that the diffusion propagation transport is more dominant compared with the advection propagation rate. Hence, by increasing the values of the Peclet number, the motile micro-organisms' profile $\chi(\eta)$ increases.

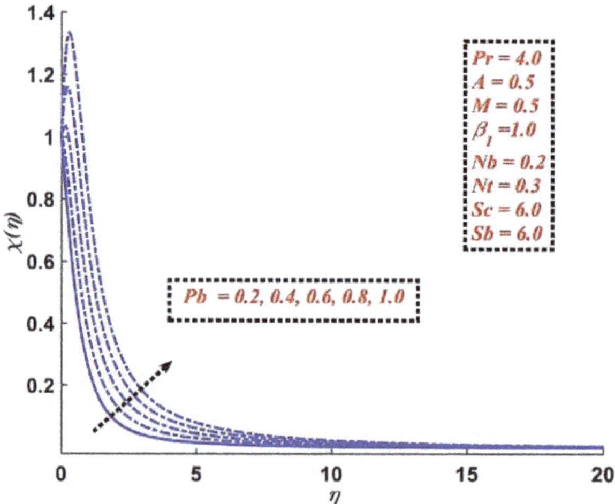

Figure 13. Influence of the bio-convective Peclet number on $\chi(\eta)$.

4.7. Effects of Various Parameters on Motile Microorganisms' Number

Figures 14–17 are discussed to show the variations in the micro-organisms' number, $Mn_s Re_s^{-\frac{1}{2}}$ with $Nt, Nb, Pb,$ and Sb. In Figure 14, Sb is varied between the range $5 \leq Sb \leq 7$ along the thermophoresis parameter in the range $0.2 \leq Nt \leq 0.6$. The variations clearly show that $Mn_s Re_s^{-\frac{1}{2}}$ decreases for Nt and increases for Sb. Similar effects are observed in Figure 15; by fixing the values of Sb, Nb is changed between $0.2 \leq Nb \leq 0.6$. This is because the thermophoretic diffusion and Brownian motion diminish the concentration of the motile micro-organism gradient of the flowing fluid, as the mobility of the micro-organism increases. The fluctuations in the microorganisms' number with Pb, along with Nt and Nb, are described in Figures 16 and 17. We follow the same range of values for Nt and Nb, whereas Pb is changed between $0 \leq Pb \leq 1$. As shown by the fluctuations, $Mn_s Re_s^{-\frac{1}{2}}$ decreases with Nt, Nb, and Pb. For the values $Pb < 1$ diffusion is more dominant than convection. Hence, we see the micro-organisms' number as a decreasing function.

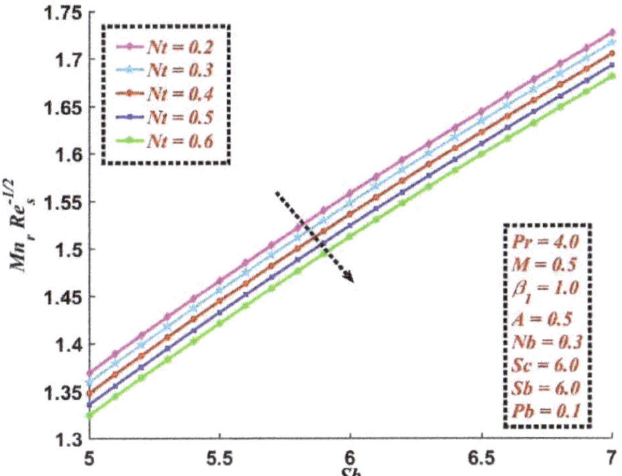

Figure 14. Variation of the motile microorganisms' number with Nt and Sb.

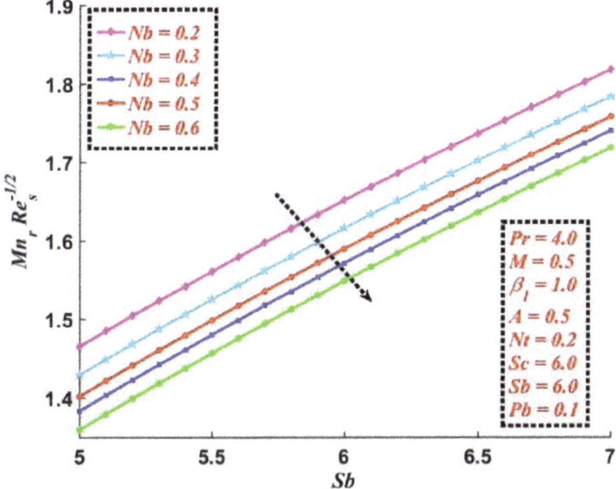

Figure 15. Variation of the motile microorganisms' number with Nb and Sb.

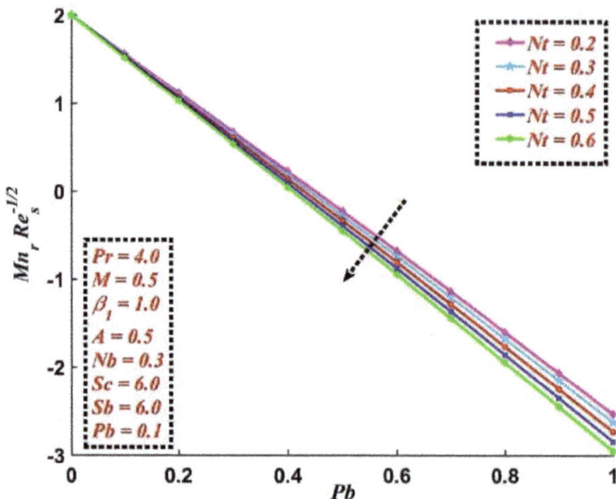

Figure 16. Variation of the motile microorganisms' number with Nt and Pb.

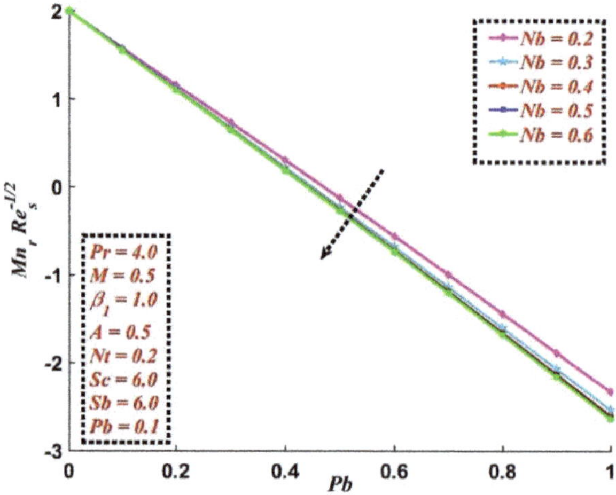

Figure 17. Variation of the motile microorganisms' number with Nb and Pb.

5. Conclusions

A numerical study is carried out concerning the bio-convection heat transfer of nanofluid flow near a curved stretched sheet containing gyrotactic micro-organisms. This research marks the impact of thermophoresis and Brownian motion in nanofluids that contains both nanoparticles and gyrotactic microorganisms, utilizing the well-known Buongiorno model. Two-dimensional Navier-Stokes, energy, and concentration equations are solved using the BVP4c integrated MATLAB package. The effects of various design parameters on the MHD flow and heat transfer are investigated. The following are the main observations of this study:

- The curvature parameter reduces the profiles of velocity $F'(\eta)$, temperature $\theta(\eta)$, concentration $\phi(\eta)$, and concentration of motile micro-organisms $\chi(\eta)$, and their respective boundary layer thicknesses.
- There is a rise in the profiles of temperature $\theta(\eta)$, concentration $\phi(\eta)$, and concentration of motile micro-organisms $\chi(\eta)$, along with a decrement in the velocity profile $F'(\eta)$ as the magnetic parameter is increased. A similar trend is noticed for the slip parameter.

- The profiles of temperature $\theta(\eta)$ and concentration $\phi(\eta)$ tend to diminish due to the impact of the Prandtl number.
- The Brownian motion has opposite effects on the profiles of the temperature $\theta(\eta)$ (i.e., increasing function) and concentration $\phi(\eta)$ (i.e., decreasing function). However, the thermophoresis parameter rises the temperature and concentration distributions.
- The increasing values of Schmidt and bio-convection Schmidt numbers decrease the profiles of concentration $\phi(\eta)$ and concentration of motile micro-organisms $\chi(\eta)$.
- The augmenting values of the Peclet number improve significantly the profile of motile micro-organisms' concentration $\chi(\eta)$.
- The motile micro-organisms' number is reduced with the increasing values of the Brownian motion parameter, the thermophoresis parameter, and the Peclet number, whereas it enhances with the bio-convection Schmidt number.

Many fields, including pharmacodynamics, drug delivery methods, tumor treatment, hemodynamics, biological polymer synthesis, bacteria-powered micro-mixers, bio-energy systems, pollution dispersion in aquifers, and others [43–47], could benefit from the use of the aforementioned problem. Increasing a nanofluid's stability as a suspension is another justification for including microorganisms in it. The same flagella that propel microorganisms will also cause some mixing at the micro-scale (on a scale that is similar to the size of a nanoparticle and a bacterium), which may prevent nanoparticles from aggregating and agglomerating, and also lead to the macroscopic motion of the host fluid. In this way, the relevance of bioconvection effects in the boundary layer close to the wall has been highlighted by the application of our model to nanofluid heat transfer in the laminar domain.

Author Contributions: Conceptualization, P.R., N.A.A., A.W., N.A.S. and Y.J.; methodology, P.R., N.A.A., A.W., N.A.S. and Y.J. software, P.R., N.A.A., A.W., N.A.S. and Y.J.; validation, P.R., N.A.A., A.W., N.A.S. and Y.J.; formal analysis, P.R., N.A.A., A.W., N.A.S. and Y.J.; investigation, P.R., N.A.A., A.W., N.A.S. and Y.J.; resources, P.R., N.A.A., A.W., N.A.S. and Y.J.; writing—original draft preparation, P.R., N.A.A., A.W., N.A.S. and Y.J.; writing—review and editing, P.R., N.A.A., A.W., N.A.S. and Y.J.; visualization, P.R., N.A.A., A.W., N.A.S. and Y.J.; supervision, P.R., N.A.A., A.W., N.A.S. and Y.J.; funding acquisition, Y.J. All authors have read and agreed to the published version of the manuscript.

Funding: This study was supported by the National Research Foundation of Korea (NRF) funded by the Korean government (MSIT) [NRF-2021R1I1A3047845, NRF-2022R1A4A3023960] and BK21 Four program through the National Research Foundation of Korea (NRF) funded by the Ministry of Education of Korea (Center for Creative Leaders in Maritime Convergence).

Data Availability Statement: Not applicable.

Conflicts of Interest: The authors declare no conflict of interest.

Abbreviations

BL	Boundary Layer
MBL	Momentum Boundary Layer
TBL	Thermal Boundary Layer
CBL	Concentration Boundary Layer
MMBL	Motile Micro-organisms' Boundary Layer

Nomenclature

Alphabets

A	Curvature parameter
a	Stretching rate constant
b	Chemotaxis constant
$\{C, C_w, C_\infty\}$	Concentration characteristics
C_P	Specific heat capacity
C_f	Skin friction coefficient
D_B	Brownian diffusion coefficient
D_T	Thermophoresis diffusion coefficient
D_m	Motile micro-organisms' diffusion coefficient
$\{F, F'\}$	Dimensionless nanofluid velocity components
k	Thermal conductivity
M	Magnetic parameter
Mn_s	Local motile micro-organisms' number
$\{N, N_w, N_\infty\}$	Motile micro-organisms' concentration characteristics
Nb	Brownian motion parameter
Nt	Thermophoresis parameter
Nu_s	Local Nusselt number
p	Pressure
P	Dimensionless pressure
Pb	Bio-convective Peclet number
Pr	Prandtl number
q_w	Wall heat flux
q_j	Wall mass flux
q_m	Wall motile micro-organisms flux
R	Radius of curvature
Re	Reynolds number
(r, s)	Curvilinear coordinates
Sb	Bio-convective Schmidt number
Sc	Schmidt number
Sh_s	Local Sherwood number
$\{T, T_w, T_\infty\}$	Temperature characteristics
U_w	Stretching sheet velocity
(u, v)	$s-$ and $r-$ velocity components
W_c	Maximum cell speed

Greek Letters

β	Slip length
β_1	Slip parameter
σ	Nanofluid's electrical conductivity
ρ	Nanofluid's density
v	Nanofluid's kinematic viscosity
μ	Nanofluid's dynamic viscosity
τ_w	Surface shear stress
θ	Non-dimensional nanofluid temperature
ϕ	Non-dimensional nanofluid concentration
χ	Non-dimensional motile micro-organisms' concentration
η	Similarity variable

Subscripts

X'	Ordinary differentiation of X w.r.t η

References

1. Hady, F.M.; Mahdy, A.; Mohamed, R.A.; Zaid, O.A.A. Effects of viscous dissipation on unsteady MHD thermo bioconvection boundary layer flow of a nanofluid containing gyrotactic microorganisms along a stretching sheet. *World J. Mech.* **2016**, *6*, 505–526. [CrossRef]
2. Pal, D.; Mondal, S.K. MHD nanofluid bioconvection over an exponentially stretching sheet in the presence of gyrotactic microorganisms and thermal radiation. *BioNanoScience* **2018**, *8*, 272–287. [CrossRef]

3. Yasmin, A.; Ali, K.; Ashraf, M. Study of heat and mass transfer in MHD flow of micropolar fluid over a curved stretching sheet. *Sci. Rep.* **2020**, *10*, 4581. [CrossRef] [PubMed]
4. Nagaraja, B.; Gireesha, B.J. Exponential space-dependent heat generation impact on MHD convective flow of Casson fluid over a curved stretching sheet with chemical reaction. *J. Therm. Anal. Calorim.* **2021**, *143*, 4071–4079. [CrossRef]
5. Haq, F.; Saleem, M.; UR Rahman, M. Investigation of natural bio-convective flow of Cross nanofluid containing gyrotactic microorganisms subject to activation energy and magnetic field. *Phys. Scr.* **2020**, *95*, 105219. [CrossRef]
6. Koriko, O.K.; Shah, N.A.; Saleem, S.; Chung, J.D.; Omowaye, A.J.; Oreyeni, T. Exploration of bioconvection flow of MHD thixotropic nanofluid past a vertical surface coexisting with both nanoparticles and gyrotactic microorganisms. *Sci. Rep.* **2021**, *11*, 16627. [CrossRef]
7. Nabwey, H.A.; El-Kabeir, S.M.M.; Rashad, A.M.; Abdou, M.M.M. Effectiveness of Magnetized Flow on Nanofluid Containing Gyrotactic Micro-Organisms over an Inclined Stretching Sheet with Viscous Dissipation and Constant Heat Flux. *Fluids* **2021**, *6*, 253. [CrossRef]
8. Shah, N.A.; Wakif, A.; El-Zahar, E.R.; Ahmad, S.; Yook, S.-J. Numerical simulation of a thermally enhanced EMHD flow of a heterogeneous micropolar mixture comprising (60%)-ethylene glycol (EG), (40%)-water (W), and copper oxide nanomaterials (CuO). *Case Stud. Therm. Eng.* **2022**, *35*, 102046. [CrossRef]
9. Kessler, J.O. Hydrodynamic focusing of motile algal cells. *Nature* **1985**, *313*, 218–220. [CrossRef]
10. Lovecchio, S.; Zonta, F.; Marchioli, C.; Soldati, A. Thermal stratification hinders gyrotactic micro-organism rising in free-surface turbulence. *Phys. Fluids* **2017**, *29*, 053302. [CrossRef]
11. Croze, O.A.; Sardina, G.; Ahmed, M.; Bees, M.A.; Brandt, L. Dispersion of swimming algae in laminar and turbulent channel flows: Consequences for photobioreactors. *J. R. Soc. Interface* **2013**, *10*, 20121041. [CrossRef] [PubMed]
12. Durham, W.M.; Kessler, J.O.; Stocker, R. Disruption of vertical motility by shear triggers formation of thin phytoplankton layers. *Science* **2009**, *323*, 1067–1070. [CrossRef] [PubMed]
13. Durham, W.M.; Climent, E.; Barry, M.; Lillo, F.D.; Boffetta, G.; Cencini, M.; Stocker, R. Turbulence drives microscale patches of motile phytoplankton. *Nat. Commun.* **2013**, *4*, 2148. [CrossRef] [PubMed]
14. Alharbi, F.M.; Naeem, M.; Zubair, M.; Jawad, M.; Jan, W.U.; Jan, R. Bioconvection Due to Gyrotactic Microorganisms in Couple Stress Hybrid Nanofluid Laminar Mixed Convection Incompressible Flow with Magnetic Nanoparticles and Chemical Reaction as Carrier for Targeted Drug Delivery through Porous Stretching Sheet. *Molecules* **2021**, *26*, 3954. [CrossRef]
15. Mondal, S.K.; Pal, D. Computational analysis of bioconvective flow of nanofluid containing gyrotactic microorganisms over a nonlinear stretching sheet with variable viscosity using HAM. *J. Comput. Des. Eng.* **2020**, *7*, 251–267. [CrossRef]
16. Kairi, R.R.; Shaw, S.; Roy, S.; Raut, S. Thermosolutal marangoni impact on bioconvection in suspension of gyrotactic microorganisms over an inclined stretching sheet. *J. Heat Transf.* **2021**, *143*, 031201. [CrossRef]
17. Khan, M.N.; Nadeem, S. Theoretical treatment of bio-convective Maxwell nanofluid over an exponentially stretching sheet. *Can. J. Phys.* **2020**, *98*, 732–741. [CrossRef]
18. Abdelmalek, Z.; Khan, S.U.; Waqas, H.; Riaz, A.; Khan, I.A.; Tlili, I. A mathematical model for bioconvection flow of Williamson nanofluid over a stretching cylinder featuring variable thermal conductivity, activation energy and second-order slip. *J. Therm. Anal. Calorim.* **2021**, *144*, 205–217. [CrossRef]
19. Shafiq, A.; Lone, S.A.; Sindhu, T.N.; Al-Mdallal, Q.M.; Rasool, G. Statistical modeling for bioconvective tangent hyperbolic nanofluid towards stretching surface with zero mass flux condition. *Sci. Rep.* **2021**, *11*, 13869. [CrossRef]
20. Chu, Y.-M.; ur Rahman, M.; Khan, M.I.; Kadry, S.; Rehman, W.U.; Abdelmalek, Z. Heat transport and bio-convective nanomaterial flow of Walter's-B fluid containing gyrotactic microorganisms. *Ain Shams Eng. J.* **2021**, *12*, 3071–3079. [CrossRef]
21. Xia, W.-F.; Haq, F.; Saleem, M.; Khan, M.I.; Khan, S.U.; Chu, Y.-M. Irreversibility analysis in natural bio-convective flow of Eyring-Powell nanofluid subject to activation energy and gyrotactic microorganisms. *Ain Shams Eng. J.* **2021**, *12*, 4063–4074. [CrossRef]
22. Aneja, M.; Sharma, S.; Kuharat, S.; Beg, O.A. Computation of electroconductive gyrotactic bioconvection from a nonlinear inclined stretching sheet under nonuniform magnetic field: Simulation of smart bio-nanopolymer coatings for solar energy. *Int. J. Mod. Phys. B* **2020**, *34*, 2050028. [CrossRef]
23. Magagula, V.M.; Shaw, S.; Kairi, R.R. Double dispersed bioconvective Casson nanofluid fluid flow over a nonlinear convective stretching sheet in suspension of gyrotactic microorganism. *Heat Transf.* **2020**, *49*, 2449–2471. [CrossRef]
24. Manan, A.; Rehman, S.U.; Fatima, N.; Imran, M.; Ali, B.; Shah, N.A.; Chung, J.D. Dynamics of Eyring–Powell Nanofluids When Bioconvection and Lorentz Forces Are Significant: The Case of a Slender Elastic Sheet of Variable Thickness with Porous Medium. *Mathematics* **2022**, *10*, 3039. [CrossRef]
25. Wang, C.Y. Flow due to a stretching boundary with partial slip-an exact solution of the Navier-Stokes equations. *Chem. Eng. Sci.* **2002**, *57*, 3745–3747. [CrossRef]
26. Noghrehabadi, A.; Pourrajab, R.; Ghalambaz, M. Effect of partial slip boundary condition on the flow and heat transfer of nanofluids past stretching sheet prescribed constant wall temperature. *Int. J. Therm. Sci.* **2012**, *54*, 253–261. [CrossRef]
27. Rauf, A.; Mushtaq, A.; Shah, N.A.; Botmart, T. Heat transfer and hybrid ferrofluid flow over a nonlinearly stretchable rotating disk under the influence of an alternating magnetic field. *Sci Rep.* **2022**, *12*, 17548. [CrossRef]
28. Hayat, T.; Khan, S.A.; Alsaedi, A.; Zai, Q.Z. Computational analysis of heat transfer in mixed convective flow of CNTs with entropy optimization by a curved stretching sheet. *Int. Commun. Heat Mass Transf.* **2020**, *118*, 104881. [CrossRef]

29. Raza, R.; Mabood, F.; Naz, R. Entropy analysis of non-linear radiative flow of Carreau liquid over curved stretching sheet. *Int. Commun. Heat Mass Transf.* **2020**, *119*, 104975. [CrossRef]

30. Madhukesh, J.K.; Kumar, R.N.; Gowda, R.J.P.; Prasannakumara, B.C.; Ramesh, G.K.; Khan, M.I.; Khan, S.U.; Chu, Y.-M. Numerical simulation of AA7072-AA7075/water-based hybrid nanofluid flow over a curved stretching sheet with Newtonian heating: A non-Fourier heat flux model approach. *J. Mol. Liq.* **2021**, *335*, 116103. [CrossRef]

31. Gireesha, B.J.; Nagaraja, B.; Sindhu, S.; Sowmya, G. Consequence of exponential heat generation on non-Darcy-Forchheimer flow of water based carbon nanotubes driven by a curved stretching sheet. *Appl. Math. Mech.* **2020**, *41*, 1723–1734. [CrossRef]

32. Zhang, X.-H.; Abidi, A.; Ahmed, A.E.-S.; Khan, M.R.; El-Shorbagy, M.A.; Shutaywi, M.; Issakhov, A.; Galal, A.M. MHD stagnation point flow of nanofluid over curved stretching/shrinking surface subject to the influence of Joule heating and convective condition. *Case Stud. Therm. Eng.* **2021**, *26*, 101184. [CrossRef]

33. Qian, W.-M.; Khan, M.I.; Shah, F.; Khan, M.; Chu, Y.-M.; Khan, W.A.; Nazeer, M. Mathematical Modeling and MHD Flow of Micropolar Fluid Toward an Exponential Curved Surface: Heat Analysis via Ohmic Heating and Heat Source/Sink. *Arab. J. Sci. Eng.* **2021**, *47*, 867–878. [CrossRef]

34. Afsar Khan, A.; Batool, R.; Kousar, N. Examining the behavior of MHD micropolar fluid over curved stretching surface based on the modified Fourier law. *Sci. Iran.* **2021**, *28*, 223–230. [CrossRef]

35. Rehman, S.U.; Fatima, N.; Ali, B.; Imran, M.; Ali, L.; Shah, N.A.; Chung, J.D. The Casson Dusty Nanofluid: Significance of Darcy–Forchheimer Law, Magnetic Field, and Non-Fourier Heat Flux Model Subject to Stretch Surface. *Mathematics* **2022**, *10*, 2877. [CrossRef]

36. Kempannagari, A.K.; Buruju, R.R.; Naramgari, S.; Vangala, S. Effect of Joule heating on MHD non-Newtonian fluid flow past an exponentially stretching curved surface. *Heat Transf.* **2020**, *49*, 3575–3592. [CrossRef]

37. Asogwa, K.K.; Goud, B.S.; Shah, N.A.; Yook, S.-J. Rheology of electromagnetohydrodynamic tangent hyperbolic nanofluid over a stretching riga surface featuring dufour effect and activation energy. *Sci Rep.* **2022**, 14602. [CrossRef]

38. Rasool, G.; Shah, N.A.; El-Zahar, E.R.; Wakif, A. Numerical investigation of EMHD nanofluid flows over a convectively heated riga pattern positioned horizontally in a Darcy-Forchheimer porous medium: Application of passive control strategy and generalized transfer laws. *Waves Random Complex Media* **2022**, 1–20. [CrossRef]

39. Ardekani, A.M.; Doostmohammadi, A.; Desai, N. Transport of particles, drops, and small organisms in density stratified fluids. *Phys. Rev. Fluids* **2017**, *2*, 100503. [CrossRef]

40. Lillo, D.F.; Cencini, M.; Durham, W.M.; Barry, M.; Stocker, R.; Climent, E.; Boffetta, G. Turbulent fluid acceleration generates clusters of gyrotactic microorganisms. *Phys. Rev. Lett.* **2014**, *112*, 044502. [CrossRef]

41. Zeng, L.; Pedley, T.J. Distribution of gyrotactic micro-organisms in complex three-dimensional flows. Part 1. Horizontal shear flow past a vertical circular cylinder. *J. Fluid Mech.* **2018**, *852*, 358–397. [CrossRef]

42. Buongiorno, J. Convective Transport in Nanofluids. *J. Heat Transf.* **2006**, *128*, 240–250. [CrossRef]

43. Sokolov, A.; Goldstein, R.E.; Feldchtein, F.I.; Aranson, I.S. Enhanced mixing and spatial instability in concentrated bacterial suspensions. *Phys. Rev. E* **2009**, *80*, 031903. [CrossRef] [PubMed]

44. Tsai, T.-H.; Liou, D.-S.; Kuo, L.-S.; Chen, P.-H. Rapid mixing between ferro-nanofluid and water in a semi-active Y-type micromixer. *Sens. Actuators A Phys.* **2009**, *153*, 267–273. [CrossRef]

45. Uddin, M.J.; Khan, W.A.; Qureshi, S.R.; Beg, O.A. Bioconvection nanofluid slip flow past a wavy surface with applications in nano-biofuel cells. *Chin. J. Phys.* **2017**, *55*, 2048–2063. [CrossRef]

46. Shaijumon, M.M.; Ramaprabhu, S.; Rajalakshmi, N. Platinum/multiwalled carbon nanotubes–platinum/carbon composites as electrocatalysts for oxygen reduction reaction in proton exchange membrane fuel cell. *Appl. Phys. Lett.* **2006**, *88*, 253105. [CrossRef]

47. Naskar, S.; Sharma, S.; Kuotsu, K. Chitosan-based nanoparticles: An overview of biomedical applications and its preparation. *J. Drug Deliv. Sci. Technol.* **2019**, *49*, 66–81. [CrossRef]

Review

Role of Metaheuristic Approaches for Implementation of Integrated MPPT-PV Systems: A Comprehensive Study

Amit Kumar Sharma [1], Rupendra Kumar Pachauri [2], Sushabhan Choudhury [2], Ahmad Faiz Minai [3], Majed A. Alotaibi [4,5,*], Hasmat Malik [6,*] and Fausto Pedro García Márquez [7]

[1] Electrical Engineering Department, Savitri Bai Phule Government Girls Polytechnic, Saharanpur 247001, Uttar Pradesh, India
[2] Electrical and Electronics Engineering Department, SOE, University of Petroleum and Energy Studies, Dehradun 248007, Uttarakhand, India
[3] Electrical Engineering Department, Integral University, Lucknow 226026, Uttar Pradesh, India
[4] Department of Electrical Engineering, College of Engineering, King Saud University, Riyadh 11421, Saudi Arabia
[5] K.A. CARE Energy Research and Innovation Center at Riyadh, Riyadh 11451, Saudi Arabia
[6] Department of Electrical Power Engineering, Faculty of Electrical Engineering, University Technology Malaysia (UTM), Johor Bahru 81310, Malaysia
[7] Ingenium Research Group, Universidad Castilla-La Mancha, 13071 Ciudad Real, Spain
* Correspondence: majedalotaibi@ksu.edu.sa (M.A.A.); hasmat.malik@gmail.com (H.M.)

Abstract: An effective MPPT approach plays a significant role in increasing the efficiency of a PV system. Solar energy is a rich renewable energy source that is supplied to the earth in surplus by the sun. Solar PV systems are designed to utilize sunlight in order to meet the energy needs of the user. Due to unreliable climatic conditions, these PV frames have a non-linear characteristic that has a significant impact on their yield. Moreover, PSCs also affect the performance of PV systems in yielding maximum power. A significant progression in solar PV installations has resulted in rapid growth of MPPT techniques. As a result, a variety of MPPT approaches have been used to enhance the power yield of PV systems along with their advantages and disadvantages. Thus, it is essential for researchers to appraise developed MPPT strategies appropriately on regular basis. This study is novel because it provides an in-depth assessment of the current state of MPPT strategies for PV systems. On account of novelty, the authors analyzed the successive growth in MPPT strategies along with working principles, mathematical modeling, and simplified flow charts for better understanding by new learners. Moreover, the taxonomy and pro and cons of conventional and AI-based MPPT techniques are explored comprehensively. In addition, a comparative study based on key characteristics of PV system of all MPPT algorithms is depicted in a table, which can be used as a reference by various researchers while designing PV systems.

Keywords: MPPT; solar PV system; optimization techniques

MSC: 68W50

Citation: Sharma, A.K.; Pachauri, R.K.; Choudhury, S.; Minai, A.F.; Alotaibi, M.A.; Malik, H.; Márquez, F.P.G. Role of Metaheuristic Approaches for Implementation of Integrated MPPT-PV Systems: A Comprehensive Study. *Mathematics* **2023**, *11*, 269. https://doi.org/10.3390/math11020269

Academic Editors: Valeriu David and Camelia Petrescu

Received: 16 November 2022
Revised: 13 December 2022
Accepted: 20 December 2022
Published: 4 January 2023

1. Introduction

As our civilization advances in technology, it necessitates a greater use of energy in today's world. Renewable energy sources have the potential to cater the increasing demand for energy in various forms. In near future, demand for renewable energy will rise in all sectors, including heating, power, and transportation, etc. Solar power is more admired than other renewable energy sources due to its widespread availability and well-established technology. This is because of recent developments in increasing accuracy and tracking speed for maximum energy harvesting [1].

Direct current is generated when photons from sunlight strike the solar cells. A series-parallel combination of these cells gives rise to a PV module, which when further combined together forms a PV array. The literature reveals that the characteristics of solar cells are non-linear [2], which degrades their conversion efficiency. Therefore, it is required to extract all the power accessible from the PV module. Moreover, a PV module does not supply power constantly on account of various factors such as temperature, irradiance, geographical conditions, and so on [3].

The P–V curve of any solar module has an optimal point, i.e., the global maximum power point (GMPP), that varies depending on temperature and solar irradiance. The PV module produces the most power at that point [4]. To confirm that the PV module is always operating at GMPP, MPPT techniques come into picture. MPPT techniques are algorithms that are implemented via software and power electronics hardware combination in any solar controller. These algorithms aid in ensuring that the output of solar array is always at its peak. MPPT techniques perform this task by continuous power tracking methodology to determine the best operating power point from solar array. Since the maximum power of a solar array varies in accordance with many environmental conditions, tracking this power is crucial for utmost utilization of solar energy. The MPPT system's aim is to sample the output of the PV array and apply the appropriate resistance to obtain maximum power for any given environmental conditions. Thus, these techniques function as an impedance-matching device between the array and load with the help of varying the duty cycle of the DC-DC converter. The whole process is controlled by software and a micro-controller. MPPT-equipped controllers have numerous advantages over other controllers, such as the following:

- More efficiency;
- Capability of optimizing voltage differences as well as DC load optimization;
- Best for larger systems where solar panel output exceeds battery voltage by a significant margin;
- Enhances the system's output and hence its capacity.

There are several approaches to achieving MPPT, which are discussed in this article.

Many researchers have published their findings on MPPT algorithms. Refs. [5–7] compare various MPPT approaches for uniform irradiance and PSCs for solar PV systems, whereas [8,9] focus specifically on PSCs. Traditional MPPT techniques such as P&O [10], INC [11], and HC [12] are proficient for uniform irradiance with a unique peak. They are unsuitable when the PV system is subjected to PSCs. The researchers attempted to improve on traditional MPPT algorithms by combining them with advanced strategies [13–15]. Figure 1a,b show a generalized block diagram of standalone and grid-connected PV systems.

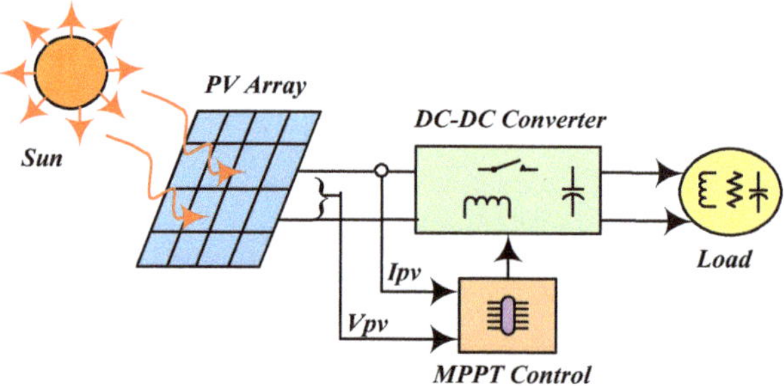

(a)

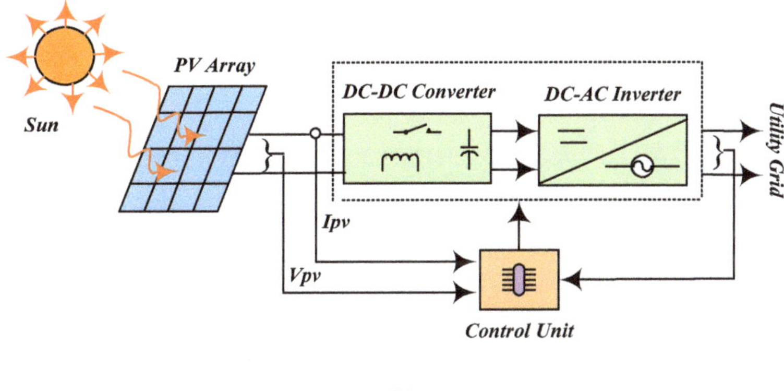

Figure 1. Generalized block diagram of (**a**) standalone PV system and (**b**) grid-connected PV system.

However, the choice of a specific MPPT approach is still an ambiguity. As a result, there is strong need to investigate and reassess the developed strategies on regular basis, as this will help in the selection of a specific technique based on the context. Different conventional and AI-based meta-heuristic MPPT techniques are reviewed and compared in this article based on a variety of factors such as tracking time, complexity, oscillations around GMPP, implementation cost, and so on. BI [16,17], SI [18,19], ANN, FLC, and ECI are explained and reviewed by authors on various parameters.

The novelty of this work can be summarized as an approach to presenting qualitative comparative analysis and set-theoretic research, with emphasis on tabular presentation (technical datasheet presentation) of the chief attributes of conventional and AI-based MPPT techniques.

This data positioning approach is most appropriate format for reading and understanding the data. Quantifying these data helps in comprehensive analysis and comparing different data sets, thereby bringing out the most important and widely used conventional, metaheuristic, and other AI-based MPPT techniques, wherein various parameters such as array size, irradiance levels, techniques considered, % boost in GMPP using best technique, and tracking time, etc., are considered.

This research work is novel from other aspects as well, such as the following:

- Ease of representation: In distinct sections, the work summarizes the main characteristics of traditional and AI-based metaheuristic techniques in a simplified style using simplified flowcharts;
- Ease of analysis: A technical datasheet was created after reviewing all the major attributes required to design any PV system of recently reported conventional MPPT techniques, AI-based metaheuristic approaches, and other AI-based MPPT techniques. This datasheet provides a bare-bones description that facilitates even a new learner to understand the performances of these metaheuristic MPPT techniques, particularly PV systems in PSCs;
- Ease of modification: The technical datasheet highlights the pros and cons of all reviewed works of each category, which enables the user to identify the research gap as discussed above and helps them to modify a particular algorithm to meet the requirement of good PV system;
- Qualitative comparative analysis: The technical datasheet facilitates comparison of all MPPT approaches based on the key characteristics required while incorporating them in any PV system, which helps the readers to select the most suitable technique for any particular application.

Structure of this work is as follows: The modeling of the PV cell is elaborated upon in Section 2 along with the effects of environmental factors. The partial shading effect is discussed in Section 3. MPPT techniques and their classification are elaborated upon in Section 4. Research gap findings are reported in Section 5. Challenges and further scope of the conducted effort are pointed out in Section 6, and paper is concluded in Section 7.

2. Modeling of PV Cell

Ideally, a parallel combination of a current source and a diode represents a solar cell. For practical applications, the model also incorporates shunt and series resistances to take into account manufacturing defects and contact resistances [20], as illustrated in Figure 2a.

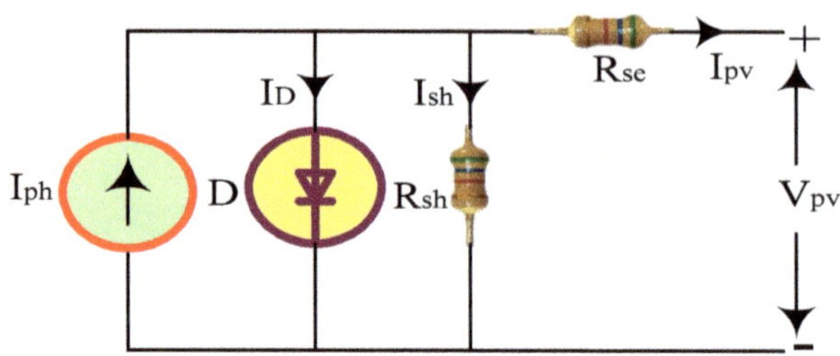

(a)

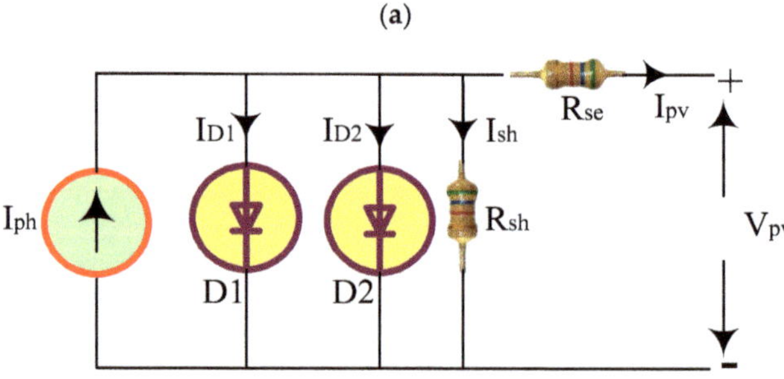

(b)

Figure 2. Solar cell: (**a**) single-diode model and (**b**) double-diode model.

The current generated by the solar cell can be computed by Equation (1).

$$I_{pv} = I_{ph} - I_D - I_{sh} \tag{1}$$

The Shockley equation and Ohm's law can be used to calculate the current through a diode and shunt resistor, as shown in Equations (2) and (3), respectively.

$$I_D = I_0 \left[\exp\left(\frac{q}{N_{cs}KT} \left(V_{pv} + I_{pv}R_{se} \right) \right) - 1 \right] \tag{2}$$

$$I_{sh} = \frac{V_{pv} + I_{pv}\,R_{se}}{R_{sh}} \tag{3}$$

Thus, the distinctive Equation of solar cell output current can be written as

$$I_{pv} = I_{ph} - I_0 \left[\exp\left(\frac{q}{nkT} \left(V_{pv} + I_{pv}R_{se} \right) \right) - 1 \right] - \frac{V_{pv} + I_{pv}\,R_{se}}{R_{sh}} \tag{4}$$

The ideality factor "n" is assumed to be constant in single-diode model, but this factor is a function of voltage at the device terminals. Its value is close to one at high voltages and becomes two at low voltages because of recombination in junction. This effect can be modelled by connecting another diode in parallel with the first diode, giving rise to the double-diode model, as shown in Figure 2b. The ideality factor is set to "2" for the double-diode model.

Figure 3 shows the PV module (I–V) and (P–V) characteristic curves. It details the solar energy conversion capability and efficiency for a particular atmospheric condition. Since short- and open-circuit circumstances have no effect on power generation, there must be a point somewhere in the middle where the solar module produces most power and is located close to the bend in the characteristic curves. P_{max} is generated by a specific combination of voltage and current, and the combination's coordinates represent the MPP.

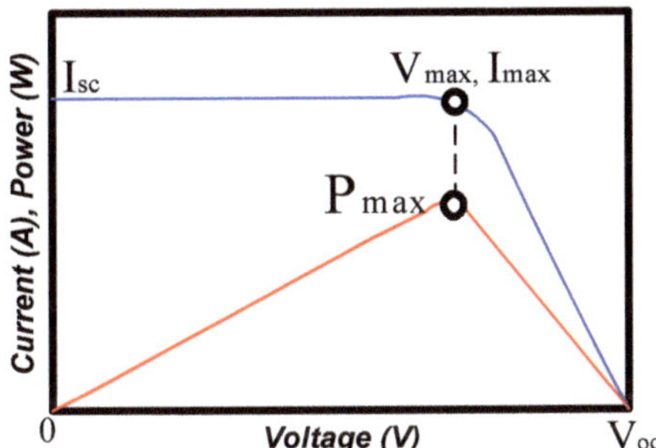

Figure 3. PV module characteristic curves (I–V) and (P–V).

A slight change in atmospheric temperature and irradiance affects the module's performance. Since module Voc decreases as temperature rises [21], the power output yield of the PV system will decrease. Figure 4a,b show the temperature variation effect on PV module (I–V) and (P–V) curves.

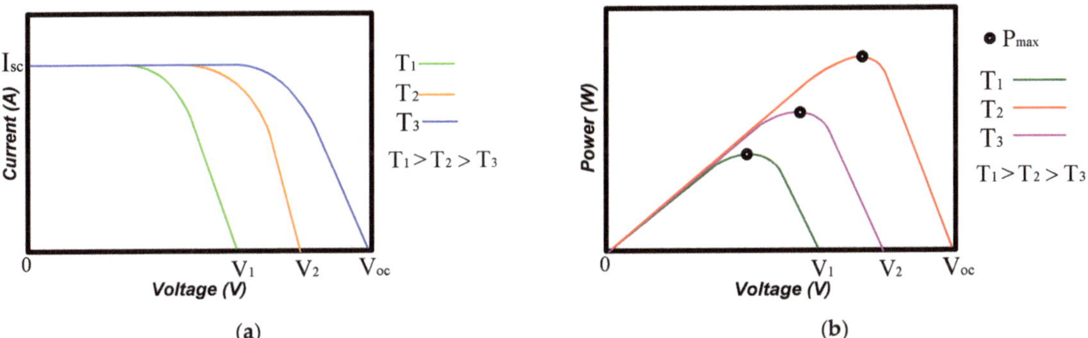

Figure 4. Temperature variations effect on PV module: (**a**) I–V curve and (**b**) P–V Similarly, the output of PV modules is also affected by the change in solar irradiance "W w/m^2", as the output current of PV module depends on irradiance. As irradiance increases, the PV module output current also increases. Thus, the PV module can generate more output power. Figure 5a,b show the effect of irradiance change on PV module (I–V) and (P–V) curves.

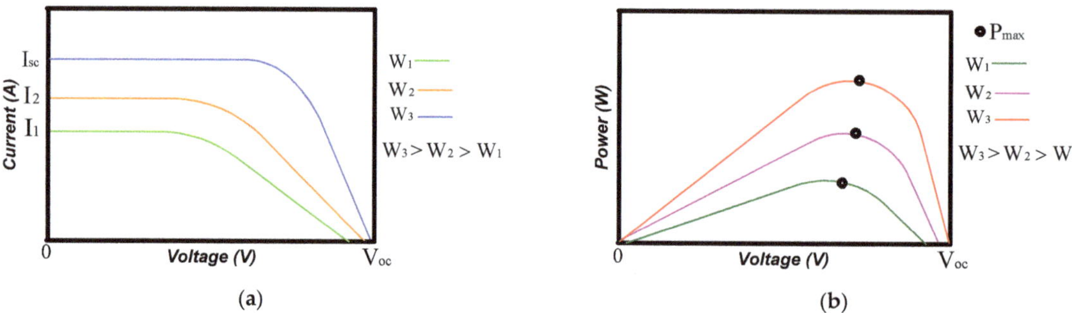

Figure 5. Irradiance variation effect on PV module: (**a**) I–V curve and (**b**) P–V curve.

3. Partial shading Effect

PV systems are extremely susceptible to partial shading. On account of various environmental conditions such as rain, clouds, and storms, it is not possible to obtain uniform irradiance at all times. In addition, PV array also suffers shading from nearby buildings and trees. This shading effect leads the PV module to yield less output power [22]. PSCs can lead to the following:

- Non-linear PV module (I–V) characteristic curve with multiple LMPP. As a result, shading causes hot spots and damages the solar cells;
- Current and voltage mismatch in PV array;
- Many peaks in the (P–V) characteristic curve with an increase in shading conditions.

Shading one cell results in a drop of current flowing through it when compared to the unshaded cells of its string. As a result, unshaded cells are forced to carry high current, and shaded cells will be restricted to the string current. This leads to a drop in the output power of the PV string. A bypass diode is connected across the shaded cell string to moderate the effect of shading. Through this, unidirectional flow of current is achieved. Figure 6a,b shows the effect of partial shading on (I–V) and (P–V) characteristics of PV system.

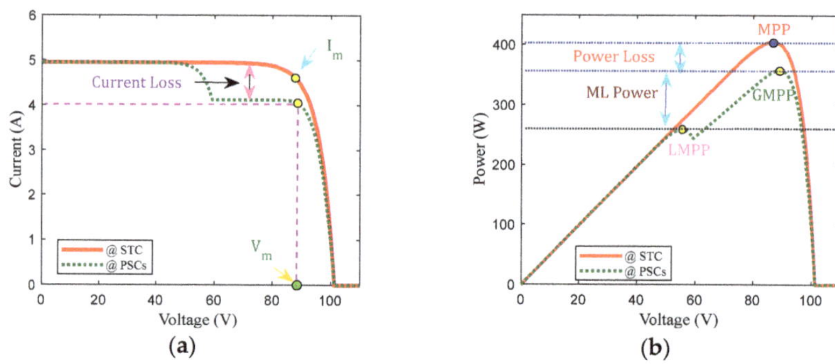

Figure 6. Characteristics of (**a**) I–V and (**b**) P–V under PSCs.

4. MPPT Algorithms

Each PV module has a different MPP in different atmospheric conditions. Thus, to extract maximum power from it, MPPT algorithms are used. These algorithms are imposed through electronic converters. Though these techniques enhance the performance of PV system, designers are generally concerned about tracking GMPP under PSCs. These algorithms are implemented through microcontrollers. The duty ratio of the DC converter employed is adjusted by these algorithms after frequent sampling of some PV module parameters. This changes the impedance seen by the PV module, resulting in achieving maximum power. These MPPT techniques are classified as shown in Figure 7. The following sections explain the basics of these techniques comprehensively, while recent advancements in each are listed in the tables at the end of each classification separately.

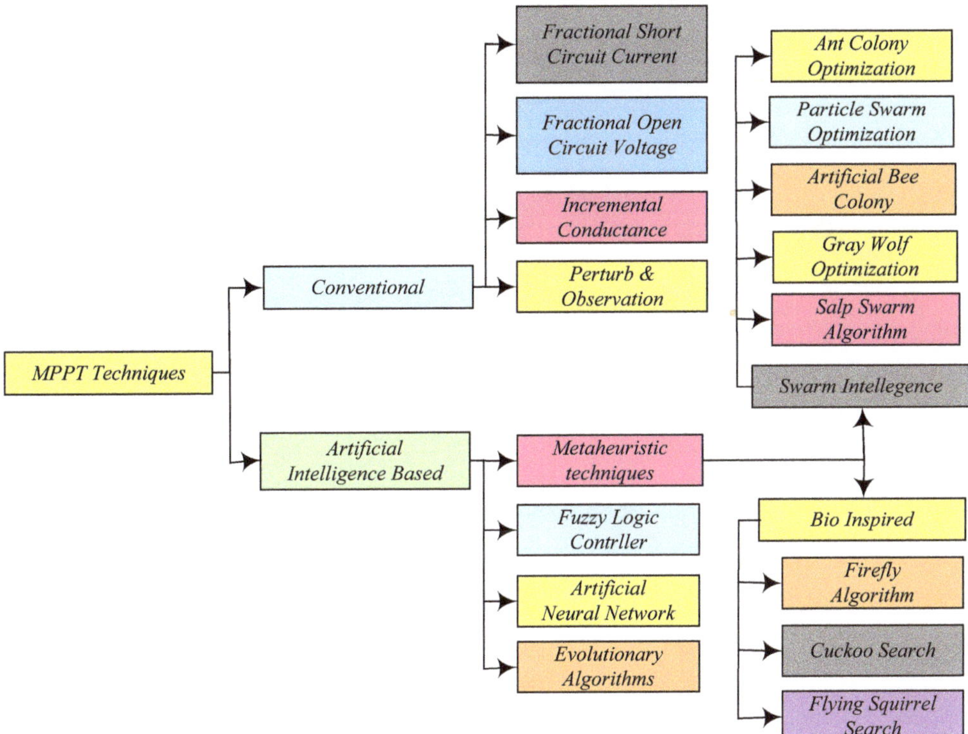

Figure 7. MPPT Techniques Classifications.

4.1. Conventional MPPT Techniques

4.1.1. Perturb and Observe

The P&O MPPT technique is widely used due to its simplicity, ease of implementation, fewer sensor requirements, and low actualized costs [23,24]. It is an iterative method of tracking MPP. This technique works on the principle of minor change in PV array voltage and monitors the resulting impact on power. This is achieved by varying the duty cycle of the DC–DC converter employed in the system. With these perturbations, the change in power can be determined. If power is increased by increasing the voltage, the operating point of the PV module is on the left side of the P–V curve. If, on the other hand, power is reduced with the increase in voltage, the PV module operating point is on the right side of the P–V curve. As a result, for tracking MPP, the direction of perturbation must be such that it converges towards a precise end. Thereafter, this iteration process is continued until MPP is reached. Though the conventional P&O technique works well in stable environmental conditions, it fails to track MPP in PSCs [25]. To overcome this drawback, P&O are modified, as reported in [26]. Steps to demonstrate the working of this technique are shown in Figure 8.

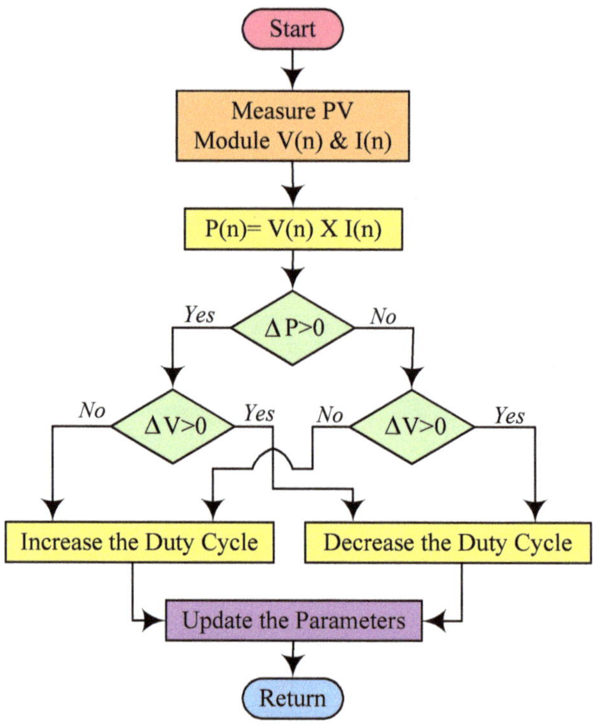

Figure 8. P&O-based MPPT technique [24].

4.1.2. Incremental Conductance

This technique is an improved version of P&O and can track MPP in a rapidly changing environment [27,28]. The principle fact of this technique is based on computing the slope of power "p" on the P–V curve. Since instantaneous power is given as the product of instantaneous voltage and current,

$$p = v \times i \tag{5}$$

The P–V curve slope can be computed as

$$\partial p / \partial v = \frac{\partial (v \times i)}{\partial v}$$

$$= i + v \left(\frac{\partial i}{\partial v} \right) \tag{6}$$

The following conditions can be drawn from Equation (6):

If $\partial i/\partial v = -v/i$	$\partial p/\partial v = 0$	At MPP
If $\partial i/\partial v < -v/i$	$\partial p/\partial v < 0$	At the right side of MPP
If $\partial i/\partial v > -v/i$	$\partial p/\partial v > 0$	At the left side of MPP

As a result, the INC approach tracks MPP by comparing incremental conductance with instantaneous one [28]. Although INC can show zero oscillations in steady state, it acts the same as the P&O technique in transition states. Figure 9 shows the flowchart of the INC approach for tracking MPP.

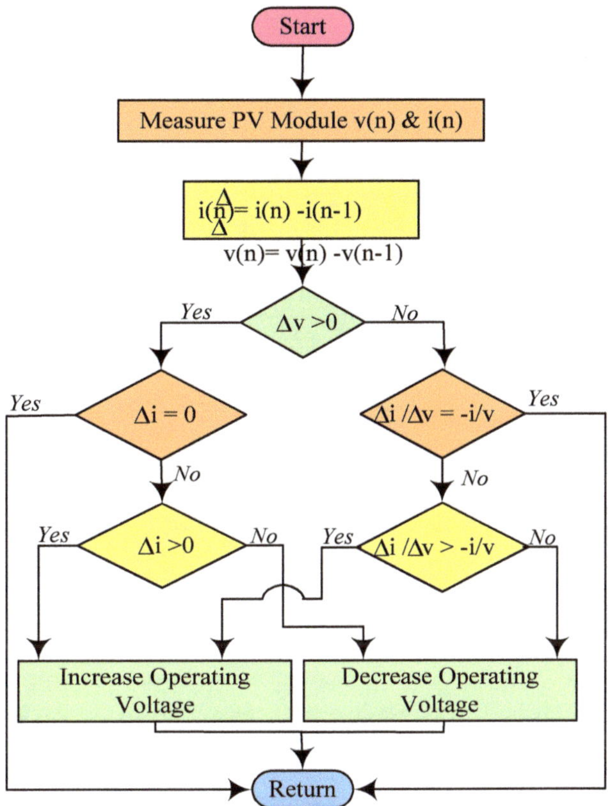

Figure 9. INC-based MPPT technique [27].

4.1.3. Fractional Open-Circuit Voltage Technique

FOCV MPPT technique is an indirect scheme to track MPP and can be utilized for low-power functions. This technique utilizes the principle that shows linear relationship between V_{mpp} and V_{oc}:

$$V_{mpp} \approx b \times V_{oc} \tag{7}$$

"b" lies in a range of $0.71 < b < 0.78$ [29]. Its value is mainly dependent on module and environmental conditions. Although the technique is simple, FOCV suffers from power loss while sampling V_{oc}. A flowchart of the FOCV method is shown in Figure 10.

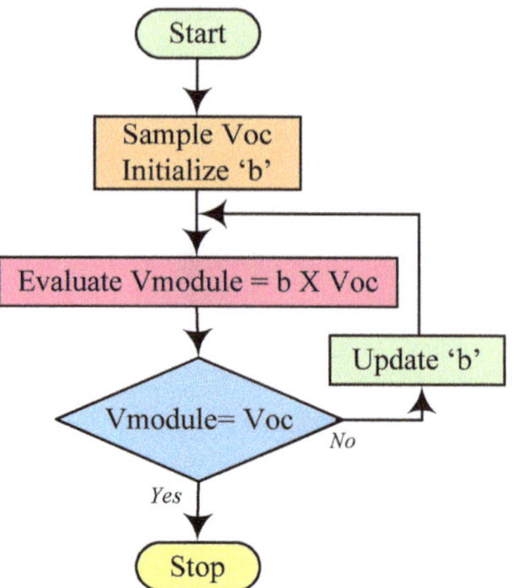

Figure 10. FOCV-based MPPT technique [29].

4.1.4. Fractional Short-Circuit Current Technique

This technique is also an indirect method for tracking MPP and is similar to FOCV. The FSCC technique utilizes the fact that there exists a linear association between I_{mpp} and I_{sc}:

$$I_{mpp} \approx d \times I_{sc} \tag{8}$$

The range of "d" lies in $0.78 < d < 0.92$ [30]. This technique also suffers from the drawback of power loss while measuring I_{sc} during MPPT. A flowchart of the FSCC technique is shown in Figure 11.

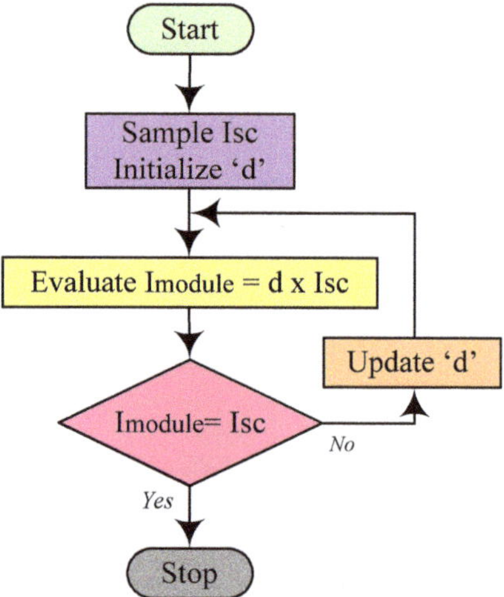

Figure 11. FSCC-based MPPT technique [30].

These conventional techniques are still used as a baseline for tracking GMPP in PSCs. Table 1 summarizes recently reported works based on these principles, followed by a discussion of their pros and cons in Table 2.

Table 1. Taxonomy on recent reported work on conventional techniques to track GMPP.

Authors [Reference No.]	Optimization Techniques	Best optimization Techniques	PV Module P_m (W)	PV System Size	GMPP (W)	Improved GMPP (%)	Irradiance (W/m²)	Shading Patterns	Tracking Time (s)
Numan BA et al. [31]	P&O Variable-step P&O	Variable-step P&O	71.8	2 PV module in series	29.22, 116.1, 106.2	0	200, 700, 800	Uniform	2, 4.8
Gil-Velasco A et al. [32]	P&O, ACO, ACO-P&O, Proposed	Proposed	250	5 PV module in series	44.97, 30.49	102.9, 35.15	1000–200	Uniform	1.12
Efendi MZ et al. [33]	P&O, Modified P&O	Modified P&O	50	3 PV module in series	6037, 5387, 7051, 7385,6322	8.30, 31.19, 61.42, 31.63, 27.69	946–828	Uniform	NA
Shang L et al. [34]	Conventional INC Proposed INC	Proposed INC	49.8	1 PV module	25.1, 40.18 25.1, 27.61	0.039, 0.424, 0.199, 0.217	800–300	Uniform	0.3, 0.35, 0.16, 0.05
Zand SJ et al. [35]	INC SP-INC	SP-INC	100.17	1X1	98.981, 94.097, 81.292	1.811, 1.179, 1.615	1000–800	Uniform	NA
Baimel D et al. [36]	FOCV PC SPC	SPC	NA	NA	27.11, 15.76, 04.83	0.93, 11.01, 0.89 10.98, 0.83, 11.03	1000–200	Uniform	NA
Hua C et al. [37]	CSAM Proposed	Proposed	60	4 PV module in series	470.95	7.27	1000–300	Uniform	0.043, 0.049
Nadeem A et al. [38]	Analytical FOCV Offline FOCV, Proposed	Proposed	245.328	3 PV module in series	438.15	89.67, 0.51	1000–600	Uniform	NA
Fapi CBN et al. [39]	FSCC, Proposed	Proposed	145	1PV module	85	13.33	NA	NA	0.7
Sarika EP et al. [40]	Proposed, VSS P&O, VSS fuzzy	Proposed	100	1PV module	76.50, 65.27	4.08, 2.99	1000–600	Non uniform	0.01
Li C et al. [41]	Proposed INC Fixed-step INC Variable-step INC	Proposed INC	178.4	NA	175.6	1.738	1000–0	Non uniform	0.38, 0.14, 0.165
Owusu-Nyarko I et al. [42]	Proposed, Variable-step-size methods	Proposed	60	NA	596.9	0.285	1000–400	Non uniform	0.0126
Sarwar S et al. [43]	PSO, DFO, INC, Hybrid, CS, FA, ACO	Hybrid	315.072	4X1	511.4, 780.4	57.35, 9.6	1000–200	Non uniform	0.48, 0.20
Hafeez M A et al. [44]	Hybrid, DFO, ACS, WCA, PSO, P&O.	Hybrid	NA	4 PV module in series	1259.9, 794.8, 593.2, 1077.0	1.933, 0.353, 7.32, 0.937	1000–200	Non uniform	0.16, 0.25, 0.4, 0.17
González-Castaño C et al. [45]	SPF-P&O, P&O	SPF-P&O	200	4 PV module in series	405.63, 331.85	4.59, 30.53	1000–120	Uniform & Non uniform	NA

Table 2. Pros and cons of recent work based on conventional techniques.

Authors [Reference No.]	Pros	Cons
Numan BA et al. [31]	• Less computationally complex	• Oscillations around GMPP • Power loss while tracking GMPP • High tracking time
Gil-Velasco A et al. [32]	• High convergence time • High tracking efficiency	• Oscillations around GMPP • Power loss due to oscillations around GMPP
Efendi MZ et al. [33]	• Additional current Voltage sensors are required	• No record of tracking time is given
Shang L et al. [34]	• Ability to judge the correct direction of disturbance • High tracking accuracy	• Low oscillations around GMPP results in power loss • Significant boost in GMPP is observed
Zand SJ et al. [35]	• Simple to implement • High tracking efficiency	• Oscillations are GMPP cannot be removed • Tracking time is not recorded
Baimel D et al. [36]	• Improves overall system efficiency	• Power loss include switching loss, switches loss, and output power of semi pilot cell
Hua C et al. [37]	• Accurate tracking • Low tracking time	• Additional sensor is required • Low oscillations around MPP
Nadeem A et al. [38]	• Can continuously measure Voc without disconnecting PV module • High tracking efficiency	• Three sensors are required to sense Voc • Computationally more complex • No record of tracking time
Fapi CBN et al. [39]	• Low ripples in output power • Improved tracking efficiency	• Two sensors are required for current and irradiance measurement • Initial setting of more parameters are required
Sarika EP et al. [40]	• Low tracking time • Low ripples in output current	• Oscillations around GMPP • .
Li C et al. [41]	• Automatically regulated step size enhances the tracking performance • Fast dynamic response	• Oscillations in steady state • Highly intricate in design
Owusu-Nyarko I et al. [42]	• Dynamic performance is enhanced by adjusting scaling factor in accordance with irradiance. • Low overshoot.	• Oscillations in steady state • .
Sarwar S et al. [43]	• High tracking efficiency • Low settling time.	• Oscillations around GMPP • Highly intricate in design.
Hafeez M A et al. [44]	• High tracking efficiency • Ability to handle complex partial scenarios	• Oscillations around GMPP • Computationally more complex
González-Castaño C et al. [45]	• Robust and fast tracking response • No oscillations in steady state under PSCs	• Low tracking factor at the time of system start up • High settling time

4.2. Swarm Intelligence MPPT Techniques

This section of the paper explains various swarm intelligence MPPT techniques in detail and reports the recent work done with these techniques to enhance MPPT along with their pros and cons in Tables 3 and 4 respectively.

4.2.1. Ant colony Optimization

Ants' cooperative search behavior for the shortest path between source food and their colony motivates ACO. Firstly, ants scurry about aimlessly. When any ant finds a food source, they return to their home along with the food, leaving pheromone trails at their back. This pheromone is composed of particular artificial compounds that are received by living organisms to send messages or codes to other members of the same class. If other colony ants come across such a route, they will follow it to the food source rather than roaming randomly.

They leave pheromones when they return to their territory, boosting the existing pheromone strength. The potency of the pheromone is condensed as pheromone dissipates over time. The ants ultimately regulate and find the shortest path to the food source.

The procedure starts with a single colony of (artificial) ants that has been randomly positioned in that colony. Suppose ants are represented by N parameters. Each ant in the colony uses its magnetic power to entice another ant. They travel from the lower potency zone to the higher potency zone on the basis of attractive force. The attractive power resolute after each iteration cycle and the ants travel in the direction of the best option based on the results.

Consider a problem in which "n" artificial ants (parameters) must be tuned so that $A \geq n$. The solution register stores "A", which represents the primarily created arbitrary solutions. The result afterwards sited according to their fitness significance, f (si), is shown in Equation (9):

$$f(s_1) \leq f(s_2) \leq f(s_3) \leq f(s_4) \ldots\ldots\ldots\ldots\ldots \leq f(s_n) \tag{9}$$

Similarly, fresh arrangements are created to determine the placements of these ants with the help of Gaussian kernel function sampling for ith dimensions and kth solution as [46]

$$\hat{G}_i(x) = \sum_{k=1}^{A} w_k \hat{g}_k^i(x) = \sum_{k=1}^{A} w_k \frac{1}{\sqrt{2\pi}\tilde{\alpha}_k^i} e^{\left[-\frac{(x-\hat{\mu}_k^i)^2}{2(\hat{\alpha}_k^i)^2}\right]} \tag{10}$$

$\tilde{\alpha}_k^i$, $\hat{\mu}_k^i$, and w_k can be evaluated as

$$\tilde{\alpha}_k^i = \epsilon \sum_{k=1}^{A} \frac{|s_k^i - s_k^i|}{A-1} \tag{11}$$

$$\hat{\mu}_k^i = \left[\hat{\mu}_1^i, \hat{\mu}_2^i, \ldots\ldots\hat{\mu}_k^i, \ldots\ldots, \hat{\mu}_A^i\right] = \left[s_1^i, s_2^i, \ldots\ldots s_k^i, \ldots\ldots s_A^i\right] \tag{12}$$

$$w_k = \frac{1}{\varnothing A \sqrt{2\pi}} e^{\left[-\frac{(k-1)^2}{2(\varphi A)^2}\right]} \tag{13}$$

The investigative cycle will be continual depending on the quantity of parameters that needs to be improved. First, we generate "B" novel solutions that sum up the initial "A" solutions. Afterwards, A + B solutions must be placed in the search box. Soon after, A's most effective arrangements are re-established. The entire cycle is thus re-hashed for the required amount of iterations [47]. Effective tracking of GMPP, high convergence rate, and a lesser number of iteration makes ACO more advantageous than traditional MPPT techniques. A flowchart of ACO is shown in Figure 12.

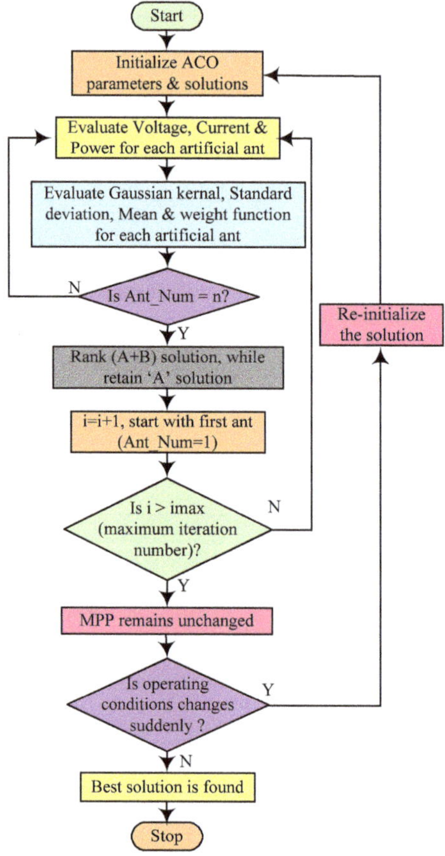

Figure 12. ACO-based MPPT technique [47].

4.2.2. Particle Swarm Optimization

PSO is a random search technique. It utilizes the principle of maximizing nonlinear continuous function. It follows the rules of natural manner of fish schooling and flock gathering. Several combined birds are used in this technique, each of which represents a particle. In search space, every particle has a fitness value mapped by a vector of position and velocity. The direction and steps of every particle are determined by their fitness value. Following that, all particles present a solution by combining the information gathered during their own search process to arrive at the optimal solution. This technique starts with random solution groups based on particles position and velocity in the search area. With the help of cerebral and social trade-off, the fitness value of particles is adjusted after each iteration. Because of the trade off, shifts in individual and community best position are obtained. Individual particles' best position is also remembered by every particle while also accumulating the global best position [48].

After each cycle, the swarm tries to determine the optimum solution by stimulating the position and velocity. Following that, a global maximum is swiftly achieved by each particle. For the kth cycle, the nth molecule refreshes the condition with position "Y" and velocity "v" as given below

$$v_n(k+1) = \omega v_n(k) + \alpha_1 \mu_1 \left(p_{p,best-k} - Y_n(k) \right) + \alpha_2 \mu_2 \left(p_{g,best} - Y_n(k) \right) \tag{14}$$

$$Y_n(k+1) = Y_n(k) + v_n(k+1) \tag{15}$$

$$n = 1, 2, 3, \ldots\ldots\ldots\ldots, N$$

If, with an improvised scenario as in Equation (16), the initialization requirement is satisfied, the technique update is in line with Equation (17):

$$ft(Y_{n-k}) > ft\left(p_{p,\,best-k} \right) \tag{16}$$

$$p_{p,\,best-k} = Y_{n-k} \tag{17}$$

"ft" must be maximized. Figure 13 shows the flowchart of the PSO algorithm to track GMPP.

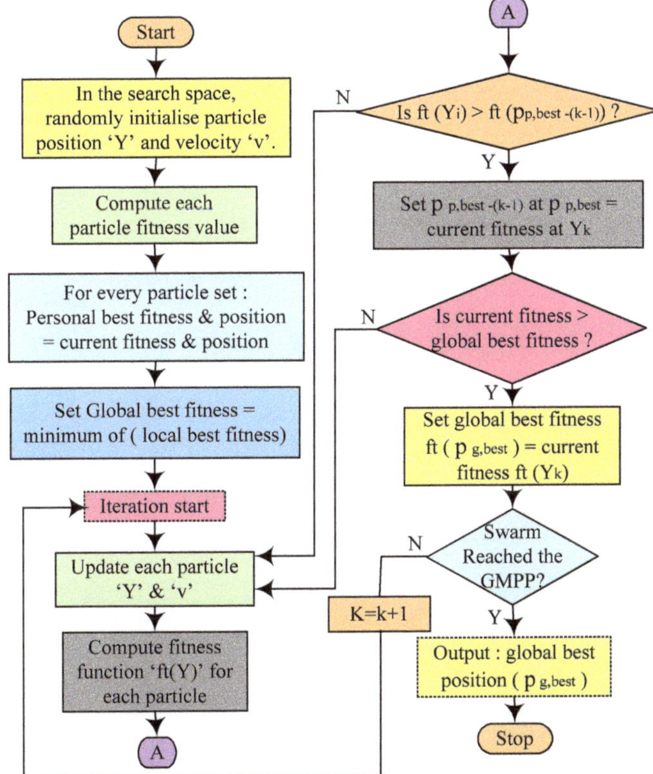

Figure 13. PSO-based MPPT technique [48].

4.2.3. Artificial Bee Colony

The ABC approach is based on honey bees' foraging intelligence. This approach is a sensible, modern, and speculative global optimization technique. Honey bees reside inside their hives and use a chemical exchange (pheromones) and the shake dance for their communication. If a bee finds a honey source (food), it takes food back to its hive by performing a shake dance to trade off the food-source site. The potency and duration of the shake dance show the richness of the food source discovered.

Three classes of artificial bee are formed by ABC algorithm, i.e., employed, scouts, and spectator bees. The hive is divided equally between employed and spectator bees. The main aim of whole bees group is to find the best honey source. Employed bees seek out a honey source (food) initially. They revisit their hive and communicate their findings with other groups of bees through shake dance movements. By carefully examining the shake dance of employee bees, spectator bees try to find the food source, while scout bees imprecisely search for new food sources. Thus, with this communication and coordination amongst them, artificial honey bees arrive at ideal solutions in the possible shortest time [49,50]. The ABC algorithm uses five phases to track GMPP as discussed below.

Phase 1: Initialization phase

First, create N_s food sources at random in the hunt arena. The algorithm's performance improves with the increase in size of the group. Each solution Y_i is an n-dimensional vector that dispenses the entire employed bee equivalent to each distinctive source of food as per Equation (18) with n optimization parameter numbered as

$$Y_{i,k} = Y_{min,i} + rand[0,1](Y_{max,i} - Y_{min,i}) \tag{18}$$

$$i = 1,2,3,\ldots\ldots N_S \& k = 1,2,3,\ldots\ldots\ldots n$$

Phase 2: Employed bee phase

The goal is to chase the food source location in the exploration region with the most nectar accessible (i.e., GMPP). Every employed bee progresses to its new position (X_i, k) in the immediate space by means of the previous position value (Y_i) to maintain the previous position value (Y_i) securely in memory according to Equation (19):

$$X_{i,k} = Y_{i,k} + \alpha_{i,k}\left(Y_{i,k} - Y_{j,k}\right); \quad j = 1,2,3,\ldots\ldots N_s \tag{19}$$

Y_j is other than Y_i, i.e., $i \neq j$, and $\alpha_{i,k}$ ranges from $[-1, 1]$.

A gluttonous assortment method is adopted by employed bees after they search a new food source. The quantity of nectar present at the previous and latest sites is compared in this technique. As a result, a better option is preserved.

Phase 3: Spectator bee phase

On the basis of the information of the food source obtained by spectator bees from employed bees with their shake dance, spectator bees use a probabilistic selection mechanism in order to identify food sources (solutions) with f(x) fitness factor according to Equation (20).

$$\hat{p}_i = \frac{f(x_i)}{\sum_{n=1}^{N_s} f(x_i)}; i = 1,2,3, \ldots\ldots, N_s \tag{20}$$

Phase 4: Scout bee phase

Scout bees can locate fresh feasible solutions on the basis of Equation (20) in the vicinity of the chosen food source. In any event, even after a thorough investigation of the entire investigated area by employed and spectator bees, the food-source fitness value remains unaffected for the existing step. The same employed bees turn into scout bees, and the scout bees use Equation (18) to hunt for new possible solutions in the next step.

Phase 5: Conclusion phase

In case that output power does not show any further improvement, the method comes to an end. The procedure, on the other hand, will restart when there is a fluctuation in output power on account of various factors. Irradiance variation is one amongst them, and such changes can be represented as

$$\left| \frac{P_{pv} - P_{pv\,old}}{P_{pv\,old}} \right| \geq \Delta P_{pv}\% \tag{21}$$

If Equation (21) is satisfied, ABC again starts searching GMPP. Hence, ABC works well in PSCs. Figure 14 shows a flowchart of the ABC technique.

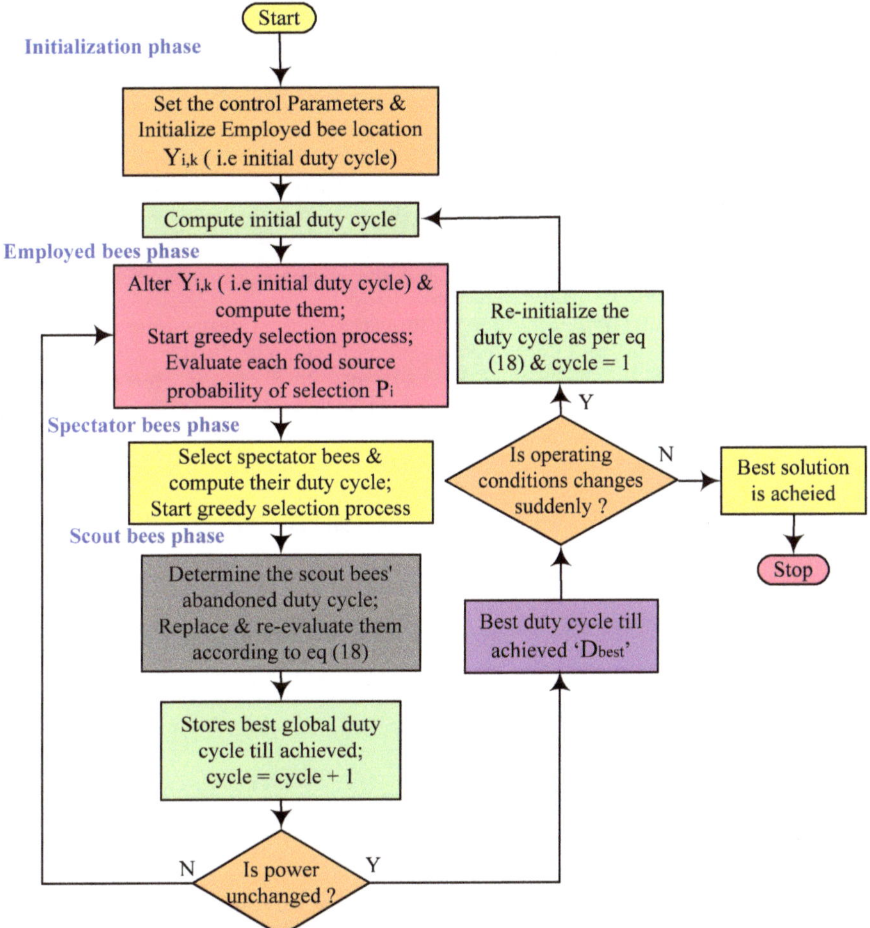

Figure 14. ABC-based MPPT technique [50].

4.2.4. Grey Wolf Optimization

The GWO technique was proposed in 2014. It is motivated by social stratification and the gray wolf's behavioral hunting personality [51]. Grey wolves, as a whole, live in packs with typical size of around 5–12. According to the hierarchical chain shown in Figure 15, grey wolves are classified into four categories based on their community supremacy. Alpha (α) wolves are the pioneer at the peak and are thus regarded as the best sources of solutions for a given optimization problem. Beta (β) wolves pursue the (α) and assist them in fulfilling their tasks. They take (α) wolves' position if the (α) wolves die. The delta (δ) wolves make up the pack's hunters, keepers, and explorers and are the second end-class. As a result, (β) and (δ) wolves represent the second- and third-best solutions, correspondingly. Omega (ω) wolves are the last group, which make up the youngest members and therefore stand for the residual solution [52].

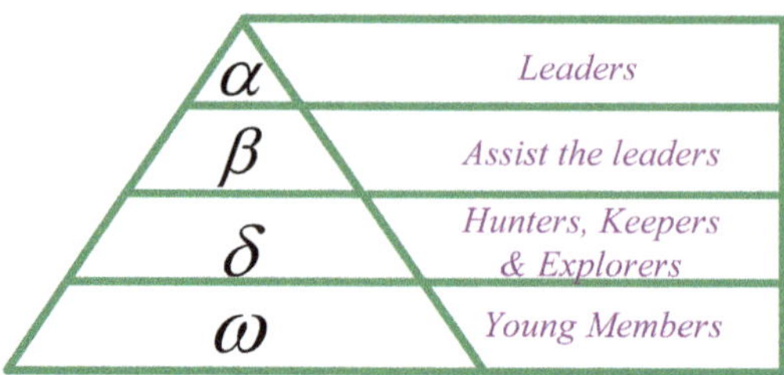

Figure 15. Grey wolves hierarchy sequence.

The supremacy of wolves is reduced as the position of the wolves lowers in the hierarchical order from top to bottom. Aside from the community order of wolves, the grey wolf's social behavior is also heavily influenced by aggregation hunting. On the basis of this, the GWO algorithm's mathematical model analyzes the following measure [52]:

Step-1: Social Hierarchy

The GWO technique presumes (α) as the fittest solution, followed by (β) and (δ) as the second- and third-finest solutions, to simulate the hierarchical system of wolves. (ω) is thought to represent the left-over contender solutions. Thus α, β and δ wolves guide the hunting process with ω wolves trailing behind.

Step-2: Tracking and Encircling the Prey

Grey wolves frequently encircle prey all through the hunting phase, expressed mathematically by Equations (22) and (23) (with iteration "i"). Equation (22) calculates a wolf's distance vector $\vec{d}$ from prey with current iteration.

$$\vec{d} = \left| \vec{B}.\vec{X}_{P_{GW}}(i) - \vec{X}_P(i) \right| \tag{22}$$

$$\vec{X}_P(i+1) = \vec{X}_{P_{GW}}(i) - \vec{A}.\vec{d} \tag{23}$$

$$\vec{A} = 2\vec{a}.\vec{r}_1 - \vec{a} \tag{24}$$

$$\vec{B} = 2\vec{r}_2 \tag{25}$$

$\vec{r}_1 \& \vec{r}_2$ ranges between [0, 1], and $\vec{a}$ = linearly decreases from 2 to 0 during each iteration.

Step-3: Hunting

Using arbitrary vectors $\vec{r}_1$ and $\vec{r}_2$, any place in between the points can be reached by a wolf. The first three best solutions (i.e., α, β, and δ wolves' locations) are initially saved. Other probing wolves alter their locations based on the top solution knowledge. As a result, a grey wolf can use this technique to improve its position in any arbitrary direction.

Step-4: Attack the Prey

Since in each cycle, the $\vec{a}$ drops linearly from 2 to 0, therefore, when $|A| < 1$ is achieved, the prey comes to a standstill in an unchanging position, and the grey wolves attack it.

Step-5: Searches for Prey

If condition $|A| > 1$ is achieved, grey wolves are compelled to look for the prey. The exploration approach is depicted in this procedure where the wolves wander away from each other in search of prey, then return to attack the prey.

In addition to this, a flowchart to explain the operation of the GWO-based MPPT technique is depicted in Figure 16.

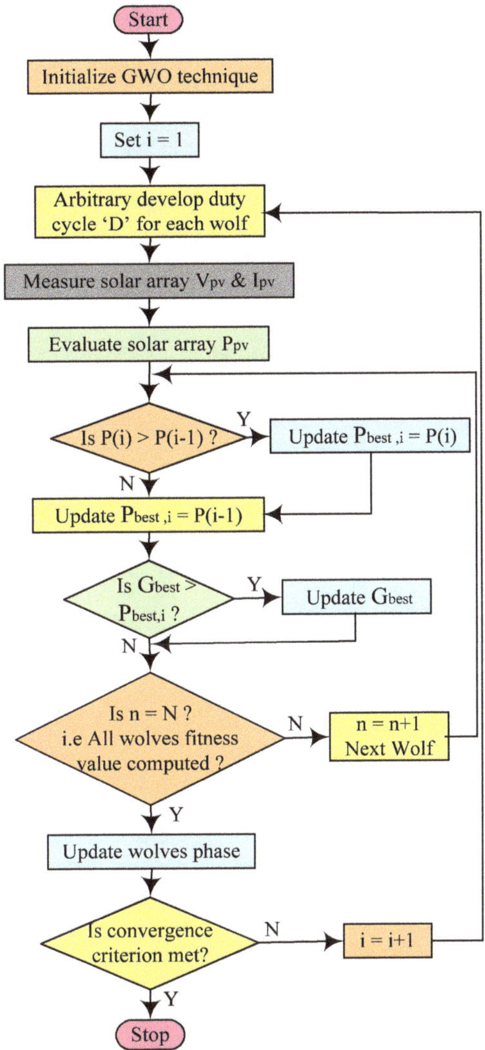

Figure 16. GWO-based MPPT technique [52].

4.2.5. Salp Swarm Algorithm (SSA)

SSA was proposed in 2017 and mimics the salps' swarm behavior. Salps are barrel-shaped, jellylike zooplankton with jellylike bodies, and they live in the deep, warm waters of the ocean. It moves by swimming with its gelatinous body, which pumps water all the way through it. It moves by constructing a chain formation of one leader, and rest follow in the chain [53]. Figure 17 shows its flowchart.

At first, a candidate solution for the leader is updated and then for the followers with the solutions found for the leaders. Let the entire chain's primary solution be given by $X_{m,n}$, where $m = 1, 2, 3, \ldots\ldots, M$ and $n = 1, 2, 3, \ldots\ldots, N$ represent salp chain size and verdict variable numbers, respectively. The leader's candidate solutions are rationalized by

$$X_{m,n}^{new} = P_n + a_1\left\{\left(X_n^+ - X_n^-\right)a_2 + X_n^-\right\}a_3 \geq 0.5 \tag{26}$$

$$X_{m,n}^{new} = P_n - a_1\left\{\left(X_n^+ - X_n^-\right)a_2 + X_n^-\right\}a_3 < 0.5 \tag{27}$$

Random numbers a_2 and a_3 are distributed evenly between [0, 1], as per the following Equation:

$$a_1 = 2e^{-(4i/I)^2} \tag{28}$$

where i= current iteration, and I= iterations maximum count.

This solution aids in updating the followers' candidate solutions:

$$X_{m,n}^{new} = \frac{X_{m,n} + X_{m-1,n}}{2} \tag{29}$$

If, after modifying the candidate solutions as recommended in Equations (26), (27), and (29), the entire chain candidate solutions still breach the minimum and maximum standards of verdict variables, the candidate solutions must be reinitialized at the appropriate minimum and maximum values of verdict variables.

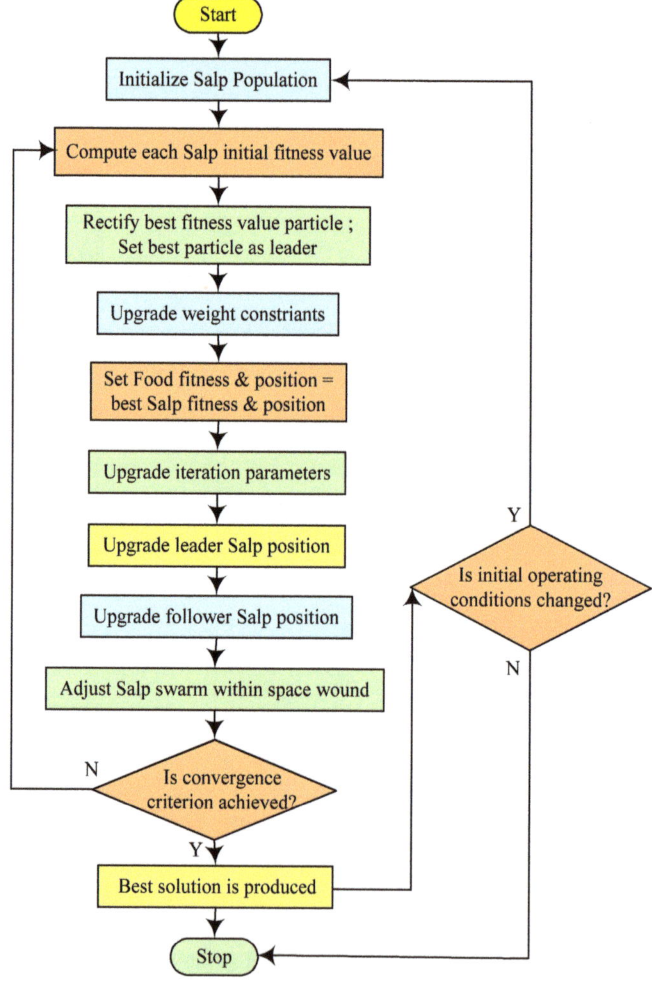

Figure 17. SSA-based MPPT technique [46].

Table 3. Taxonomy on recent reported work on swarm intelligence techniques to track GMPP.

Authors [Reference No.]	Optimization Techniques	Best Optimization Techniques	PV Module P_m (W)	PV System Size	GMPP (W)	Improved GMPP (%)	Irradiance (W/m²)	Shading Patterns	Tracking Time (s)
Krishnan SG et al. [54]	Proposed, ACO, PSO, P&O	Proposed ACO	20	4 × 4 3 × 6	63, 48.75	1.00, 32.29	NA	Non uniform	1.5, 1.56
Sridhar R et al. [55]	ACO, P&O	ACO	NA	3 PV module in series	61.4	261.1	NA	Non uniform	0.076
Alshareef M et al. [56]	APSO, PSO, P&O	APSO	NA	NA	40.56, 73.33, 76.51	13.07, 4.29, 73.49	NA	NA	1.9–2.4
Panda KP et al. [57]	Modified PSO PSO, P&O	Modified PSO	60	4 × 1	116.4	105.3	1000–400	Non uniform	0.9
Gopalakrishnan SG et al. [58]	Proposed PSO PSO, P&O	Proposed PSO	20	4 × 4 3 × 6	56.25, 48.75	18.42, 32.29	NA	Non uniform	1.9, 1.7
Mao M et al. [59]	Proposed, PSO	Proposed	83.2824	3 × 1	245.31, 60.8, 148.38	−0.28, 32.83, 1.54	1000–300	Non uniform	0.012–0.016
Koad RBA et al. [60]	LIPSO, P&O INC, PSO	LIPSO	NA	4 × 1	60.64, 48.76, 36.58, 24.29, 11.67	4.98, 12.79, 8.80, 16.23	1000–200	Uniform	NA
Belghith OB et al. [61]	PSO Fuzzy_TS P&O	PSO	150	1 PV module	148.46, 122.81, 55.67	1.48, 2.36, 5.69	1000–400	Non uniform	0.003–0.043
Obukhov S et al. [62]	VCPSO, CFPSO	VCPSO	320.4	3 PV module in series, 4 PV module in series, 8 PV module in series	960.2, 478.8, 477.8, 312.3	0.376, 0.041, 0.378, 0.192	1000–100	Non uniform	0.48–0.66
Li H et al. [63]	OD-PSO Firefly, P&O-PSO	OD-PSO	101.3	3 PV module in series	112.85, 110.85	−10.48, 4.00	1000–300	Non uniform	1.64, 2.08
Suhardi D et al. [64]	GWO INC	GWO	200	NA	203.2, 142.2, 35.9	112.19, 54.76, −50.72	1000–400	Non uniform	0.55
Kumar CS [65]	EGWO GWO PSO	EGWO	200	4 PV module in series, 2 × 2	522.629, 401.044, 522.763, 401.027	0.938, 2.707, −0.05, 7.91	1000–400	Non uniform	3.6–4.8
Shi JY et al. [66]	P&O, PSO GWO, GWO-P&O GWO-GSO	GWO-GSO	60	4 × 1	100.72	100.95	1000–300	Non uniform	0.64
Ilyas M [67]	Modified GWO GWO	Modified GWO	100	4 PV module in series, 2 × 2	444.65, 435.76	0.234, 0.045	NA	Non uniform	0.189, 0.21
Kraiem H et al. [68]	PSO, GWO	PSO	249	4 PV module in series	645.6, 633.9, 359.1	0.077, 0.939, 0.447	1000–200	Non uniform	0.0561–0.071
Jamaludin MNI et al. [69]	SSA PSO GOA GWO BOA HC	SSA	59.85	4 × 1	136.3, 114.3, 176.9	23.5, 107.7, 58.93	1000–500	Non uniform	0.22, 2.3, 4.2
Dagal I et al. [70]	Hybrid SSPSO P&O FA DE ISSA	SSPSO	60	4 PV module in series	124.09	6.55	1000–400	Non uniform	0.29

Table 3. *Cont.*

Authors [Reference No.]	Optimization Techniques	Best Optimization Techniques	PV Module P_m (W)	PV System Size	GMPP (W)	Improved GMPP (%)	Irradiance (W/m^2)	Shading Patterns	Tracking Time (s)
Krishnan S et al. [71]	SSO WOA GWO	SSO	220.5	3 PV module in series 2X2	294.8, 41.8, 525.4, 38.5, 445.2, 02.7	5.58, 10.04, 39.92, 14.67, 14.97, 28.43	750–500	Non uniform	0.0245–0.0749
Farzaneh J et al. [72]	P&O, FFA, PSO, DE, SSA, ISSA	ISSA	60	4 PV module in series	115.59	6.53	1000–400	Non uniform	1.22
Ali MHM [73]	P&O, SSO	SSO	NA	NA	843.5	2.55	200	Uniform	0.72
Balaji V et al. [74]	Hybrid SSPO SS, PO	Hybrid SSPO	50	4 PV module in series	50.3, 85.1, 78.2, 96.1	27.66, 0.09, 24.32, 51.10	1000–200	Non uniform	0.52–0.57
Restrepo C et al. [75]	ABC-P&O GMPPT P&O	ABC-P&O	200.143	4 PV module in series	597.95	54.19	900–120	Non uniform	NA
Sawant PT et al. [76]	ABC, PSO	ABC	75	NA	74, 61	2.77, 3.38	1000–800	Non uniform	NA
Li N et al. [77]	P&O, PSO ABC, MABC	Modified MABC	NA	2 PV module in series	850	70.68	1000–800	Non uniform	0.39
Wan Y et al. [78]	SSA-GWO, P&O, PSO, SSA	SSA-GWO	35	3 PV module in series	104.88, 44.55, 69.32	0.788, 28.60, 1.612	1000–300	Non uniform	0.46, 0.53, 0.47
Hayder W et al. [79]	IPSO, PSO-P&O, ANN-PSO	IPSO	120	NA	119.9720, 69.9888, 94.9073, 45.3924	NA	1000–400	Non uniform	1.5
Almutairi A et al. [80]	OGWO, P&O	OGWO	60	NA	60, 47.8, 23	32.77	NA	Non uniform	0.5, <1,
Sharma A et al. [81]	TSA-PSO, FPA, GWO, TSA, PSO, P&O	TSA-PSO	85	3 PV module in series	103.36, 122.88, 156.84	22.20, 5.97, 13.11	1000–300	Non uniform	0.38, 0.54, 0.40
Chao K-H et al. [82]	I-ABC, PSO, P&O, ABC	I-ABC	20	4 × 3	246.6, 198.6, 148.8, 107.1, 77.1	0.08, 2.00, 0.881, 17.43, 66.88	NA	Non uniform	0.38, 0.63, 0.89, 1.48, 1.14
Alaraj M et al. [83]	HGWO, PSO, INC	HGWO	450	5 × 5	8256, 6441, 6347, 5567	13.23, 13.09, 20.50, 22.86	1000–400	Non uniform	0.08, 0.07
Windarko N A et al. [84]	Proposed, DE, FF, PSO, GWO	Proposed	100	3 PV module in series	172.9, 170.9, 80.9	5.81, 65.60, 226.2	1000–100	Non uniform	0.45, 0.41, 0.52
Chawda G S et al. [85]	ICPSO, P&O, INC, GA-based FLC, PSO-based FLC PSO-GA-FLC	ICPSO	NA	NA	97.3, 60, 94.2	7.955, 11.77	1000–300	Non uniform	0.1

Table 4. Pros and cons of recent work based on swarm intelligence techniques.

Authors [Reference No.]	Pros	Cons
Krishnan SG et al. [54]	• High tracking efficiency • Less iterations are required to achieve GMPP • Less ripples in output power	• Convergence time can further be reduced • Computationally complex
Sridhar R et al. [55]	• Ability to achieve high GMPP in PSCs	• Tracking time is high when compared with conventional technique • Required more numbers of iterations
Alshareef M et al. [56]	• Can distinguish between LMPP and GMPP • Fast dynamic response	• Tracking time can further be improved • Oscillations around GMPP
Pandal KP et al. [57]	• No oscillations in steady state • Both good and worst position of particle is considered	• High computational complexity • Required more number of iterations
Gopalakrishnan SK et al. [58]	• Ability to achieve true GMPP in PSCs	• Oscillations in steady state • High tracking time
Mao M et al. [59]	• With adaptive inertia factor, tracking time is improved • Low MPP tracking error in PSCs	• Computationally more complex • Oscillations around GMPP • Require more number of iterations
Koad RBA et al. [60]	• High tracking efficiency • Less iterations are required to reach at GMPP	• Algorithm estimates three sets of duty cycle making it more intricate in design
Belghith OB et al. [61]	• Takes less time to reach at MPP • High accuracy	• Cannot track GMPP in some changing irradiance condition
Obukhov S et al. [62]	• Optimal parameters of PSO is conveniently selected	• Time to track GMPP can be further improved
Li H et al. [63]	• Required less number of iterations • Low power fluctuations	• High tracking time • Trapped in LMPP is some cases when tested on hardware

Table 4. *Cont.*

Authors [Reference No.]	Pros	Cons
Suhardi D et al. [64]	• Low power loss while tracking GMPP	• Cannot achieve GMPP is some shading conditions • Tracking time can further be improved
Kumar CS et al. [65]	• Low standard deviation	• Very high tracking time • Trapped in local GMPP
Shi JY et al. [66]	• Highly accurate • Hunting process is accelerated by varying decision weight	• Comparatively more iterations are required results in power loss • Intricate to design
Ilyas M et al. [67]	• High tracking efficiency • Algorithm modified the surrounding and hunting behavior that finds the optimum solution correctly	• Oscillations around GMPP • Computationally more complex
Kraiem H et al. [68]	• Low tracking time • Low oscillations around GMPP	• High computational complexity • .
Jamaludin MNI et al. [69]	• High accuracy • Zero steady state oscillations • High convergence speed	• Inability to deal with rapidly changing environment conditions • Information regarding change in landscape fitness is not considered while tracking GMPP • Required periodic tuning
Dagal I et al. [70]	• High tracking efficiency	• Not tested on hardware setup
Krishnan S et al. [71]	• No periodic tuning is required • Low computational complexity in comparison to other metaheuristic approaches	• Oscillations around GMPP • Requires large number of iterations
Farzaneh J et al. [72]	• No oscillations around GMPP • High tracking efficiency	• High tracking time • Computationally more complex to design
Ali MHM [73]	• High tracking efficiency	• Oscillations around GMPP

Table 4. *Cont.*

Authors [Reference No.]	Pros	Cons
Balaji V et al. [74]	• fewer initializations of parameters • reduced oscillations in initial stage of tracking	• Hardware validation is not done • .
Restrepo C et al. [75]	• Rapid control loops • Quick response	• High computational constraint
Sawant PT et al. [76]	• Highly accurate	• Intricate to design • Hardware validation is not done
Li N et al. [77]	• High tracking efficiency	• Computationally more complex to design
Wan Y et al. [78]	• Accurate GMPP tracking • Low power fluctuations	• Parameter initialization is required • Low oscillations in steady state
Hayder W et al. [79]	• High accuracy	• Temperature effect is neglected in testing
Almutairi A et al. [80]	• Low fluctuation of power in steady state around MPP	• High tracking time • More number of iterations are required
Sharma A et al. [81]	• Fast tracking capability • Less number of iteration is required	• High computational complexity
Chao K-H et al. [82]	• Low power losses during power-generation process	• High tracking time in complex PSCs
Alaraj M et al. [83]	• Low convergence factor • Low rise and settling time	• Highly intricate to design
Windarko N A et al. [84]	• High energy tracking capability • Random calculations are avoided which minimize unnecessary duty cycle	• High cost of implementation
Chawda G S et al. [85]	• Low tracking time • INC is utilized to update particle position and velocity, resulting in high dynamic response	• Computationally more complex

4.3. Bio Inspired Techniques

This part of the paper elaborates various MPPT techniques inspired by biological behavior of different organism. Additionally, various recent works done to track MPP incorporating these techniques are tabulated in Tables 5 and 6.

4.3.1. Firefly MPPT Algorithm

Fireflies are beetles emitting light in the night and communicate amongst themselves using a special light pattern. The light color formed by each species is unique. The FFA's hunting tactic is governed by firefly attraction, which is equivalent to brightness. A dimmer firefly approaches a brighter one, and if their brightness level is the same as that of a certain firefly, it will shift at random [86]. The key purpose of flashing in the FFA tactic is to allure other fireflies and attract their target. The charm of fireflies is governed by the intensity of the firefly along with the objective function value. The value of attraction "μ" is resolute by the evaluation of other fireflies and is diverge on the basis of "i" and "j" fireflies' distance "D_{ij}". Both can be evaluated as per Equations (30) and (31), with "D" as the distance between two fireflies, "β" as an arbitrary constant that lies between 0.1 and 10, and "n" as the dimension number.

$$\mu = \mu_0 \ e^{-\beta D^2} \tag{30}$$

$$D_{ij} = |x_i - x_j| = \sqrt[2]{\sum_{y=1}^{n}(x_{i,y} - x_{j,y})^2} \tag{31}$$

$D = 1$ is taken in MPPT problems because it is a one-dimensional case. A flowchart of FFA is shown in Figure 18.

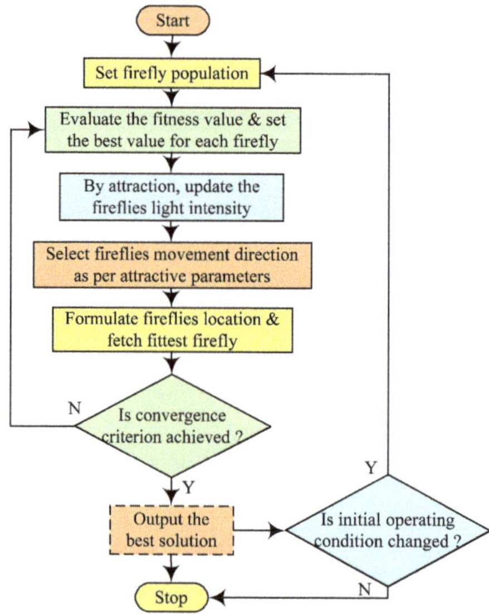

Figure 18. FFA-based MPPT technique [46].

4.3.2. Cuckoo Search

This bio-inspired technique was reported in 2009 and is inspired by the cuckoo species' parasitic imitation tactic (brood-parasitism) [87]. Certain birds, such as cuckoos (Tapera), engage in social parasitism. The Tapera is a knowledgeable winged creature that fits in with the host fowls, and with this tactic, next-generation endurance is encouraged. Rather than building its own nest, the cuckoo places its eggs in the nests of other flying species. Primarily, the cuckoo bird (female) flies erratically in search of a nest with similar egg characteristics to their own. After finding the best nest, cuckoo eggs have the utmost opportunity of hatching, ensuring the new generation. The cuckoo makes a few attempts by assisting the incubating bird in laying their eggs in a suitable location and hence gives itself a better chance. The cuckoo may occasionally throw the eggs of the host species from the nest because host birds could be readily duped into recognizing the strange eggs. If the host bird comes to know about the foreign eggs, the eggs will definitely be dumped outside the nest. The host bird may even demolish the nest.

For optimization objectives, the CS approach is an effective meta-heuristic method. Three idealized principles used to accomplish this strategy are as follows:

- Every cuckoo bird merely lays one egg at a time in a hastily chosen host nest;
- The cuckoos' subsequent generation will be carried on by the superior eggs' nest (i.e., the best solutions);
- In the hunt area, the entire number of reachable host nests is fixed.

Cuckoo birds represent the particles relegated to find the solution in the CS strategy implementation, and their eggs indicate the current iteration's solution to an optimization problem. Searching for a nest is comparable to searching for food, and in CS, it is described by Levy flight. A Levy flight "y" is an arbitrary stride where Levy distribution is used to evaluate sizes of steps by using a power law [88]:

$$y = L^{-\gamma} \, ; \, (1 < \gamma < 3) \tag{32}$$

Thus, "y" has an infinite variance. The new cuckoo solution $\left(x^{i+1}\right)$ for ith iteration cycle "i" and the nth particle "n" can be generated as

$$x_n^{i+1} = x_n^i + z(\, levy\,(\gamma)) \tag{33}$$

"z" is a mathematical operator that represents the multidimensional problem's entrywise multiplication.

In each iteration cycle, all particles transmit Levy flights until they find GMPP. Figure 19 shows the flowchart of the CS algorithm to track GMPP.

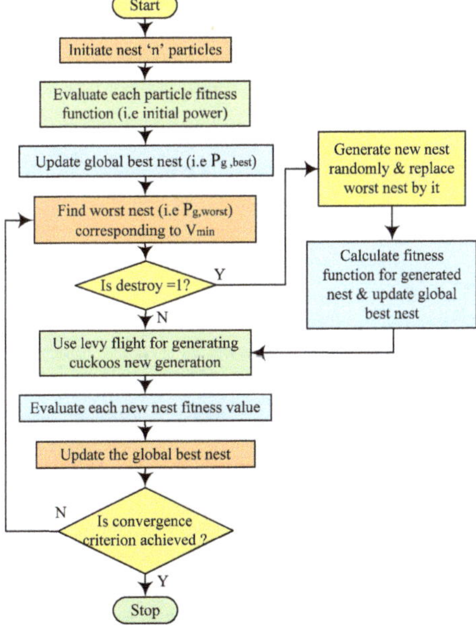

Figure 19. CS-based MPPT technique [87].

4.3.3. Flying Squirrel Search Optimization

This bio-inspired optimization approach to track GMPP was introduced in 2020 and mimics the highly effective hunting tactic used by southern flying squirrels [89]. This approach also mimics the squirrels' manner of buoyant headways in the air. The posture of FS is referenced to as the feasible outcome vector and the comparable wellness is typical food source, respectively.

The posture is divided into three districts addressing sets based on wellness value:

- BS (hickory nut tree);
- CBS (acorn nut tree);
- US (ordinary tree).

Following assumptions are made while incorporating FSSO [89] in tracing GMPP:
The food supply point is similar to the power yield from PV;
DC converter duty ratio (∂) in the MPPT approach is regarded as option variable, i.e., the posture;
To reduce the tracking time, the FSSO approach is custom-fitted by eliminating the occurrence of hunters.

The following steps are taken into account while implementing the FSSO technique.

Starting: Initially, FSs "N" numbers are placed at various locations. In the solution area, the duty ratio of the DC converter can be estimated for "i" iteration count by these points as follows:

$$\partial_i = \partial_{min} + \frac{(i-1)(\partial_{max} - \partial_{min})}{N} \quad ; i = 1, 2, 3, \ldots \ldots N \tag{34}$$

Wellness evaluation: The DC converter employed is gradually running with each duty ratio in this progression (i.e., with each FS posture). Each food source feature shows instantaneous power yield PV (∂) for each "∂". This sequence is repeated for all "∂", whereas MPPT goal wellness function "$f(\partial)$" can be determined as

$$f(\partial) = \max\,(PV(\partial)) \tag{35}$$

- Declaration and categorization: The duty cycle at which the system yields maximum power is considered as hickory tree, while acorn trees are considered as the most excellent FS positions;
- Posture update: After the examination of occasional observing situation, the duty cycle is updated, and wellness is assessed from that point.

Important conditions followed in FSSA are as follows:
Occasional observing conditions: These conditions help FSSA to avoid being stuck in LMPP. The cyclic constant (O_C) and its base value (O_{min}) for a single-dimensional space with "i and i_m" as the count of the present and maximum number of cycles allowed are

$$O_C^i = \left| x_{at}^i - x_{ht} \right| \tag{36}$$

$$O_{min} = 10e^{-6}/365^{i/i_m} \tag{37}$$

For investigating the superior search area, Levy distribution is employed. As a result, the OTFS duty cycle is relocated.

- Groove contemporized: Squirrels of hickory tree maintain their position. The squirrels on acorn tree, on the other hand, find a way to access the hickory tree. The arbitrarily chosen squirrel (ATFS) from normal trees chooses the hickory tree, while the leftover (NTFS-ATFS) is pressed to the acorn tree. The duty cycle is changed:

$$\partial_{at}^{i+1} = \partial_{at}^i + H_c h_d \left(\partial_{ht}^i - \partial_{at}^i \right) \tag{38}$$

$$\partial_{ot}^{i+1} = \partial_{ot}^{i} + H_c h_d \left(\partial_{ht}^{i} - \partial_{ot}^{i} \right) \tag{39}$$

$$\partial_{ot}^{i+1} = \partial_{ot}^{i} + H_c h_d \left(\partial_{at}^{i} - \partial_{ot}^{i} \right) \tag{40}$$

- Convergence Resolution: If the utmost number of iterations has been reached, the algorithm is terminated and gives the duty cycle at the point where the converter follows GMPP.
- Re-initialization: In rapidly changing environmental conditions, the duty ratio (FSs posture) is reinitialized to hunt new GMPP in accordance with Equation (41).

$$\frac{P_{pv}^{i+1} - P_{pv}^{i}}{P_{pv}^{i+1}} \geq \Delta P \ (\%) \tag{41}$$

The complete steps of FSSO algorithm in tracking GMPP are depicted in Figure 20.

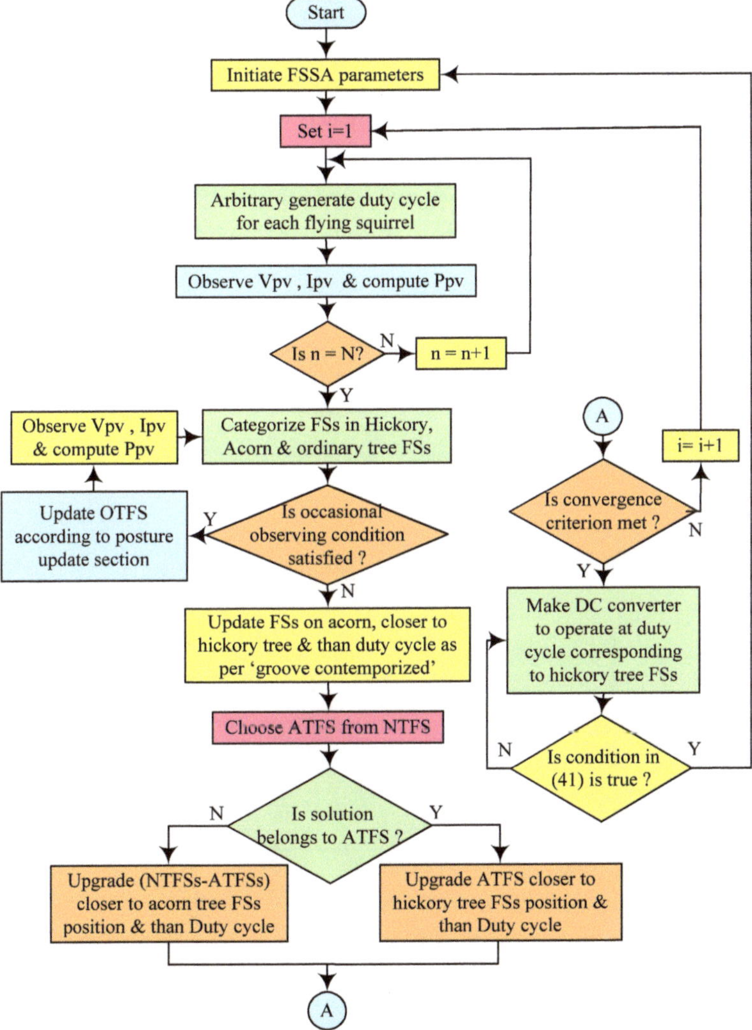

Figure 20. FSSO-based MPPT technique [89].

Table 5. Taxonomy on recent reported work on bio-inspired techniques to track GMPP.

Authors [Reference No.]	Optimization Techniques	Best Optimization Techniques	PV Module P_m (W)	PV System Size	GMPP (W)	Improved GMPP (%)	Irradiance (W/m²)	Shading Patterns	Tracking Time (s)
Saad W et al. [90]	Proposed FA, P&O	Proposed	200	1PV module	201.7 37.7	2.40, 8.02	1000 and 200	Non uniform	NA
Farzaneh J et al. [91]	MFA, P&O PSO, FA	MFA	200.143	4 PV module in series	397.52	9.41	1000–400	Non uniform	2.22
Nusaif AI et al. [92]	MFA, P&O PSO, FA	MFA	265.737	3 × 3	1264, 1206, 1582, 834	1.77, 31.08, 17.70, 27.91	1000–100	Non uniform	0.085–0.124
Abo-Khalil AG et al. [93]	OFA, FA P&O	OFA	NA	NA	48, 36.5, 29	0.418, 2.24, 34.88	NA	Non uniform	0.2–0.33
Shi J-Y [94]	INC-FA, P&O INC, FA	INC-FA	60	4 × 1	81.4	76.19	1000–100	Non uniform	0.98
Omar FA et al. [95]	Proposed FA P&O	Proposed FA	NA	3 PV module in series	100,150,200, 300,400,500	25.00, 2.04, 108.33, 100, 110.52, 170.27	NA	Non uniform	1.3
Chitra A et al. [96]	INC, FA, MFA	MFA	200.143	2 PV module in series	330, 255	6.24, 3.23	1000–600	Non uniform	0.0018–0.0064
Mosaad MI et al. [97]	CS, NN, INC	CS	59.9	1PV module	60.47, 48.24	2.68, 3.36	1000–800	uniform	NA
Shi J-Y et al. [98]	ICS, CS PSO, P&O	ICS	60	4 PV module in series	87.547	74.97	1000–200	Non uniform	0.88
Hidayat T et al. [99]	CSA, P&O	CSA	72	2 PV module in series	97, 107.92, 107.63, 114.94, 124.56, 74.53, 72.58	45.86, 70.75, 63.99, 77.89, 81.52, 5.40, 0.276	944–495	Non uniform	NA
Bilgin N et al. [100]	FFO, PSO, CSO, BOA	FFO	NA	3 PV module in series	531.46, 377.63	5.73, 4.26	1000–278	Non uniform	NA
Ibrahim A-W et al. [101]	CSA, MPSO, MP&O, ANN	CSA	250	4 PV module in series	699.6, 928.5, 534.7, 694.7	67.93, 29.40, 13.25, 4.215	1000–400	Non uniform	0.5–0.7
Bentata K et al. [102]	DCSA, CSA	DCSA	249	2 × 2, 4 PV module in series, 3 × 2, 6 PV module in series	989.29, 482.06, 797.3, 656.45	0.00, 13.31, 6.40, 16.09	1000–200	Non uniform	0.046- 0.085
Singh N et al. [103]	FSSO, P&O, PSO, GWO	FSSO	40	4 PV module in series, 2 × 2	61.66, 48.65, 79.75, 35.37	107.53, 85.68, 61.73, 3.23	900–100	Non uniform	0.3–1.8
Fares D et al. [104]	ISSA, SSA, PSO, GA	ISSA	135	3 PV module in series	227.83, 142.82, 98.79	0.065, 0.098, 0.050	900–100	Non uniform	0.2
Al-Shammaa A A et al. [105]	CS, PSO	CS	NA	4 PV module in series	293.57, 415.38, 578.96	0.00, 0.67, 0.52	1000–200	Non uniform	1.32, 1.29, 1.28
Watanabe R B et al. [106]	FF, P&O	FF	213.15	3 PV module in series	638.7, 553.1, 316.9	0.251, 31.87, 58.05	1000–300	Non uniform	0.18, 0.22, 0.21

Table 6. Pros and cons of recent work based on bio-inspired techniques.

Authors [Reference No.]	Pros	Cons
Saad W et al. [90]	• Zero oscillations around GMPP • High tracking efficiency	• Algorithm is not validated on hardware • Highly intricate to design
Farzaneh J et al. [91]	• Requires no periodic tuning • High accuracy	• Very high tracking time
Nusaif AI et al. [92]	• Varying population size is adapted in each iteration, resulting in improved tracking time and efficiency	• Oscillations around GMPP
Abo-Khalil AG et al. [93]	• High tracking efficiency • Able to process examine MPP	• Power oscillations around GMPP
Shi JY [94]	• High switching speed during shaded to unshaded conditions • No oscillations in steady state	• High tracking time • Computationally complex compared to other MPPT approaches
Omar FA et al. [95]	• High tracking efficiency • Less complex to implement	• High convergence time • Required sensors for its operation
Chitra A et al. [96]	• Very low tracking time	• Low tracking efficiency • Many parameters initializations are required
Mosaad MI et al. [97]	• Randomization process makes the algorithm more effective	• Required tuning of parameters
Shi J-Y et al. [98]	• Tracking ability is enhanced by introducing adaptive step concept • Random steps of CS are eliminated	• High computational complexity
Hidayat T et al. [99]	• Track MPP efficiently in different PSCs	• Levy flight affects the convergence level • Oscillations around GMPP
Bilgin N et al. [100]	• High tracking efficiency	• No record of tracking time in different PSCs • Large no of iterations are required
Ibrahim A-W et al. [101]	• Not dependent on initial location	• Low oscillations around GMPP
Bentata K et al. [102]	• Initial particles are independent • Requires smaller number of iterations which saves power	• Requires higher number of particles • Highly intricate to design
Singh N et al. [103]	• Predators are eliminated for modifying squirrel positions	• High tracking time • High computational cost
Fares D et al. [104]	• High tracking efficiency	• High execution intricacy • Oscillations around GMPP
Al-Shammaa A A et al. [105]	• Only two control parameters are required • No initial situations are assumed for working	• High tracking time • Oscillations in steady state.
Watanabe R B et al. [106]	• Low tracking time	• Power variations in steady state.

4.4. Other AI-Based MPPT

This section of the paper explains other artificial intelligence methods applied in the field of tracking maximum power from the PV array along with a report of the various latest research performed concerning it in Tables 7 and 8 respectively.

4.4.1. Fuzzy Logic Control

FLC converts its analog input to digital values. This technique examines the output power of PV array for every sample. If the change fraction is greater than zero, voltage is enhanced by FLC by adjusting the duty cycle and vice versa. As a result, the maximum power ratio is zero. FLC inputs error "e", and its change "∂e" with samples in time "k_i" can be computed as

$$e = \frac{P_{pv}(k) - P_{pv}(k-1)}{V_{pv}(k) - V_{pv}(k-1)} \tag{42}$$

$$\partial e = e(k) - e(k-1) \tag{43}$$

Figure 21 shows a block diagram of FLC control. The input variables are changed to linguistic variables by using different distinct membership functions. Thereafter, they are manipulated on the basis of the "if-then" rule by applying the required conduct of the scheme. Finally, they are converted to their numerical equivalent [107]. This approach shows fewer oscillations, fast response [108], and high tracking efficiency in contrast to conventional MPPT approaches. However, it suffers from high computational complexity.

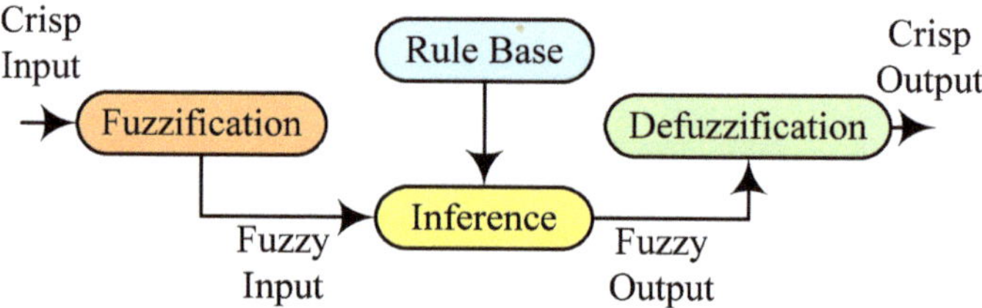

Figure 21. Block representation of FLC-based MPPT.

4.4.2. Artificial Neural Network

An ANN is a set of static learning models. For anticipating a precise output for each input, this approach simulates a biological neural system. Figure 22 shows the three-layered structure of ANN in which the neuron quantity in each layer varies depending on the situation.

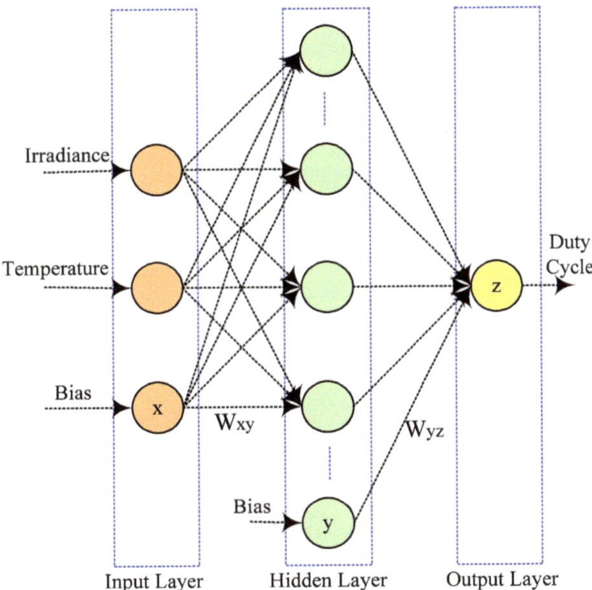

Figure 22. Three-layer structure of ANN [109].

These networks are used as an MPP system to predict the best possible values of power or voltage that can be produced at a given time. These values act as base values in deciding the converter's duty cycle. The PV module parameters and atmospheric parameters are included in the input variables and then processed by hidden layers in the network. The procreation algorithm is retroactive and grades in a mishap. Thereafter, utilizing neurons of center layer, it feeds back the output through the input neurons. The following Equation is used to calculate the presence of hidden neurons:

$$n_h = \frac{1}{2}(n_i + n_o) + \sqrt{n_t} \tag{44}$$

A complete experimental setup assists in data collection. The dataset is then obtained by feeding atmospheric conditions and array parameters into the ANN to find output V_m and P_m. This set is then transformed into an instructional one, which moves into the premeditated ANN, where it is taught how to perform. Moreover, the functions of input data serve as instruction data for the ANN model that was created. Then, the model learns how to execute on its own. The assessment datasets examine the performance of the constructed ANN after the instruction phase, and the errors are sent back to the ANN until all of the neurons' weights are changed correctly. MPPT using ANN is more accurate and shows less oscillation around MPP [109]. These algorithms suffer from the drawback of high computational complexity.

4.4.3. Evolutionary Computational Techniques

Evolutionary computation is an area of artificial intelligence and soft computing that studies a family of algorithms for global optimization inspired by biological evolution. GA and DE are ones amongst them used to track MPP.

GA is a computer model that is inspired by evolution and consists of chromosomes. These chromosomes include information on a potential solution to a problem. Each chromosome has its own set of characteristics. This algorithm is used in wide applications. In contrast to tracking MPP, it is able to boost the PV voltage, which represents the chromosomes and their fitness value that corresponds to PV power. The main idea is to make genetic changes to a population of people and discover the ideal ones corresponding to the fitness function. Figure 23 shows the flowchart of GA.

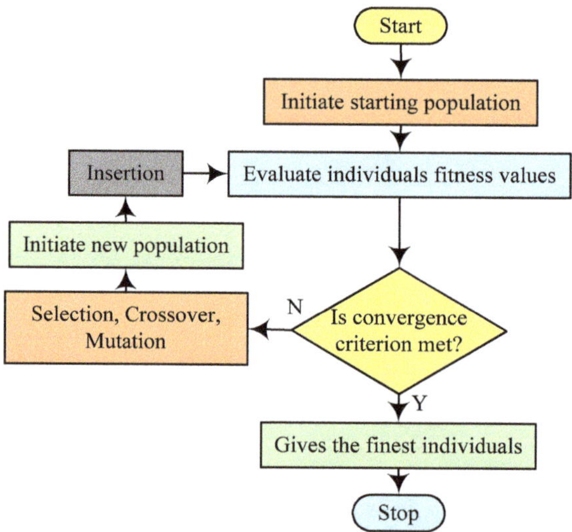

Figure 23. Flowchart of GA [110].

DE is another evolutionary computational algorithm applied to problems based on global optimization. It is applicable to track GMPP in PSCs due to its simpler execution and wide search freedom. The DC converter duty cycle is used as a target vector "∂_n" by this approach. Initially, the target vector with two dimensions is initialized as "∂_n" for each iteration and generation as the population. It chooses three random particles after one generation in order to reduce the execution time. Following that, the selected duty cycles are used to calculate the PV array's associated powers "P_n". "P_{best}" is picked as the maximum power in the set of "P_n", and "∂_{best}" is chosen as the corresponding "∂_n". The weight difference between any two target vectors is then used by a mutation factor (M) and forms the mutated particle by adding this difference to the remaining target vector. The mutated particle is also called the donor vector "DV_n". The mutation's way should be towards "P_{best}". Following mutation, donor and target vectors are combined by a crossover procedure to create trial vector "TV_n" and estimate the PV array's power.

Table 7. Taxonomy on recent reported work on other artificial intelligence techniques to track GMPP.

Authors [Reference No.]	Optimization Techniques	Best Optimization Techniques	PV Module P_m (W)	PV System Size	GMPP (W)	Improved GMPP (%)	Irradiance (W/m²)	Shading Patterns	Tracking Time (s)
Verma P et al. [111]	AFLC, FLC P&O	AFLC	360	3 PV module in series	521.5, 250.6, 198.1	7.30, 0.642, 4.26	900–100	Non uniform	0.1–0.19
Rahman MM et al. [112]	PSO-ANN PSO	PSO-ANN	60.53	4 PV module in series	135.9, 202.1	0.00, −0.04	900–400	Non uniform	0.22, 0.21
Farzaneh J [113]	Proposed P&O, PSO	Proposed	60	3 PV module in series	87.12, 116.74	46.00, 94.17	1000–300	Non uniform	0.15, 0.1
Manikandan PV [114]	Proposed P&O	Proposed	320	1 PV module	36.88, 37.2, 37.66	53.73, 50.12, 51.36	1200–400	Non uniform	NA
Al-Majidi SDet al. [115]	ANFIS FLC, P&O	ANFIS	185	5 PV module in series	924	0.2168	1000	Uniform	0.07
Aymen J et al. [116]	Neuro fuzzy Fuzzy	Neuro fuzzy	60	1PV module	50.262, 45.736, 40.856, 35.633, 30.156	0.001, −0.004, 0.0171, 0.0533, 0.0763	1000–600	Non uniform	NA
Farajdadian S [117]	AF-FA AF-PSO SF, PSO, P&O	AF-FA	220.7	NA	220.5, 175.1, 124.3	1.37, 20.26, 72.87	1000–600	Non uniform	NA
Eltamalya AM et al. [118]	GWO-FLC PSO	GWO-FLC	185.22	NA	54.6, 92.8	40.00, 20.51	1000–200	Non uniform	NA
Chen Y-T et al. [119]	Proposed fixed-step INC FLC-HC ASVSS	Proposed	60	NA	157.3,46.83	5.92, 2.51	1000 and 300	Non uniform	0.42, 0.52
Raj A et al. [120]	ANN-INC INC, P&O	ANN-INC	NA	NA	450	6.13	NA	Non uniform	NA
Abdellatif WSE et al. [121]	FB, P&O, INC	FB	305.226	NA	100.38, 80.17, 59.87	3.14, 3.13, 3.11	1000–600	Non uniform	NA
Mohammed SS et al. [122]	GA fuzzy Fuzzy ANFICS	GA fuzzy	60	1 PV module	44.17, 36.11, 41.68, 41.70, 24.07	0.546, 5.64, 0.506, 0.870, 11.22	791–481.1	Non uniform	NA
Tandel BG et al. [123]	GA, P&O	GA	200.143	16 PV module in series	1319.12	81.16	1000–250	Non uniform	NA
Karthika S et al. [124]	GA-tuned PI PI	GA-tuned PI	200	7 × 7	7020	56.69	1000 and 200	Non uniform	0.001
Dehghani M et al. [125]	PSO-GA PSO, GA INC, P&O	PSO-GA	1S	NA	98.85, 78.69, 58.64	9.67, 9.30, 9.23	1000–600	Non uniform	< 0.3
Bendary FM et al. [126]	ANFIS-GA ANFIS, NN, FLC	ANFIS-GA	40.9081	NA	40.90, 27.78, 19.28	15.24, 0.908, 1.10	1000–500	Non uniform	< 0.3
Firmanza AP et al. [127]	Proposed DE PSO	Proposed DE	100	2 PV module in series	170.5, 87.9, 152, 130.9	1.66, −0.34, 0.462, 0.383	1000–400	Non uniform	0.233- 0.371

Table 7. *Cont.*

Authors [Reference No.]	Optimization Techniques	Best Optimization Techniques	PV Module P_m (W)	PV System Size	GMPP (W)	Improved GMPP (%)	Irradiance (W/m^2)	Shading Patterns	Tracking Time (s)
Neethu M. et al. [128]	DE PSO	DE	215	4 PV module in series	663.8	81.41	900–600	Non uniform	366
Kamaruddina NI et al. [129]	DE, P&O	DE	125	3×3	489.3, 497.2	39.87, 56.40	1000–250	Non uniform	NA
Joisher M et al. [130]	Proposed, PSO, DE	Proposed	95	2 PV module in series	11, 20.33, 13.88	120.0, 18.40, 16.5	NA	Non uniform	1.0
Algarín C R et al. [131]	FLC P&O	FLC	65	1 PV module	11.7, 24.4, 37.7, 51.3, 64.9	0.00	1000–200	Non uniform	NA
Cheng P-C et AL. [132]	Asymmetrical FLC, Symmetrical FLC, P&O	Asymmetrical FLC	220	NA	44.12, 222.18	6.134, 04.53	1000 and 200	Non uniform	0.7, 5.6
Liu C-L et al. [133]	Asymmetrical FLC, Symmetrical FLC, P&O	Asymmetrical FLC	220	NA	222.69	7.63	1000	Uniform	0.91
Kececioglu O F et al. [134]	Proposed, AIC	Proposed	250	1 PV module	249.4, 244.2	0.605, 0.825,	1000–600	Non uniform	0.008
Hayder W et al. [135]	NN-P&O IPSO	NN-P&O	120	1 PV Module	90.2943, 55.2495, 73.076, 98.6604	0.00	1100–600	Uniform	0.2003, 0.0003, 0.7003, 0.0003
Hua C-C et al. [136]	Proposed, P&O+PSO, GA	Proposed	21.31	3 PV module in series	42.90, 37.38, 32.56, 26.73, 22.06	2.21, 0.402, 0.618, 0.074, 5.499	1000–300	Non uniform	12, 15, 16
Zhang P et al. [137]	Improved DE, DE, PSO	Improved DE	NA	4X3	644.57, 857.56	0.041, 0.282	800–350	Non uniform	0.019, 0.02
Bakkar M et al. [138]	DSM-based FLC, FLC	DSM-based FLC	80	1 PV module	80	122.2	700	Non uniform	NA
Batainesh K et al. [139]	Hybrid, FLC+P&O, FLC	Hybrid FLC+P&O	270	1 PV module	127.9, 57.9, 126.2, 46.1	4.40, 3.02, 18.16, 21.31	1000–100	Non uniform	NA
Guerra M I S et al. [140]	ANIFS, P&O, ANN, Fuzzy	ANN	245	NA	956.6, 1674, 2190, 1631	0.525, 0.600, 0.274, 0.803	548–303	Non uniform	NA

Table 8. Pros and cons of recent work based on other artificial intelligence techniques.

Authors [Reference No.]	Pros	Cons
Verma P et al. [111]	• Low shading losses • Low settling time	• Complicate to design
Rahman MM et al. [112]	• Improvement in tracking time • High tracking efficiency	• GMPP is not improved • Not tested on hardware setup
Farzaneh J [113]	• Highly accurate • Requires fewer numbers of training data, which eliminates tracking error	• Highly intricate to design
Manikandan PV [114]	• Enhanced optimal solution	• Low tracking efficiency • Oscillations around GMPP
Al-Majidi SD et al. [115]	• Drift problem is avoided • Low converging time	• Oscillations in steady state • High cost of implementation
Aymen J et al. [116]	• High reliability • Combines advantages of FLC flexibility and ANN learning capacity	• Computationally more complex • High cost of implementation
Farajdadian S [117]	• High accuracy in tracking GMPP • Lower percentage MPP error	• Power fluctuations • Highly complex to intricate
Eltamalya AM et al. [118]	• Re-initializing process enables searching agents to follow new GMPP	• Array size is not specified • No record of tracking time • Oscillations in output power
Chen Y-T et al. [119]	• High tracking capability • Low tracking time	• Array size is not specified • High cost of implementation
Raj A et al. [120]	• Low ripples in output power	• Low tracking efficiency
Abdellatif WSE et al. [121]	• Oscillations in steady state is reduced	• Size of PV array is not specified • Highly intricate to design
Mohammed SS et al. [122]	• High tracking efficiency • Highly accurate	• Computationally more complex
Tandel BG et al. [123]	• Highly accurate in detecting GMPP	• Requires large numbers of iterations
Karthika S et al. [124]	• Ability to track GMPP in vary short duration of time	• Tested in only single change in irradiance
Dehghani M et al. [125]	• Quick response time • High accuracy	• Not tested on hardware • Highly intricate to design
Bendary FM et al. [126]	• High tracking efficiency	• High cost of implementation
Firmanza AP et al. [127]	• High convergence speed due to mutation factor	• Algorithm loses GMPP tracking in some cases • Oscillations around GMPP
Neethu M. et al. [128]	• Low oscillations around GMPP	• High tuning time • High computational cost
Kamaruddina NI et al. [129]	• Able to track true GMPP • Required minimum control parameters	• More values of iterations required • Intricate to design
Joisher M et al. [130]	• Able to track true GMPP	• Power oscillations at output • Computationally more complex
Algarín C R et al. [131]	• Fewer oscillations in steady state • No power loss	• Computationally more complex • Generates error in measuring low powers

Table 8. *Cont.*

Authors [Reference No.]	Pros	Cons
Cheng P-C et al. [132]	• Increased tracking performance without increase in calculation burden	• High tracking time • Low accuracy
Liu C-L et al. [133]	• Improved tracking accuracy • Asymmetrical membership function improved the MPPT performance	• Oscillations around GMPP • High transient time • Computationally more complex
Kececioglu O F et al. [134]	• Oscillations in steady-state output are eliminated	• Computationally more complex
Hayder W et al. [135]	• Low transient time	• If irradiance remains constant for long, algorithm does not show better performance • Computationally more complex in design
Hua C-C et al. [136]	• No oscillations in steady state	• High tracking time • High computational cost
Zhang P et al. [137]	• Mutation factor is modified to limit the random search • Low tracking time	• Comparatively requires large numbers of iterations • Computationally complex
Bakkar M et al. [138]	• Highly accurate	• Issues in determining safe operating region • High cost of computation
Batainesh K et al. [139]	• Highly accurate • No trapping in LMPP	• Oscillations around GMPP • High cost of implementation
Guerra M I S et al. [140]	• Negligible oscillations around GMPP • Fast tracking response	• High cost of implementation • Computationally more complex

After having the deep analysis of all these MPPT techniques, a concluded comparative study has been depicted in Table 9 for better understanding as

Table 9. Comparative analysis of various MPPT.

Categorization	Technique	Execution Cost			Accuracy			Tracking Speed			Oscillations Around MPP				Computational Complexity			Analog/Digital	
		L	M	H	L	M	H	L	M	H	L	M	H	~Z	L	M	H	D	A/D
Conventional	P&O		●		●			●					●		●				●
	INC			●		●			●			●				●		●	
	FOCV	●			●					●			●		●				●
	FSCC	●			●					●	●					●			●
AI-Based Metaheuristic techniques	ACO	●				●				●				●	●			●	
	PSO		●			●			●			●				●			●
	ABC			●		●				●				●			●		●
	GWO		●				●	●						●	●				●
	SSA		●				●	●						●	●				●
	FFA		●				●	●						●	●				●
	CS		●			●				●				●		●			●
	FSSO		●			●				●				●		●			●
Other AI	FLC	●				●				●				●			●		●
	ANN		●			●			●					●			●		●
	GA		●			●			●					●			●		●
	DE	●				●			●					●		●			●

L, low; M, medium; H, high; ~Z, nearly zero; D, digital; A/D, analog/digital.

5. Research Gap and Findings

There are total 16 techniques reported in this paper. In 23 papers conventional MPPT techniques, 42 papers swarm intelligence MPPT techniques, 21 papers bio-inspired, and in 35 papers other AI-based techniques are discussed. Therefore, a total of 121 papers were mainly studied, which are focused on these MPPT techniques. The remaining 23 out of 144 papers were used in other important sections. The classification of papers focusing on different techniques can be seen in Figure 24.

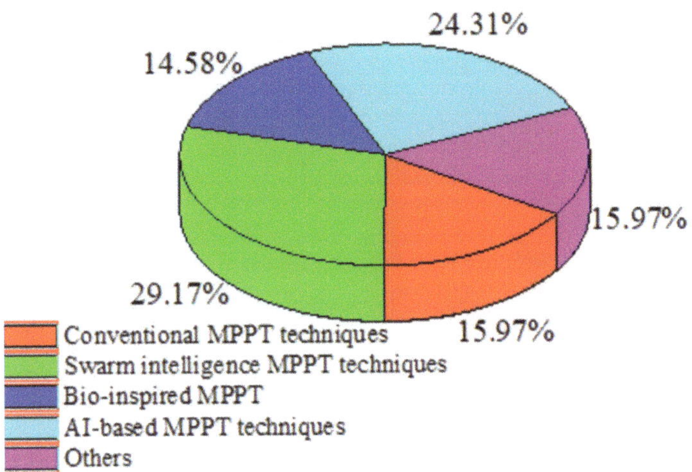

Figure 24. Papers focused on different MPPT techniques.

The authors are mainly classified concerning conventional MPPT techniques, metaheuristic AI techniques, and other AI-based techniques. Further, conventional MPPT techniques are classified as perturb and observe, incremental conductance, fractional open-circuit voltage, and fractional short-circuit current; particle swarm optimization, artificial bee colony, grey wolf optimization, and salp swarm algorithm fall under swarm intelligence MPPT techniques; and firefly MPPT algorithm, cuckoo search, and flying squirrel search optimization techniques are classified as bio-inspired techniques [141–144]. While swarm intelligence and bio-inspired techniques are metaheuristic AI techniques, other AI-based MPPT techniques are fuzzy logic control, artificial neural network, and evolutionary computational techniques (genetic algorithm and differential evolution).

After conducting a thorough analysis of metaheuristic MPPT approaches based on conventional and AI techniques in this paper, one can easily find the following gaps in this area:

- Despite the fact that conventional techniques are simpler and work better in unshaded spaces, they have the downside of slow response. In their findings, oscillations around GMPP are observed;
- Even though these methods are frequently modified, power loss still occurs while monitoring open-circuit voltage or short-circuit current. Additionally, these methods need a large number of sensors to function, but those numbers can be decreased;
- In PSCs, AI approaches are effective, but they have the disadvantage of having high computational complexity;
- These methods require a great deal of time to track GMPP because of the large number of iterations. Despite the fact that many of these are only tested on virtual platforms, real-world validation is still crucial;
- Most of the reported work ignores the effect of load variation, which is crucial for building any PV system.

6. Challenges and Future Work

This paper comprehensively elaborates many recently reported works to track GMPP in PSCs in detail along with their pros and cons. Presently, over eighty MPPT optimization techniques have been published, and more than four new techniques are published each year. This article covers the recent findings in each MPPT technique in a tabular form. Because there are so many optimization strategies in the literature, picking one becomes quite challenging. Avoiding local MPP and local hotspots of PV array is critical for any optimization strategy. Moreover, when these algorithms are built, there is a requirement to manage energy. Research on efficient MPPT techniques can be rationalized in the future by considering many other critical factors such as local hotspots, array reconfigurations, and cell materials, which contribute to producing maximum power during PSCs. With the aid of smartphones, an MPPT application can also be set to work at any time via the Internet.

7. Conclusions

Solar PV systems are regarded as the most capable energy source in renewable power-generation systems due to the copious availability of sunlight. However, unpredictable weather makes their working efficiency low. Thus, MPPT techniques are used to yield maximum power from these systems in any weather conditions. Much research has been done till now in this field, but selecting an appropriate technique for specific circumstances has always been difficult. For the mentioned reason, this study reassesses the art of various MPPT optimization strategies developed by various researchers so far in a different manner. Conventional and AI-based MPPT techniques are elaborated separately with simplified flowcharts in respective sections with the aim to understand their basic principles in detail for new learners. Following the appropriate evaluation of each study, a tabular summary was created on important attributes of PV systems under PSCs, such as array size, % improvement in GMPP, level of irradiance, and tracking time, forming novel datasheets. In this paper, the reported taxonomy of MPPT techniques can help new learners, researchers, amd professional engineers to interpret the performance of each MPPT approach under different climatic scenarios. After careful analysis, it is easy to conclude that traditional techniques are less complex and work well in unshaded environmental conditions. However, they have the disadvantage of slow response. AI techniques perform well in PSCs with negligible oscillations in a steady state, with high accuracy and high tracking efficiency, but they suffer from high computational complexity. With the tabulated pros and cons of each reviewed article, new learners can easily find the research gaps that still exist in this field. With the help of the comparison table based on important parameters, while incorporating any MPPT in PV system, one can select most appropriate MPPT approach in a specific application. Furthermore, this analysis reveals that AI-based MPP controllers are the best option to deal with PSCs. As a result, a large research area has opened up for new researchers. To summarize, this review paper will be a useful resource for researchers or industrialists to utilize in choosing the most appropriate MPPT method for a certain objective.

Author Contributions: Conceptualization, A.K.S., R.K.P., S.C., A.F.M., M.A.A., H.M. and F.P.G.M.; Data curation, A.K.S., R.K.P., S.C., A.F.M., M.A.A., H.M. and F.P.G.M.; Formal analysis, A.K.S., R.K.P., S.C., A.F.M., M.A.A., H.M. and F.P.G.M.; Funding acquisition, H.M., M.A.A. and F.P.G.M.; Investigation, A.K.S., R.K.P., S.C., A.F.M., M.A.A., H.M. and F.P.G.M.; Methodology, A.K.S., R.K.P., S.C., A.F.M., M.A.A., H.M. and F.P.G.M.; Project administration, H.M., M.A.A. and F.P.G.M.; Resources, H.M., M.A.A. and F.P.G.M.; Software, H.M., M.A.A. and F.P.G.M.; Supervision, H.M., M.A.A., R.K.P., S.C. and F.P.G.M.; Validation, A.K.S., R.K.P., S.C., A.F.M., M.A.A., H.M. and F.P.G.M.; Visualization, A.K.S., R.K.P., S.C., A.F.M., M.A.A., H.M. and F.P.G.M.; Writing—original draft, A.K.S., R.K.P., S.C., A.F.M., M.A.A., H.M. and F.P.G.M.; Writing—review & editing, A.K.S., R.K.P., S.C., A.F.M., M.A.A., H.M. and F.P.G.M. All authors have read and agreed to the published version of the manuscript.

Funding: The work reported here in has been financially supported by the Intelligent Prognostic Private Limited Delhi, India under Research Grant XX-02/2022.

Data Availability Statement: Data will be provided on request.

Acknowledgments: This study was supported by the Universiti Teknologi Malaysia—"Development of Adaptive and Predictive ACMV/HVAC Health Monitoring System Using IoT, Advanced FDD, and Weather Forecast Algorithms" (Q.J130000.3823.31J06). The authors would like to acknowledge the support from Ingenium Research Group, Universidad Castilla-La Mancha, 13071 Ciudad Real, Spain, support from Integral University, Lucknow, support from Universiti Teknologi Malaysia (UTM), and support from Intelligent Prognostic Private Limited Delhi, India researcher's supporting Project.

Conflicts of Interest: The authors declare no conflict of interest.

Abbreviations

MPPT	Maximum power point tracking	PV	Photovoltaic
PSCs	Partial shading conditions	RES	Renewable energy sources
P–V	Power–voltage	GMPP	Global maximum power point
P&O	Perturb and observe	INC	Incremental conductance
HC	Hill climbing	BI	Bio-inspired
SI	Swarm intelligence	AI	Artificial intelligence
ANN	Artificial neural networks	FLC	Fuzzy logic control
ECI	Evolutionary computational intelligence	I–V	Current–voltage
MPP	Maximum power point	LMPP	Local maximum power points
DC	Direct current	CS	Cuckoo search
FOCV	Fractional open-circuit voltage	FSCC	Fractional short-circuit current
ACO	Ant colony optimization	ACO-P&O	Ant colony optimization–perturb and observe
SP-INC	Self-predictive incremental conductance	SPC	Semi pilot cell
PC	Pilot cell	CSAM	Current Sensorless Method with Auto-modulation
VSS	Variable step size	PSO	Particle swarm optimization
ABC	Artificial Bee Colony	GWO	Grey wolf optimization
SSA	Salp swarm algorithm	APSO	Accelerated PSO
LIPSO	Lagrange interpolation PSO	TS	Takagi–Sugeno
VCPSO	Variable coefficients PSO	CFPSO	Constriction factor-based PSO
OD-PSO	Overall distribution PSO	P&O-PSO	Perturb and observe-PSO
EGWO	Enhanced GWO	GWO-GSO	GWO–golden-section optimization
GWO-P&O	GWO–Perturb and observe	GOA	Grasshopper optimization algorithm
BOA	Bat algorithm	SSPSO	Series salp PSO
FA	Firefly elgorithm	ISSA	Improved salp swarm algorithm
DE	Differential Evolution	WOA	Whale optimization algorithm
SSO	Salp swarm optimization	ISSA	Improved salp swarm algorithm
SSPO	Hybrid salp swarm–perturb and observe	ABC-P&O	Artificial bee colony–perturb and observe
GMPPT	Global maximum power point tracking	MABC	Modified artificial bee colony
AIC	Angle of incremental conductance	IPSO	Improved particle swarm optimization
OGWO	Opposition-based learning GWO	DFO	Dragonfly optimization
TSA-PSO	Tunicate swarm algorithm with PSO	IABC	Improved artificial bee colony
SPF-P&O	Surface-sased polynomial fitting P&O	HGWO	Hybrid grey wolf optimization
DSM	Dynamic safty margin	ICPSO	Incremental conductance-based PSO
FSSO	Flying squirrel search optimization	BS	Best solution

Nomenclature

I_{pv}	PV output current
I_{ph}	Photocurrent
I_{sh}	Shunt current
I_D	Diode current
I_0	Diode reverses saturation current
q	Electron charge
N_{cs}	Number of cells in series
$\dot{K}$	Boltzmann constant
T	Temperature
V_{pv}	PV output voltage
R_{se}	Series resistance
R_{sh}	Shunt resistance
P_{max}	Maximum power
V_{oc}	Open-circuit voltage
I_{sc}	Short-circuit current
ΔP	Change in power
ΔV	Change in voltage
Δi	Change in current
V_{mpp}	Voltage at maximum power point
b	Proportionality constant
I_{mpp}	Current at maximum power point
d	Constant current factor
P_m	Maximum power
$\hat{G}_i(x)$	Gaussian kernel solution
$\hat{g}_k^i$	Sub-Gaussian function
$\tilde{\mu}_k^i$	Mean value
α_k^i	Standard deviation
w_k	Weight factor
ϕ	Best optimal operating solution
$\in$	Convergence rate
$p_{p,best}$	Individual best position
$p_{g,best}$	Swarm optimum position
Y_n	nth particle position
v_n	nth particle velocity
ω	Inertia burden
$\alpha_1 \& \alpha_2$	Social and cognitive acceleration coefficients
$\mu_1 \& \mu_2$	Arbitrary variables that are uniformly distributed between zero and one in terms of their assessments
ft	Target function
$Y_{max,i} \& Y_{min,i}$	Nth-dimension maximum and minimum values.
Y_j	Arbitrarily selected food source
$\alpha_{i,k}$	Arbitrary number between
$\overrightarrow{X_P}$	Prey vector
$\overrightarrow{X_{P_{GW}}}$	Position vector of grey wolf
$\overrightarrow{A} \& \overrightarrow{B}$	Coefficient vectors
$\overrightarrow{r_1} \& \overrightarrow{r_2}$	Random variables
$X_{m,n}^{new}$	$X_{m,n}$-rationalized candidate solution
P_n	Position of food source

$X_n^+ \& X_n^-$	Decemberision variables maximum and minimum value
μ_0	Initial call
$x_{i,y} \& x_{j,y}$	i^{th} and j^{th} fireflies spatial coordinate "y" components
L	Step length
γ	Variance
$\partial_{max} \& \partial_{min}$	Maximum and minimum duty cycle
$X_{at} \& X_{ht}$	Squirrels' posture address at hickory and acorn trees
H_C	Hovering constant (~1.90)
h_d	Hovering distance
P_{pv}	PV output power
V_m	Maximum voltage
n_h	Hidden neuron numbers
n_i	Injected input neurons numbers
n_o	Output neurons numbers
n_t	Instruction samples numbers

References

1. Kermadi, M.; Salam, Z.; Eltamaly, A.M.; Ahmed, J.; Mekhilef, S.; Larbes, C.; Berkouk, E.M. Recent Developments of MPPT Techniques for PV Systems under Partial Shading Conditions: A Critical Review and Performance Evaluation. *IET Renew. Power Gener.* **2020**, *17*, 3401–3417. [CrossRef]
2. Singh, N.; Goswami, A. Study of P-V and I-V Characteristics of Solar Cell in MATLAB/Simulink. *Int. J. Pure Appl. Math.* **2018**, *118*, 24.
3. Selvan, S.; Nair, P.; Umayal, A. Review on Photo Voltaic MPPT Algorithms. *Int. J. Electr. Comput. Eng.* **2016**, *6*, 567–582.
4. Xu, L.; Cheng, R.; Yang, J. A New MPPT Technique for Fast and Efficient Tracking under Fast Varying Solar Irradiation and Load Resistance. *Int. J. Photoenergy* **2020**, *2020*, 6535372. [CrossRef]
5. Gupta, A.K.; Chauhan, Y.K.; Pachauri, R.K. A comparative investigation of maximum power point tracking methods for solar PV system. *Sol. Energy* **2016**, *136*, 236–253. [CrossRef]
6. Baba, A.O.; Liu, G.; Chen, X. Classification and Evaluation Review of Maximum Power Point Tracking Methods. *Sustain. Futures* **2020**, *2*, 100020. [CrossRef]
7. Belhachat, F.; Larbes, C. A review of global maximum power point tracking techniques of photovoltaic system under partial shading conditions. *Renew. Sustain. Energy Rev.* **2018**, *92*, 513–553. [CrossRef]
8. Podder, A.K.; Roy, N.K.; Pota, H.R. MPPT methods for solar PV systems: A critical review based on tracking nature. *IET Renew. Power Gener.* **2019**, *13*, 1615–1632. [CrossRef]
9. Verma, D.; Nema, S.; Agrawal, R.; Sawle, Y.; Kumar, A. A Different Approach for Maximum Power Point Tracking (MPPT) Using Impedance Matching through Non-Isolated DC-DC Converters in Solar Photovoltaic Systems. *Electronics* **2022**, *11*, 1053. [CrossRef]
10. Szemes, P.T.; Melhem, M. Analyzing and modeling PV with "P&O" MPPT Algorithm by MATLAB/SIMULINK. In Proceedings of the 3rd International Symposium on Small-Scale Intelligent Manufacturing Systems (SIMS) 2020, Gjovik, Norway, 10–12 June 2020; pp. 1–6.
11. Christopher, I.W.; Ramesh, R. Comparative Study of P&O and InC MPPT Algorithms. *Am. J. Eng. Res.* **2013**, *2*, 402–408.
12. Jately, V.; Azzopardi, B.; Joshi, J.; Venkateswaran, B.V.; Sharma, A.; Arora, S. Experimental Analysis of hill-climbing MPPT algorithms under low irradiance levels. *Renew. Sustain. Energy Rev.* **2021**, *150*, 111467. [CrossRef]
13. Ali, A.; Almutairi, K.; Padmanaban, S.K.; Tirth, V.; Algarni, S.; Irshad, K.; Islam, S.; Zahir, M.H.; Shafiullah, M.; Malik, M.Z. Investigation of mppt techniques under uniform and non-uniform solar irradiation condition-a retrospection. *IEEE Access* **2020**, *8*, 127368–127392. [CrossRef]
14. Batarseh, M.G.; Za'ter, M.E. Hybrid maximum power point tracking techniques: A comparative survey, suggested classification and uninvestigated combinations. *Sol. Energy* **2018**, *169*, 535–555. [CrossRef]
15. Sundareswaran, K.; Vigneshkumar, V.; Palani, S. Development of a hybrid genetic algorithm/perturb and observe algorithm for maximum power point tracking in photovoltaic systems under non-uniform insolation. *IET Renew. Power Gener.* **2015**, *9*, 757–765. [CrossRef]
16. Li, G.; Jin, Y.; Akram, M.W.; Chen, X.; Ji, J. Application of bio-inspired algorithms in maximum power point tracking for PV systems under partial shading conditions—A review. *Renew. Sustain. Energy Rev.* **2018**, *81*, 840–873. [CrossRef]
17. Pathy, S.; Subramani, C.; Sridhar, R.; Thentral, T.M.T.; Padmanaban, S. Nature-Inspired MPPT Algorithms for Partially Shaded PV Systems: A Comparative Study. *Energies* **2019**, *12*, 1451. [CrossRef]
18. Pilakkat, D.; Kanthalakshmi, S.; Navaneethan, S. A comprehensive review of swarm optimization algorithms for MPPT control of PV systems under partially shaded conditions. *Electronics* **2020**, *24*, 3–14. [CrossRef]
19. Rezk, H.; Fathy, A.; Abdelaziz, A.Y. A comparison of different global MPPT techniques based on meta-heuristic algorithms for photovoltaic system subjected to partial shading conditions. *Renew. Sustain. Energy Rev.* **2017**, *74*, 377–386. [CrossRef]

20. Tamrakar, R.; Gupta, A. A Review: Extraction of solar cell modelling parameters. *Int. J. Innov. Res. Electr. Electron. Instrum. Control Eng.* **2015**, *3*, 55–60.

21. Singh, P.; Vinay, T.R.; Balyan, A.; Gangadhara; Sandeep, P.M. P-V and I-V Characteristics of Solar Cell. *Design Eng.* **2021**, *6*, 520–528.

22. Bayrak, F.; Ertürk, G.; Oztop, H.F. Effects of partial shading on energy and exergy efficiencies for photovoltaic panels. *J. Clean. Prod.* **2017**, *164*, 58–69. [CrossRef]

23. Nkambule, M.; Hasan, A.; Ali, J.A. Proportional study of Perturb & Observe and Fuzzy Logic Control MPPT Algorithm for a PV system under different weather conditions. In Proceedings of the IEEE 10th GCC Conference and Exhibition, Kuwait City, Kuwait, 19–23 April 2019.

24. Reddy, D.C.K.; Satyanarayana, S.; Ganesh, V. Design of Hybrid Solar Wind Energy System in a Microgrid with MPPT Techniques. *Int. J. Electr. Comput. Eng.* **2018**, *8*, 730–740.

25. Hajighorbani, S.; Amran, M.; Radzi, M.; Kadir, M.Z.A.A.; Shafie, S. Dual Search Maximum Power Point (DSMPP) Algorithm Based on Mathematical Analysis under Shaded Conditions. *Energies* **2015**, *8*, 12116–12146. [CrossRef]

26. Ahmed, J.; Salam, Z. A Modified P&O Maximum Power Point Tracking Method with Reduced Steady-State Oscillation and Improved Tracking Efficiency. *IEEE Trans. Sustain. Energy* **2016**, *7*, 1506–1515.

27. Sera, D.; Kerekes, T.; Teodorescu, R.; Blaabjerg, F. Improved MPPT Algorithms for Rapidly Changing Environmental Conditions. In Proceedings of the 2006 12th International Power Electronics and Motion Control Conference, Portoroz, Slovenia, 30 August–1 September 2006; pp. 1614–1619.

28. Bouksaim, M.; Mekhfioui, M.; Srifi, M.N. Design and Implementation of Modified INC, Conventional INC, and Fuzzy Logic Controllers Applied to a PV System under Variable Weather Conditions. *Designs* **2021**, *5*, 71. [CrossRef]

29. Babu, C.S.; Kumari, J.S.; Kullayappa, T.R. Design and Analysis of Open Circuit Voltage Based Maximum Power Point Tracking for Photovoltaic System. *Int. J. Adv. Sci. Technol.* **2011**, *2*, 51–60.

30. Kumari, J.S.; Ch, S.B.; Yugandhar, J. Design and Investigation of Short Circuit Current Based Maximum Power Point Tracking for Photovoltaic System. *Int. J. Res. Rev. Electr. Comput. Eng.* **2011**, *1*, 63–68.

31. Numan, B.A.; Shakir, A.M.; Ahmed, B.M. Enhancement of P&O algorithm for MPPT for partially shading PV systems. In Proceedings of the Academicsera International Conference, Antalya, Turkey, 21–22 January 2021.

32. Gil-Velasco, A.; Aguilar-Castillo, C. A modification of the perturb and observe method to improve the energy harvesting of PV systems under partial shading conditions. *Energies* **2021**, *14*, 2521. [CrossRef]

33. Efendi, M.Z.; Suhariningsih Murdianto, F.D.; Inawati, E. Implementation of modified P&O method as power optimizer of solar panel under partial shading condition for battery charging system. *AIP Conf. Proc.* **2018**, *1977*, 020002.

34. Shang, L.; Guo, H.; Zhu, W. An improved MPPT control strategy based on incremental conductance algorithm. *Prot. Control. Mod. Power Syst.* **2020**, *5*, 14. [CrossRef]

35. Zand, S.J.; Hsia, K.H.; Eskandarian, N.; Mobayen, S. Improvement of Self-Predictive Incremental Conductance Algorithm with the Ability to Detect Dynamic Conditions. *Energies* **2021**, *14*, 1234. [CrossRef]

36. Baimel, D.; Tapuchi, S.; Levron, Y.; Belikov, J. Improved fractional open circuit voltage MPPT methods for PV systems. *Electronics* **2019**, *8*, 321–340. [CrossRef]

37. Hua, C.; Chen, W.; Fang, Y. A hybrid MPPT with adaptive step-size based on single sensor for photovoltaic systems. In Proceedings of the 2014 International Conference on Information Science, Electronics and Electrical Engineering, Sapporo, Japan, 26–28 April 2014; pp. 441–445.

38. Nadeem, A.; Sher, H.A.; Murtaza, A.F. Online fractional open-circuit voltage maximum output power algorithm for photovoltaic modules. *IET Renew. Power Gener.* **2020**, *14*, 188–198. [CrossRef]

39. Fapi, C.B.N.; Wira, P.; Kamta, M. Real-time experimental assessment of a new MPPT algorithm based on the direct detection of the short-circuit current for a PV system. In Proceedings of the 19th International Conference on Renewable Energies and Power Quality (ICREPQ'21), Almeria, Spain, 28–30 July 2021.

40. Sarika, E.P.; Jacob, J.; Mohammed, S.; Paul, S. A novel hybrid maximum power point tracking technique with zero oscillation based on P&O algorithm. *Int. J. Renew. Energy Res.* **2020**, *10*, 1962–1973.

41. Li, C.; Chen, Y.; Zhou, D.; Liu, J.; Zeng, J. A High-Performance Adaptive Incremental Conductance MPPT Algorithm for Photovoltaic Systems. *Energies* **2016**, *9*, 288. [CrossRef]

42. Owusu-Nyarko, I.; Elgenedy, M.A.; Abdelsalam, I.; Ahmed, K.H. Modified Variable Step-Size Incremental Conductance MPPT Technique for Photovoltaic Systems. *Electronics* **2021**, *10*, 2331. [CrossRef]

43. Sarwar, S.; Javed, M.Y.; Jaffery, M.H.; Arshad, J.; Ur Rehman, A.; Shafiq, M.; Choi, J.-G. A Novel Hybrid MPPT Technique to Maximize Power Harvesting from PV System under Partial and Complex Partial Shading. *Appl. Sci.* **2022**, *12*, 587. [CrossRef]

44. Hafeez, M.A.; Naeem, A.; Akram, M.; Javed, M.Y.; Asghar, A.B.; Wang, Y. A Novel Hybrid MPPT Technique Based on Harris Hawk Optimization (HHO) and Perturb and Observer (P&O) under Partial and Complex Partial Shading Conditions. *Energies* **2022**, *15*, 5550.

45. González-Castaño, C.; Restrepo, C.; Revelo-Fuelagán, J.; Lorente-Leyva, L.L.; Peluffo-Ordóñez, D.H. A Fast-Tracking Hybrid MPPT Based on Surface-Based Polynomial Fitting and P&O Methods for Solar PV under Partial Shaded Conditions. *Mathematics* **2021**, *9*, 2732.

46. Verma, P.; Alam, A.; Sarwar, A.; Tariq, M.; Vahedi, H.; Gupta, D.; Ahmad, S.; Mohamed, A.S.N. Meta-Heuristic optimization techniques used for maximum power point tracking in solar PV system. *Electronics* **2021**, *10*, 2419. [CrossRef]
47. Jiang, L.L.; Maskell, D.L.; Patra, J.C. A novel ant colony optimization-based maximum power point tracking for photovoltaic systems under partially shaded conditions. *Energy Build.* **2013**, *58*, 227–236. [CrossRef]
48. Oliveira, F.M.; da Silva, S.A.O.; Durand, F.R.; Sampaio, L.P. Application of PSO method for maximum power point extraction in photovoltaic systems under partial shading conditions. In Proceedings of the 2015 IEEE 13th Brazilian Power Electronics Conference and 1st Southern Power Electronics Conference (COBEP/SPEC), Fortaleza, Brazil, 29 November–2 December 2015; pp. 1–6.
49. Benyoucef, A.S.; Chouder, A.; Kara, K.; Silvestre, S.; Sahed, O.A. Artificial bee colony based algorithm for maximum power point tracking (MPPT) for PV systems operating under partial shaded conditions. *Appl. Soft Comput.* **2015**, *32*, 38–48. [CrossRef]
50. Mohapatra, A.; Nayak, B.; Das, P.; Mohanty, K.B. A review on MPPT techniques of PV system under partial shading condition. *Renew. Sustain. Energy Rev.* **2017**, *80*, 854–867. [CrossRef]
51. Rezaei, H.; Bozorg-Haddad, O.; Chu, X. Grey Wolf Optimization (GWO) Algorithm. In *Studies in Computational Intelligence*; Springer: Berlin/Heidelberg, Germany, 2017; pp. 81–91.
52. Mohanty, S.; Subudhi, B.; Ray, P.K. A New MPPT Design Using Grey Wolf Optimization Technique for Photovoltaic System Under Partial Shading Conditions. *IEEE Trans. Sustain. Energy* **2016**, *7*, 181–188. [CrossRef]
53. Faris, H.; Mirjalili, S.; Aljarah, I.; Mafarja, M.; Heidari, A.A. Salp Swarm Algorithm: Theory, Literature Review, and Application in Extreme Learning Machines. In *Nature-Inspired Optimizers. Studies in Computational Intelligence*; Springer: Cham, Switzerland, 2019; Volume 811, pp. 185–199.
54. Krishnan, G.S.; Kinattingal, S.; Simon, S.P.; Nayak, P.S.R. MPPT in PV systems using ant colony optimisation with dwindling population. *IET Renew. Power Gener.* **2020**, *14*, 1105–1112. [CrossRef]
55. Sridhar, R.; Vishnuram, P.; Bindu, D.H.; Divya, A. Ant Colony Optimization based Maximum Power Point Tracking (MPPT) for Partially Shaded Standalone PV System. *IJCTA* **2016**, *9*, 8125–8133.
56. Alshareef, M.; Lin, Z.; Ma, M.; Cao, W. Accelerated Particle Swarm Optimization for Photovoltaic Maximum Power Point Tracking under Partial Shading Conditions. *Energies* **2019**, *12*, 623. [CrossRef]
57. Panda, K.P.; Anand, A.; Bana, P.R.; Panda, G. Novel PWM Control with Modified PSO-MPPT Algorithm for Reduced Switch MLI Based Standalone PV System. *Int. J. Emerg. Electr. Power Syst.* **2018**, *19*, 20180023. [CrossRef]
58. Gopalakrishnan, S.K.; Kinattingal, S.; Simon, S.P. MPPT in PV Systems Using PSO Appended with Centripetal Instinct Attribute. *Electr. Power Compon. Syst.* **2020**, *48*, 881–891. [CrossRef]
59. Mao, M.; Zhang, L.; Duan, Q.; Oghorada, O.J.K.; Duan, P.; Hu, B. A Two-Stage Particle Swarm Optimization Algorithm for MPPT of Partially Shaded PV Arrays. *Int. J. Green Energy* **2017**, *4*, 694–702. [CrossRef]
60. Koad, R.B.A.; Zobaa, A.F.; El-Shahat, A. A Novel MPPT Algorithm Based on Particle Swarm Optimization for Photovoltaic Systems. *IEEE Trans. Sustain. Energy* **2017**, *8*, 468–476. [CrossRef]
61. Belghith, O.B.; Sbita1, L.; Bettaher, F. MPPT Design Using PSO Technique for Photovoltaic System Control Comparing to Fuzzy Logic and P&O Controllers. *Energy Power Eng.* **2016**, *8*, 349–366.
62. Obukhov, S.; Ibrahim, A.; Zaki Diab, A.A.; Al-Sumaiti, A.S.; Aboelsaud, R. Optimal Performance of Dynamic Particle Swarm Optimization Based Maximum Power Trackers for Stand-Alone PV System Under Partial Shading Conditions. *IEEE Access* **2020**, *8*, 20770–20785. [CrossRef]
63. Li, H.; Yang, D.; Su, W.; Lü, J.; Yu, X. An Overall Distribution Particle Swarm Optimization MPPT Algorithm for Photovoltaic System Under Partial Shading. *IEEE Trans. Ind. Electron.* **2019**, *66*, 265–275. [CrossRef]
64. Suhardi, D.; Syafaah, L.; Irfan, M.; Yusuf, M.; Effendy, M.; Pakaya, I. Improvement of maximum power point tracking (MPPT) efficiency using grey wolf optimization (GWO) algorithm in photovoltaic (PV) system. *IOP Conf. Ser. Mater. Sci. Eng.* **2019**, *674*, 012038. [CrossRef]
65. Kumar, C.S.; Rao, R.S. Enhanced Grey Wolf Optimizer Based MPPT Algorithm of PV System Under Partial Shaded Condition. *Int. J. Renew. Energy Dev.* **2017**, *6*, 203–212.
66. Shi, J.Y.; Zhang, D.Y.; Ling, L.T.; Xue, F.; Li, Y.J.; Qin, Z.J.; Yang, T. Dual-Algorithm Maximum Power Point Tracking Control Method for Photovoltaic Systems based on Grey Wolf Optimization and Golden-Section Optimization. *J. Power Electron.* **2018**, *18*, 841–852.
67. Ilyas, M.; Ghazal, H.K.E. Design of a MPPT System Based on Modified Grey Wolf Optimization Algorithm in Photovoltaic System under Partially Shaded Condition. *Int. J. Comput.* **2021**, *40*, 36–49.
68. Kraiem, H.; Aymen, F.; Yahya, L.; Triviño, A.; Alharthi, M.; Ghoneim, S.S.M. A Comparison between Particle Swarm and GreyWolf Optimization Algorithms for Improving the Battery Autonomy in a Photovoltaic System. *Appl. Sci.* **2021**, *11*, 7732. [CrossRef]
69. Jamaludin, M.N.I.; Tajuddin, M.F.N.; Ahmed, J.; Azmi, A.; Azmi, S.A.; Ghazali, N.H.; Babu, T.S.; Alhelou, H.H. An Effective Salp Swarm Based MPPT for Photovoltaic Systems Under Dynamic and Partial Shading Conditions. *IEEE Access* **2021**, *9*, 34570–34589. [CrossRef]
70. Dagal, I.; Akın, B.; Akboy, E. A novel hybrid series salp particle Swarm optimization (SSPSO) for standalone battery charging applications. *Ain Shams Eng. J.* **2022**, *13*, 101747. [CrossRef]
71. Krishnan, S.; Sathiyasekar, K. A Novel Salp Swarm Optimization MPP Tracking Algorithm for the Solar Photovoltaic Systems under Partial Shading Conditions. *J. Circuits Syst. Comput.* **2020**, *29*, 2050017. [CrossRef]

72. Farzaneh, J.; Karsaz, A. Application of Improved Salp Swarm Algorithm Based on MPPT for PV Systems under Partial Shading Conditions. *Int. J. Ind. Electron. Control Optim.* **2020**, *3*, 415–429.

73. Ali, M.H.M.; Mohamed, M.M.S.; Ahmed, N.M.; Zahran, M.B.A. Comparison between P&O and SSO techniques based MPPT algorithm for photovoltaic systems. *Int. J. Electr. Comput. Eng.* **2022**, *12*, 32–40.

74. Balaji, V.; Fathima, A.P. Enhancing the Maximum Power Extraction in Partially Shaded PV Arrays Using Hybrid Salp Swarm Perturb and Observe Algorithm. *Int. J. Renew. Energy Res.* **2020**, *10*, 898–911.

75. Restrepo, C.; Yanez-Monsalvez, N.; González-Castaño, C.; Kouro, S.; Rodriguez, J. A Fast Converging Hybrid MPPT Algorithm Based on ABC and P&O Techniques for a Partially Shaded PV System. *Mathematics* **2021**, *9*, 2228.

76. Sawant, P.T.; Tejasvi, P.C.; Bhattar, L.; Bhattar, C.L. Enhancement of PV System Based on Artificial Bee Colony Algorithm under dynamic Conditions. In Proceedings of the IEEE International Conference on Recent Trends In Electronics Information Communication Technology 2016, Bangalore, India, 20–21 May 2016; pp. 1251–1255.

77. Li, N.; Mingxuan, M.; Yihao, W.; Lichuang, C.; Lin, Z.; Qianjin, Z. Maximum Power Point Tracking Control Based on Modified ABC Algorithm for Shaded PV System. In Proceedings of the 2019 AEIT International Conference of Electrical and Electronic Technologies for Automotive (AEIT AUTOMOTIVE), Turin, Italy, 2–4 July 2019; pp. 1–5.

78. Wan, Y.; Mao, M.; Zhou, L.; Zhang, Q.; Xi, X.; Zheng, C. A Novel Nature-Inspired Maximum Power Point Tracking (MPPT) Controller Based on SSA-GWO Algorithm for Partially Shaded Photovoltaic Systems. *Electronics* **2019**, *8*, 680. [CrossRef]

79. Hayder, W.; Ogliari, E.; Dolara, A.; Abid, A.; Hamed, M.B.; Sbita, L. Improved PSO: A Comparative Study in MPPT Algorithm for PV System Control under Partial Shading Conditions. *Energies* **2020**, *13*, 2035. [CrossRef]

80. Almutairi, A.; Abo-Khalil, A.G.; Sayed, K.; Albagami, N. MPPT for a PV Grid-Connected System to Improve efficiency under Partial Shading Conditions. *Sustainability* **2020**, *12*, 10310. [CrossRef]

81. Sharma, A.; Sharma, A.; Jately, V.; Averbukh, M.; Rajput, S.; Azzopardi, B. A Novel TSA-PSO Based Hybrid Algorithm for GMPP Tracking under Partial Shading Conditions. *Energies* **2022**, *15*, 3164. [CrossRef]

82. Chao, K.-H.; Li, J.-Y. Global Maximum Power Point Tracking of Photovoltaic Module Arrays Based on Improved Artificial Bee Colony Algorithm. *Electronics* **2022**, *11*, 1572. [CrossRef]

83. Alaraj, M.; Kumar, A.; Alsaidan, I.; Rizwan, M.; Jamil, M. An Advanced and Robust Approach to Maximize Solar Photovoltaic Power Production. *Sustainability* **2022**, *14*, 7398. [CrossRef]

84. Windarko, N.A.; Nizar Habibi, M.; Sumantri, B.; Prasetyono, E.; Efendi, M.Z.; Taufik, A. New MPPT Algorithm for Photovoltaic Power Generation under Uniform and Partial Shading Conditions. *Energies* **2021**, *14*, 483. [CrossRef]

85. Chawda, G.S.; Mahela, O.P.; Gupta, N.; Khosravy, M.; Senjyu, T. Incremental Conductance Based Particle Swarm Optimization Algorithm for Global Maximum Power Tracking of Solar-PV under Nonuniform Operating Conditions. *Appl. Sci.* **2020**, *10*, 4575. [CrossRef]

86. Teshome, D.F.; Lee, C.H.; Lin, Y.W.; Lian, K.L. A Modified Firefly Algorithm for Photovoltaic Maximum Power Point Tracking Control Under Partial Shading. *IEEE J. Emerg. Sel. Top. Power Electron.* **2017**, *5*, 661–671. [CrossRef]

87. Nugraha, D.A.; Lian, K.L.; Suwarno. A Novel MPPT Method Based on Cuckoo Search Algorithm and Golden Section Search Algorithm for Partially Shaded PV System. *Can. J. Electr. Comput. Eng.* **2019**, *42*, 173–182. [CrossRef]

88. Assis, A.; Mathew, S. Cuckoo Search Algorithm Based Maximum Power Point Tracking For Solar PV Systems. *Int. J. Adv. Electr. Power Syst. Inf. Technol.* **2016**, *2*, 20–28.

89. Jain, M.; Singh, V.; Rani, A. A novel nature-inspired algorithm for optimization: Squirrel search algorithm. *Swarm and Evolutionary Computation* **2019**, *44*, 148–175. [CrossRef]

90. Saad, W.; Hegazy, E.; Shokair, M. Maximum power point tracking based on modified firefly scheme for PV system. *SN Appl. Sci.* **2022**, *4*, 94. [CrossRef]

91. Farzaneh, J.; Keypour, R.; Khanesar, M.A. A New Maximum Power Point Tracking Based on Modified Firefly Algorithm for PV System Under Partial Shading Conditions. *Technol. Econ. Smart Grids Sustain. Energy* **2018**, *3*, 9. [CrossRef]

92. Nusaif, A.I.; Mahmood, A.L. MPPT Algorithms (PSO, FA, and MFA) for PV System Under Partial Shading Condition, Case Study: BTS in Algazalia, Baghdad. *Int. J. Smart Grid* **2020**, *10*, 100–110.

93. Abo-Khalil, A.G.; Alharbi, W.; Al-Qawasmi, A.R.; Alobaid, M.; Alarifi, I.M. Maximum Power Point Tracking of PV Systems under Partial Shading Conditions Based on Opposition-Based Learning Firefly Algorithm. *Sustainability* **2021**, *13*, 2656. [CrossRef]

94. Shi, J.-Y.; Ling, L.-T.; Xue, F.; Qin, Z.-J.; Li, Y.-J.; Lai, Z.-X.; Yang, T. Combining incremental conductance and firefly algorithm for tracking the global MPP of PV arrays. *J. Renew. Sustain. Energy* **2017**, *9*, 023501. [CrossRef]

95. Omar, F.A.; Kulaksiz, A.A. Experimental evaluation of a hybrid global maximum power tracking algorithm based on modified firefly and perturbation and observation algorithms. *Neural Comput. Appl.* **2021**, *33*, 17185–17208. [CrossRef]

96. Chitra, A.; Yogitha, G.; Sivaramakrishnan, K.; Sultana, W.R.; Sanjeevikumar, P. Modified Firefly-Based Maximum Power Point Tracking Algorithm for PV Systems Under Partial Shading Conditions. In *Artificial Intelligent Techniques for Electric and Hybrid Electric Vehicles*; Scrivener Publishing LLC: Beverly, MA, USA, 2020; pp. 143–164.

97. Mosaad, M.I.; Abed el-Raouf, M.O.; Al-Ahmar, M.A.; Banakher, F.A. Maximum Power Point Tracking of PV system Based Cuckoo Search Algorithm; review and comparison. *Energy Procedia* **2019**, *162*, 117–126. [CrossRef]

98. Shi, Y.-J.; Xue, F.; Qin, Z.-J.; Zhang, W.; Ling, L.-T.; Yang, T. Improved Global Maximum Power Point Tracking for Photovoltaic System via Cuckoo Search under Partial Shaded Conditions. *J. Power Electron.* **2016**, *16*, 287–296. [CrossRef]

99. Hidayat, T.; Efendi, M.Z.; Murdianto, F.D. Maximum Power Point Tracking Interleaved Boost Converter Using Cuckoo Search Algorithm on The Nano Grid System. *J. Adv. Res. Electr. Eng.* **2021**, *5*, 41–46. [CrossRef]

100. Bilgin, N.; Yazici, I. Comparison of Maximum Power Point Tracking Methods Using Metaheuristic Optimization Algorithms for Photovoltaic Systems. *Sak. Univ. J. Sci.* **2021**, *25*, 1075–1085. [CrossRef]

101. Ibrahim, A.-W.; Fang, Z.; Ameur, K.; Min, D.; Shafik, M.B.; Al-Muthanna, G. Comparative Study of Solar PV System Performance under Partial Shaded Condition Utilizing Different Control Approaches. *Indian J. Sci. Technol.* **2021**, *14*, 1864–1893. [CrossRef]

102. Bentata, K.; Mohammedi, A.; Benslimane, T. Development of rapid and reliable cuckoo search algorithm for global maximum power point tracking of solar PV systems in partial shading condition. *Arch. Control Sci.* **2021**, *31*, 495–526.

103. Singh, N.; Gupta, K.K.; Jain, S.K.; Dewangan, N.K.; Bhatnagar, P. A Flying Squirrel Search Optimization for MPPT Under Partial Shaded Photovoltaic System. *IEEE J. Emerg. Sel. Top. Power Electron.* **2021**, *9*, 4963–4978. [CrossRef]

104. Fares, D.; Fathi, M.; Shams, I.; Mekhilef, S. A novel global MPPT technique based on squirrel search algorithm for PV module under partial shading conditions. *Energy Convers. Manag.* **2021**, *230*, 113773. [CrossRef]

105. Al-Shammaa, A.A.; Abdurraqeeb, A.M.; Noman, A.M.; Alkuhayli, A.; Farh HM, H. Hardware-In-the-Loop Validation of Direct MPPT Based Cuckoo Search Optimization for Partially Shaded Photovoltaic System. *Electronics* **2022**, *11*, 1655. [CrossRef]

106. Watanabe, R.B.; Ando Junior, O.H.; Leandro PG, M.; Salvadori, F.; Beck, M.F.; Pereira, K.; Brandt MH, M.; De Oliveira, F.M. Implementation of the Bio-Inspired Metaheuristic Firefly Algorithm (FA) Applied to Maximum Power Point Tracking of Photovoltaic Systems. *Energies* **2022**, *15*, 5338. [CrossRef]

107. Pandey, A.K.; Singh, V.; Jain, S. Chapter eleven—Study and comparative analysis of perturb and observe (P&O) and fuzzy logic based PV-MPPT algorithms. In *Applications of AI and IOT in Renewable Energy*; Academic Press: Cambridge, MA, USA, 2022; pp. 193–209.

108. Almajid, S.; Al-Raweshidy, H.; Abbod, M. A Novel Maximum Power Point Tracking Technique based on Fuzzy logic for Photovoltaic Systems. *Int. J. Hydrogen Energy* **2018**, *43*, 14158–14171. [CrossRef]

109. Jyothy, L.P.N.; Sindhu, M.R. An Artificial Neural Network based MPPT Algorithm for Solar PV System. In Proceedings of the 4th International Conference on Electrical Energy Systems (ICEES), Chennai, India, 7–9 February 2018; pp. 375–380.

110. Selivanov, S.G.; Poezjalova, S.N.; Gavrilova, O.A. The Use of Artificial Intelligence Methods of Technological Preparation of Engine-Building Production. *Am. J. Ind. Eng.* **2014**, *2*, 10–14.

111. Verma, P.; Garg, R.; Mahajan, P. Asymmetrical fuzzy logic control-based MPPT algorithm for stand-alone photovoltaic systems under partially shaded conditions. *Sci. Iran.* **2020**, *27*, 3162–3174.

112. Rahman, M.M.; Islam, M.S. PSO and ANN Based Hybrid MPPT Algorithm for Photovoltaic Array under Partial Shading Condition. *Eng. Int.* **2020**, *8*, 9–24. [CrossRef]

113. Farzaneh, J. A Hybrid Modified FA-ANFIS-P&O Approach for MPPT in Photovoltaic Systems under PSCs. *Int. J. Electron.* **2019**, *107*, 703–718.

114. Manikandan, P.V.; Selvaperuma, S. EANFIS-based Maximum Power Point Tracking for Standalone PV System. *IETE J. Res.* **2022**, *68*, 4218–4231. [CrossRef]

115. Al-Majidi, S.D.; Abbod, M.F.; Al-Raweshidy, H.S. Design of an Efficient Maximum Power Point Tracker Based on ANFIS Using an Experimental Photovoltaic System Data. *Electronics* **2019**, *8*, 858. [CrossRef]

116. Aymen, J.; Ons, Z.; Crăciunescu, A.; Popescu, M. Comparison of Fuzzy and Neuro-Fuzzy Controllers for Maximum Power Point Tracking of Photovoltaic Modules. *Renew. Energy Power Qual. J.* **2016**, *1*, 796–800. [CrossRef]

117. Farajdadian, S.; Hosseini, S.M.H. Design of an optimal fuzzy controller to obtain maximum power in solar power generation system. *Sol. Energy* **2019**, *182*, 161–178. [CrossRef]

118. Eltamalya, A.M.; Farh, H.M.H. Dynamic global maximum power point tracking of the PV systems under variant partial shading using hybrid GWO-FLC. *Sol. Energy* **2019**, *177*, 306–316. [CrossRef]

119. Chen, Y.-T.; Jhang, Y.-C.; Liang, R.-H. A fuzzy-logic based auto-scaling variable step-size MPPT method for PV systems. *Sol. Energy* **2016**, *126*, 53–63. [CrossRef]

120. Raj, A.; Gupta, M. Numerical Simulation and Performance Assessment of ANN-INC Improved Maximum Power Point Tracking System for Solar Photovoltaic System Under Changing Irradiation Operation. *Ann. Rom. Soc. Cell Biol.* **2021**, *25*, 790–797.

121. Abdellatif, W.S.E.; Mohamed, M.S.; Barakat, S.; Brisha, A. A Fuzzy Logic Controller Based MPPT Technique for Photovoltaic Generation System. *Int. J. Electr. Eng. Inform.* **2021**, *13*, 394–417.

122. Mohammed, S.S.; Devaraj, D.; Ahamed, T.P.I. GA-Optimized Fuzzy-Based MPPT Technique for Abruptly Varying Environmental Conditions. *J. Inst. Eng. Ser. B* **2021**, *102*, 497–508. [CrossRef]

123. Tandel, B.G.; Vora, D.R. MPP Detection Based on Genetic Algorithm for PV System in Partial Shading Condition. *Int. J. Res. Dev. Technol.* **2016**, *5*, 107–115.

124. Karthika, S.; Rathika, P.; Devaraj, D. Evaluation of GA Tuned PI Controller for Maximum Power Point Tracking for Solar PV System under Partially Shaded Conditions Based on Two Diode Model. *World Appl. Sci. J.* **2017**, *35*, 2580–2590.

125. Dehghani, M.; Taghipour, M.; Gharehpetian, G.B.; Abedi, M. Optimized Fuzzy Controller for MPPT of Grid-connected PV Systems in Rapidly Changing Atmospheric Conditions. *J. Mod. Power Syst. Clean Energy* **2021**, *9*, 376–383. [CrossRef]

126. Bendary, F.M.; Saied, E.M.; Mohamed, W.A.; Afifi, Z.E. Optimal Maximum Power Point Tracking of PV Systems based Genetic-ANFIS Hybrid Algorithm. *Int. J. Sci. Eng. Res.* **2016**, *7*, 830–836.

127. Firmanza, A.P.; Habibi, M.N.; Windarko, N.A.; Yanaratri, D.S. Differential Evolution-based MPPT with Dual Mutation for PV Array under Partial Shading Condition. In Proceedings of the 2020 10th Electrical Power, Electronics, Communications, Controls and Informatics Seminar (EECCIS), Malang, Indonesia, 26–28 August 2020; pp. 198–203.
128. Neethu, M.; Senthilkumar, R. Comparison Method of PSO and DE Optimization for MPPT in PV Systems under Partial Shading Conditions. *Int. Energy J.* **2020**, *20*, 291–298.
129. Kamaruddina, N.I.; Haron, A.R.; Chua, B.L.; Tan, M.K.; Lim, K.G.; Teo, K.T.K. Differential Evolution Based Maximum Power Point Tracker for Photovoltaic Array Under Non-Uniform Illumination Condition. *ICTACT J. Soft Comput.* **2020**, *10*, 2076–2083.
130. Joisher, M.; Singh, D.; Taheri, S.; Espinoza-Trejo, D.R.; Pouresmaeil, E.; Taheri, H. A Hybrid Evolutionary-Based MPPT for Photovoltaic Systems Under Partial Shading Conditions. *IEEE Access* **2020**, *8*, 38481–38492. [CrossRef]
131. Algarín, C.R.; Giraldo, J.T.; Álvarez, O.R. Fuzzy Logic Based MPPT Controller for a PV System. *Energies* **2017**, *10*, 2036. [CrossRef]
132. Cheng, P.-C.; Peng, B.-R.; Liu, Y.-H.; Cheng, Y.-S.; Huang, J.-W. Optimization of a Fuzzy-Logic-Control-Based MPPT Algorithm Using the Particle Swarm Optimization Technique. *Energies* **2015**, *8*, 5338–5360. [CrossRef]
133. Liu, C.-L.; Chen, J.-H.; Liu, Y.-H.; Yang, Z.-Z. An Asymmetrical Fuzzy-Logic-Control-Based MPPT Algorithm for Photovoltaic Systems. *Energies* **2014**, *7*, 2177–2193. [CrossRef]
134. Kececioglu, O.F.; Gani, A.; Sekkeli, M. Design and Hardware Implementation Based on Hybrid Structure for MPPT of PV System Using an Interval Type-2 TSK Fuzzy Logic Controller. *Energies* **2020**, *13*, 1842. [CrossRef]
135. Hayder, W.; Sera, D.; Ogliari, E.; Lashab, A. On Improved PSO and Neural Network P&O Methods for PV System under Shading and Various Atmospheric Conditions. *Energies* **2022**, *15*, 7668.
136. Hua, C.-C.; Zhan, Y.-J. A Hybrid Maximum Power Point Tracking Method without Oscillations in Steady-State for Photovoltaic Energy Systems. *Energies* **2021**, *14*, 5590. [CrossRef]
137. Zhang, P.; Sui, H. Maximum Power Point Tracking Technology of Photovoltaic Array under Partial Shading Based on Adaptive Improved Di_erential Evolution Algorithm. *Energies* **2020**, *13*, 1254. [CrossRef]
138. Bakkar, M.; Aboelhassan, A.; Abdelgeliel, M.; Galea, M. PV Systems Control Using Fuzzy Logic Controller Employing Dynamic Safety Margin under Normal and Partial Shading Conditions. *Energies* **2021**, *14*, 841. [CrossRef]
139. Bataineh, K.; Eid, N. A Hybrid Maximum Power Point Tracking Method for Photovoltaic Systems for Dynamic Weather Conditions. *Resources* **2018**, *7*, 68. [CrossRef]
140. Guerra MI, S.; Ugulino de Araújo, F.M.; Dhimish, M.; Vieira, R.G. Assessing Maximum Power Point Tracking Intelligent Techniques on a PV System with a Buck–Boost Converter. *Energies* **2021**, *14*, 7453. [CrossRef]
141. Minai, A.F.; Khan, A.A.; Pachauri, R.K.; Malik, H.; Márquez, F.P.G.; Jiménez, A.A. Performance Evaluation of Solar PV-Based Z-Source Cascaded Multilevel Inverter with Optimized Switching Scheme. *Electronics* **2022**, *11*, 3706. [CrossRef]
142. Minai, A.F.; Malik, H. Metaheuristics Paradigms for Renewable Energy Systems: Advances in Optimization Algorithms. Springer Nature Book: Metaheuristic and Evolutionary Computation: Algorithms and Applications. In *Metaheuristic and Evolutionary Computation: Algorithms and Applications*; Studies in Computational Intelligence; Springer: Singapore, 2020; pp. 35–61.
143. Chankaya, M.; Hussain, I.; Ahmad, A.; Fausto, P.; García, M. Multi-Objective Grasshopper Optimization Based MPPT and VSC Control of Grid-Tied PV-Battery System. *Electronics* **2021**, *10*, 2770. [CrossRef]
144. Tajjour, S.; Chandel, S.S.; Alotaibi, M.A.; Ustun, T.S.A. Novel Metaheuristic Approach for Solar Photovoltaic Parameter Extraction Using Manufacturer Data. *Photonics* **2022**, *9*, 858. [CrossRef]

 *mathematics*

Article

Upper Limb Joint Angle Estimation Using Wearable IMUs and Personalized Calibration Algorithm

Md. Mahmudur Rahman [1,2], **Kok Beng Gan** [3,*], **Noor Azah Abd Aziz** [4], **Audrey Huong** [5] **and Huay Woon You** [6]

1   Department of Electrical, Electronic and Systems Engineering, Universiti Kebangsaan Malaysia,
    Bangi 43600, Malaysia
2   Department of Electrical and Electronic Engineering, Daffodil International University,
    Dhaka 1216, Bangladesh
3   Medical Engineering and Systems Research Group, Department of Electrical, Electronic and Systems
    Engineering, Universiti Kebangsaan Malaysia, Bangi 43600, Malaysia
4   Department of Family Medicine, Faculty of Medicine, Universiti Kebangsaan Malaysia Medical Centre,
    Kuala Lumpur 56000, Malaysia
5   Department of Electronic Engineering, Universiti Tun Hussein Onn Malaysia, Parit Raja 86400, Malaysia
6   Pusat GENIUS@Pintar Negara, Universiti Kebangsaan Malaysia, Bangi 43600, Malaysia
*   Correspondence: kbgan@ukm.edu.my

Abstract: In physical therapy, exercises improve range of motion, muscle strength, and flexibility, where motion-tracking devices record motion data during exercises to improve treatment outcomes. Cameras and inertial measurement units (IMUs) are the basis of these devices. However, issues such as occlusion, privacy, and illumination can restrict vision-based systems. In these circumstances, IMUs may be employed to focus on a patient's progress quantitatively during their rehabilitation. In this study, a 3D rigid body that can substitute a human arm was developed, and a two-stage algorithm was designed, implemented, and validated to estimate the elbow joint angle of that rigid body using three IMUs and incorporating the Madgwick filter to fuse multiple sensor data. Two electro-goniometers (EGs) were linked to the rigid body to verify the accuracy of the joint angle measuring algorithm. Additionally, the algorithm's stability was confirmed even in the presence of external acceleration. Multiple trials using the proposed algorithm estimated the elbow joint angle of the rigid body with a maximum RMSE of 0.46°. Using the IMU manufacturer's (WitMotion) algorithm (Kalman filter), the maximum RMSE was 1.97°. For the fourth trial, joint angles were also calculated with external acceleration, and the RMSE was 0.996°. In all cases, the joint angles were within therapeutic limits.

Keywords: inertial measurement unit; accelerometer; gyroscope; magnetometer; electro-goniometer; joint angle; rigid body; sensor fusion; Madgwick filter; Kalman filter

MSC: 92-10

Citation: Rahman, M.M.; Gan, K.B.; Aziz, N.A.A.; Huong, A.; You, H.W. Upper Limb Joint Angle Estimation Using Wearable IMUs and Personalized Calibration Algorithm. *Mathematics* **2023**, *11*, 970. https://doi.org/10.3390/math11040970

Academic Editors: Camelia Petrescu and Valeriu David

Received: 17 November 2022
Revised: 10 January 2023
Accepted: 11 January 2023
Published: 14 February 2023

1. Introduction

Stroke is considered to be a leading cause of upper body limb disability among adults, particularly the elderly. It results in immobility and can be deadly in severe cases [1,2]. Numerous factors, such as age, gender, level of physical activity, and others, affect the movement of the upper body limbs [3]. People started experiencing a wide range of health issues that altered their way of life, and their regular activities became more difficult due to their inability to use their upper limbs [4]. One of the leading causes of mobility loss in middle-aged and older people is the age-related decline of the musculoskeletal system caused by chronic aging illnesses [2,5]. The early commencement of the degeneration of body limb mobility can be usefully predicted by the joint data. Thus, the quantification of human mobility-related parameters can assist in making decisions about human health status and performance [6], and measuring joint characteristics such as joint angles, angular accelerations, etc., can contribute a vital role in accurately assessing the human body's stability and functional capacity.

It is important that a human motion capture system used in a therapeutic setting be easy to use, portable, and inexpensive while also being accurate in addressing the problems [7]. Marker-based optical motion capture systems, like VICON, are often considered state of the art for conducting such studies. These systems can give position and orientation with extremely high accuracy by directly measuring the positions of the markers [8]. Reconstructing a person's spatial posture is the primary function of the optical system, which primarily employs a high-speed camera to record the locations of reflecting markers on the surface of the body. Due to its ability to ensure precision, the optical system is sometimes referred to as the industry standard. Issues such as light, occlusion, location, cost, lengthy preparation, setup time, etc., are the primary constraints of this technology [9,10]. However, these systems are impractical outside of institutional settings such as hospitals and large-scale laboratories due to the high price, highly complicated design, and requirements for professional personnel [6].

Micro-electromechanical systems (MEMS) technology has made low-cost, energy-efficient, and sensitive tiny sensors possible in the real world. Nowadays, smartphones, smartwatches, and fitness trackers have MEMS-based IMUs, which include various sensors such as accelerometers, gyroscopes, magnetometers, and so on [11–13]. In comparison to an optoelectronic system, they offer portability and convenience of use due to their small size, low cost, and light weight. The validity and reliability of wearable sensors in motion analysis were examined in several studies. IMU sensors can analyze gait, lower limb joint and pelvic angle kinematics, upper limb motion and joint parameters, and total body motion [14]. Many commercially available IMU systems, including Xsens, IMeasureU, BioSyn Systems, and Shimmer Sensing, were developed specifically for motion analysis. Among those systems, the precision of 3D kinematics was validated [15,16]. Moreover, due to the ability to detect strength, angular velocity, and orientation of the body limbs, the IMU is one of the options that was often selected [17]. Low-power, small IMUs can be integrated with smart textiles to create wearable, noninvasive elderly health monitoring devices, which will allow remote healthcare workers to monitor, assess, and retain data on their patients' mobility, activity, physical fitness, and rehabilitation [18,19].

However, inertial measurement units (IMUs) have their own challenges. There is a possibility that the data produced by an IMU may be insufficient, imprecise, or contaminated with errors. The data from the accelerometer can be inaccurate due to a gravitational force [20]. Typically, the orientation of a segment is determined by integrating the gyroscope measurement (angular velocity). The translational acceleration detected by the accelerometers is double-integrated to determine the position. One of the most critical problems with integration is that measurement errors quickly add up, and the precision of the outcome reduces. The magnetometer suffers from the interference generated by the surrounding magnetic fields and the presence of ferromagnetic materials close to the magnetometer [21].

Because of the aforementioned difficulties, human kinematics-related research using accelerometers, gyroscopes, or magnetometers was severely restricted. To solve these problems, a tri-axial gyroscope, accelerometer, and magnetometer were integrated into a single device, and a fusion algorithm was also developed to accompany the device. Integrating the data obtained from sensors can help decrease measurement error and produce a more precise estimate of the motion [22]. For the purpose of performing sensor fusion, several methods were reported in the various scientific literature. These methods include the Kalman filter (KF) and its variants, such as the extended Kalman filter (EKF), particle filter, unscented Kalman filter (UKF), complementary filter and its variants, and so on [23]. A nonlinear variation of the KF is the EKF, considered to be a common attitude estimate technique among researchers [24,25]. In fact, the Kalman filter (KF) maintains its undisputed coverage in industrial applications and is an ideal filtering strategy in terms of minimum mean squared error [26]. However, there are still several issues with traditional KF techniques. The state and observation models must be linear for classical KF to work. Additionally, the noise sources of these two models must be uncorrelated white Gaussian noise [27]. In contrast to actual engineering practice, where the system is typically nonlinear, the traditional Kalman filtering theory is only applicable to linear systems and demands linear observation equations. As a result, Bucy and Sunahara developed the Extended Kalman filter (EKF) in the 1970s. It is necessary to linearize the nonlinear system before using the generalized Kalman filter to estimate its state. The linearization procedure adds errors to the nonlinear system, which reduces the accuracy of the final state estimation [28,29]. Thus, researchers focused on the complementary filter (CF) to overcome problems related to the KF [30]. However, it became necessary to use a nonlinear complementary filter (NCF) since linear complementary filters are also unable to adjust the changing bias of low-cost sensors [31]. For attitude estimation, Madgwick offered a gradient-descent-based CF in 2011 [32], while Mahony proposed a version of the CF in a particular orthogonal group in 2008 [33]. In terms of execution time, the Madgwick filter requires less time than the EKF, which happens due to the higher computational load in the EKF [34]. The EKF was recommended for reliable tilt measurements at higher angular speeds, while the Madgwick filter appeared to be the best for angular velocities up to $100\text{--}150° \text{ s}^{-1}$ [35]. To find a reliable and efficient sensor fusion technique, a number of fusion algorithms were compared in [36], where the authors concluded that the Madgwick filter performs marginally better than all other evaluated algorithms based on the root mean square error (RMSE).

The inevitable consequence is that calibration of the sensors is a concerning issue that affects the measurement's outcome, and the angle measurement from the individual sensors is not exact. Though a sensor fusion technique is required to prevent individual problems with the accelerometer, gyroscope, and magnetometer, most operational algorithms have numerous problems which have been mentioned in the previous section. Excessive external acceleration and distortion in magnetometer data may cause errors in the computed joint angles, and contemporary works did not address external acceleration. So, in this work, a two-stage algorithm was proposed to estimate the joint angles of the upper limbs, utilizing three IMUs, and this two-stage algorithm improves the accuracy and reduces the bias for joint angle calculation, addressing these gaps. In the first step, an estimation of each IMU sensor's orientation was made using the sensor fusion algorithm. The second step included deriving the joint angle from these IMUs' orientations, which were less susceptible to noise introduced by external acceleration. The rest of this article is organized as follows: The experimental setup and general methodology are covered in Section 2. The specifics of the proposed algorithm have also been discussed in Section 2. Section 3 then discusses and evaluates the algorithm's performance. In Section 4, some final findings and a discussion on potential possibilities are drawn for further study using the suggested algorithm.

2. Materials and Methods

2.1. Experimental Scenario and Platform

This system comprised three wireless sensor nodes, each of which was equipped with a relatively inexpensive MEMS inertial sensor MPU9250. This MPU9250 is a low-cost 9-axis MEMS IMU made by WitMotion Company. The inertial sensor comprises a gyroscope with three axes, an accelerometer with three axes, and a magnetometer with three axes. The dimensions of the inertial sensor are 51.3 mm × 36 mm × 15 mm, and the net weight is 20 g. Table 1 provides a comprehensive summary of the IMU's numerous features and parameters.

Figure 1a,b depicts the hardware configuration of the inertial motion capture system used in this study. BLE 5.0 multiple connection software was utilized to link a PC with IMU sensors, which has a 50 m coverage range (without obstacles like walls). This software can retrieve and save CSV files containing data from accelerometers, gyroscopes, and magnetometers.

Table 1. IMU specifications. Source: https://www.wit-motion.com/. Accessed on 5 September 2022.

Parameter	Technical Specification
Dimension	51.3 mm × 36 mm × 15 mm
Net Weight	20 g
Chip	nRF52832 Bluetooth chip
Processor	Cortex-M0 core processor
IMU	MPU9250
Voltage	3.3–5 V
Output	3-axis Acceleration + Angle + Angular Velocity + Magnetic Field + Quaternion
Range	Acceleration (±16 g), Gyroscope (±2000°/s), Magnet Field (±4900 µT)
Angle	X, Y-axis: 0.05° (Static)
Accuracy	X, Y-axis: 0.1° (Dynamic)

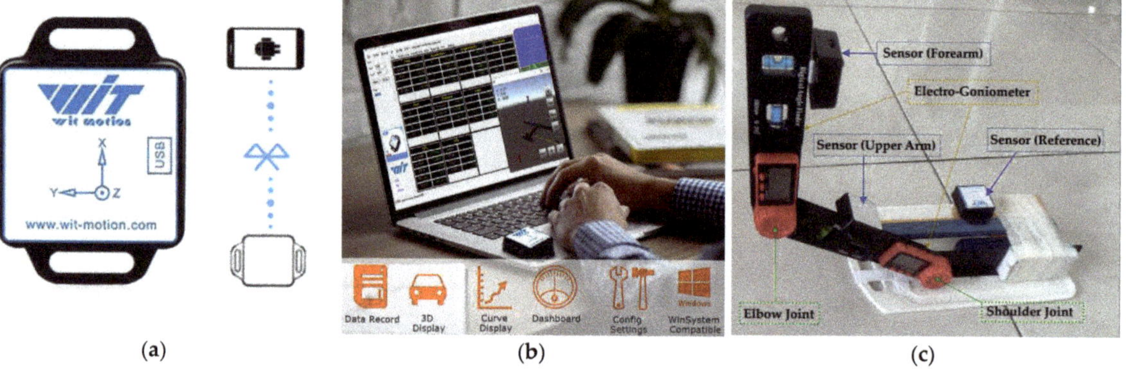

Figure 1. (**a**,**b**) The hardware of the motion capture system. Source: https://www.wit-motion.com/. (**c**) Three-dimensional rigid body structure.

The elbow joint angle of the human body was represented by a 3D rigid body, shown in Figure 1c, which resembles an arm of the human body. The rigid body was designed and developed utilizing two electro-goniometers that were joined together using a strong adhesive, as shown in Figure 1c. The electro-goniometers have an accuracy of 0.5° with a measuring range of 0–200°. This structure was then placed on a platform to develop a complete arrangement. This rigid body has three segments or arms. One arm represents the upper arm, the second arm represents the forearm, and the third arm represents the shoulder part of the human body. Sensors were attached to each arm of the rigid body and raw sensor data were collected at a rate of 10 samples per second. These IMU sensor data were used to determine the elbow joint angle of the rigid body during static and dynamic conditions.

2.2. Joint Angle Measurement Algorithm

In this study, we proposed a two-stage orientation measurement algorithm that can estimate the joint angles of the elbow joint using the accelerometer, gyroscope, and magnetometer raw data from three IMUs. Among them, two IMUs were attached above and below the elbow joint of the rigid body, and the third IMU acted as a reference, placed in the shoulder position (static). At the beginning of the proposed algorithm, each IMU sensor's data were calibrated, and in the first stage, all sensor data were fused using the Madgwick filter, which returns output in quaternion form. In the second stage, the joint angle was estimated by fusing the quaternion data of all IMUs obtained in the first stage. Finally, to eliminate the high frequency components from the estimated angle, the joint angle was passed through a fourth-order Butterworth low-pass filter. Algorithm 1 outlines the procedure that has been proposed for estimating the joint angle. The proposed algorithm is represented as a block diagram in Figure 2.

Algorithm 1 Proposed Joint Angle Measurement Algorithm

---

1 Initialization and calibration of the forearm, upper arm, and reference sensor:

    Accelerometer data: a^i

    Gyroscope data: g^i

    Magnetometer data: m^i

2 Collection of Accelerometer, Gyroscope, and Magnetometer raw data

3 Measurement of bias correction vector (b_i) from acceleration data

4 Calibration of Accelerometer data using bias correction vector:

$$a_c^k = (a^k - b_i)$$

5 Conversion of Magnetometer data (m^i) from local frame to global frame

6 Calibration and correction of the Magnetometer data in global frame:

$$m_c^k = [q_b \quad q_c \quad q_d]$$

7 First Stage: Use of Madgwick filter for all three sensors' orientation estimation

Output:

Forearm Sensor $\rightarrow q_{FA}$

Upper Arm Sensor $\rightarrow q_{UA}$

Reference Sensor $\rightarrow q_R$

8 Second Stage: Calculation of Joint Angle (θ) from the three quaternions

9 Filtering of Joint Angle (θ) using Fourth-Order Butterworth Filter

---

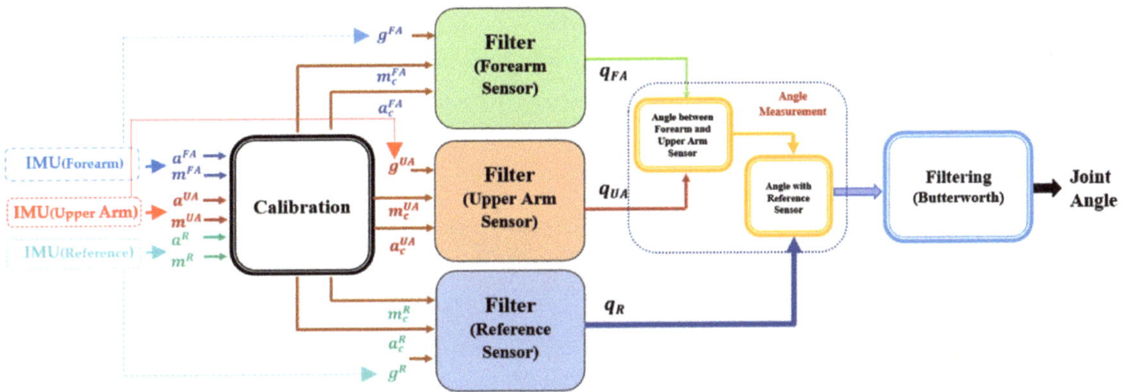

Figure 2. Proposed algorithm for joint angle estimation.

2.2.1. Calibration

When an IMU is at rest, the accelerometer should only measure gravity, and the gyroscope should show zero rotational velocity. In contrast, they always show some data while still in real-world circumstances. On the other hand, the magnetometer has issues with magnetic interference [21]. To minimize these issues, calibration was therefore required for the magnetometer, gyroscope, and accelerometer. With the aid of WitMotion's built-in software, each of the three sensors—accelerometer, gyroscope, and magnetometer—were calibrated. Gyroscope calibration was sufficient using WitMotion software, but the accelerometer and magnetometer required more than this procedure. In light of this, further calibration of these two sensors was essential, and an additional simple calibration was performed as an early step in the algorithm to reduce or eliminate the bias in data after performing calibration using the manufacturer software. If the sensor was not calibrated using this two-stage algorithm, the results would be different from the actual value.

This calibration process and the calculation are simple, less time-consuming, and easy to follow. Thus, this extra process did not increase the calculation burden. Table 2 depicts the shortcomings of various calibration techniques described in other research articles and the advantages of this proposed calibration process over the previous research.

Table 2. Inertial sensor calibration shortcomings mentioned in the previous literature and advantages of the proposed calibration process.

Ref.	Year	Shortcomings of Calibration Process (Previous Literature)	Advantages of Proposed Calibration Process
[14]	2022	• Cumbersome calibration procedure	
[37]	2022	• Deep convolutional neural network Calib-Net was implemented, where internal algorithms are more difficult to interpret from a physical and geometric perspective	
[38]	2020	• A total of thirty positions are needed for the process, which is a laborious task	• The procedure and calculation are simple • Requires small dataset • Positioning the sensor for calibration purposes is straightforward, and rotation of the sensor is not required
[39]	2020	• Training necessitates a substantial dataset at the beginning	
[40]	2017	• Numerical integration could result in inaccuracies	• The process is not time consuming • Each sensor calibration process is independent
[41]	2017	• Difficult procedure • Inconvenient for engineering application	
[42]	2015	• Gyroscope precision is dependent on the calibration accuracy of the accelerometer	

The acceleration (a^i), angular velocity (g^i), and magnetic field strength (m^i) of the IMU about the x, y, and z axes were measured with a tri-axis accelerometer, gyroscope, and magnetometer, and they were expressed as

$$a^i = \begin{bmatrix} a_{xi} & a_{yi} & a_{zi} \end{bmatrix} \tag{1}$$

$$g^i = \begin{bmatrix} \omega_{xi} & \omega_{yi} & \omega_{zi} \end{bmatrix} \tag{2}$$

$$m^i = \begin{bmatrix} m_{xi} & m_{yi} & m_{zi} \end{bmatrix} \tag{3}$$

where i = 1 (for forearm sensor), 2 (for upper arm sensor), 3 (for reference sensor).

In this system, the accelerometer was calibrated using the bias correction vector. During the measurement, the sensors were in static condition for at least 10 s. The first hundred raw accelerometer data were used for determining the bias correction vector for the calibration of the accelerometer. The bias correction vector and calibrated value of the accelerometer were calculated from Equations (4) and (5), respectively.

$$b_i = \begin{bmatrix} \dfrac{\sum_0^{100}\left(a_{xi_{bias}}\right)}{100} & \dfrac{\sum_0^{100}\left(a_{yi_{bias}}\right)}{100} & \dfrac{\sum_0^{100}\left(a_{zi_{bias}}\right)}{100} \end{bmatrix} \tag{4}$$

$$a_c^k = (a^k - b_i) \tag{5}$$

where

b_i = bias in accelerometer readings;

a^k = accelerometer reading after calibration by WitMotion software;

a_c^k = calibrated accelerometer data.

When there was a value of roll and pitch, the magnetometer data in the local coordinate system were transferred to the global coordinate system. This transformation was performed using Equations (6)–(8), where m_{Gx}, m_{Gy}, and m_{Gz} are the magnetometer measurements in the global coordinate frame in X, Y, and Z axes.

$$m_{Gx} = m_{xi} \cos\theta + m_{yi} \sin\theta \sin\varphi + m_{zi} \sin\theta \cos\varphi \tag{6}$$

$$m_{Gy} = m_{yi} \cos\varphi - m_{zi} \sin\varphi \tag{7}$$

$$m_{Gz} = -m_{xi} \sin\theta + m_{yi} \sin\varphi \cos\theta + m_{zi} \cos\varphi \cos\theta \tag{8}$$

The yaw angle, calculated using Equations (6)–(8), is the heading of the sensor with respect to the magnetic north. However, the magnetometer data were converted to get the initial zero yaw angle using Equations (9)–(14).

$$m_{i(avg)} = \begin{bmatrix} m_{xi_{avg}} & m_{yi_{avg}} & m_{zi_{avg}} \end{bmatrix} = \begin{bmatrix} \dfrac{\sum_0^{100}\left(m_{xi_j}\right)}{100} & \dfrac{\sum_0^{100}\left(m_{yi_j}\right)}{100} & \dfrac{\sum_0^{100}\left(m_{zi_j}\right)}{100} \end{bmatrix} \tag{9}$$

$$heading = \begin{bmatrix} 0 & 0 & Atan2\left(m_{yi_{avg}}, m_{xi_{avg}}\right) \end{bmatrix} \tag{10}$$

$$q_h = \begin{bmatrix} q_{h0} & q_{h1} & q_{h2} & q_{h3} \end{bmatrix} \tag{11}$$

$$q_{m_k} = \begin{bmatrix} 0 & m_{Gx} & m_{Gy} & m_{Gz} \end{bmatrix} \tag{12}$$

$$q_{m_c^k} = \left(q_h \otimes q_{m_k}\right) \otimes q_h^* = \begin{bmatrix} q_a & q_b & q_c & q_d \end{bmatrix} \tag{13}$$

$$m_c^k = \begin{bmatrix} q_b & q_c & q_d \end{bmatrix} \tag{14}$$

where

$m_{i(avg)}$ = average of first hundred data of magnetometer along X, Y, and Z axes;

q_h = quaternion corresponding to the heading angle;

$q_{m_c^k}$ = quaternion corresponding to the corrected magnetometer data;

m_c^k = corrected magnetometer data.

2.2.2. First Stage: Estimation of Orientation from Sensor Fusion Technique

The Madgwick algorithm (MAD) was implemented in this study as an orientation filter. The MAD is a sensor fusion algorithm that combines the data from the accelerometer, gyroscope, and magnetometer in a quaternion form. This algorithm computes a quaternion derivative of the IMU, which can be converted to Euler angles. Although the sample rate restricts the range of the motion or joint angle measurement accuracy, satisfactory behavior was recorded even when utilizing low sampling rates, close to 10 Hz, and this level of accuracy may be suitable for applications involving human motion [32]. The Madgwick filter is an algorithm based on gradient descent that can compensate gyroscope drift [32]. The advantages of the Madgwick filter are its low computational load and complexity, low sampling rate requirement, that it can compensate for magnetic distortion, and that it has a simple tuning method where there is only one adjustable parameter. Since MAD uses a quaternion representation, the filter is not subjected to the gimbal lock problem associated with Euler angle representation. The Madgwick algorithm is also very convenient for small-size, low-cost, and low-energy-consumption microprocessors.

The implementation of the proposed algorithm was carried out with the assistance of Matlab R2022a. After going through the calibration steps, the data from three IMUs (forearm, upper arm, and reference) acted as an input for the Madgwick filter. The filter's output was three different sets of quaternions for the upper arm, forearm, and reference sensors. These three sets of quaternions were utilized to compute the joint angle of the rigid body. The Madgwick filter's precise details are stated in Algorithm 2.

Algorithm 2 Madgwick Filter [32]

First Step: Computation of the orientation from the gyroscope.

Gyroscope measurement: $S_\omega = [0 \quad \omega_x \quad \omega_y \quad \omega_z]$

Quaternion derivative: $^S_E\dot{q}_{w,t} = \frac{1}{2}{}^S_E\hat{q}_{est,t-1} \otimes S_{\omega t}$

Orientation from Gyroscope, $^S_E q_{\omega,t} = \frac{1}{2}{}^S_E\hat{q}_{est,t-1} + {}^S_E\dot{q}_{w,t}\Delta t$

Second Step: Use of accelerometer data to get the orientation quaternion.

Sensor Orientation: $^S_E\hat{q} = [q_1 \quad q_2 \quad q_3 \quad q_4]$

Predefined reference direction of the field in the earth frame:

$$E_{\hat{d}} = [0 \quad d_x \quad d_y \quad d_z]$$

Measurement of the field in the sensor frame, $S_{\hat{s}} = [0 \quad s_x \quad s_y \quad s_z]$

The sensor orientation $^S_E\hat{q}$ can be formulated as an optimization problem by

$$\min_{^S_E\hat{q}\, \in R^4} f(^S_E\hat{q}, E_{\hat{d}}, S_{\hat{s}})$$

where the objective function $f(^S_E\hat{q}, E_{\hat{d}}, S_{\hat{s}})$ can be calculated by

$$(^S_E\hat{q}^* \otimes E_{\hat{d}} \otimes {}^S_E\hat{q} - S_{\hat{s}})$$

Using Gradient Descent algorithm, estimated orientation based on previous one and μ step size:

$$^S_E\hat{q}_{k+1} = {}^S_E\hat{q}_k - \mu \frac{\nabla f(^S_E\hat{q}, E_{\hat{d}}, S_{\hat{s}})}{\|\nabla f(^S_E\hat{q}, E_{\hat{d}}, S_{\hat{s}})\|}$$

where $\nabla f(^S_E\hat{q}, E_{\hat{d}}, S_{\hat{s}}) = J^T(^S_E\hat{q}_k, E_{\hat{d}}) f(^S_E\hat{q}, E_{\hat{d}}, S_{\hat{s}})$

For accelerometer, the Objective function and the Jacobian matrix are $f_g(^S_E\hat{q}, S_{\hat{a}})$ and $J_g(^S_E\hat{q})$.

Third Step: Use of magnetometer data.

Earth's magnetic field: $E_{\hat{b}} = [0 \quad b_x \quad 0 \quad b_z]$

Magnetometer measurement: $S_{\hat{m}} = [0 \quad m_x \quad m_y \quad m_z]$

For Magnetometer the Objective function and the Jacobian matrix are $f_b(^S_E\hat{q}, E_{\hat{b}}, S_{\hat{m}})$ and $J_b(^S_E\hat{q}, E_{\hat{b}})$ respectively.

Complete solution considering accelerometer and magnetometer:

Objective function: $f_{g,b}(^S_E\hat{q}, S_a, E_{\hat{b}}, S_{\hat{m}}) = \begin{pmatrix} f_g(^S_E\hat{q}, S_{\hat{a}}) \\ f_b(^S_E\hat{q}, E_{\hat{b}}, S_{\hat{m}}) \end{pmatrix}$

Jacobian matrix: $J_{g,b}(^S_E\hat{q}, E_{\hat{b}}) = \begin{pmatrix} J_g(^S_E\hat{q}) \\ J_b(^S_E\hat{q}, E_{\hat{b}}) \end{pmatrix}$

Estimated Orientation, $^S_E q_{\nabla,t} = \frac{1}{2}{}^S_E q_{est,t-1} - \mu \frac{\nabla f}{\|\nabla f\|}$

where, $\nabla f = J^T_{g,b}(^S_E\hat{q}, E_{\hat{b}}) f_{g,b}(^S_E\hat{q}, S_a, E_{\hat{b}}, S_{\hat{m}})$ and $\mu = \alpha\, ^S_E\dot{q}_{w,t}\Delta t$, $\alpha > 1$

Final Step: Final estimation of the orientation:

$$^S_E q_{est,t} = \gamma t\, ^S_E q_{\nabla,t} + (1 - \gamma)^S_E q_{w,t}$$

The simple expression after some simplifications and assumptions:

$$^S_E q_{est,t} = -\beta \frac{\nabla f}{\|\nabla f\|} \Delta t + {}^S_E\hat{q}_{est,t-1} + {}^S_E\dot{q}_{w,t}\Delta t$$

2.2.3. Second Stage: Measurement of Angle

The quaternions for the forearm, upper arm, and reference from the first stage were denoted by q_{FA}, q_{UA}, and q_R, respectively.

$$q_{FA} = [q_{F0} \quad q_{F1} \quad q_{F2} \quad q_{F3}] \tag{15}$$

$$q_{UA} = [q_{U0} \quad q_{U1} \quad q_{U2} \quad q_{U3}] \tag{16}$$

$$q_R = [q_{R0} \quad q_{R1} \quad q_{R2} \quad q_{R3}] \tag{17}$$

If the upper arm is completely static, it is possible to calculate the joint angle from the initial and final quaternion of the forearm sensor. However, as the upper arm sensor may move with the movement of the forearm, the actual angle between the upper arm and forearm can be found by using the quaternion of two sensors placed on the forearm and upper arm. Considering this, the quaternion corresponding to the angle (θ_1) between these two sensors was found using Equation (18).

$$q_{UF} = q_{UA} \times q_{FA}^{*} = [q_{UF0} \quad q_{UF1} \quad q_{UF2} \quad q_{UF3}] \tag{18}$$

The angle (θ_1) between the forearm and upper arm sensors was obtained from the quaternion q_{UF} using Equation (19).

$$\text{Angle } (\theta_1) = \left[Atan2 \left((1 - (q_{UF2}^2 + q_{UF3}^2)), \ 2(q_{UF0}q_{UF3} + q_{UF1}q_{UF2}) \right) \right] \times 57.3 \tag{19}$$

Moreover, the impact of the movement of the upper arm could be found by using Equation (20).

$$q_{UFR} = q_{UF} \times q_{R}^{*} = [q_0 \quad q_1 \quad q_2 \quad q_3] \tag{20}$$

The more precise joint angle (θ_2) was obtained from the quaternion q_{UFR} using Equation (21).

$$\text{Joint Angle, } \theta_2 = \left[Atan2 \left((1 - (q_2^2 + q_3^2)), \ 2(q_0 q_3 + q_1 q_2) \right) \right] \times 57.3 \tag{21}$$

2.2.4. Filtering

An accelerometer can accurately calculate roll and pitch angles for a stationary object on Earth. If the sensor moves, acceleration will alter rotation computation. Additionally, the adjacent magnetic fields' impact causes the magnetometer's results to be inaccurate. Therefore, filtering is quite important, and this particular design filters the final angle. The data filtering process was carried out using a fourth-order Butterworth filter.

3. Results and Discussion

The effectiveness of the proposed algorithm is evaluated and discussed in this section.

3.1. Joint Angle Measurement

The performance of the proposed joint monitoring algorithm was first tested to obtain the elbow joint angle of the rigid body using two sensors, one in the forearm and another in the upper arm, shown in Figure 3.

The forearm sensor was moved for five consecutive trials, while the upper arm sensor attached to the rigid body was in a static posture. Each time, the forearm was moved around 40°, and the respective joint angle was around 140°. Through the use of the WitMotion software, the raw motion data from the accelerometer, gyroscope, and magnetometer was recorded and gathered. The accelerometer, gyroscope, and magnetometer raw data were collected at 10 samples per second. Following that, the accelerometer and magnetometer sensor data were subjected to a second step of calibration. Then the accelerometer, gyroscope, and magnetometer data were used to calculate quaternion for both sensors, and after that, the joint angle created by the rigid body was calculated using Equation (19). Two electro-goniometers (EGs) were attached with the forearm and the upper arm of the rigid body to measure the joint angle at the same time (shown in Figure 1c) and the angle calculated using the two EGs was considered as the reference value. The WitMotion software itself calculated the orientation of the sensors using the KF. The joint angle from the proposed algorithm (PA) and calculated from the KF outcomes of WitMotion software (WM) for two sensors were compared with the measurement of joint angle from two EGs.

The performance of the proposed algorithm (PA), using two sensors, was evaluated with respect to the angle measurement value of the EGs and the angle measured from the KF outcomes of WitMotion software (WM) in terms of root mean square error (RMSE), which are presented in Table 3. Figure 4 shows joint angle graphical representations obtained from the proposed algorithm with two sensors and WitMotion outcomes for five different trials. In this case, the RMSEs for PA and WM were 0.26° and 0.43°, respectively. It can be seen that the proposed joint angle measurement system using two sensors and the Madgwick filter gives a more accurate estimation in this case.

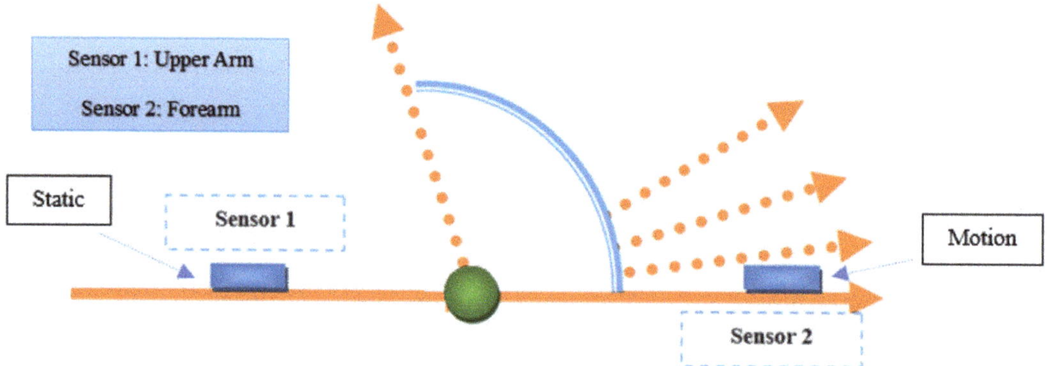

Figure 3. Joint angle (two sensors).

Table 3. Angle measurement comparison (RMSE in degrees) between the proposed algorithm (PA) and WitMotion (WM).

EG	PA	WM	Error (PA)	Error (WM)	RMSE (PA)	RMSE (WM)
139.25	139.55	138.86	−0.3	0.39		
139.5	139.72	139.01	−0.22	0.49		
139.2	139.38	138.75	−0.18	0.45	0.26	0.43
139.65	139.93	139.23	−0.28	0.42		
139.2	139.51	138.82	−0.31	0.38		

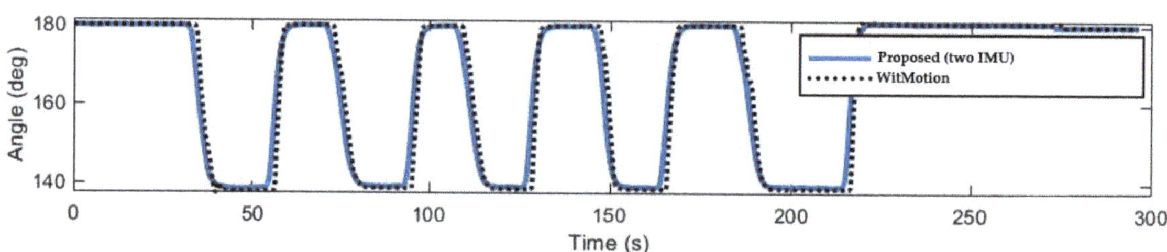

Figure 4. Measured angle from proposed algorithm (PA) and WitMotion (WM) using two IMUs.

In the subsequent case, three sensors were used for more precise measurement of the joint angle between the forearm and the upper arm. The forearm of the body was also moved for four separate trials, where the forearm was moved by approximately 30°, 45°, 60°, and 90° in these four trials, respectively, and the upper arm was moved by 30° in every trial. During the movement of the forearm of the rigid body, shown in Figure 5 (also shown in Figure 1c), the upper arm remained in a stationary position. After the predefined movement of the forearm, the movement of the upper arm was executed. In each trial, the forearm and the upper arm were moved five times, and with the rotation of the upper arm, the final rotation of forearm was shifted to 60°, 75°, 90°, and 120° in the four trials, respectively. Thus, in these trials, the joint angles between the forearm and the upper arm were approximately 150°, 135°, 120°, and 90°.

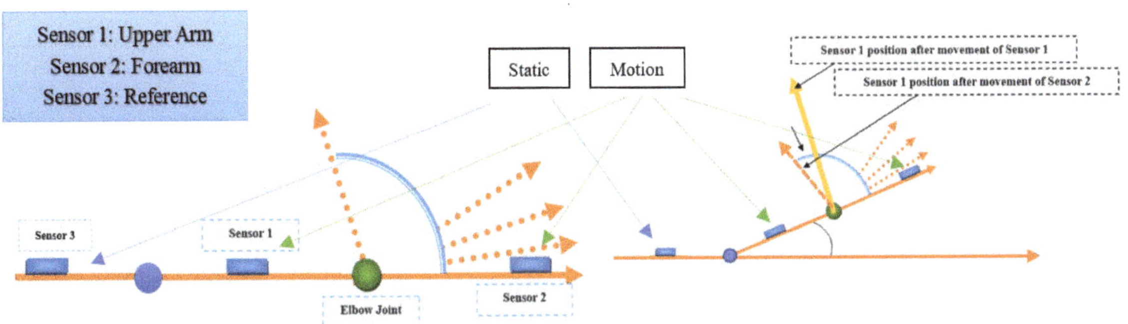

Figure 5. Joint angle (three sensors).

In each case or trial, the angle between the forearm and upper arm was calculated from the data of the two EGs attached to the forearm and upper arm of the rigid body. The angle calculated with the EGs was considered to be the reference value. Additionally, the raw data from the accelerometer, gyroscope, and magnetometer were collected and used as the input of the proposed algorithm (PA) after executing the calibration process. Three sensors provide three orientations in quaternion form, and using Equations (15)–(21), the more accurate joint angle between the forearm and upper arm was calculated.

In the first trial, at first the forearm was moved by about 30°, and then the upper arm was moved by about 30°. Thus, the angle was approximately 150° between the forearm and upper arm. The angles calculated from the EGs, PA, and WM are presented in Table 4, and Figure 6 shows joint angle graphical representations obtained from the PA and WM for the first trial. In the second trial, the forearm was moved by about 45°, and then the upper arm was moved by about 30°. Thus, the angle was approximately 135° between the forearm and upper arm. The angles calculated from the EGs, PA, and WM are presented in Table 5, and Figure 7 shows joint angle graphical representations obtained from the PA and WM for the second trial.

Table 4. RMSE (°) of the joint angle (first trial).

EG	PA	WM	Error (PA)	Error (WM)	RMSE (PA)	RMSE (WM)
149.70	149.32	148.53	−0.38	−1.17		
149.40	148.91	148.23	−0.49	−1.17		
149.65	149.23	148.49	−0.42	−1.16	0.46	1.19
149.50	148.98	148.29	−0.52	−1.21		
149.75	149.27	148.52	−0.48	−1.23		

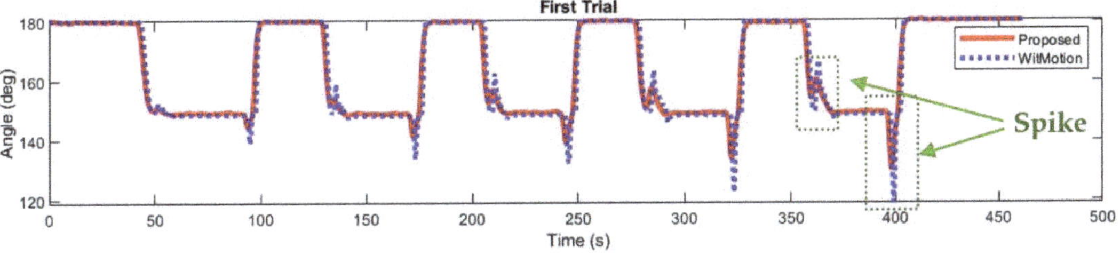

Figure 6. Measured angle using proposed algorithm (PA) and WitMotion (WM) (first trial).

Table 5. RMSE (°) of the joint angle (second trial).

EG	PA	WM	Error (PA)	Error (WM)	RMSE (PA)	RMSE (WM)
134.05	134.12	132.30	0.07	−1.75		
134.65	134.76	132.67	0.11	−1.98		
134.70	134.83	132.73	0.13	−1.97	0.10	1.97
134.80	134.93	132.74	0.13	−2.06		
134.60	134.65	132.54	0.05	−2.06		

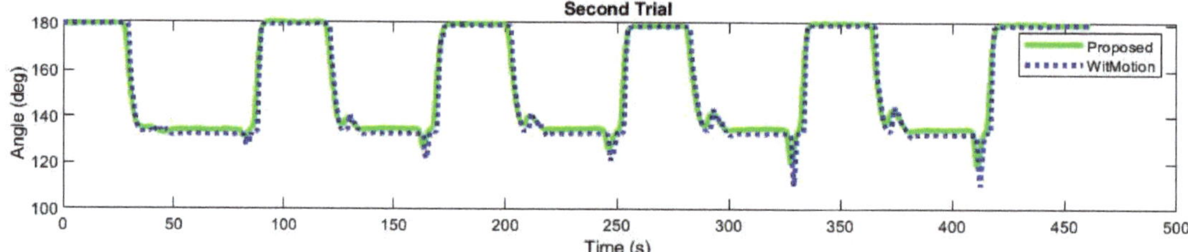

Figure 7. Measured angle using proposed algorithm (PA) and WitMotion (WM) (second trial).

In the same way, the outcome of the third and fourth trials is given in Tables 6 and 7, respectively, and graphically represented in Figures 8 and 9, respectively. In the third trial, the forearm was moved by about 60°, and then the upper arm was moved by about 30°. Additionally, in the fourth trial, the forearm was moved by about 90°, and then the upper arm was moved by about 30°.

Table 6. RMSE (°) of the joint angle (third trial).

EG	PA	WM	Error (PA)	Error (WM)	RMSE (PA)	RMSE (WM)
120.00	120.19	118.69	0.19	−1.31		
119.85	120.00	118.48	0.15	−1.37		
119.95	120.07	118.58	0.12	−1.37	0.18	1.40
119.85	119.94	118.35	0.09	−1.50		
119.95	120.23	118.50	0.28	−1.45		

In these four trials, the RMSEs for the PA and WM were calculated with respect to the joint angle calculated using EGs, and all the results were compared. The calculated RMSEs for the joint angle using the PA were 0.46°, 0.10°, 0.18°, and 0.03°, respectively, and for the WM, the RMSEs were 1.19°, 1.97°, 1.40°, and 0.29°, respectively. The comparison of the RMSE between the PA and WM showed that the proposed joint angle measurement system using the Madgwick filter gave a more accurate estimation for all the trials. Moreover, the RMSE resided within the clinically acceptable threshold of 5° in all cases. There are two spikes during each motion of all the trials, which was only mentioned in Figure 6. This problem was developed as different sensor units' data alter differently while in motion. The experiments were conducted under the same environmental conditions, and the same posture was used for this experiment. Table 8 shows a performance comparison between several existing studies and the proposed algorithm, and for this comparison table, articles only with artificially developed structures were considered.

Table 7. RMSE (°) of the joint angle (fourth trial).

EG	PA	WM	Error (PA)	Error (WM)	RMSE (PA)	RMSE (WM)
89.20	89.27	88.89	0.07	−0.31		
89.95	89.96	89.73	0.01	−0.22		
89.90	89.88	89.62	−0.02	−0.28	0.03	0.29
89.85	89.85	89.59	0.00	−0.26		
89.80	89.79	89.42	−0.01	−0.38		

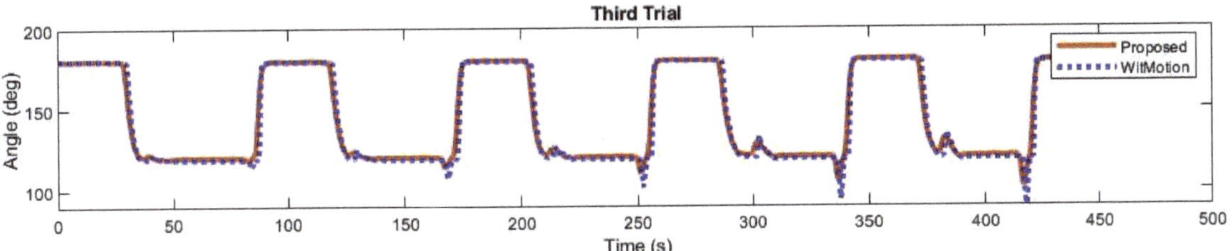

Figure 8. Measured angle using proposed algorithm (PA) and WitMotion (WM) (third trial).

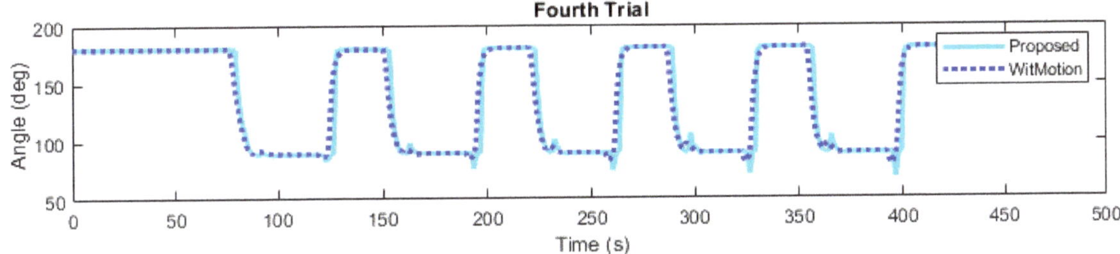

Figure 9. Measured angle using proposed algorithm (PA) and WitMotion (WM) (fourth trial).

Table 8. Performance comparison.

Ref.	Year	Structure	Comparison Parameter (RMSE/ Max. Deviation)
[43]	2022	UR3 Robot	RMSE: 1.0029°
[44]	2022	Two links joined by a magnetic encoder	ADXL345 (RMSE) Analytical (3.61° to 11.67°), EKF (3.09° to 7.95°), UKF (3.03° to 7.92°) ADXL357 (RMSE) Analytical (4.7° to 11.39°), EKF (4.8° to 11.42°), UKF (4.8° to 11.37°) BNO055 (RMSE) Analytical (2.99° to 17.72°), EKF (3.47° to 10.52°), UKF (3.45° to 10.51°)
[45]	2022	ROMSS	Max. Deviation: 0.87°
[46]	2021	Artificial joint	Max. Deviation: 0.60°
Proposed Algorithm		3D Rigid body	RMSE: 0.03° to 0.46° Max. Deviation: 0.52°

3.2. Joint Angle Measurement Considering External Acceleration

In the presence of an external acceleration, the proposed algorithm's effectiveness was verified by simulating zero-mean white Gaussian noise to the acceleration measurements of all three IMUs. Zero-mean Gaussian noise was used to create external acceleration as IMU noise is best fitted by a Gaussian distribution, and the noise in IMU is white Gaussian in nature [13,47]. Figure 10a shows the sample raw accelerometer data without external noise, and Figure 10b displays the sample raw accelerometer data with external noise, which was contaminated at 20 dB signal-to-noise ratio (SNR) for one wearable IMU.

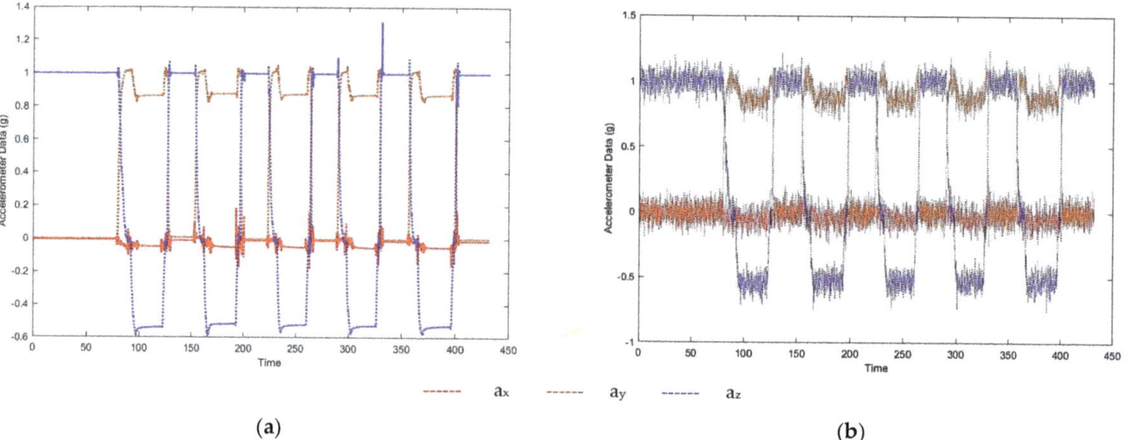

(a) (b)

Figure 10. Raw accelerometer data (**a**) without noise and (**b**) with external noise.

In Figure 11, the joint angle is shown, estimated using the proposed algorithm that takes into account the noisy accelerometer data, and compared to the angle obtained using the proposed algorithm with clean accelerometer data. Table 9 displays the root mean square error associated with calculated joint angles when an external acceleration is present. Figure 11 and Table 9 both demonstrate that the suggested algorithm was exceptionally resistant to the effects of acceleration from the environment, as the RMSE was $0.996°$ after the addition of external noise. Moreover, the RMSE value was below the threshold of $5°$, which is considered clinically acceptable [13].

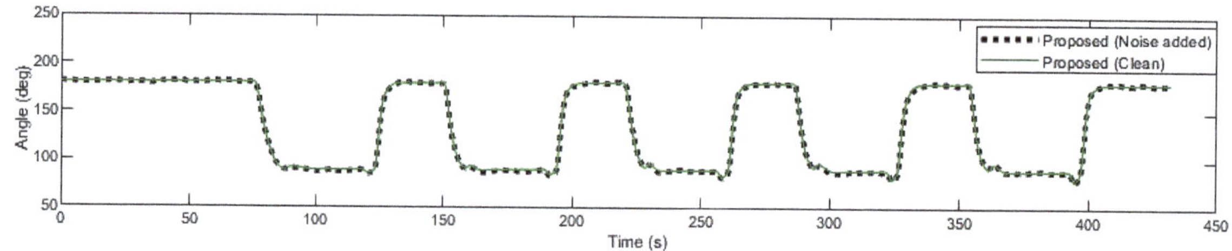

Figure 11. Measured angle using proposed algorithm (PA) with and without external noise.

Table 9. RMSE (°) of the joint angle (external noise added).

EG	PA	Error (PA)	RMSE (PA)
89.20	88.02	1.18	
89.95	88.42	1.53	
89.90	89.58	0.32	0.996
89.85	88.87	0.98	
89.80	89.40	0.40	

3.3. Limitations

In this experiment, the attachment location of the sensors was not precisely regulated, especially the shoulder sensor; nonetheless, while the measurements were being taken, they were aligned approximately in the sagittal plane. The reference sensor may face unwanted motion in real-world scenarios. Thus, this straightforward way of attaching sensors is significant for real-world clinical applications, but to get a high level of measurement accuracy in real-world clinical applications, the sensors themselves need to be precisely positioned, or their positions need to be measured. On the other hand, determining the placements of the sensors to achieve high measurement accuracy with patients may be challenging. In this study, the joint angle measurement error was minimized. However, the motion speed was not detected while the rigid body was in motion. Here, the sensor movement caused by the muscles or tendons was not considered. Moreover, this study only focused on the joint angles in the sagittal plane. However, it is desirable to measure the abduction and adduction angles and internal and external rotation angles. In addition, there is a possibility of challenges in dealing with stroke patients, especially those suffering from upper limb tightening or contracture. Nevertheless, the developed system in this study is thought to have attained a good level of accuracy when practical applications are taken into consideration.

4. Conclusions

This study implemented the Madgwick filter-based joint angle measurement algorithm to construct a wireless wearable sensor system for simplified joint angle measurement. The design and development of a 3D rigid body included the attachment of three IMU sensors to the body's arms. The proposed algorithm was tested against a gold standard EG system and also compared with the outcomes of WitMotion software (WM). The comparison confirms that the proposed algorithm performed better for joint angle measurement, which is necessary for clinical acceptance. The suggested approach successfully predicted the elbow joint angle with a maximum root mean square error (RMSE) of $0.46°$. The joint angles were also determined using external acceleration, and the RMSE was $0.996°$. All the RMSE values were within the range of acceptable joint angles appropriate for medical applications. Still, there are some critical issues and possibilities for future investigation. In this analysis, a rigid body was used to assess how efficiently the proposed algorithm performed. Therefore, in future work, the measurement in real-world scenarios (with the human body upper limb joint angle) will be used to assess the efficacy. For quantitative risk assessment of the human upper limb joints, we will incorporate a real-time feedback system with this proposed system. A focus may be given to semi-permanent tissue implantation with a remote sensor for accurate measurement, and in this way, researchers will have round-the-clock total body measurements. Finally, a comprehensive wearable system based on IMU will be developed to monitor all upper body joints at home.

Author Contributions: Conceptualization, M.M.R., K.B.G. and N.A.A.A.; Methodology, M.M.R. and K.B.G.; Software, M.M.R. and K.B.G.; Validation, M.M.R., K.B.G. and N.A.A.A.; Formal analysis, M.M.R., K.B.G. and N.A.A.A.; Investigation, M.M.R. and K.B.G.; Resources, M.M.R.; Data curation, M.M.R.; Writing—original draft, M.M.R.; Writing—review & editing, M.M.R., K.B.G., N.A.A.A., A.H. and Y.H.W.; Visualization, M.M.R., K.B.G. and N.A.A.A.; Supervision, K.B.G.; Project administration, K.B.G.; Funding acquisition, K.B.G. All authors have read and agreed to the published version of the manuscript.

Funding: This research was funded by "Ministry of Higher Education under Fundamental Research Grant Scheme, grant number FRGS/1/2020/TK0/UKM/02/14" and "Research University Grant, grant number GUP-2018-048".

Data Availability Statement: The data presented in this study are available on request from the corresponding author.

Conflicts of Interest: The authors declare no conflict of interest. The funders had no role in the design of the study; in the collection, analyses, or interpretation of data; in the writing of the manuscript; or in the decision to publish the results.

References

1. Ramlee, M.H.; Beng, G.K.; Bajuri, N.; Abdul Kadir, M.R. Finite element analysis of the wrist in stroke patients: The effects of hand grip. *Med. Biol. Eng. Comput.* **2018**, *56*, 1161–1171. [CrossRef] [PubMed]
2. Ponvel, P.; Singh, D.K.A.; Beng, G.K.; Chai, S.C. Factors affecting upper extremity kinematics in healthy adults: A systematic review. *Crit. Rev. Phys. Rehabil. Med.* **2019**, *31*, 101–123. [CrossRef]
3. Ramlee, M.H.; Gan, K.B. Function and biomechanics of upper limb in post-stroke patients—A systematic review. *J. Mech. Med. Biol.* **2017**, *17*, 1750099. [CrossRef]
4. Faisal, A.I.; Majumder, S.; Mondal, T.; Cowan, D.; Naseh, S.; Deen, M.J. Monitoring methods of human body joints: State-of-the-art and research challenges. *Sensors* **2019**, *19*, 2629. [CrossRef] [PubMed]
5. Zheng, R.; Zhang, Y.; Zhang, K.; Yuan, Y.; Jia, S.; Liu, J. The Complement System, Aging, and Aging-Related Diseases. *Int. J. Mol. Sci.* **2022**, *23*, 8689. [CrossRef] [PubMed]
6. McGrath, T.; Stirling, L. Body-Worn IMU-Based Human Hip and Knee Kinematics Estimation during Treadmill Walking. *Sensors* **2022**, *22*, 2544. [CrossRef] [PubMed]
7. Vincent, A.C.; Furman, H.; Slepian, R.C.; Ammann, K.R.; Maria, C.D.; Chien, J.H.; Siu, K.C.; Slepian, M.J. Smart Phone-Based Motion Capture and Analysis: Importance of Operating Envelope Definition and Application to Clinical Use. *Appl. Sci.* **2022**, *12*, 6173. [CrossRef]
8. Lee, J.K.; Jung, W.C. Quaternion-based local frame alignment between an inertial measurement unit and a motion capture system. *Sensors* **2018**, *18*, 4003. [CrossRef]
9. Li, J.; Liu, X.; Wang, Z.; Zhao, H.; Zhang, T.; Qiu, S.; Zhou, X.; Cai, H.; Ni, R.; Cangelosi, A. Real-Time Human Motion Capture Based on Wearable Inertial Sensor Networks. *IEEE Internet Things J.* **2022**, *9*, 8953–8966. [CrossRef]
10. Sung, J.; Han, S.; Park, H.; Cho, H.M.; Hwang, S.; Park, J.W.; Youn, I. Prediction of lower extremity multi-joint angles during overground walking by using a single IMU with a low frequency based on an LSTM recurrent neural network. *Sensors* **2022**, *22*, 53. [CrossRef]
11. Basso, M.; Galanti, M.; Innocenti, G.; Miceli, D. Pedestrian Dead Reckoning Based on Frequency Self-Synchronization and Body Kinematics. *IEEE Sens. J.* **2017**, *17*, 534–545. [CrossRef]
12. Majumder, S.; Mondal, T.; Deen, M.J. A Simple, Low-Cost and Efficient Gait Analyzer for Wearable Healthcare Applications. *IEEE Sens. J.* **2019**, *19*, 2320–2329. [CrossRef]
13. Majumder, S.; Member, G.S.; Deen, M.J.; Fellow, L. Wearable IMU-Based System for Real-Time Monitoring of Lower-Limb Joints. *IEEE Sens. J.* **2021**, *21*, 8267–8275. [CrossRef]
14. Shuai, Z.; Dong, A.; Liu, H.; Cui, Y. Reliability and Validity of an Inertial Measurement System to Quantify Lower Extremity Joint Angle in Functional Movements. *Sensors* **2022**, *22*, 863. [CrossRef]
15. Al-Amri, M.; Nicholas, K.; Button, K.; Sparkes, V.; Sheeran, L.; Davies, J.L. Inertial measurement units for clinical movement analysis: Reliability and concurrent validity. *Sensors* **2018**, *18*, 719. [CrossRef]
16. Brouwer, N.P.; Yeung, T.; Bobbert, M.F.; Besier, T.F. 3D trunk orientation measured using inertial measurement units during anatomical and dynamic sports motions. *Scand. J. Med. Sci. Sport.* **2021**, *31*, 358–370. [CrossRef]
17. Lim, X.Y.; Gan, K.B.; Aziz, N.A.A. Deep convlstm network with dataset resampling for upper body activity recognition using minimal number of imu sensors. *Appl. Sci.* **2021**, *11*, 3543. [CrossRef]
18. Majumder, S.; Mondal, T.; Deen, M.J. Wearable sensors for remote health monitoring. *Sensors* **2017**, *17*, 130. [CrossRef]
19. Majumder, S.; Aghayi, E.; Noferesti, M.; Memarzadeh-Tehran, H.; Mondal, T.; Pang, Z.; Deen, M.J. Smart homes for elderly healthcare—Recent advances and research challenges. *Sensors* **2017**, *17*, 2496. [CrossRef]
20. Vijayan, V.; Connolly, J.; Condell, J.; McKelvey, N.; Gardiner, P. Review of wearable devices and data collection considerations for connected health. *Sensors* **2021**, *21*, 5589. [CrossRef]
21. Longo, U.G.; De Salvatore, S.; Sassi, M.; Carnevale, A.; De Luca, G.; Denaro, V. Motion Tracking Algorithms Based on Wearable Inertial Sensor: A Focus on Shoulder. *Electronics* **2022**, *11*, 1741. [CrossRef]
22. Rigoni, M.; Gill, S.; Babazadeh, S.; Elsewaisy, O.; Gillies, H.; Nguyen, N.; Pathirana, P.N.; Page, R. Assessment of shoulder range of motion using a wireless inertial motion capture device—A validation study. *Sensors* **2019**, *19*, 1781. [CrossRef] [PubMed]
23. Chiella, A.C.B.; Teixeira, B.O.S.; Pereira, G.A.S. Quaternion-based robust attitude estimation using an adaptive unscented Kalman filter. *Sensors* **2019**, *19*, 2372. [CrossRef] [PubMed]
24. Yuan, X.; Yu, S.; Zhang, S.; Wang, G.; Liu, S. Quaternion-based unscented kalman filter for accurate indoor heading estimation using wearable multi-sensor system. *Sensors* **2015**, *15*, 10872–10890. [CrossRef]
25. Kottath, R.; Poddar, S.; Das, A.; Kumar, V. Window based Multiple Model Adaptive Estimation for Navigational Framework. *Aerosp. Sci. Technol.* **2016**, *50*, 88–95. [CrossRef]
26. Kalman, R.E. A new approach to linear filtering and prediction problems. *J. Fluids Eng. Trans. ASME* **1960**, *82*, 35–45. [CrossRef]
27. Wu, J.; Zhou, Z.; Fourati, H.; Li, R.; Liu, M. Generalized Linear Quaternion Complementary Filter for Attitude Estimation From Multisensor Observations: An Optimization Approach. *IEEE Trans. Autom. Sci. Eng.* **2019**, *16*, 1330–1343. [CrossRef]

28. Urrea, C.; Agramonte, R. Kalman Filter: Historical Overview and Review of Its Use in Robotics 60 Years after Its Creation. *J. Sensors* **2021**, *2021*, 9674015. [CrossRef]
29. Kim, J.; Lee, K. Unscented kalman filter-aided long short-term memory approach for wind nowcasting. *Aerospace* **2021**, *8*, 236. [CrossRef]
30. Poddar, S.; Narkhede, P.; Kumar, V.; Kumar, A. PSO Aided Adaptive Complementary Filter for Attitude Estimation. *J. Intell. Robot. Syst. Theory Appl.* **2017**, *87*, 531–543. [CrossRef]
31. Kottath, R.; Narkhede, P.; Kumar, V.; Karar, V.; Poddar, S. Multiple Model Adaptive Complementary Filter for Attitude Estimation. *Aerosp. Sci. Technol.* **2017**, *69*, 574–581. [CrossRef]
32. Madgwick, S.O.H.; Harrison, A.J.L.; Vaidyanathan, R. Estimation of IMU and MARG orientation using a gradient descent algorithm ACT Profile Report: State. Graduating Class 2012. In Proceedings of the 2011 IEEE International Conference on Rehabilitation Robotics, Zurich, Switzerland, 29 June–1 July 2011; pp. 1–7.
33. Mahony, R.; Hamel, T.; Morin, P.; Malis, E. Nonlinear complementary filters on the special linear group. *Int. J. Control* **2012**, *85*, 1557–1573. [CrossRef]
34. Ludwig, S.A.; Burnham, K.D. Comparison of Euler Estimate using Extended Kalman Filter, Madgwick and Mahony on Quad-copter Flight Data. In Proceedings of the 2018 International Conference on Unmanned Aircraft Systems (ICUAS), Dallas, TX, USA, 12–15 June 2018; pp. 1236–1241. [CrossRef]
35. Fayat, R.; Betancourt, V.D.; Goyallon, T.; Petremann, M.; Liaudet, P.; Descossy, V.; Reveret, L.; Dugué, G.P. Inertial measurement of head tilt in rodents: Principles and applications to vestibular research. *Sensors* **2021**, *21*, 6318. [CrossRef] [PubMed]
36. Rahman, M.M.; Gan, K.B. Range of Motion Measurement Using Single Inertial Measurement Unit Sensor: A Validation and Comparative Study of Sensor Fusion Techniques. In Proceedings of the IEEE 20th Student Conference on Research and Development (SCOReD), Bangi, Malaysia, 8–9 November 2022; pp. 114–118. [CrossRef]
37. Li, R.; Fu, C.; Yi, W.; Yi, X. Calib-Net: Calibrating the Low-Cost IMU via Deep Convolutional Neural Network. *Front. Robot. AI* **2022**, *8*, 772583. [CrossRef]
38. Bao, Q. A Field Calibration Method for Low-Cost MEMS Accelerometer Based on the Generalized Nonlinear Least Square Method. *Multiscale Sci. Eng.* **2020**, *2*, 135–142. [CrossRef]
39. Soriano, M.A.; Khan, F.; Ahmad, R. Two-Axis Accelerometer Calibration and Nonlinear Correction Using Neural Networks: Design, Optimization, and Experimental Evaluation. *IEEE Trans. Instrum. Meas.* **2020**, *69*, 6787–6794. [CrossRef]
40. Sarkka, O.; Nieminen, T.; Suuriniemi, S.; Kettunen, L. A Multi-Position Calibration Method for Consumer-Grade Accelerometers, Gyroscopes, and Magnetometers to Field Conditions. *IEEE Sens. J.* **2017**, *17*, 3470–3481. [CrossRef]
41. Wang, S.M.; Meng, N. A new Multi-position calibration method for gyroscope's drift coefficients on centrifuge. *Aerosp. Sci. Technol.* **2017**, *68*, 104–108. [CrossRef]
42. Ding, Z.; Cai, H.; Yang, H. An improved multi-position calibration method for low cost micro-electro mechanical systems inertial measurement units. *Proc. Inst. Mech. Eng. Part G J. Aerosp. Eng.* **2015**, *229*, 1919–1930. [CrossRef]
43. Franco, T.; Sestrem, L.; Henriques, P.R.; Alves, P.; Varanda Pereira, M.J.; Brandão, D.; Leitão, P.; Silva, A. Motion Sensors for Knee Angle Recognition in Muscle Rehabilitation Solutions. *Sensors* **2022**, *22*, 7605. [CrossRef]
44. Woods, C.; Vikas, V. Joint angle estimation using accelerometer arrays and model-based filtering. *IEEE Sens. J.* **2022**, *22*, 19786–19796. [CrossRef]
45. Tuan, C.C.; Wu, Y.C.; Yeh, W.L.; Wang, C.C.; Lu, C.H.; Wang, S.W.; Yang, J.; Lee, T.F.; Kao, H.K. Development of Joint Activity Angle Measurement and Cloud Data Storage System. *Sensors* **2022**, *22*, 4684. [CrossRef]
46. González-Alonso, J.; Oviedo-Pastor, D.; Aguado, H.J.; Díaz-Pernas, F.J.; González-Ortega, D.; Martínez-Zarzuela, M. Custom imu-based wearable system for robust 2.4 ghz wireless human body parts orientation tracking and 3d movement visualization on an avatar. *Sensors* **2021**, *21*, 6642. [CrossRef] [PubMed]
47. Nirmal, K.; Sreejith, A.G.; Mathew, J.; Sarpotdar, M.; Suresh, A.; Prakash, A.; Safonova, M.; Murthy, J. Noise modeling and analysis of an IMU-based attitude sensor: Improvement of performance by filtering and sensor fusion. *Adv. Opt. Mech. Technol. Telesc. Instrum. II* **2016**, *9912*, 99126W. [CrossRef]

 *mathematics*

Article

Estimation of the Spatial and Temporal Distribution of Magnetic Fields around Overhead Power Lines—A Case Study

Ionel Pavel, Camelia Petrescu *, Valeriu David and Eduard Lunca

Faculty of Electrical Engineering, "Gheorghe Asachi" Technical University of Iasi, 700050 Iasi, Romania; ionel.pavel@academic.tuiasi.ro (I.P.); valeriu.david@academic.tuiasi.ro (V.D.); costel-eduard.lunca@academic.tuiasi.ro (E.L.)
* Correspondence: camelia-mihaela.petrescu@academic.tuiasi.ro

Abstract: Due to the growing number, diversity and spreading of magnetic field sources, an increasing need to determine the field levels of human exposure has arisen. Some of the most encountered sources are the overhead power lines (OPL) and the determination of spatial and temporal variation of the magnetic fields produced by OPLs is a challenge. In this paper a hybrid method for the estimation of the temporal and spatial distribution of the magnetic flux density B caused by OPLs, based on experimental measurements and on numerical and analytical simulations, is presented. Thus, using a small number of simultaneous spot measurements correlated with a long-term survey, maps of the magnetic flux density distribution on extended areas are established, for several time instances. The proposed method is verified using two sets of different measurements and the results obtained through simulation. The difference between the estimated and simulated values of B is under 5.5%, which is considered acceptable considering that B spans over a large set of values (724 nT ÷ 1375 nT) in the location of the long-term survey procedure. The possibilities and limitations of the proposed method are discussed.

Keywords: magnetic field survey; experimental determination of magnetic fields; modeling and simulation of OPLs

MSC: 94C60

Citation: Pavel, I.; Petrescu, C.; David, V.; Lunca, E. Estimation of the Spatial and Temporal Distribution of Magnetic Fields around Overhead Power Lines—A Case Study. *Mathematics* **2023**, *11*, 2292. https://doi.org/10.3390/math11102292

Academic Editor: Jacques Lobry

Received: 23 April 2023
Revised: 10 May 2023
Accepted: 13 May 2023
Published: 15 May 2023

1. Introduction

Electrical energy transport and distribution is done through overhead power lines (OPLs) as well as, where necessary, through underwater sea cables buried in the sea bed. The development of industrial and household applications both in urban and in rural areas lead to an expansion of the distribution networks so as to satisfy consumer demands. This means a network of high voltage power lines, as well as medium and low voltage lines is geared towards the end consumer. Overhead power lines, which host currents in the order of hundreds of amps, produce magnetic fields whose levels must be monitored due to the possible adverse effects on people and other living beings.

Overhead power lines work in the extra low frequency domain of the electromagnetic spectrum (ELF), i.e., 30–300 Hz. The current view, resulting from numerous researches and measurements, is to achieve a prudent avoidance of the exposure to electric and magnetic fields, both in occasional and in occupational situations.

Even if the maximum admissible values recommended by several international regulating authorities are rather large (of the order of 100 μT for the magnetic flux density), in cases of exposure for long periods of time, the threshold for B must be significantly smaller, especially for children, hence the necessity of a long-term survey and that of a complete characterization of the magnetic field exposure for the general population [1–4].

Numerous researches addressed the problem of determining, both analytically and experimentally, the electric and magnetic field produced by OPLs, trying to include various aspects such as ground proximity or the proximity of other conductors, the deformation of line conductors due to gravity, etc. In the following, a brief overview of some recent papers that address this subject is given.

In [5], the formulae for computing the electric and magnetic field produced by a line current at high altitudes (110 km above the Earth's surface) are developed. The model considers a flat Earth surface and a multilayer soil structure, with different electric properties, and uses a series expansion technique and the complex image method, as well as exact integral expressions for $\overline{E}$ and $\overline{B}$ components based on Maxwell's equations and boundary conditions at the Earth's surface.

In [6], the authors use double complex numbers to incorporate in one expression the components of $\overline{B}$, B_x and B_y (and the fact that these are complex numbers). Closed form expressions are derived for $\overline{B}$, based on the Biot Savart Laplace (BSL) formula.

In [7], the relations for the computation of the electric and magnetic fields produced by finite length OPLs, using the classical expression for the magnetic vector potential, are established.

Paper [8] considers a 3D model of OPLs, with deformation of the lines due to gravity. The study combines the classical simulation current method (SCM) which replaces the actual unknown distribution of currents with simulated currents (in order to determine the magnetic fields) with two stochastic optimization methods, Particle Swarm (PS) and Differential Evolution (DE), used to optimize (determine) the position and number of simulated currents.

Another optimization method, Ant Lion Optimization (ALO), is used in [9] to determine the position of the overhead power line conductors that minimize both the electric and magnetic fields at a height of 1 m above the ground. This method of field reduction implies, however, additional costs, due to the necessity to re-design OPLs.

In [10], the authors propose a method for the analysis of multi-circuit overhead transmission lines using artificial neural networks (ANN) trained to estimate the real and imaginary parts of B_x and B_y at arbitrary points (x, y). The results are compared with BSL simulations and experimental measurements.

The magnetic field produced by submarine power cables is studied in papers such as [11], where closed form solutions for thin wires with a helical shape are established, as well as in [12], where both modelled and measured results for B are presented and the geomagnetic field is also taken into account.

The main objective of the present paper is to obtain a complete characterization of the magnetic field generated by overhead power lines in cases of long-term exposure, taking into account that B (rms) has large and unpredictable variations in time. The originality and novelty of the paper resides in the proposed hybrid method for estimating B using a correlation between spot measurements and long-term survey data. Both these measurements are made simultaneously using two measuring devices realized by the authors. Thus, maps with the spatial distribution of B in a large area near the OPL can be obtained for any moment of time, without the need of using a large network of sensors for measuring the magnetic flux density.

The results obtained using the proposed hybrid method and our instruments are in good agreement with the results obtained in simulations.

The organization of the paper is as follows: Section 2 presents the materials and methods used in the study, Section 3 presents the performed measurements, Section 4 presents the results of simulations, Section 5 discusses the obtained results and Section 6 is reserved for the conclusions of the paper.

2. Materials and Methods

Magnetic flux density can be expressed in a three-orthogonal system as:

$$B = \sqrt{B_1^2 + B_2^2 + B_3^2} \tag{1}$$

where B_1, B_2 and B_3 are the rms values of the components along the orthogonal directions. If the orthogonal system is Oxyz, then the three components are B_x, B_y and B_z. This simple observation ensures the fact that if the measurements are done with a sensor that determines the rms value of B, then the result is the same, irrespective of the sensor orientation.

The usual approach in monitoring the magnetic field produced by OPL is to trace a longitudinal and a transversal profile of B. If a mesh with a step size of 1 m is considered and measurements are conducted using only one instrument, the map for B is correct, if the current in the OPL is constant (rms) during the entire survey. Due to the fact that line currents are unpredictable, the magnetic field may vary significantly in the observation points, so a time variation for B (rms) must be also determined.

The method proposed in this paper takes into account both the spatial and the temporal variation of B (rms). The results are based on experimental determinations onsite and also on measurements and simulations (being thus a hybrid method). The experimental results are compared with the results obtained through numerical simulations that use the OPL configuration and the values of the line currents.

As a result of applying the proposed method, the spatial distribution (map) for B is obtained in a rectangular region with the dimensions (in this case study) of 60 m in transversal direction and 282 m in longitudinal direction, for any observation time during the automatic monitoring interval.

The geometric configuration of the OPL (2D transversal view) is outlined in Figure 1a and in Figure 1b. The real view of the line, with the measuring instruments, is presented.

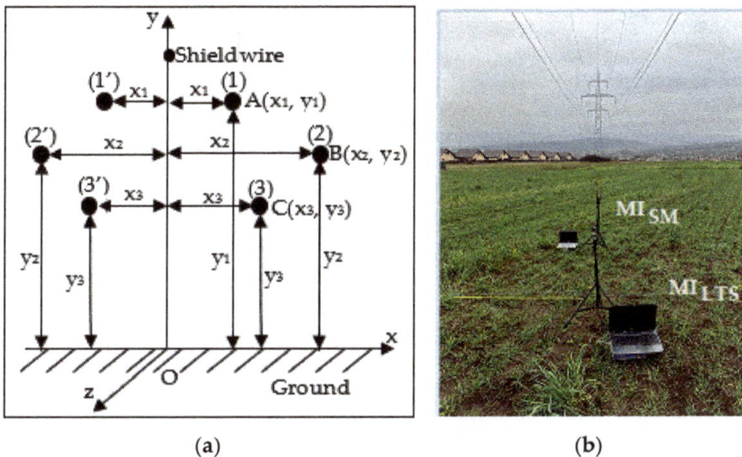

(a)   (b)

Figure 1. (**a**) 2D cross section of the overhead power line, (**b**) real view of the OPL with the two measuring instruments (MI_{LTS} and MI_{SM}).

2.1. Measurement Procedure

The measurements for B are carried out using two instruments for automatic survey of the magnetic field, which were designed by the authors and are presented in Section 3.1 (Instrumentation). One of the instruments, MI_{LTS}, used for long-term survey, is placed in a fixed point under the geometric center of the OPL, at the mid-distance between two consecutive pillars. This instrument performs a survey for several hours, but this time can be increased to days or even months if proper housing and power supply is available.

The long-term survey performed by MI_{LTS} records the rms values of B for almost 6 h (5 h and 31 min) with a time step of about 1 s.

The second measurement instrument, MI_{SM} (Figure 1b), realizes spot measurements for B in the specified points of the longitudinal (LD) and transversal (TD) directions (with respect to the OPL), at points 1 m apart for TD and 3 m apart for LD. Unlike the procedure presented by the authors in [13], which used a simple commercial instrument for spot measurements, the procedure used in this paper is based on two automatic monitoring systems.

In this way, besides a very good synchronization between the two instruments (MI_{SM} and MI_{LTS}), i.e., the spot measurements data and the long-term survey data necessary for the proposed hybrid method, supplementary information regarding B are obtained in all the observation points.

The time for completing the spot measurements with MI_{SM} is approximately 20 min for the transversal profile and 40 min for the longitudinal profile, in the case studied experimentally in this paper. Two transversal profiles were traced, one at the pillar ($z = 0$) and one at the mid-distance between consecutive pillars ($z = d/2$), where d is the distance between the two pillars. The second transversal profile was traced in order to verify and compare the results obtained with the proposed method, as will be later detailed.

The number of spot measurements in longitudinal direction can be reduced to one half due to the symmetry of the magnetic field with respect to the transversal middle plane $z = d/2$. A total of 61 spot measurements were taken in transversal direction at times t_{T1}, t_{T2},..., t_{T61} and 95 measurements in longitudinal direction at times t_{L1}, t_{L2},..., t_{L95}.

2.2. Proposed Hybrid Method

Due to the fact that the current rms values have a permanent variation, in this paper, a method is proposed for the estimation of the magnetic field produced by the OPL both in transversal and in longitudinal directions for a specified time, e.g., t_{T1}, for the entire transversal profile ($EP_T(t_{T1})$) and similarly at t_{L1} for the entire longitudinal profile ($EP_L(t_{L1})$).

The estimated magnetic flux density, B_e, is determined using the measured values B_m and, also, taking into account the time variation of B (rms) recorded in one single fixed point ($z = d/2$) during the long-term survey, B_{LTS}.

The transversal profile is traced sequentially, resulting in a set of data for B_m in 61 evenly spaced locations, namely B_m measured at point P_1 at time t_{T1}, and so on, $B_m(P_1, t_{T1})$, $B_m(P_2, t_{T2})$,..., $B_m(P_{61}, t_{T61})$. In the transversal profile estimated at time t_{T1} ($EP_T(t_{T1})$), the estimated value coincides with the measured value only at the first point P_1:

$$B_e(P_1, t_{T1}) = B_m(P_1, t_{T1}) \qquad (2)$$

The next values will be estimated based on the values measured with MI_{SM} in subsequent points P_2, P_3, . . . , P_{61}, taking into account the time variation of B recorded with MI_{LTS} at the fixed point. Thus, at point P_2 the estimated value B_e is the following:

$$B_e(P_2, t_{T1}) = B_m(P_2, t_{T2}) * B_{LTS}(P, t_{T1})/B_{LTS}(P, t_{T2}) \qquad (3)$$

Relation (3) is based on system linearity and can be obviously rewritten in the form:

$$\frac{B_e(P_2, t_{T1})}{B_m(P_2, t_{T2})} = \frac{B_{LTS}(P, t_{T1})}{B_{LTS}(P, t_{T2})} \qquad (4)$$

A similar procedure is employed for estimating the longitudinal profile, $EP_L(t)$, at a given time t, using the data measured with MI_{SM} for B along the line and the values recorded by MI_{LTS} in a fixed observation point P.

According to this procedure, the estimated values should be the same as those measured simultaneously in all the 61 discretization points for the transversal profile and in all the 95 points for the longitudinal profile (if such an experiment were realized), but this would require a very large number of instruments (MI_{SM}), thus being impractical.

Using the consecutive measurements for one transversal profile (P_T) and one longitudinal profile (P_L), measured with MI_{SM}, and the values for B obtained during the long-term survey in a fixed point (measured with MI_{LTS}), the transversal profiles for any $z = k \cdot d/N, k = \overline{0, N}$, where d/N is the step size in longitudinal direction, can be estimated for any moment of time. At the same time, the longitudinal profiles for any time during the observation procedure with MI_{LTS} can be also estimated.

Using this method, a matrix of 61×95 points (for the considered step size), containing the estimated values of B in a rectangular region under the OPL covering an area of $60 \text{ m} \times 282 \text{ m}$, is obtained for any moment of time during the survey with MI_{LTS}. Maps with the estimated values of B can be generated in MATLAB using these matrices.

2.3. OPL Modeling

The transversal view of the overhead power line is presented in Figure 1. In order to determine the magnetic flux density, both an analytical and a numerical approach can be used. In this paper the focus is on the magnetic field (the electric field is not monitored), so that the ground proximity of the line conductors plays a less important role since the Earth's magnetic permeability is close to μ_0. Moreover, as stated before, the OPL works at 50 Hz (extra low frequency domain) which further simplifies the analysis. At such a low frequency, the wavelength is of the order of thousands of km, and the propagation of the electromagnetic field, which occurs in direction Oz (along the line) is characterized by the Poynting vector S.

$$\overline{S} = \overline{E} \times \overline{H} = \left(E_x \overline{i} + E_y \overline{j} \right) \times \left(H_x \overline{i} + H_y \overline{j} \right) = \left(E_x H_y - E_y H_x \right) \overline{k} \tag{5}$$

where $\overline{i}$, $\overline{j}$ and $\overline{k}$ are the unit vectors of the three axes Ox, Oy and Oz. In sinusoidal steady state, the vectors are complex. Comparing the dimensions of the line, which may be of the order of tens of kilometers, to the wavelength, we can assert that the line is in quasi-stationary magnetic regime. This means that the time variation of the electric field is negligible, and the equations for the determination of the magnetic field are the same as in stationary regime:

$$\nabla \times \overline{H} = \overline{J} \; ; \overline{B} = \mu \overline{H} \; ; \nabla \cdot \overline{B} = 0 \tag{6}$$

Thus, in an environment of constant permeability μ_0, the magnetic flux density produced by a thin conductor can be determined using the Biot–Savart–Laplace formula (BSL):

$$\overline{B}(P) = \frac{\mu_0 i}{4\pi} \oint_\Gamma \frac{\overline{dl} \times \overline{R}}{R^3} \tag{7}$$

which, for the long line conductor, becomes (Figure 2b) the following:

$$\underline{\overline{B}}_k = \frac{\mu_0 \underline{I}_k \left[(y - y_k)\overline{i} + (x_k - x)\overline{j} \right]}{2\pi \left[(x - x_k)^2 + (y - y_k)^2 \right]} \tag{8}$$

In (8), $\underline{I}_k$ is the complex rms value of the current in conductor k. In the case of the OPL line, there are six conductors which may or may not be current-carrying conductors (some currents may be zero).

The total magnetic field is obtained by superposition:

$$\underline{\overline{B}} = \sum_{k=1}^{6} \underline{\overline{B}}_k \tag{9}$$

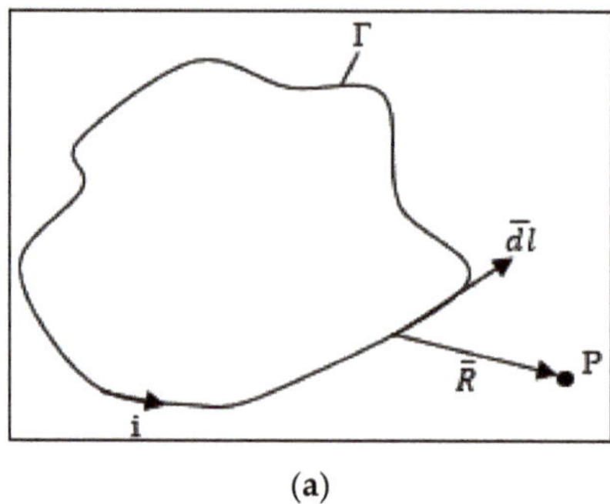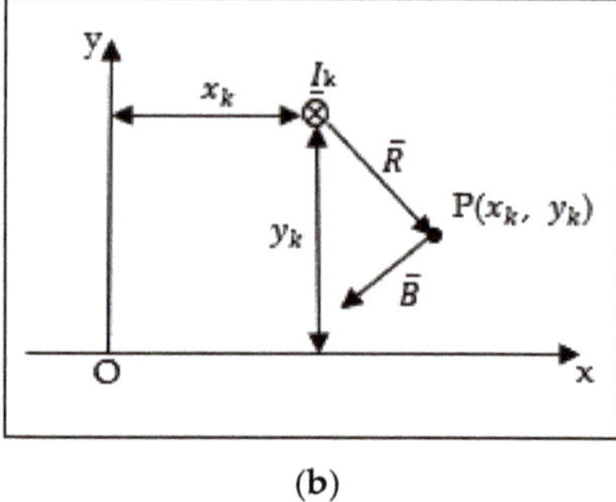

(a)   (b)

Figure 2. Determination of the magnetic flux density with the BSL formula: (**a**) general case, (**b**) line conductors.

3. Measurements

3.1. Instrumentation

The proposed hybrid method is based on the data obtained during the automatic long-term survey performed using the two instruments MI_{SM} and MI_{LTS}. These new/original instruments were designed, realized and calibrated by the authors [14–16] for the purpose of measuring magnetic fields, being suitable in monitoring magnetic field exposure for the general population.

Although there are small differences between MI_{SM} and MI_{LTS}, each of the two instruments consists of an isotropic field sensor (three linear coils), an electronic signal processing circuit (amplifier and integrator), a data acquisition module and a laptop that hosts several virtual instruments realized in LabVIEW.

Both measurement systems record and process the waveforms for the three components of B. The processing and LabVIEW module can perform a frequency analysis and compute the rms and peak-to-peak values, as well as a statistical post-processing of the recorded data. These two instruments can perform a long-term survey of the magnetic field, recording samples of B every second for a frequency range of the B components up to 100 kHz, which is appropriate for observing the biological effects of the magnetic field.

The calibration of these instruments was conducted using a reference magnetic field (standard-field method), with an uncertainty of less than 5%. This uncertainty of the measurement instrument was also verified by comparison with commercial instruments.

The experimental recording performed with MI_{LTS} lasted for 5 h and 31 min, between 9:37 am and 3:08 p.m. At the same time interval, the transversal profiles near the pillar (in $z = 0$) and at the mid-distance between two pillars ($z = d/2$), and also the longitudinal profile B $(0, y, z)$, $z \in [0, d]$, were traced with MI_{SM} at a height $y = 1$ m above the ground.

The OPL considered in experiments (Figure 1b) is a double three-phase line 2×220 kV with RST-RST phase disposition, situated in Iasi County, Romania. The geometrical configuration of the line as well as the current rms values are known and are used in the numerical simulations.

3.2. Measurement Results

During the experiments, two profiles for B were obtained: one in transversal direction for $z = 0$, P_T, and a longitudinal profile P_L for $z \in [0, d]$. A supplementary verification and validation of these results is performed using measurements taken for a transversal profile at the mid-distance between two consecutive pillars, P_{TM}.

Figure 3 depicts the transversal profile near the pillar using 61 consecutive measurements in points 1 m apart, at different moments of time (since only one instrument MI_{SM} was used). The maximum value for $|B|$ is obtained at approximately 5 m from the central symmetry plane of the OPL, due to the fact that the currents in the second line (conductors $(1')$, $(2')$ and $(3')$ in Figure 1) were zero (line out of service).

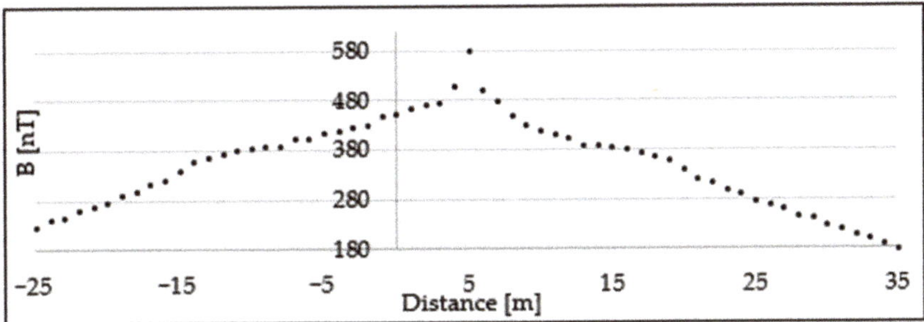

Figure 3. Transversal profile for |B| obtained in successive measurements near one pillar (z = 0).

The longitudinal profile between two pillars, P_L, was traced using spot measurements in points 3 m apart for the distance d = 282 m, Figure 4. In the considered case, the experimental procedure for P_L lasted 40 min.

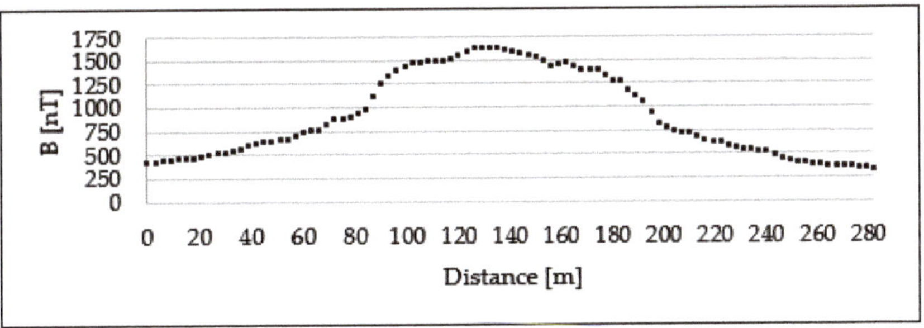

Figure 4. Longitudinal profile for |B| obtained in successive measurements (P_L).

The plots in Figures 3 and 4 show rather large variations of |B|, even for neighboring points. This is due to the variation of $|I_k|$ in time, allowing for the instrument MI_{SM} to be moved to the next position.

However, most of these variations can be smoothed (leveled) using the proposed method for estimating the magnetic field profile at a given time, this being equivalent to the case when all the measurements are carried out simultaneously. Some irregularities in |B| still persist even after applying this method due to errors produced by the fact that the Earth's surface is not flat (small differences in the distance between the line and the instrument occur).

Although the profiles P_T and P_L give sufficient data in order to plot a map of |B| in a rectangular region beneath the line, a second transversal profile P_{TM} was recorded at a distance z = d/2. This profile, represented in Figure 5, is used to verify the proposed method for field estimation. The procedure is based on the comparison of the data in P_{TM} with the transversal profile estimated using the data in P_T, taken in z = 0, the data in P_L and the time variation of B obtained with MI_{LTS} during the long-term survey.

Thus far, only the data from spot measurements with MI_{SM} were presented. In the following, the data from the long-term survey performed with MI_{LTS} will be presented and discussed. Figure 6 presents the recordings made for B rms with MI_{LTS} for the entire observation interval of 5 h and 31 min. In this recording, a significant temporal variation of the magnetic field can be observed, justified by the time variation of the rms current in the line. These variations can be correlated with the variations of B identified in the measured data for the longitudinal profile (plotted in Figure 4).

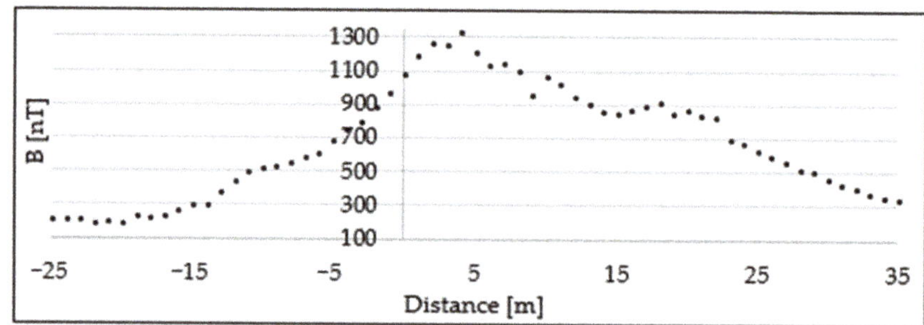

Figure 5. Transversal profile measured experimentally at the mid-distance between two pillars.

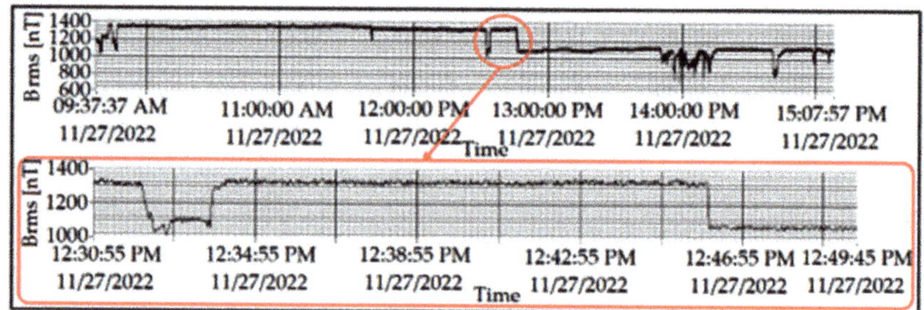

Figure 6. Values recorded for B (rms) during the long-term survey at a fixed point.

Using the long-term survey instrument, MI_{LTS}, a time and frequency analysis of the recorded signal can be performed. Figure 7 presents both the time variation and the spectral analysis for the field components B_x, B_y and B_z.

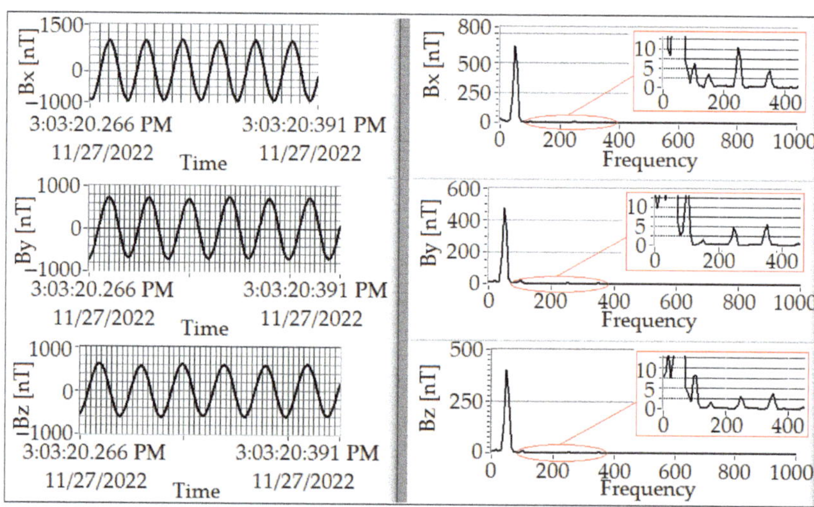

Figure 7. Waveforms and spectral analysis for the B components.

A statistical post-processing of the recorded results over the observation time interval can be also performed. Table 1 presents the results of post-processing, i.e., date and time of observation, number of measurements, minimum, maximum and average values of B, standard deviation, number of recorded data larger than the average value and percentage of exceeding values.

Table 1. Post-processing statistical results for the data recorded with MI_{LTS}.

Survey Period [hh:mm]	Number of Measurements	Min.	B_{rms} [nT] Average	Max.	Standard Dev.	$\frac{t_{over\ average}}{t_{survey}} \times 100(\%)$
[05:31]	17,530	724	1223	1375	132.3	54.67

The currents in the line, further used in simulations, are known only for six moments in time (10 a.m., 11 a.m.,..., 3 p.m.), but the number of values recorded for B during the long time survey is 17,530, with a time step of about 1 s (17,530 measurements in 19,860 s). Moreover, if the range for the current rms values is from 118 to 196 A, the range of values for B recorded by MI_{LTS} is from 724 to 1375 nT.

4. Modeling and Simulation Results

4.1. Estimation Based on "In Situ" Field Measurements

Due to the time variation of the magnetic field rms value, tracing the transversal and longitudinal values is difficult to achieve using only one instrument. The objective of this paper is to obtain an estimation of the magnetic field at each point of a rectangular mesh beneath the OPL at a particular moment of time. This estimation is realized using the values of B obtained with the two instruments MI_{LTS} and MI_{SM} and then applying a correction to the values obtained at successive moments in time. In this way, all the values for B in each profile are estimated at the same moment of time as if simultaneous measurements were made in 61 points for the transversal profile and 95 points for the longitudinal profile.

Figure 8 presents three estimations of B for the transversal profile near the pillar at moments t_{Ti}, t_{Tj} and t_{Tk} (11 a.m., 12 a.m. and 1 p.m.), determined from the successive measurements recorded in P_T, performed with MI_{SM} and estimated according to relation (3). In Figure 8, the data from P_T (represented in Figure 3) are also included in order to observe the possibilities of the proposed method.

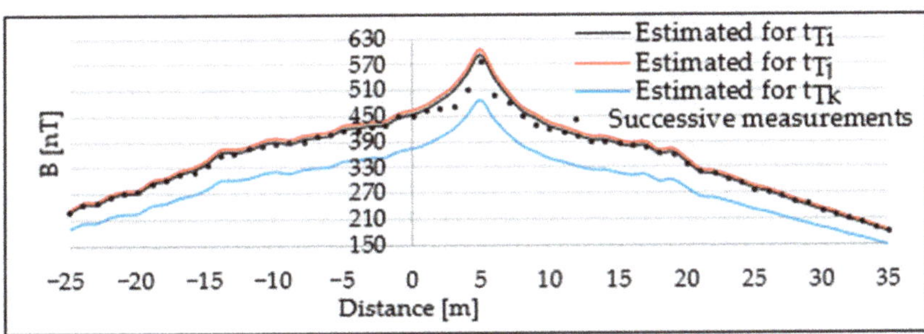

Figure 8. Transversal profiles near the pillar estimated at times t_{Ti}, t_{Tj} and t_{Tk}, compared to the results from spot measurements.

Using the same method, estimations for the longitudinal profile were also made at the moments t_{Li}, t_{Lj} and t_{Lk} (11 a.m., 12 a.m. and 1 p.m.). The estimated longitudinal profiles, as well as the original profile, are presented in Figure 9. As may be seen, the original large variations of B from Figure 4 are corrected, and the estimation results present a rather smooth variation.

In order to verify the proposed estimation method, similar estimations were made for the transversal profile P_{TM} (corresponding to $z = d/2$) for the chosen moments t_{TMi}, t_{TMj} and t_{TMk} (11 a.m., 12 a.m. and 1 p.m.). The resulting plots, as well as the original profile P_{TM}, are presented in Figure 10.

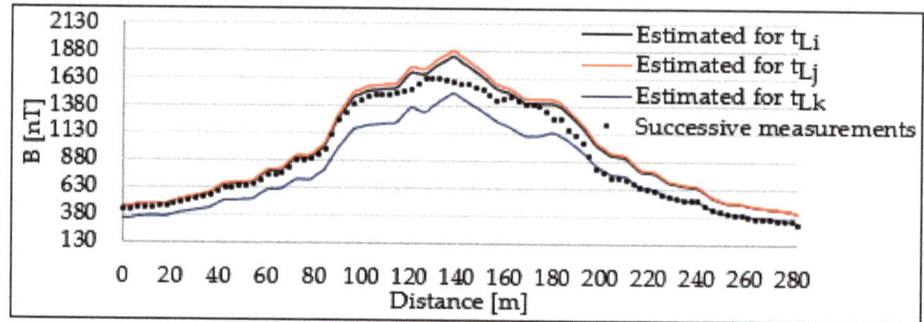

Figure 9. Estimated longitudinal profiles at times t_{Li}, t_{Lj} and t_{Lk} compared to the results from spot measurements.

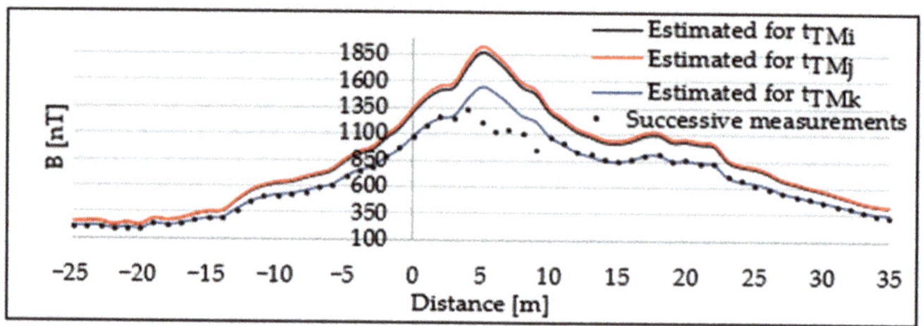

Figure 10. Transversal profiles at the mid-distance between the pillars, estimated at the moments t_{TMi}, t_{TMj} and t_{TMk}, compared with the experimental profile.

As mentioned before, the transversal profile P_{TM} was traced for $z = d/2$, but similar transversal profiles can be determined experimentally and then estimated according to (3) for any value $z \in [0,\, d]$.

Figure 11 presents two plots that estimate the transversal profile for B in $z = d/2$ at the same moment t_k (in the considered case at 1 p.m.), using two separate sets of experimental data, namely:

1. Data for the transversal profile at the pillar ($z = 0$) and for the longitudinal profile (obtained with MI_{SM}), taking also into account the temporal variation of B obtained in the long-term survey, thus resulting, firstly, in the estimated profiles $EP_T(t_k)$ and $EP_L(t_k)$ and finally the estimated transversal profile at the distance $z = d/2$ at time t_k;
2. Data from the experimental transversal profile P_{TM} at $z = d/2$, considering also the time variation recorded with MI_{LTS} at $z = d/2$, thus resulting in the estimated transversal profile at time t_k (as it was presented in Figure 10).

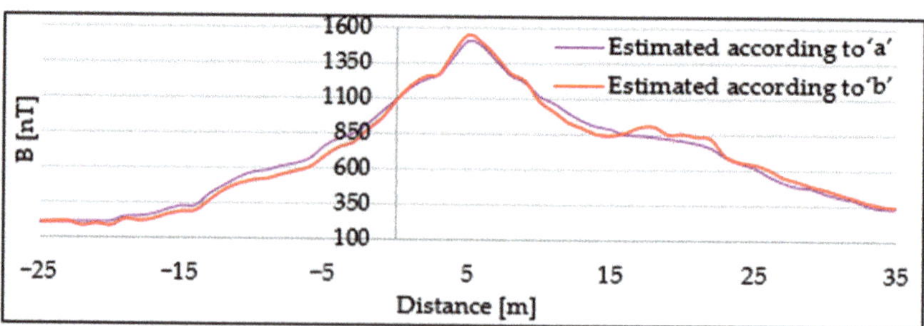

Figure 11. Estimated transversal profile at the mid-distance between two towers, based on two different sets of data correlated with the continuous recording of B_{LTS}.

Comparing the two plots in Figure 11, a relative deviation of under 9% is observed in the conditions in which the range of the recorded values for B is from 724 to 1375 nT, and other factors, such as instrument error (under 5%), terrain oscillations, small errors in positioning the instrument MI_{SM}, etc., affect the measured values of B.

In a similar manner, the transversal profiles for any value of z can be obtained using one transversal profile (P_T) measured at a fixed point z_0, the longitudinal profile P_L and the time recordings for B conducted with MI_{LTS}.

Using this method for estimating the magnetic field in transversal direction for any $z \in [0, d]$, maps of the magnetic field in a rectangular region beneath the OPL can be obtained for any of the 17,530 moments of time for which recordings of B performed with MI_{LTS} exist (Table 1).

Figures 12 and 13 represent a map of $|B|$ in the region $z \in [0, d]$, $x \in [-x_{max}, x_{max}]$, with d = 282 m, x_{max} = 30 m, in two cases: for a time t_X when the estimated value of B is equal to the maximum value obtained in the long-time survey, and for a time t_y when the estimated value of B is equal to the minimum recorded value of B. These maps can be obtained using only one longitudinal and one transversal profile, resulting in a significant reduction of the number of spot measurements.

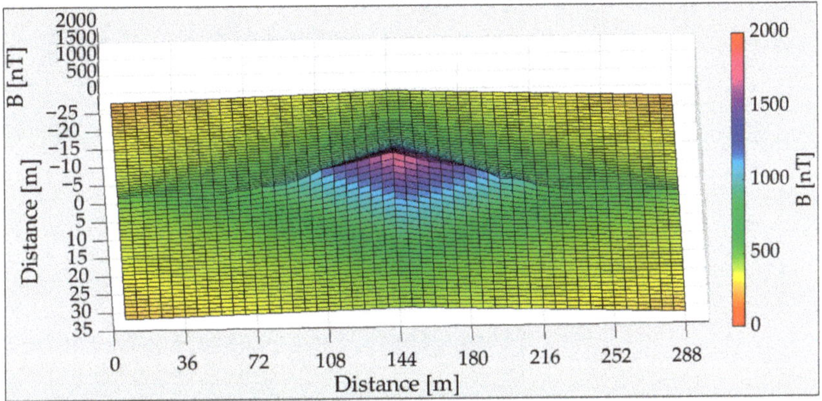

Figure 12. Magnetic flux density map for the maximum recorded value of B.

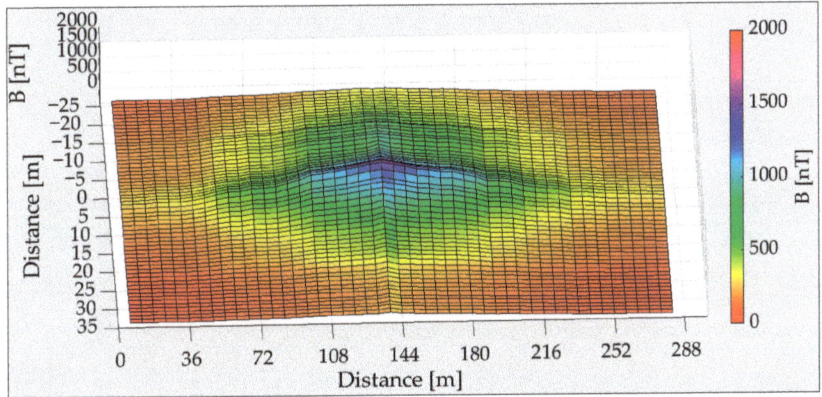

Figure 13. Magnetic flux density map for the minimum recorded value of B.

4.2. Results of Analytical and Numerical Simulations

The transversal profile for the norm of the magnetic flux density

$$\left|\underline{\overline{B}}\right| = \sqrt{\left|\underline{B}_x\right|^2 + \left|\underline{B}_y\right|^2} \tag{10}$$

calculated with relations (8)–(10), is presented in Figure 14 for the cases in which the experimental data obtained with MI_{LTS} were available and the values of the rms line currents are known. Conductors (1)–(3) (Figure 1a) carry a symmetric three-phase current, with values specified in Figure 14 (three cases), while the current in the conductors (1′), (2′) and (3′) are zero (line not in service). The geometric coordinates considered in simulations, corresponding to the position of the three conductors at the pillar, are $x_1 = 5$ m, $y_1 = 35$ m, $x_2 = 8$ m, $y_2 = 28.5$ m, $x_3 = 5$ m and $y_3 = 22$ m.

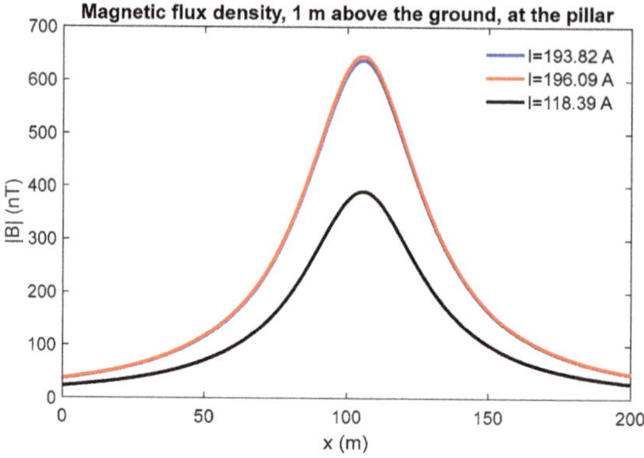

Figure 14. Transversal profile of | B | at the pillar—simulations based on analytical results.

A numerical simulation of the line was also performed using COMSOL Multiphysics 6.1. In this case, the electrical constants for the soil, ε_r and σ can be also taken into account, but these constants depend on the content of water in the soil [17]. In the numerical simulations, the considered values were $\sigma_{\text{soil}} = 0.5$ S/m and $\varepsilon_{r\,\text{soil}} = 10$.

The transversal profile for the magnetic flux density at the height of 1 m and 1.8 m, respectively, above the ground, was computed using the same geometric coordinates for the conductors as before (conductors near the pillar), and the results are presented in Figure 15. Simulations for other numerical values of σ_{soil} and $\varepsilon_{r\,\text{soil}}$ were also carried out since their value in the onsite experiment is uncertain, but it was found that they have a small influence over B.

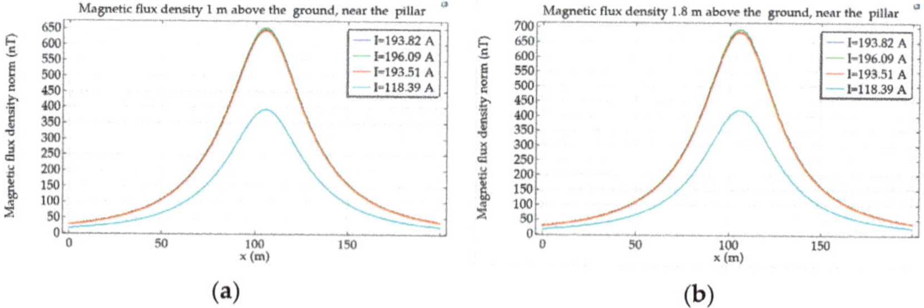

Figure 15. Transversal profile of | B | at the pillar—simulations in COMSOL: (**a**) at a height of 1 m above the ground, (**b**) at a height of 1.8 m above the ground.

In Figures 14 and 15 the geometric plane of symmetry of the OPL is the plane x = 100 m. In the COMSOL simulations, the physics module magnetic and electric fields (mef) was used, performing a frequency analysis [18]. The plots in Figure 15 correspond to 50 Hz. This physics module takes into account the displacement currents, besides the conduction currents, making the study more accurate. The dimensions of the entire analyzed domain were 400 m in the direction of Ox and 300 m in the direction of Oy, with a 150 m region under the ground.

The results obtained in the COMSOL simulations are in very good agreement with the analytical results. For example, the largest value of B, obtained for I = 193.82 A, is B_{max} = 646 nT in COMSOL and 638 nT in MATLAB (analytical results), giving a maximum relative difference between analytical and numerical simulations of 1.2%.

Comparing the results obtained in simulations with the estimated values of B obtained using the hybrid method (Section 4.1), the similarity of the plots in Figures 8 and 14 (or Figure 15) can be observed with inherent irregularities in the curve based on the experiment, due to the particular onsite conditions (as mentioned in 4.1). At the same time, the maximum value of B is 638 nT in the analytical simulations (for I = 193.82 A) and from the estimations based on the measurements B_{max} = 605 nT, leading to a maximum relative difference between the simulated and estimated B of 5.4%.

5. Discussions

In order to obtain a complete map of the magnetic flux density produced by an overhead power line (OPL), a large number of simultaneous measurements taken over a significant time interval would be necessary. This approach that takes into account the spatial and temporal variation of B (rms) is not feasible due to the large number of instruments necessary in the survey and the complexity of the entire operation.

That is why characterization of the magnetic fields produced by the OPL is usually performed using a transversal and a longitudinal profile obtained in successive measurements in a number of observation points. This approach is easier to implement and needs only one measurement instrument, but it is not complete because it does not distinguish between the spatial and temporal variations of B and becomes incorrect when the magnetic field has large variations in time, which happens in most cases.

The transversal profile P_T obtained through successive measurements and presented in Figure 3 is able to characterize the magnetic field in the direction perpendicular to the line, since B has small variations at the time these data were collected. The small deviations from the real values can be caused by terrain oscillations of levels and small errors in positioning the instrument.

In contrast, the longitudinal profile P_L, obtained experimentally through successive measurements and presented in Figure 4, cannot characterize correctly the spatial variation of B along the line in direction Oz, due to the large variations of B during the experiment.

That is why, in this paper, a new method for estimating the longitudinal profile and the transversal profiles for B at different positions along the line (z ∈ [0,d]) is proposed, thus allowing for spatial maps of B to be represented at different moments of time. In the case considered in this study, the map for B covers an area of 60 m × 282 m. In order to obtain the estimated profiles for B, two instruments are used, one for spot measurements in different points (MI_{SM}) and one for a long-term survey (MI_{LTS}), which record automatically and continuously the values of B in a fixed point. Thus, using only two instruments, 156 values for B are collected using MI_{SM} (61 for P_T and 95 for P_L) and, using MI_{LTS}, the values of B can be estimated in 5795 points at any moment of time (17,530 instances of time, according to Table 1). Some of the estimated results are presented in Figures 8–11. Two maps for the magnetic flux density are also presented in Figures 12 and 13, at moments corresponding to the maximum and minimum recorded values of B, respectively.

The first validation of the proposed method is conducted within the method by obtaining two estimated transversal profiles at the mid-distance between two consecutive pillars P_{TM} (Figure 5). The plots in Figure 11 show that the two estimations for the same profile at the same moment of time, obtained using two separate sets of data, are almost identical, with relative differences between the two profiles of under 9%.

In order to verify or validate the proposed method, calculations for B using analytical and numerical methods were also used. The maximum relative difference between the hybrid method and data from analytical simulations, using estimations of the transversal profile at the pillar, was 5.4%.

The two instruments MI_{SM} and MI_{LTS} were designed, realized and calibrated by the authors, with an uncertainty in the measured value of B of under 5%. Supplementary measurement uncertainty may also occur due to errors in positioning the instrument both in horizontal and in vertical directions and also due to possible errors in the time synchronization of the two instruments.

The proposed hybrid method of estimation may be used to map other sources of electromagnetic field, and, by using an automatic recording of the magnetic flux density and of the electric field, maps for both B and E can be obtained [14,15].

6. Conclusions

This paper presents a new hybrid method to estimate and map the magnetic flux density produced by overhead power lines in a large region beneath the OPL and for a long period of time using a minimized number of spot measurements and a long-term survey of B. The method is based on the correlation of data from a transversal profile and those from a longitudinal profile of B, obtained by successive measurements made in a short time interval, with the data from the long-term survey, both sets of data being obtained with instruments developed by the authors.

In order to validate the results of the estimations, simulations are carried out based on the analytical and numerical methods for magnetic field determination. The relative difference between the estimation and simulation results is under 5.5%.

All the measured, estimated and calculated values in the analyzed case are below the threshold imposed by international regulations for human exposure to magnetic fields. It is to be mentioned, however, that there are reports suggesting that long time exposure of children to magnetic fields in the ELF domain must be limited to much lower values than those recommended by international regulating organizations, this being a subject of ongoing research.

Thus, the need for estimating and mapping the magnetic field produced by OPL (an important source of magnetic fields) and characterizing the human field exposure to complex fields is a topic of major interest that relates to public health concerns.

Author Contributions: Conceptualization, V.D.; methodology, V.D., C.P. and I.P.; software, C.P.; validation, I.P., C.P. and V.D.; formal analysis, I.P. and C.P.; investigation, I.P.; resources, I.P. and E.L.; writing—original draft preparation, V.D. and C.P.; writing—review and editing, C.P.; visualization, C.P. and I.P.; supervision, V.D. All authors have read and agreed to the published version of the manuscript.

Funding: This research received no external funding.

Data Availability Statement: Not applicable.

Acknowledgments: This work was achieved through the Advanced Research postdoctoral program within IOSUD-TUIASI: "Performance and Excellence in postdoctoral Research—2022". The first author would like to thank for the support obtained through the project "Network of excellence in applied research and innovation for doctoral and postdoctoral programs"/InoHubDoc, a project co-funded by the European Social Fund.

Conflicts of Interest: The authors declare no conflict of interest.

Nomenclature

OPL	Overhead Power Line
B	magnetic flux density
rms value	root mean square value
MI_{LTS}	Measurement Instrument for Long-Term Survey
MI_{SM}	Measurement Instrument for Spot Measurements
P_L	Longitudinal profile (obtained from successive measurements)
P_T	Transversal profile (obtained from successive measurements)
P_{TM}	Transversal profile at the mid-distance between two consecutive pillars
$t_{T1}, t_{T2}, \ldots, t_{T61}$	times at which measurements were made in 61 points for the transversal profile
$t_{L1}, t_{L2}, \ldots, t_{L95}$	times at which measurements were made in 95 points for the longitudinal profile
$EP_T\,(t_{T1})$	estimated (whole or completed) transversal profile for time t_{T1}
$EP_L\,(t_{L1})$	estimated (whole or completed) longitudinal profile for time t_{L1}
d	distance between consecutive pillars of the OPL
B_e	estimated magnetic flux density
B_m	measured magnetic flux density in successive measurements with MI_{SM}
B_{LTS}	values of B measured with MI_{LTS} during the long-term survey

References

1. Directive 2013/35/EU of the European Parliament and of the Council. *Off. J. Eur. Union* **2013**, *179*, 12–18.
2. Tourab, W.; Babouri, A. Measurement and modeling of personal exposure to the electric and magnetic fields in the vicinity of high voltage power lines. *Saf. Health Work.* **2016**, *7*, 102–110. [CrossRef] [PubMed]
3. Garrido, C.; Otero, A.; Cidras, J. Low frequency magnetic fields from electrical appliances and power lines. *IEEE Trans. Power Deliv.* **2003**, *18*, 1310–1319. [CrossRef]
4. Bravo-Rodriguez, J.C.; del-Pino-Lopez, J.C.; Cruz-Romero, P. A survey on optimization techniques applied to magnetic field mitigation in power systems. *Energies* **2019**, *12*, 1332. [CrossRef]
5. Pirjola, R.; Boteler, D. Calculation methods of the electric and magnetic fields at the Earth's surface produced by a line current. *Radio Sci.* **2002**, *37*, 1–9. [CrossRef]
6. Filippopoulos, G.; Tsanakas, D. Analytical calculation of the magnetic field produced by electric power lines. *IEEE Trans. Power Deliv.* **2005**, *20*, 1474–1482. [CrossRef]
7. Vujevic, S.; Sarajcev, P.; Botica, A. Computation of overhead power line electromagnetic field. In Proceedings of the 16th International Conference on Software, Telecommunications and Computer Networks, Split-Dubrovnik, Croatia, 25–27 September 2008.
8. OuYang, W.; Zhang, J.; Hu, J.; Lv, W.; Wang, D. PSO/DE combined with simulation current method for the magnetic field under transmission lines in 3D calculation model. *Meas. Control.* **2022**, *55*, 1097–1109. [CrossRef]
9. Al Salameh, M.; Alnemrawi, S. Ant Lion optimization to minimize emissions of power transmission lines. *Progress Electromagn. Res.* **2022**, *110*, 171–184. [CrossRef]
10. Mujezinovic, A.; Turajlic, E.; Alihodzic, A.; Dautbasic, N.; Dedovic, M.M. Novel method for magnetic flux density estimation in the vicinity of multi-circuit overhead transmission lines. *IEEE Access* **2022**, *10*, 18169–18181. [CrossRef]
11. Scott, G.; Pooley, M.; Cotts, B. Numerical and analytical modeling of electromagnetic fields from offshore power distribution cables. *IEEE Trans. Magn.* **2023**, *59*, 1–5. [CrossRef]
12. Kavet, R.; Wyman, M.; Klimley, P. Modeling magnetic fields from a DC power cable buried beneath San Francisco bay, based on empirical measurements. *PLoS ONE* **2016**, *11*, e0148543. [CrossRef] [PubMed]
13. David, V.; Pavel, I.; Lunca, E. A method for estimating the magnetic fields generated by the overhead power lines. In Proceedings of the 11th International Conference and Exposition on Electrical and Power Engineering (EPE), Iași, Romania, 22–23 October 2020.
14. David, V.; Nica, I. A measurement system for an automatic survey of low frequency magnetic and electric fields. *Rev. Sci. Instrum.* **2012**, *83*, 105102. [CrossRef] [PubMed]
15. David, V.; Nica, I. System for Determination of Low Frequency Magnetic and Electric Fields. Patent 127139/30.09, 30 September 2014.
16. David, V.; Lunca, E.; Pavel, I. Automatic Monitoring for the Magnetic Fields with the Detection and Characterization of Transient Fields. Patent RO-BOPI 8/2019, 30 August 2019. pp. 36–37.
17. Scott, J. *Electric and Magnetic Properties of Rock and Soil*; Open-File Report 83-915; United States Department of the Interior Geological Survey: Reston, VA, USA, 1983. [CrossRef]
18. COMSOL Multiphysics v. 6.1 Documentation, AC/DC Module User's Guide. Available online: www.comsol.com (accessed on 1 February 2023).

 *mathematics*

Article

Simulation of Light Scattering in Automotive Paints: Role of Particle Size

Sergey Ershov, Alexey Voloboy * and Vladimir Galaktionov

Keldysh Institute of Applied Mathematics RAS, 125047 Moscow, Russia; ersh@gin.keldysh.ru (S.E.);
vlgal@gin.keldysh.ru (V.G.)
* Correspondence: voloboy@gin.keldysh.ru

Abstract: Nowadays, computer simulation is being used to develop new materials. Many of them are dispersed media (e.g., paints, and 3D printer inks). Modern automotive paints are of great interest in research works. They contain colorant particles and thin flat metallic or pearlescent flakes distributed in a clear varnish. There are two main approaches to simulation of light scattering in a dispersed media. The first one is based on the continuous medium model. This model is faster but less accurate. The second approach is the simulation of light propagation through an ensemble of paint flakes and particles represented as an explicit geometry. This model correctly calculates light scattering but is rather time-consuming. In our study, we investigated the dependence of the painted surface luminance on particle size and compared both the approaches. We prove that the effect of coarse particles can emerge even in a model where positions of these particles are not correlated; this is different from the mainstream studies which have only concentrated on the role of these correlations. Then, we suggest a semi-analytical model of dependence on particle size. This model not only allows to more accurately simulate visual appearance but also admits intuitive comprehension of how it is affected by various medium parameters. In case of the divergence between the results of LTE and accurate approaches, we propose a simple approximation that allows to improve the accuracy of the LTE results for coarse particles.

Keywords: light scattering; dispersed medium; lighting simulation; paint realistic rendering; BRDF

MSC: 78-10; 78A55

Citation: Ershov, S.; Voloboy, A.; Galaktionov, V. Simulation of Light Scattering in Automotive Paints: Role of Particle Size. *Mathematics* **2023**, *11*, 2429. https://doi.org/10.3390/math11112429

Academic Editors: Camelia Petrescu and Valeriu David

Received: 29 April 2023
Revised: 18 May 2023
Accepted: 22 May 2023
Published: 24 May 2023

1. Introduction

Nowadays, the use of computer simulation to develop new materials has become a widespread practice. From the point of view of the visual perception of the material, it is important to model the interaction of light with it. Many modern materials are dispersed media, i.e., they consist of optically contrasting particles distributed in the volume of a transparent substance. Such media are used in modern light sources (diffusers in flat sources, luminous linear sources and devices in car interior), and they are also the basis of modern paints, auto glass, plastics, and inks for 3D printers.

Visual appearance is the main characteristic of paint and it manifests itself through the human perception of objective optical properties, such as color, brightness (reflection coefficient), glossiness, texture (spatial heterogeneity), etc. Hence, simulation and visualization of optically complex materials, such as multilayer paints with a complex microstructure (like pearlescent and metallic paints) in the automotive industry, have been developed in recent years. Advanced software allows one to simulate light propagation through a paint composed of clear varnish with pigment particles and flakes (metallic or interference ones) dispersed in it. The color of these paints depends on the observation and illumination directions. Therefore, its visual appearance should be described by a bidirectional reflectance distribution function (BRDF). The primary task is to calculate how the paint with given composition looks under given illumination and observation directions [1].

We consider two main approaches of calculating light scattering in dispersed media. The first one is based on the continuous medium model [2]. In this model, any infinitesimal volume scatters light proportionally to that volume. This model leads to the differential light transport equation (LTE) (or Radiative Transfer Equation in [2]). There are several methods within this approach. For example, deterministic methods, the method of discrete ordinates [3], finite difference, and matrix methods like doubling/adding [4]. Additionally, it can be solved via stochastic (Monte Carlo) integration. The continuous medium approximation (i.e., LTE) works pretty well for atmosphere for which it was originally created. Presently, it is quite popular and widely applied to a wide class of turbid media. However, this approach becomes inaccurate when the pigment particles are large or are packed densely in the paint.

The second approach is the simulation of light propagation through an ensemble of paint flakes and particles represented as an explicit geometry. Here, we can solve it by using the Monte Carlo ray tracing (MCRT) [5]. It is possible to either create a huge sample geometry that includes billions of randomly distributed particles or use many random samples of a rather small piece of paint geometry (corresponding to small area of paint layer) and average over them. This approach is straightforward but rather resource and time consuming. However, it does provide accurate solution, and thus we call it the "accurate approach".

Comparing the measurements of real paint samples with simulation, we found that for effect pigments (e.g., metallic flakes), the LTE solution cannot correctly predict the total integral reflectance [6]. Moreover, the measured BRDFs, while generally running more or less closely to the simulated ones, show a strong deviation for nearly normal incidence and observation. The LTE seriously underestimates it, while ray tracing through an ensemble of flakes gives a more accurate result. This is a major problem for the simulation of automotive metallic and pearlescent paints that must look bright. Thus, investigating the reasons of this problem and development of a possible numerical solution is the main motivation of our research.

Our study shows that this effect is due to the correlations between close incident and scattered rays and not the correlations between particles. The mathematical method was borrowed from a thought experiment of perfectly aligned flakes. We consider a ray that goes down to some depth where it is reflected upward by the flake and leaves the layer. We calculate the probability of this event and thus obtain the attenuation (extinction) of the light. It does not follow the usual exponential attenuation in a continuous medium, i.e., it is an anomalous extinction. It is not the one found in the studies of correlated particles. Having the probability of such light path, we calculate the statistical properties of the single scattered light. Then, we take the LTE results as the sum of the scattering orders and replace the first of them with the one given above, leaving the higher orders unchanged. It provides a very good approximation to the results of the accurate model. This allows to obtain near-accurate results much faster than the Monte Carlo ray tracing and without its noise. Additionally, the correction term is almost an analytic function that allows to understand the role and effect of various paint parameters and predict some nontrivial effects. It also predicted that the BRDF could deviate greatly (up to twofold) from the LTE results, even for tiny particles, in the case of near-normal illumination and observation. That is, there is no simple good convergence to the LTE results when the particle size approaches 0.

Initially, these ideas had been applied to the simplified case when all flakes have equal size and are opaque [7]. However, in reality, flakes vary in size and are not always opaque; for example, mica flakes are semi-translucent. This paper aims to remove these limitations and thus considers a general case.

Continuous medium approximation works with the product "area times concentration" and thus do not use the flake size separately. It means that for this approximation, the mean surface luminance is exactly the same for particles n-times larger area in n-times lower concentration. In this paper, we investigated the dependence of the painted surface luminance (BRDF) on the flake size. We compared LTE with a more reliable and accurate (yet expensive) simulation. This simulation is MCRT in the explicit paint geometry that contains an ensemble of individual flakes, instead of replacing their scattering with the phase function of the continuous medium.

The main contribution of this paper is that it proves that the effect of coarse particles can emerge even in a model where positions of these particles are not correlated. This is different from the mainstream studies which have only concentrated on the role of these correlations to describe the effect of coarse particles. Moreover, we suggest a semi-analytical model of dependence based on particle size which not only allows to calculate a more accurate BRDF but also admits an intuitive comprehension of how various parameters of medium affect the BRDF. In case of the divergence in results of LTE and accurate approaches, we propose a simple approximation that allows to improve the accuracy of the LTE results for coarse particles.

The remainder of the paper is organized as follows. Section 2 describes related studies. The proposed method is introduced in Section 3. Section 4 presents the results calculated using the proposed method and their comparison with other methods. In Section 5, discussion and conclusions are stated.

2. Related Works

Many studies are devoted to the simulation of paints or 3D printer inks as disperse media. Simulated BRDF of paint layer is then used for visualization of a virtual car. Some works propose the paint models and try to realistically visualize the paint appearance based on the paint composition. An approximate model for predicting the car paint appearance by the paint composition is presented in the paper [8]. Therein, authors proposed to use a modified version of the micro-flake model based on double-sided specularly reflecting flakes. Their model provides visually satisfactory results in the appearance of multilayer automotive paint, if one is to ignore sparkling. Accurate representation of the reflectivity of metallic paint using a two-layer model with sample distribution functions of microfacets was proposed in [9]. This model provides better accuracy due to the use of the nonparametric terms and allows the analysis of the characteristics of metal particles using the analytical form built into the model.

Texture is proposed to model sparkling effect. The sparkling texture is usually calculated by modulating the BRDF with random field whose statistical characteristics are taken from light interaction with an ensemble of individual particles [1,10]. This is inevitable because continuous medium (i.e., LTE) cannot have a texture. Several approaches for obtaining the spatial variation of the luminance are considered in [11]. The basic approach based on a bidirectional texture function is compared with four variants of half-difference parametrization. With the help of a psychophysical study, the authors concluded that bivariate representations better preserve the visual accuracy of effect coatings.

Several works are devoted to paint rendering. Some of them operated with measured data either combined with analytical solution [12] or postprocessed to archive effective and realistic rendering of real car paint [13]. An interactive interpolation between measured metal paints for cars was presented in [14]. It can be used to create new realistic-looking metallic paint. The authors consider optimal transfer between types of metallic paints by clustering the color information presented in the measured bidirectional texture function responsible for the sparkling effect. The work in [15] describes the methodology of metallic paint visualization based on the measured data. The authors matched the measured spectral reflectivity of several paint samples to the BRDF analytical model to obtain its parameters. To achieve the sparkling effects, several images of the surface were taken at different light incidence.

There are many works that investigate propagation of light in a medium where positions of particles are correlated [16–19]. The authors have proven that the extinction of light beam is no longer exponential, as it would be for the classic case. Although there are sophisticated mathematical models to handle this effect, its base idea is rather intuitive and is illustrated in Figure 1 of [17], which explained it so perfectly that it was re-used in [18]. The basic LTE is then replaced by a sort of generalized equation of similar type, termed "Generalized Boltzmann Equation" [18]. Indeed, there is some similarity with the classic Boltzmann equation, at least in the integral (scattering) term. It still has the same structure as the classic LTE: a sort of convolution of the local angular intensity with the phase function. The latter is still treated as usual in the classic continuous medium approximation, i.e., it is the phase function of an isolated particle scaled to the local density. Investigation into ensembles of correlated particles is advanced in [19]. Its authors finalize their work using the numerical method of calculation of light propagation (and scattering) based on MCRT. A slightly different method of calculation of light propagation in correlated medium and resulting "anomalous extinction" can be found in [20].

While the studies [16–20] operate ray optics, there are investigations proceeding from the wave theory of light. The first thing which this is aimed at is the interference between particles. Indeed, the LTE (and even its above generalizations) requires phase function of medium, i.e., scattering by the elementary volume dV. It can contain many particles at close distance and inevitably diffraction of light by this group is different from the sum over isolated, not interacting with particles. While the phase function of medium is usually assumed proportional to the scattering of an isolated particle, it would be more accurate to compute it as a diffraction of light by the group of particles within dV. Here, it is silently assumed that the result converges as we increase dV. Such an approach is pursued in [21], wherein only the multiple body diffraction problem (scattering by many close particles) is calculated.

In [22–24], the radiative transfer problem is considered for particle agglomeration and dependent scattering. Calculations are performed for very close, particles with refraction close to the bounding medium one. The Percus–Yevick approximation is used in these works to obtain the local concentration and the rule of its change from the cluster center. Then, in [22,23], the authors calculate scattering of the wave field by this group of particles, which is effectively a piece of inhomogeneous medium with correlated variation of refraction index. This scattering gives the local phase function of the elementary volume of the medium. However, this approach still remains a hybrid of wave optics (used to compute phase function of small volume) and ray optics to handle the change of illumination by large and meso scale.

An ultimate wave optics approach would use wave optics consistently at all space scales. Additionally, an attempt of such a treatment is made in [25]. Roughly, the method of calculation of [25] is the development and extension of the single-scattering method from statistical electrodynamics [26] where we use the Born approximation of the wave equation, i.e., a homogeneous medium with volumetric source being incident wave field times the deviation of the squared local refraction from its mean value $n^2(x) - \langle n^2 \rangle$. Scattered wave field is then naturally linear in that deviation. Intensity of light is squared field averaged over the random distribution of refraction. It results in the local intensity of scattered light proportional to the spatial correlation function of refraction. Whilst the above is the first approximation, one can try to go further and improve the volumetric source by including the scattered field in it. Continuing successive approximation, we obtain the scattered field as the sum of an infinite series whose terms are local Green resolvents of homogeneous medium. This procedure is somewhat similar to the operator series of solution of the global illumination equation in ray optics [27].

The authors of [25] take the base wave equation in a stochastically inhomogeneous medium and then write its solution through the propagators of wave field. The authors investigate in detail the extreme cases of long and short wave limits. For long waves, the role of short-scale spatial variations decreases (cf. Rayleigh law) and eventually light propagates like in a homogeneous medium with effective refraction index derived from formulae [25]. The effective medium is similar to the Bruggemann formula for a molecular-level mixture of several substances. For short wave limit, they naturally approach the ray optics. Their transport equation converges to a sort of generalized LTE.

A similar approach can be found in [28]. Higher orders of scattering (scattering of scattered field) are calculated as iteration of the integral operator. The scattering operator includes the spatial correlation of the squared refraction index (= dielectric permittivity), so it also enters the higher order scattering terms.

3. Methods

There are two main approaches for calculation of scattering in paint layer. The first is the continuous medium approach. Roughly speaking, this means that a ray never hits the same flake even when it is reflected exactly backwards. In other words, scattering of two adjacent rays is statistically independent: when a ray hits a flake, the ray shifted by just a bit may miss it. The most famous method of practical calculations in this situation is the light transport equation (LTE). It can be solved via MCRT in the continuous medium when successive scattering or absorption events are independent. Such behavior takes place in the case of infinitesimal flakes (gas mode) or to be precise, in case when the vertical separation of flakes is much greater than their diameter.

When the flakes are large or are packed densely with large concentration, this assumption is violated and calculations deviate from the real flake ensemble properties. Thus, we need the second approach to calculate light interaction here. Nonetheless, MCRT still can be used but now the ray goes in an empty space populated with some individual flakes that do not overlap. If these flakes are large enough then a ray might hit the same flake several times. Since this is the same flake, the corresponding scattering events are correlated.

Below we shall compare the LTE and the accurate approaches.

3.1. Full BRDF as a Sum of BRDF Orders

To calculate paint visual appearance expressed via BRDF, we can use ray tracing which leads to the following expansion of the full BRDF:

$$f = f_1 + f_2 + f_3 + \cdots \tag{1}$$

where f_n corresponds to BRDF created by ray paths with n flake hits. It is called the n-th order of BRDF. The order equals the number of ray scattering (the changes of ray direction), so only reflections are counted but the specular transmissions that do not change ray direction and only attenuate it are not counted (Figure 1). In a sense, our BRDF orders are similar to the scattering orders in [28].

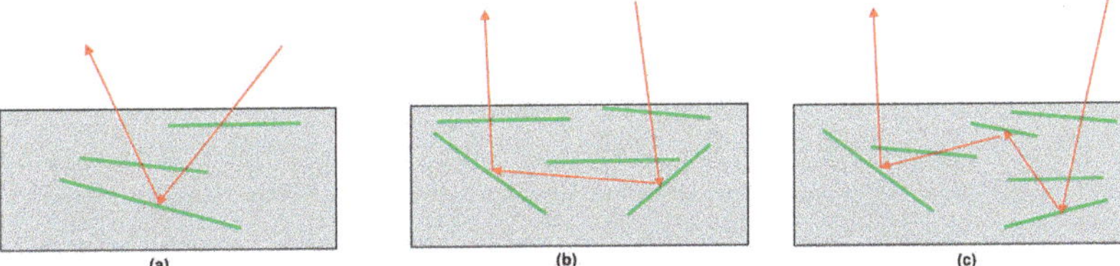

Figure 1. Side view of ray paths which form BRDF of the first (**a**), second (**b**), third (**c**) order. Light rays are shown by red arrows, flakes are thick green dashes and the binder is shaded light gray. The number of ray transmission events is irrelevant, so a random number of them are shown.

To be precise, any ray that contributes to the BRDF must penetrate the top Fresnel boundary twice, entering the paint layer and then leaving it. Thus, formally the minimal count of ray scattering events is 2, not 0, and BRDF components should be numbered as f_2, $f_3, \ldots$ We, however, do not count these two constant events in the orders.

Every BRDF order is an average over all the ray paths of the corresponding type. For f_1, this means that the ray transmits Fresnel boundary and enters the paint layer, then descends until it hits a flake. After that, it is reflected by that flake and ascends to the top boundary but not intersecting any flake. Finally, it transmits through the Fresnel boundary and leaves the paint layer (Figure 1a).

Generally, different flakes can be slightly correlated. If the flakes are well aligned and there are no forces between them, then we can neglect correlations between flakes at different depths. As a result, the flake hit event is rather independent from the obscure event (if another flake intersects the incident or reflected rays). Therefore

$$f_1(v,u) = t_F(v)t_F(u)\int_0^H a(v',u',z)\mathfrak{f}_1(v',u';z)dz \tag{2}$$

where v', u' are direction of the refracted incident and observation rays v and u, respectively, t_F is Fresnel transmittance of the binder-air boundary, $a(v',u',z)$ is the product attenuation along both ray segments and $\mathfrak{f}_1(v',u';z)dz$ is the first-order BRDF of the sublayer of thickness dz at depth z. It is independent from z in case of a homogeneous paint. We do not use its explicit form which is the same for both LTE and accurate approach (derivation is in [1]).

By definition, attenuation a is the average probability that the given fixed full path (along v' down to z then upwards along u') over all possible geometries of the flake ensemble which we can write as

$$a(v',u',z) = \langle \mathfrak{a}(v',z)\mathfrak{a}(u',z)\rangle$$

where $\mathfrak{a}$ is the probability that the given one ray goes from the surface to the depth z (or vice versa). The first term is for the incident ray, and the second is for the reflected one.

In the continuous medium approximation, it is assumed that the fates of these two rays are statistically independent, and therefore

$$a(v',u',z) = \langle \mathfrak{a}(v',z)\rangle\langle \mathfrak{a}(u',z)\rangle$$

Meanwhile calculation of the mean probability of ray transmitting the paint layer is simple and leads to

$$\langle \mathfrak{a}\rangle = e^{-(1-t)\overline{D}\overline{S}z} \tag{3}$$

(regardless of direction), and therefore

$$a(v',u',z) = e^{-2(1-t)\overline{D}\overline{S}z} \tag{4}$$

where t is the flake transmittance, $\overline{S}$ is the mean flake's area and $\overline{D}$ is the total concentration of flakes as their number in unit paint volume:

$$\overline{D} = \frac{\mathrm{PVC}}{\overline{S}h} \tag{5}$$

where PVC is the pigment volume concentration and h is flake thickness. This value determines BRDF of paint with thin planar flakes.

The formula (3) of attenuation for a single ray is very general and correct. It is true for both continuous medium approximation and ray tracing individual flakes of finite size. However, (4) is not accurate because it assumes statistical independence of the fates of the incident and reflected rays. Meanwhile, in reality they are correlated, and below we shall calculate how this affects attenuation and demonstrate large deviation from (4).

3.2. Combined Attenuation along Both Rays

Let the flakes be opaque thin disks of radius R aligned horizontally or with small inclination the horizontal plane. Figure 2 shows the cross-section of paint layer by a horizontal plane. As it is seen there, a horizontal disk of radius R at depth z' intersects a ray if its center is closer than R from the ray point at this depth, i.e., the center is within the circle of radius R and center in the ray point.

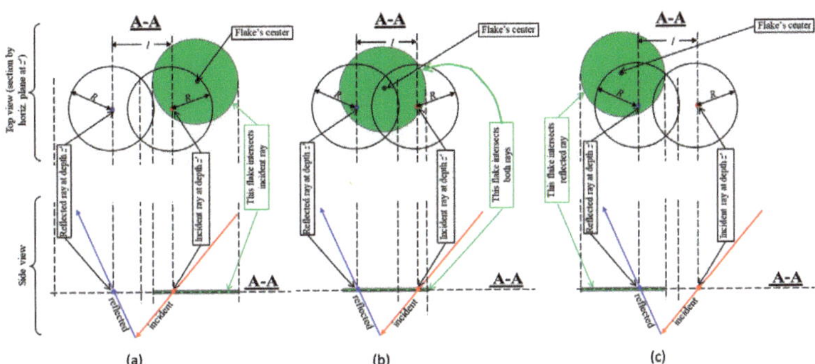

Figure 2. Cross-section of paint layer by a horizontal plane at depth z′. The top half is top view, the bottom half being side view. Flakes are represented as nearly horizontal thin disks of radius R (green). We show the three cases when the flake at depth z′ intersects (shadows) only the incident ray (**a**), when it intersects both rays (**b**) and when it intersects only the reflected ray (**c**).

Figure 3 shows the domain where the flake center intersects with the incident or reflected ray. If the flake center is in the red domain, the flake intersects the incident ray (red arrow). If the flake center is within in the blue domain, the flake intersects the reflected ray (blue arrow). If the center is in the intersection of the domains, the flake shadows both. The area of the horizontal section of the intersected domains at depth z′ is denoted by $\mathfrak{S}(z')$. As it is seen from the top panel of Figure 3, the area $\mathfrak{S}(z')$ is twice circle's area $S = \pi R^2$ minus area of intersection of these circles. The intersection is twice the area of the sector s:

$$\mathfrak{S} = 2\pi R^2 - 2s \tag{6}$$

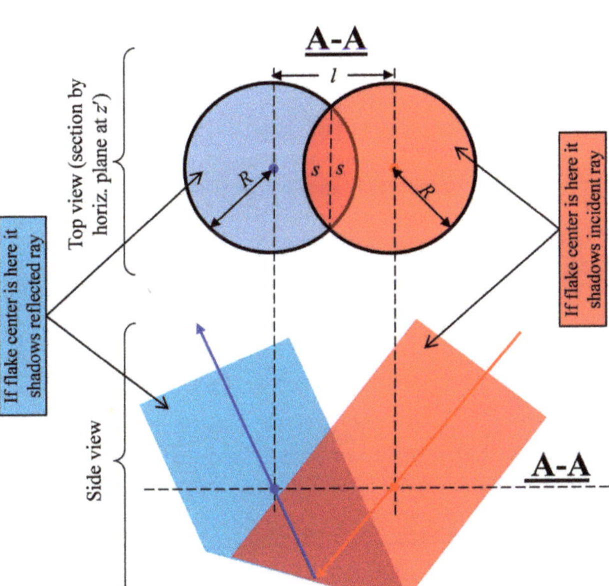

Figure 3. The center of a horizontal flake of radius R must belong to the blue domain if flake intersects the reflected ray (blue arrow) and red domain if flake intersects the incident ray (red arrow). The domain to intersect both rays is mixture (violet). The centers of the circles are the points of intersection with the reflected ray (left blue dot) and the incident ray (right red dot) at depth z′.

The area of each of this sector spanning the angle $\alpha = 2\arccos\frac{l/2}{R}$ is

$$
s = \begin{cases} R^2\left(\arccos\frac{l/2}{R} - \frac{l/2}{R}\sqrt{1 - \left(\frac{l/2}{R}\right)^2}\right), & l \leq 2R \\ 0, & l > 2R \end{cases}
\tag{7}
$$

where $l(z')$ is the distance between the points of the incident and reflected rays at depth z' and equals to

$$
l(z') = c(z - z')
$$

where z is the depth of the reflection point where both ray segments join; and c depends only on the directions of the incident and reflected rays [7].

To calculate transmission for the whole path (whose deepest point, i.e., the point of reflection is at depth z), we slice the paint's layer $[0, z]$ into horizontal thin sub-layers of thickness dz'.

Notice that if the flake has a non-zero transmittance t then if a ray intersects that flake, it still can pass with probability t. Thus, if both (incident and reflected) rays intersect a flake, the whole path still transmits with probability t^2. Then, from simple geometric considerations we can infer the following:

- The area where the center of a flake must be in order to intersect one of the rays is $\mathfrak{S}(z') - 2s$. Thus, the probability that one of the rays intersects a flake is $\mathrm{Pr}_1 = D(\mathfrak{S}(z') - 2s)dz'$; if it happens, the whole path is blocked with a probability $(1 - t)$. Thus, the total probability that the whole path is blocked is $(1 - t)\mathrm{Pr}_1$;
- The area where the center of a flake must be in order to intersect both the rays is $2s$. Thus, the probability that both of the rays intersect a flake is $\mathrm{Pr}_2 = 2Dsdz'$; if it happens, the whole path is blocked with a probability $(1 - t^2)$. Thus, the total probability that the whole path is blocked is $(1 - t^2)\mathrm{Pr}_2$.

Since $\mathfrak{S} = 2S - 2s$, see (6), the total probability that the whole path is blocked by sublayer $[z', z' + dz']$ is then

$$
\mathrm{Pr}(z, z') = (1 - t)\mathrm{Pr}_1 + \left(1 - t^2\right)\mathrm{Pr}_2 = 2(1 - t)D(S - (1 - t)s)dz'
$$

In the case of horizontal flakes, the flakes at different depths are independent and so the shadowing events at different depths are independent. The probability that the path transmits the whole layer $[0, z]$ is then the product of probabilities of transmission of each sublayer:

$$
a(v', u', z) = \prod_{z'=0}^{z}(1 - \mathrm{Pr}(z, z')) = \prod_{z'=0}^{z}(1 - 2(1 - t)D(S - (1 - t)s)dz')
$$
$$
= e^{-2(1-t)\int_0^z D(S-(1-t)s)dz'}
$$

In case there is a mixture of flakes of different area S (in different concentrations $D(S)$), the path can be blocked by either of them, so the total probability of blocking is a sum over flake species, i.e.,

$$
\begin{aligned}
\mathrm{Pr}(z, z') &= 2(1 - t)\sum_{species} D(S)(S - (1 - t)s)dz' \\
&= 2(1 - t)(\smallint D(S)SdS - (1 - t)\smallint D(S)s(l, S)dS)dz' \\
&\equiv 2(1 - t)\left(\overline{DS} - (1 - t)\overline{Ds}(l)dS\right)dz'
\end{aligned}
$$

where s is given by (7) for $R = \sqrt{S/\pi}$ and

$$
\begin{aligned}
\overline{DS} &\equiv \smallint D(S)SdS \\
\overline{Ds}(l) &\equiv \smallint D(S)s(l, S)dS
\end{aligned}
$$

So, attenuation becomes

$$
\begin{aligned}
a(v',u',z) &= e^{-2(1-t)\overline{DS}z+2(1-t^2)\int_0^z \overline{Ds}(c(z-z'))dz'} \\
&= e^{-2(1-t)\overline{DS}z+2c^{-1}(1-t)^2 \int_0^{cz} \overline{Ds}(l)dl} \\
&= e^{-4c^{-1}(1-t)\overline{DS}Z+2c^{-1}(1-t)^2 \alpha(Z)}
\end{aligned}
\tag{8}
$$

where

$$
\begin{aligned}
\alpha(Z) &\equiv \int_0^{2Z} \overline{Ds}(l)dl = \int_0^{2Z}\left(\int D(S)s(l,S)dS\right)dl \\
Z &\equiv \tfrac{cz}{2}
\end{aligned}
\tag{9}
$$

Let us calculate the above α, which in view of (7) and recalling that $R = \sqrt{S/\pi}$ can be written as

$$
\alpha(Z) \equiv \int_0^{2Z} \overline{Ds}(l)dl = \int_0^{2Z}\left(\int_{\pi(l/2)^2}^{\infty} D(S)\frac{S}{\pi}g\left(\frac{l}{2\sqrt{\frac{S}{\pi}}}\right)dS\right)dl
$$

where

$$
g(t) \equiv \arccos t - t\sqrt{1-t^2}
\tag{10}
$$

Changing the order of integration

$$
\int_0^{2Z}\left(\int_{\pi(l/2)^2}^{\infty}(\cdots)dS\right)dl = \int_0^{\pi Z^2}\left(\int_0^{2\sqrt{\frac{S}{\pi}}}(\cdots)dl\right)dS + \int_{\pi Z^2}^{\infty}\left(\int_0^{2Z}(\cdots)dl\right)dS
$$

this becomes

$$
\begin{aligned}
\alpha(Z) &= \int_0^{\pi Z^2}\left(\int_0^{2\sqrt{\frac{S}{\pi}}} D(S)\frac{S}{\pi}g\left(\frac{l}{2\sqrt{\frac{S}{\pi}}}\right)dl\right)dS + \int_{\pi Z^2}^{\infty}\left(\int_0^{2Z} D(S)\frac{S}{\pi}g\left(\frac{l}{2\sqrt{\frac{S}{\pi}}}\right)dl\right)dS \\
&= \frac{2}{\pi^{\frac{3}{2}}}\left(\int_0^1 g(x)dx\right)\int_0^{\pi Z^2} D(S)S^{\frac{3}{2}}dS + \frac{2}{\pi^{\frac{3}{2}}}\int_{\pi Z^2}^{\infty} D(S)S^{\frac{3}{2}}\left(\int_0^{\frac{Z}{\sqrt{\frac{S}{\pi}}}} g(x)dx\right)dS \\
&= \frac{2}{\pi^{\frac{3}{2}}}\left(\frac{2}{3}\int_0^{\pi Z^2} D(S)S^{\frac{3}{2}}dS + \int_{\pi Z^2}^{\infty} D(S)S^{\frac{3}{2}}G\left(\sqrt{\frac{\pi Z^2}{S}}\right)dS\right)
\end{aligned}
\tag{11}
$$

where

$$
G(x) \equiv \int_0^x g(y)dy = \frac{2}{3} + \frac{\pi}{2}x - x\cdot\arcsin x - \frac{2+x^2}{3}\sqrt{1-x^2}
\tag{12}
$$

Additionally, $s \equiv \pi Z^2$.

Complexity of (12) prevents us from obtaining the analytic dependence of the integral $\int_{\pi Z^2}^{\infty} D(S)S^{3/2}G\left(\sqrt{\frac{\pi Z^2}{S}}\right)dS$ on its parameter Z even for a simple distribution $D(S)$. This can be overcome if we find a good polynomial approximation to G, then Z could be moved out of the integral of each its term. It is reasonable to require that this approximation preserves the following properties of the exact function $G(x)$: it is 0 for $x = 0$, it is $\frac{2}{3}$ for $x = 1$, and it has zero derivative at $x = 1$. Then, the lowest degree polynomial is

$$
\frac{1}{3}\left((1-\varepsilon)\left(1-(1-x)^3\right) + (1+\varepsilon)\left(1-(1-x)^2\right)\right)
$$

The value of ε can be found from the least square fit that gives $\varepsilon = 0.091649$ and thus

$$
G(x) \approx \frac{(5-\varepsilon)x - (4-2\varepsilon)x^2 + (1-\varepsilon)x^3}{3} = 1.6361x - 1.2722x^2 + 0.30278x^3
$$

Substituting it in (11) we arrive at

$$
\begin{aligned}
\alpha(Z) \;\approx\; & \frac{2}{\pi^{\frac{3}{2}}}\left(\frac{2}{3}\int_0^{\pi Z^2} D(S)S^{\frac{3}{2}}dS + \int_{\pi Z^2}^{\infty} D(S)S^{\frac{3}{2}}\left(1.6361\sqrt{\frac{\pi Z^2}{S}} - 1.2722\frac{\pi Z^2}{S} + 0.30278\left(\frac{\pi Z^2}{S}\right)^{\frac{3}{2}} \right)dS \right) \\
=\; & \frac{4}{3\pi^{\frac{3}{2}}}\int_0^{\infty} D(S)S^{\frac{3}{2}}dS - \frac{4}{3\pi^{\frac{3}{2}}}\int_{\pi Z^2}^{\infty} D(S)S^{\frac{3}{2}}dS \\
& + \frac{2}{\pi^{\frac{3}{2}}}\left(1.6361\sqrt{\pi}Z\int_{\pi Z^2}^{\infty} D(S)SdS - 1.2722\pi Z^2\int_{\pi Z^2}^{\infty} D(S)\sqrt{S}dS + 0.30278\pi^{\frac{3}{2}}Z^3\int_{\pi Z^2}^{\infty} D(S)dS \right) \\
=\; & \frac{4}{3\pi^{\frac{3}{2}}}(\gamma_0(0) - \gamma_0(Z)) + \frac{2\cdot 1.6361}{\pi}Z\gamma_1(Z) - \frac{2\cdot 1.2722}{\sqrt{\pi}}Z^2\gamma_2(Z) + 2\cdot 0.30278Z^3\gamma_3(Z)
\end{aligned}
\tag{13}
$$

where

$$
\gamma_m(Z) \equiv \int_{\pi Z^2}^{\infty} S^{\frac{3-m}{2}} D(S)dS
$$

Remark 1. *In case the distribution of flake area is Gaussian* $Ce^{-\frac{(S-\bar{S})^2}{2\delta_S^2 \bar{S}^2}}$ *then*

$$
\gamma_m(Z) \;=\; C\bar{S}^{-\frac{5-m}{2}}\int_{\frac{\pi Z^2}{\bar{S}}}^{\infty} t^{\frac{3-m}{2}}e^{-\frac{(t-1)^2}{2\delta_S^2}}dt
$$

3.3. BRDF for Specular Flakes

The expansion in scattering order (1) works in the accurate approach and in the LTE. In most cases, the first-order term is the principal one and the latter ones are secondary corrections to it. Therefore, if we take the first-order calculated using the accurate approach and the second and other orders calculated using the LTE, we shall give a decent approximation

$$
\begin{aligned}
f \;=\; & f_1 + f_2^{(LTE)} + f_3^{(LTE)} + \cdots \\
=\; & f_1 + \left(f^{(LTE)} - f_1^{(LTE)} \right)
\end{aligned}
$$

For vertically homogeneous paint, the equation for the first-order BRDF (2) becomes

$$
f_1(v,u) = t_F(v)t_F(u)\mathfrak{f}_1(v',u')\int_0^H a(v',u',z)dz
$$

It is valid for both the LTE and the accurate approach. The pre-integral factor is the same for both approaches. The attenuation is different: (4) for the LTE and (8) for the accurate approach. So

$$
f_1(v,u) = f_1^{(LTE)}(v,u)\frac{A|_{accurate}}{A|_{LTE}}
\tag{14}
$$

where

$$
A \equiv \int_0^H a(v',u',z)dz
$$

Therefore, the final approximation to the full (all orders) BRDF becomes

$$
f \approx f^{(LTE)} + \left(\frac{A|_{accurate}}{A|_{LTE}} - 1 \right)f_1^{(LTE)}(v,u)
\tag{15}
$$

For the LTE method, the integral of attenuation (4) is

$$
A_{LTE} = \frac{1 - e^{-2DSH}}{2DS}
\tag{16}
$$

While for the accurate model, according to (8),

$$
\begin{aligned}
A &\equiv \int_0^H a(v',u',z)\,dz \\
&\approx \frac{2}{c}\int_0^{\frac{cH}{2}} e^{-2c^{-1}(1-t)(2\overline{DS}Z-(1-t)\alpha(Z))}\,dZ \\
&= 2\rho H \int_0^{\frac{1}{2\rho}} e^{-4(1-t)\rho F(\zeta-\frac{(1-t)}{\pi}\tilde{\alpha}(\zeta))}\,d\zeta
\end{aligned}
\tag{17}
$$

where

$$
\begin{aligned}
\tilde{\alpha}(\zeta) &\equiv \frac{\pi}{2c\rho F}\alpha(Z) \\
\zeta &\equiv \frac{Z}{cH\rho} = \frac{Z}{\overline{R}} \\
\rho &\equiv c^{-1}r \\
r &\equiv \frac{\overline{R}}{H} \\
\overline{R} &\equiv \sqrt{\overline{S}/\pi} \\
F &\equiv \overline{DS}H
\end{aligned}
$$

The F is a sort of a concentration parameter like PVC. It can be named PAC (pigment area concentration) because by definition F is the total area of flakes in the paint layer of the unit area. $\overline{R}$ is the effective mean radius, and $r \equiv \overline{R}/H$ is the relative effective radius. A is determined just by the three parameters ρ, F and H and depends on the directions v' and u' only through ρ which is inversely proportional to $c = c(v',u')$.

The integral (17) can be calculated only numerically.

The functions γ_m and α are determined solely by the distribution of flake area. Thus, they can be pre-calculated in advance and re-used for all color channels and all BRDF points (i.e., for all combinations of the directions of incidence and illumination) because it is only c that depends on these directions and t which depends on the color channel.

3.4. Opaque Flakes of Fixed Size as a Limiting Case

Obviously, BRDF scaling for opaque flakes of fixed size that was initially investigated in [7] can be calculated now as the limiting case when the distribution of area is a delta-function and $t = 0$.

In case this distribution is sharp, $\gamma_m(Z)$ quickly change at $Z = \overline{R}$ and

$$
\gamma_m(Z) = \overline{D}\pi^{\frac{3-m}{2}}\overline{R}^{3-m}
\begin{cases}
0, & Z > \overline{R} \\
1, & Z < \overline{R}
\end{cases}
$$

Thus,

$$
\alpha(Z) = \frac{2}{\pi}\overline{DSR}\left(1.6361\min(\zeta,1) - 1.2722(\min(\zeta,1))^2 + 0.30278(\min(\zeta,1))^3\right)
$$
$$
\zeta \equiv \frac{Z}{\overline{R}}
$$

As a result, the integral of attenuation is

$$
\int_0^H a(v',u',z)\,dz \approx \frac{2b}{\overline{DS}}\int_0^{\frac{cH}{2R}} e^{-4(1-t)b(x-(1-t)\frac{1}{\pi}(1.6361x-1.2722x^2+0.30278x^3))}\,dx
$$

where $b \equiv \frac{\overline{DSR}}{c} = \frac{F}{c}\frac{\overline{R}}{H}$ in case $\frac{cH}{2} < \overline{R}$, and

$$
\begin{aligned}
\int_0^H a(v',u',z)\,dz \approx{}& \frac{2b}{\overline{DS}}\int_0^1 e^{-4(1-t)b(x-(1-t)\frac{1}{\pi}(1.6361x-1.2722x^2+0.30278x^3))}\,dx \\
& + e^{4b(1-t)^2\frac{2}{3\pi}}\frac{e^{-4b(1-t)}-e^{-2F(1-t)}}{2\overline{DS}(1-t)}
\end{aligned}
$$

in case $\frac{cH}{2} > \overline{R}$.

For opaque flakes this gives

$$\int_0^H a(v',u',z)\,dz = \begin{cases} \frac{2b}{\overline{DS}}\int_0^{\frac{F}{2b}} e^{-4b(x-\frac{1}{\pi}(1.6361x-1.2722x^2+0.30278x^3))}\,dx, & \frac{cH}{2} < \overline{R} \\ \frac{2b}{\overline{DS}}\int_0^1 e^{-4b(x-\frac{1}{\pi}(1.6361x-1.2722x^2+0.30278x^3))}\,dx + e^{\frac{8b}{3\pi}}\frac{e^{-4b}-e^{-2F}}{2\overline{DS}}, & \frac{cH}{2} > \overline{R} \end{cases}$$

The difference from [7] is very small because $2\left(x - \frac{1}{\pi}(1.6361x - 1.2722x^2 + 0.30278x^3)\right) \approx x + 0.58x^2$.

3.5. The Effect of Variation of Size

As we can see, BRDF depends on the flake size (and its distribution) through the ratio $\frac{A|_{accurate}}{A|_{LTE}}$, see (15). Strange as it may seem, the correction scale is nearly insensitive to the distribution of flake area being determined by the average area. To understand this effect, let us consider the exponential distribution of area

$$D(S) = \overline{DS}^{-1} e^{-\frac{S}{\overline{S}}}$$

where $\overline{S}$ is the mean area and $\overline{D}$ is the "total density". This form of distribution allows to calculate α analytically.

We see that while the difference between fixed size flakes and LTE can be even twofold, the difference between fixed size flakes and variable size flakes can only reach about 3.5% for very special parameters.

According to (14), the main first-order component of BRDF is proportional to the integral of attenuation

$$A(t,\rho,F) \equiv \int_0^{\frac{1}{2\rho}} e^{-4(1-t)\rho F(\zeta - \frac{(1-t)}{\pi}\tilde{\alpha}(\zeta))}\,d\zeta$$

Therefore, the quantitative measure of the effect of the distribution of size on BRDF is the relative difference of that factor, i.e., $\frac{A_{var} - A_{fix}}{A_{var}}$. According to (13)

$$\begin{aligned}
\alpha(Z) &= \frac{2\overline{DS}^{-1}}{\pi^{3/2}}\left(\frac{2}{3}\int_0^s e^{-\frac{S}{\overline{S}}}S^{3/2}dS + 1.6361\sqrt{s}\int_s^\infty e^{-\frac{S}{\overline{S}}}S\,dS - 1.2722s\int_s^\infty e^{-\frac{S}{\overline{S}}}\sqrt{S}\,dS + 0.30278s^{3/2}\int_s^\infty e^{-\frac{S}{\overline{S}}}dS\right) \\
&= \frac{2\overline{DS}^{3/2}}{\pi^{3/2}}\left(\frac{2}{3}\int_0^\sigma x^{3/2}e^{-x}dx + 1.6361\sqrt{\sigma}\int_\sigma^\infty xe^{-x}dx - 1.2722\sigma\int_\sigma^\infty \sqrt{x}e^{-x}dx + 0.30278\sigma^{3/2}e^{-\sigma}\right) \\
&= \frac{2\overline{DS}^{3/2}}{\pi^{3/2}}\left((1.3333 \times 10^{-5}\sigma + 0.6361)\sqrt{\sigma}e^{-\sigma} - 1.1275\sigma + (0.88623 + 1.1275\sigma)\mathrm{erf}(\sqrt{\sigma})\right) \\
&= 2\frac{\overline{DS}^{3/2}}{\pi^{3/2}}\tilde{\alpha}(\zeta) = \frac{2}{\pi^{3/2}}\frac{\overline{DS}H\sqrt{\overline{S}}}{H}\tilde{\alpha}(\zeta) = \frac{2crF}{\pi}\tilde{\alpha}(\zeta) \\
\tilde{\alpha}(\zeta) &\equiv (1.3333 \times 10^{-5}\zeta^2 + 0.6361)\zeta e^{-\zeta^2} - 1.1275\zeta^2 + (0.88623 + 1.1275\zeta^2)\mathrm{erf}(\zeta)
\end{aligned}$$

where $s \equiv \pi Z^2$, $\sigma \equiv s/\overline{S}$ and $\zeta \equiv \sqrt{\frac{\pi}{\overline{S}}}Z = \sqrt{\sigma}$.

The case of fixed size flakes relates to the delta-function distribution

$$D(S) = \overline{D}\delta(S - \overline{S})$$

for which

$$\begin{aligned}
\alpha(Z) &= \frac{2\overline{DS}^{3/2}}{\pi^{3/2}}\begin{cases} 1.6361\sqrt{\frac{s}{\overline{S}}} - 1.2722\frac{s}{\overline{S}} + 0.30278\left(\frac{s}{\overline{S}}\right)^{3/2}, & s \leq \overline{S} \\ \frac{2}{3}, & s > \overline{S} \end{cases} \\
&= \frac{2\overline{DS}^{3/2}}{\pi^{3/2}}\left(1.6361\sqrt{\min(\sigma,1)} - 1.2722\min(\sigma,1) + 0.30278(\min(\sigma,1))^{3/2}\right) \\
\tilde{\alpha}(\zeta) &\equiv 1.6361\min(\zeta,1) - 1.2722(\min(\zeta,1))^2 + 0.30278(\min(\zeta,1))^3
\end{aligned}$$

The plots of $\tilde{\alpha}(\zeta)$ as a function of ζ for both cases are shown in Figure 4.

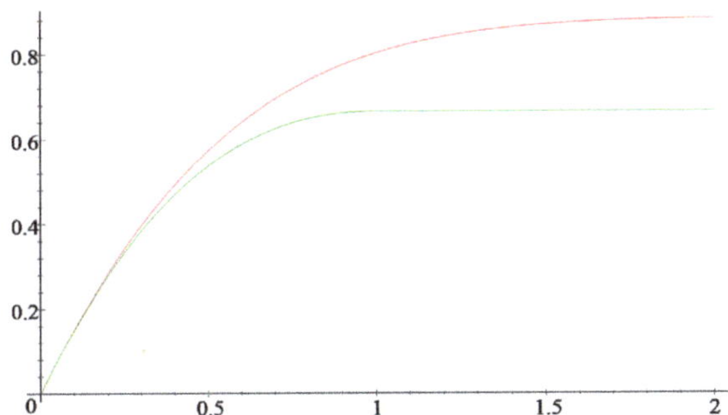

Figure 4. $\widetilde{\alpha}(\zeta)$ as a function of ζ for flakes with exponentially distributed area (red) and for the fixed-size flakes with the same mean area (green).

For $\zeta \to 0$

$$\widetilde{\alpha}_{var}(\zeta) \approx 1.6361\zeta - 1.1275\zeta^2 + O(\zeta^3)$$
$$\widetilde{\alpha}_{fixed}(Z) \approx 1.6361\zeta - 1.2722\zeta^2 + O(\zeta^3)$$

So, the two functions converge.

For $\zeta \to \infty$ both functions saturate

$$\widetilde{\alpha}_{var}(Z) \approx \frac{\overline{DS}^{3/2}}{\pi^{3/2}}$$
$$\widetilde{\alpha}_{fixed}(Z) \approx \frac{4\overline{DS}^{3/2}}{3\pi^{3/2}}$$

3.6. Back Scattering Approximation

Back scattering means that the incident ray is reflected in the exactly opposite direction, i.e., both rays go the same path. In case of the first-order BRDF, the incident and reflected rays have a common point. In this case, obviously, $c = 0$ or $\rho \to \infty$. As the reflected ray approaches the incident path, c approaches 0 and ρ diverges. For very large ρ, integration effectively ends at $\zeta < (\sim 2.5)\frac{1}{2(1-t)\rho r F} \ll 1$, where $\widetilde{\alpha}(\zeta) \approx 1.6361\zeta$, and so

$$
\begin{aligned}
A(t,\rho,F) &= \int_0^{\frac{1}{2\rho}} e^{-4(1-t)\rho F(\zeta - \frac{(1-t)}{\pi}\widetilde{\alpha}(\zeta))}\,d\zeta \\
&\approx \int_0^{\frac{1}{2\rho}} e^{-4(1-t)(1-0.52(1-t))\rho F\zeta}\,d\zeta \\
&= \frac{1 - e^{-2(1-t)(1-0.52(1-t))F}}{4(1-t)(1-0.52(1-t))\rho F}
\end{aligned}
$$

While LTE (which corresponds to $\alpha = 0$) gives

$$A(t,\rho,F) = \int_0^{\frac{1}{2\rho}} e^{-4(1-t)\rho F\zeta}\,d\zeta = \frac{1 - e^{-2(1-t)F}}{4(1-t)\rho F}$$

And thus, the ratio of the first-order BRDFs (14) is

$$s = \frac{A_{accurate}(t,\rho,F)}{A_{LTE}(t,\rho,F)} \approx \frac{1}{1-0.52(1-t)}\frac{1 - e^{-2(1-t)(1-0.52(1-t))F}}{1 - e^{-2(1-t)F}}$$

which for opaque flakes is

$$s \approx 2.08\frac{1 - e^{-0.96F}}{1 - e^{-2F}} \tag{18}$$

This asymptotic highlights a remarkable fact: the difference between continuous medium (the LTE approach) and individual particles (the accurate approach) persists even for the tiniest flakes for illumination and observation close to normal.

4. Results

The following paint structure was used in our simulation experiments: the binder refraction index is 1.5, and the paint layer thickness is $H = 100$ µm. Flakes are thin platelets with thickness of 0.5 µm and specular reflectance of 50%. Their specular transmittance is 0% (calculations for opaque flakes) or 50% (calculations for semi-transparent flakes). The angle between the paint surface normal and normal of flakes has a Gaussian distribution with a variance of 2 degrees. The concentration and size of the flakes are described by two dimensionless parameters: relative radius $r = \overline{R}/H$ and pigment area concentration $F = \overline{DS}H$, which equals to the total area of flakes in paint layer with unit area. In our calculations, r varies from 1 for large flakes to 0.01 for small flakes and F varies from 2 (high concentration) to 0.2 (low concentration). Flake area has a Gaussian distribution with center at 0 and two different widths: 4000 µm² and 40,000 µm². Effective flake radius $\overline{R}$ (such a value that $\pi\left(\overline{R}\right)^2$ equals the mean flake area) was 1 µm, 10 µm and 100 µm.

BRDF is a function of incident and outgoing directions. The azimuth of incidence is irrelevant because of the isotropy of our paint layer. The outgoing direction is taken in the coordinate system with the polar axis along the mirror reflection of the incident ray. This allows to choose high angular resolution for the sharp near-specular peak which is close to the pole regardless of σ. Hence, in our coordinate system, BRDF is a function of three angles: the angle between illumination and paint normal σ and two angles of observation, φ and ϑ, where ϑ is the angle between observation and direction of the mirror reflection and φ is the rotation of the observation direction about the mirror direction.

BRDF of the paint layer was calculated using three methods: Monte Carlo ray tracing in continuous medium (the LTE approach), ray tracing within paint layer with explicitly specified individual particles (the accurate approach) and the LTE approach with correction (15). For the accurate approach, we created a sample of paint geometry with randomly distributed and not overlapping flakes. Additionally, for comparison, we calculated the BRDF for fixed flake area (with the same mean area $\overline{S}$). However, the plots for fixed area and for the Gaussian distribution of area are indistinguishable within the line thickness; the LTE results are completely independent from flake area while the accurate ray tracing results change but very slightly, see Section 3.5.

Figure 5 shows the results of calculations using these three models for the case $F = 2$ (high concentration) and $r = 1$ (large flakes) when the difference is maximal. To fit them all in one image, we show BRDF only in the plane of incidence ($\varphi = 0°$) and for three angles of incidence $\sigma = 0°, 30°,$ and $60°$, because the other BRDF plots demonstrate nearly the same relation.

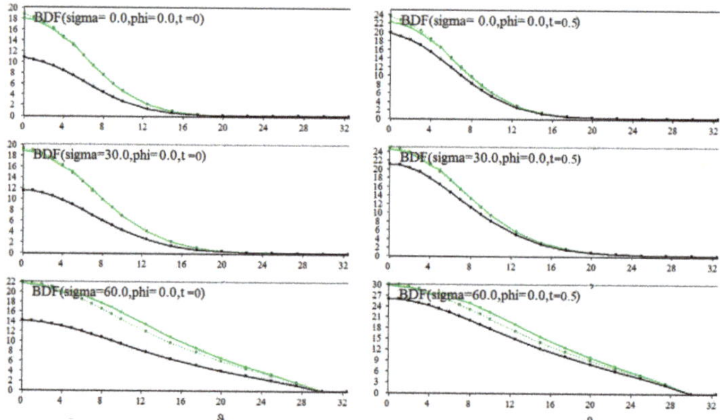

Figure 5. BRDF calculated using the accurate method (solid green), LTE (solid black) and the corrected LTE model (dashed dark green). Left column is for opaque flakes (t = 0), and right column is for semi-transparent flakes (t = 0.5). Effective mean flake radius $\overline{R}$ is 100 µm, F = 2.

In Figure 5, we can see that the correction (15) significantly improves the accuracy. Results of the accurate approach and the LTE with correction are close. Additionally, we can see that the role of size is weaker for semi-transparent flakes than for the opaque ones. This is because BRDF depends on flake size through the term α, see (17), and this term is scaled by $(1 - t)$, so for $t \to 1$ it vanishes.

The difference between the LTE and the accurate approaches increases with the increase in F or r parameters. Figure 6 shows the results of the increasing (from left to right and from top to bottom) parameters for opaque flakes. Figure 7 demonstrates the same tendency for semi-transparent flakes. It is seen that the difference from LTE increases with F and r and that the correction significantly improves the accuracy.

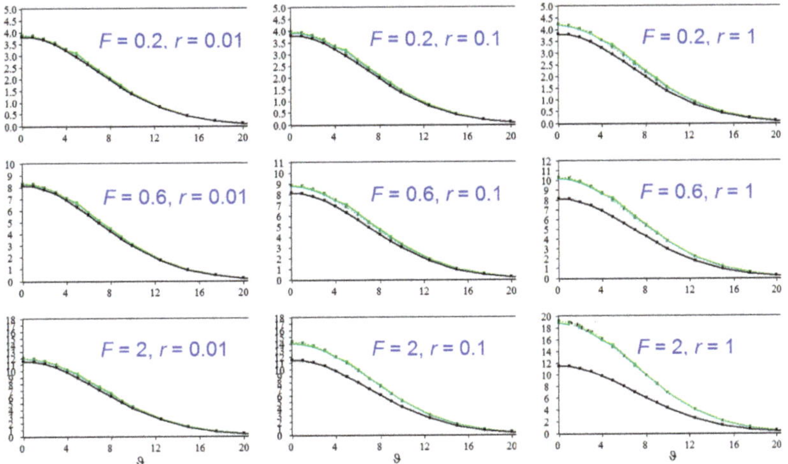

Figure 6. Dependence of BRDF on the size and concentration for opaque flakes. BRDF calculated using the accurate method (solid green), LTE (solid black) and the corrected LTE model (dashed dark green). We only show the section in the plane of incidence when the angle of incidence $\sigma = 30°$.

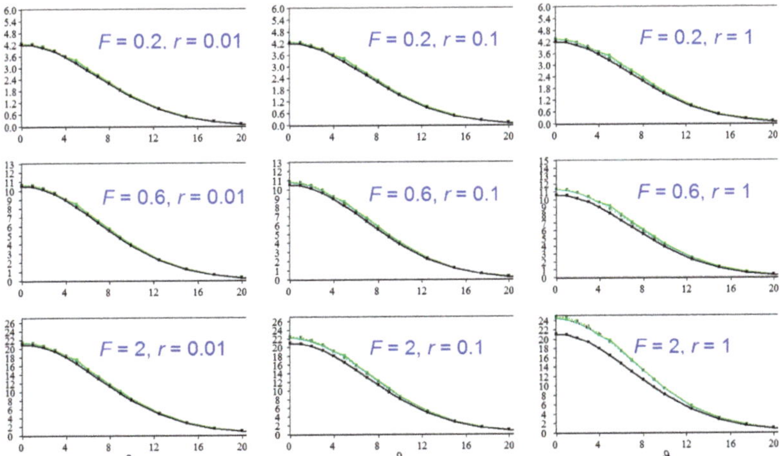

Figure 7. Dependence of BRDF on the size and concentration for semi-transparent flakes ($t = 0.5$). BRDF calculated using the accurate method (solid green), LTE (solid black) and the corrected LTE model (dashed dark green). We only show the section in the plane of incidence when the angle of incidence $\sigma = 30°$.

One can see that our method that calculates BRDF from scaling of the LTE results provides good accuracy in the wide range of flake size and concentration. Naturally, as the flake size decreases, the accurate model for individual flakes and the LTE for continuous medium converge (Figure 6, left column).

As expected from the derived formulae, the case of normal incidence is special. Indeed, for normal incidence and observation close to normal, we have nearly the back scattering when correlation effects do not vanish even for tiny flakes, see Section 3.6. Therefore, now the difference between the accurate approach (individual flakes) and the LTE (continuous medium) must persist even for tiny particles. Figures 8 and 9 demonstrate that this is really so. The effect is more pronounced for opaque flakes (Figure 8, top row) than for semi-transparent flakes (Figure 9, top row). The effect is, however, gone for $\sigma = 10°$ (bottom rows of Figures 8 and 9).

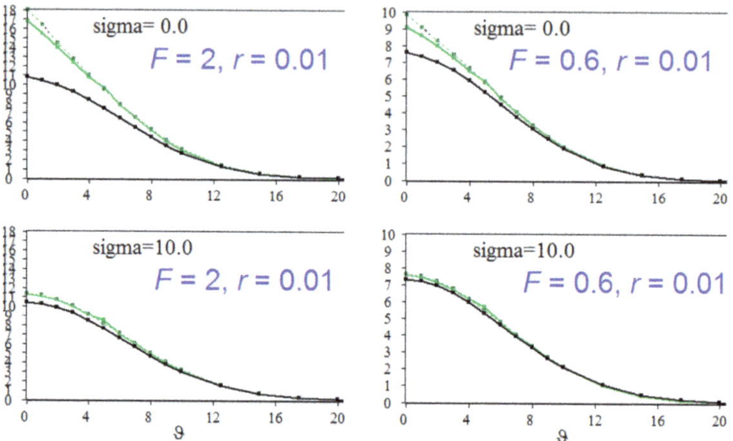

Figure 8. Singularity of the case of normal incidence for opaque flakes ($t = 0$). BRDF for the smallest flakes ($\overline{R} = 1$ μm) calculated using the accurate method (solid green), LTE (solid black) and the corrected LTE model (dashed dark green).

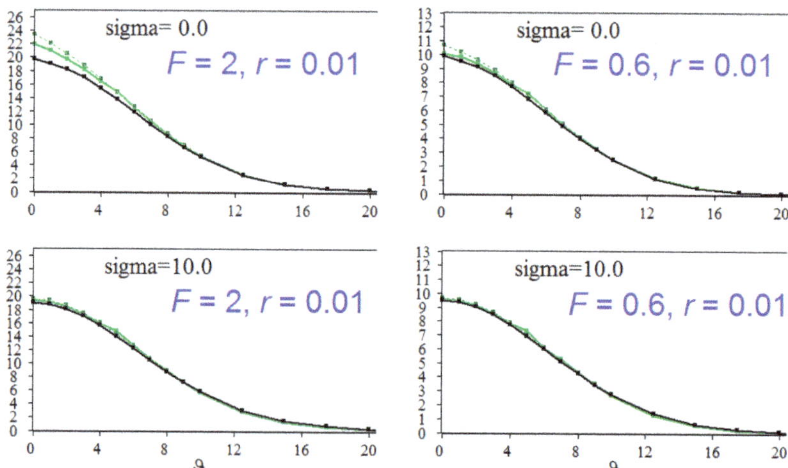

Figure 9. Singularity of the case of normal incidence for semi-transparent flakes ($t = 0.5$). BRDF for the smallest flakes ($\overline{R} = 1$ μm) calculated using the accurate method (solid green), LTE (solid black) and the corrected LTE model (dashed dark green).

Again, the effect of size is much weaker for semi-transparent flakes than for the opaque ones.

It should be noted that the back scattering occurs for any σ. It corresponds to $\varphi = 0$, and $\vartheta = 2\sigma$. Therefore, the first order BRDF for $\vartheta \to 2\sigma$ must deviate seriously from the LTE results according to (18), for example, the difference can be up to twofold for $F = 2$. However, this applies to the first-order BRDF, which for this angle is less than 10% of the full one. Meanwhile, for higher scattering orders, the reflected ray does not have a common point with the incident ray. Hence, it is spatially separated even if its direction is exactly opposite to the direction of incidence. Therefore, this effect does not apply to higher scattering orders while they dominate for, for example, $\sigma = 10°$, and $\vartheta = 20°$. This is why we do not see significant divergence of the two curves at this point (Figure 9, bottom row).

5. Discussion and Conclusions

While the mainstream studies on the deviation of light scattering in dispersed media from the continuous medium approximation concentrate on the role of correlations between particles (such as their agglutination), we demonstrate that another mechanism exists in automotive paints with "effect pigments" (metallic and pearlescent paints). Here, the light scattering deviates significantly from the continuous medium approximation even in the absence of such correlations, i.e., when the particles of an "effect pigment" are homogeneously, evenly and stochastically distributed. The deviation is caused by correlations between subsequent light scattering events. We prove that this effect is very rough and exists whenever the flakes of "effect pigment" are aligned parallel to the paint surface. This effect is very widespread because such paints are always applied to achieve exactly this alignment.

Meanwhile, correlations between particles are a more subtle effect of chemical physics, usually caused by positive or negative mutual affinity of particles. This may or may not happen depending on many factors including surfactants. It is not always known if this will happen, and it is even a more rare case if we know it quantitatively (i.e., know the potential of interaction). In this case, predictions of its effect on the optical appearance can only be qualitative.

On the contrary, the effect investigated by us is rather rough and it is not related to the subtle interaction potential. It depends on the flake size (and the law of dependence is simple and close to analytical) and on alignment. If alignment is good, we can use the asymptotic. Thus, quantitative prediction is possible and we have provided nearly analytical laws that allow very accurate calculation. Moreover, being mostly simple analytical formulae, they allow you to "intuitively feel" the effect so that you can figure out what is going to happen, even without massive computations. It is noteworthy that at normal incidence and observation, the deviation from LTE is almost twofold even for tiny flakes, i.e., there is no simple convergence as the particle size goes to 0.

We have derived a correction term which makes the paint appearance calculated using LTE very close to that of the accurate model. If we apply this correction to the first scattering-order BRDF of the LTE approach leaving the higher orders unchanged, the sum will already be very close to the full accurate BRDF. The value of the derived analytical corrections is that they are more easy to obtain numerically and even admit some analytical approximation, while the accurate approach calculations (for individual flakes) are more difficult and time consuming.

Simulation and realistic visualization of pearlescent and metallic paints have direct and inverse problems. The direct problem is calculating how the paint with given composition looks under given illumination and observation directions. The inverse problem emerges when we are looking for the paint composition whose appearance is the closest to the target one. The latter problem is more interesting for the automotive industry. It always occurs when repairing a car body. For modern paint formulations, optical characteristics have many degrees of freedom, and the dimension of the paint matching problem increases to dozens of parameters, and it is almost impossible to adjust them by mixing several basic options. This problem is solved by minimizing the discrepancy between the target appearance and the one calculated by the simulation of the direct problem.

There have been attempts to solve the inverse problem basing on LTE, for example, the radiative transfer equation is used in optical tomography [29]. For the paint visualization task, we have demonstrated that BRDF (visual appearance of paint) depends on the flake size. At the same time, LTE does not operate the flake size, and therefore cannot be used for the inverse problem of the automotive paint simulation. However, after application of our correction term, we have a "modified LTE" and can vary all parameters to find the composition for which the calculated BRDF best fits the measured one. Thus, we can solve not only the direct but also the inverse problem. This is a possible direction for future work.

This work continues [7] where the first steps of this research were taken. Herein, the method is generalized and allows the flakes to vary in size and have a transmittance. However, there are still some limitations and assumptions. First of all, we considered only the case of perfectly aligned flakes. It is assumed that for non-aligned flakes, our method should work with less accuracy. Investigation of the influence of flake alignment on the method accuracy is one of the directions of future work. Another possible study is related to the influence of the flakes with a matte/diffuse surface. In our study, they are specular and do not have a diffuse component while in reality there exists partially diffuse flakes.

Author Contributions: Conceptualization, S.E. and A.V.; methodology, A.V.; software, S.E.; validation, A.V.; formal analysis, S.E.; investigation, S.E.; resources, V.G.; data curation, V.G.; writing—original draft preparation, S.E. and A.V.; writing—review and editing, A.V. and V.G.; visualization, S.E. and A.V.; supervision, V.G.; project administration, V.G. All authors have read and agreed to the published version of the manuscript.

Funding: This research received no external funding.

Data Availability Statement: The data presented in this study are available within this paper.

Conflicts of Interest: The authors declare no conflict of interest.

References

1. Ershov, S.; Kolchin, K.; Myszkowski, K. Rendering pearlescent appearance based on paint-composition modelling. *Comput. Graph. Forum* **2001**, *20*, 227–238. [CrossRef]
2. Chandrasekhar, S. *Radiative Transfer*; Dover Publications Inc.: New York, NY, USA, 1960.
3. Budak, V.P.; Korkin, S.V. On the solution of a vectorial radiative transfer equation in an arbitrary three-dimensional turbid medium with anisotropic scattering. *J. Quant. Spectrosc. Radiat. Transf.* **2008**, *109*, 220–234. [CrossRef]
4. Hansen, J.E. Radiative transfer by doubling very thin layers. *Astrophys. J.* **1969**, *155*, 565–573. [CrossRef]
5. Pharr, M.; Jakob, W.; Humphreys, G. *Physically Based Rendering: From Theory to Implementation*, 3rd ed.; Morgan Kaufmann: Cambridge, MA, USA, 2017.
6. Voloboy, A.; Ershov, S.; Pozdnyakov, S. Interactive modelling of automotive paints. In Proceedings of the 22nd International Conference on Computer Graphics and Vision Graphicon'2012, Moscow, Russia, 1–5 October 2012; pp. 242–247. Available online: https://www.graphicon.ru/html/2012/conference/RU6%20-%20Graphics/gc2012Voloboy.pdf (accessed on 27 April 2023).
7. Ershov, S.; Voloboy, A.; Barladian, B.; Sokolov, V.; Potemin, I.; Zhdanov, D. Light scattering in automotive paints: Continuous medium approach vs correlations between particles. In Proceedings of the SPIE Conference on Illumination Optics VI, Online, 12 September 2021; Volume 11874, pp. 39–54. [CrossRef]
8. Ergun, S.; Onel, S.; Ozturk, A. A General Micro-flake Model for Predicting the Appearance of Car Paint. In Proceedings of the Eurographics Symposium on Rendering—Experimental Ideas & Implementations, Dublin, Ireland, 22–24 June 2016; pp. 65–71.
9. Kim, G.Y.; Lee, K.H. A reflectance model for metallic paints using a two-layer structure surface with microfacet distributions. *IEICE Trans. Inf. Syst.* **2010**, *93*, 3076–3087. [CrossRef]
10. Ershov, S.; Khodulev, A.; Kolchin, K. Simulation of sparkles in metallic paints. In Proceedings of the 9th international conference on Computer Graphics and Image Processing Graphicon'1999, Moscow, Russia, 26 August–1 September 1999; pp. 121–128. Available online: https://www.graphicon.ru/html/1999/Lighting_and_Photo-Realistic_Rendering/Ershov_Khodulev_Kolchin.pdf (accessed on 27 April 2023).
11. Filip, J.; Vavra, R. Image-based appearance acquisition of effect coatings. *Comput. Vis. Media* **2019**, *5*, 73–89. [CrossRef]
12. Rump, M.; Muller, G.; Sarlette, R.; Koch, D.; Klein, R. Photo-realistic rendering of metallic car paint from image-based measurements. *Comput. Graph. Forum* **2008**, *27*, 527–536. [CrossRef]
13. Gunther, J.; Chen, T.; Goesele, M.; Wald, I.; Seidel, H.P. Efficient acquisition and realistic rendering of car paint. *Vis. Model. Vis.* **2005**, *5*, 487–494.

14. Golla, T.; Klein, R. Interactive interpolation of metallic effect car paints. In Proceedings of the 23rd Symposium on Vision, Modeling, and Visualization, Stuttgart, Germany, 10–12 October 2018; pp. 11–20. [CrossRef]
15. Mih, A.; Durikovic, R. Metallic paint appearance measurement and rendering. *J. Appl. Math. Stat. Inform.* **2013**, *9*, 25–39. [CrossRef]
16. Kostinski, A.B. On the extinction of radiation by a homogeneous but spatially correlated random medium. *J. Opt. Soc. Am. A* **2001**, *18*, 1929–1933. [CrossRef] [PubMed]
17. Kostinski, A.B. On the extinction of radiation by a homogeneous but spatially correlated random medium: Reply to comment. *J. Opt. Soc. Am. A* **2002**, *19*, 2521–2525. [CrossRef]
18. Jarabo, A.; Allaga, C.; Gutierrez, D. A radiative transfer framework for spatially-correlated materials. *ACM Trans. Graph.* **2018**, *37*, 1–13. [CrossRef]
19. Bitterli, B.; Ravichandran, S.; Muller, T.; Wrenninge, M.; Novak, J.; Marschner, S.; Jarosz, W. A radiative transfer framework for non-exponential media. *ACM Trans. Graph.* **2018**, *37*, 1–17. [CrossRef]
20. Packard, C.D.; Larsen, M.L.; Cantrell, W.H.; Shaw, R.A. Light scattering in a spatially-correlated particle field: Role of the radial distribution function. *J. Quant. Spectrosc. Radiat. Transf.* **2019**, *236*, 106601. [CrossRef]
21. Mishchenko, M.I. "Independent" and "dependent" scattering by particles in a multi-particle group. *OSA Contin.* **2018**, *1*, 243–260. [CrossRef]
22. Loiko, V.A.; Berdnik, V.V. Light scattering in disperse layers with a high concentration of optically soft particles. *Opt. Spectrosc.* **2003**, *95*, 800–807. [CrossRef]
23. Loiko, V.; Berdnik, V. Light scattering by a disperse layer of closely packed two-layered spherical particles. In Proceedings of the XII Electromagnetic and Light Scattering Conference, Helsinki, Finland, 28 June–2 July 2010; pp. 130–133.
24. Ma, L.X.; Wang, C.C.; Tan, J.Y. Light scattering by densely packed optically soft particle systems, with consideration of the particle agglomeration and dependent scattering. *Appl. Opt.* **2019**, *58*, 7336–7345. [CrossRef] [PubMed]
25. Vynck, K.; Pierrat, R.; Carminati, R.; Froufe-Perez, L.S.; Scheffold, F.; Sapienza, R.; Vignolini, S.; Saenz, J.J. Light in correlated disordered media. *arXiv* **2021**, arXiv:2106.13892. [CrossRef]
26. Rytov, S.M.; Kravtsov, Y.A.; Tatarskii, V.I. *Principles of Statistical Radiophysics 1: Elements of Random Process Theory*; Springer: Berlin, Germany, 1987.
27. Ershov, S.V.; Zhdanov, D.D.; Voloboy, A.G.; Deryabin, N.B. The method of quasi-specular elements to reduce stochastic noise during illuminance simulation. *Light Eng.* **2020**, *28*, 39–47. [CrossRef]
28. Meglinski, I.V.; Romanov, V.P.; Churmakov, D.Y.; Berrocal, E.; Jermy, M.C.; Greenhalgh, D.A. Low and high order light scattering in particulate media. *Laser Phys. Lett.* **2004**, *1*, 387–390. [CrossRef]
29. Fan, Y.; Ying, L. Solving optical tomography with deep learning. *arXiv* **2019**, arXiv:1910.04756. [CrossRef]

 *mathematics*

Article

An Adaptive Controller Design for Nonlinear Active Air Suspension Systems with Uncertainties

Jinhua Zhang , Yi Yang and Cheng Hu *

School of Mechanical and Electrical Engineering, Guangzhou University, Guangzhou 510006, China
* Correspondence: c_hu@gzhu.edu.cn

Abstract: Active air spring suspensions can improve the vehicle ride comfort and meanwhile realize the vehicle height regulation, and therefore, they have been widely used and studied. However, to achieve better ride comfort and a satisfactory vehicle body height adjustment, the active air suspension controller becomes an indispensable and significant part of the system. Since the nonlinear suspension system possesses uncertainties, it is difficult to take into account both ride comfort and height regulation. This study innovatively proposes an adaptive control algorithm to specifically address the problem of vehicle height regulation and ride comfort for nonlinear active air suspension systems with uncertainties. The accurate tracking to reference vehicle body height curves is realized, and the ride comfort is also improved. Through simulations with two scenarios, it is illustrated that the active air suspension controller owns better control effectiveness than the PID controller. Compared with the PID controller, the designed controller can track the reference vehicle body height curves faster and more accurately. The result also verifies the priority of the designed controller.

Keywords: active air suspension; nonlinear systems; uncertainties; adaptive control; Lyapunov stability

MSC: 93-10

check for
updates

Citation: Zhang, J.; Yang, Y.; Hu, C. An Adaptive Controller Design for Nonlinear Active Air Suspension Systems with Uncertainties. *Mathematics* **2023**, *11*, 2626. https://doi.org/10.3390/ math11122626

Academic Editors: Camelia Petrescu and Valeriu David

Received: 22 April 2023
Revised: 6 June 2023
Accepted: 7 June 2023
Published: 8 June 2023

1. Introduction

Automotive active suspension has been developed over the last few decades, and can be controlled via a computer. An excellent automotive active suspension possesses lots of advantages. Instead of driven suspension, the height of the car body above the ground is kept at a reasonable value by adjusting its own parameters [1]. In this way, the handling stability and the ride of the car can be highly improved through the appliance of automotive active suspensions. However, the high cost and the high hardware requirements limit the popularization and application of the automotive active suspension in automobiles.

Up to now, active suspension is gradually being widely used, and many papers have proposed control methods of active suspension, such as H-infinity control [2–5]. The literature [6] proposes a synergetic law of discontinuous control of the active suspension system of the car in order to reduce the influence of hysteresis and the dead zone. In the literature [7], the paper has designed event-trigger control for the fuzzy T-S systems with parameter uncertainties and disturbances. Simulations are given for the vehicle suspension systems. Control methods such as adaptive harmonic control [8], double time-delay feedback control [9] and nonlinear robust control [10] are adopted in active suspension research. The literature [11] applies the voice coil motor (VCM) to the active suspension in order to improve robustness of active suspension. Furthermore, the active suspension is not only applied in automotive, but is also adopted in other fields. The literature [12] outlines the potential for active suspensions in railway applications, and the literature [13] investigates the lateral stability of this mobile robot when it reconfigures itself to adjust its roll angle with the active suspension.

With the development of automobile suspension technology, people's requirements for vehicle riding comfort are also increasing. The appearance of automotive air suspension meets people's needs [14,15]. The control link of the active suspension is equipped with a device that is capable of producing a jerk, which can inhibit the impact force of the road surface on the body and adjust the car body height [16]. The air suspension keeps the constant driving height of the vehicle on different road surfaces by adjusting the charging and discharging of the air suspension bag. The air suspension can also automatically adjust the height of the body according to the speed and set different vehicle damping. The research model of this paper is automotive air suspension. At the same time, many studies have performed research on air suspension. The literature [17] presents a new nonlinear adaptive sliding-mode control method for electronically controlled air suspension. The literature [18] focuses on the evaluation of the dynamic load reduction at all axles of a semi-trailer with an air suspension system. The literature [19] describes the structure and design principle of the air suspension system, and makes an analysis and a discussion on the key use effect, i.e., the damping effect. Different control methods are proposed, such as the semi-active control strategy of the vehicle [20] and interconnected state control [21].

In this paper, the backstepping method is used to design the controller. Its main idea is to recursively construct the Lyapunov function of the closed-loop system to obtain the feedback controller, and to select the control law to make the derivative of the Lyapunov function along the trajectory of the closed-loop system have a certain type of performance to ensure the boundedness and convergence of the trajectory of the closed-loop system to the equilibrium point. The method of backstepping is used in much of the literature. The literature [22] presents an adaptive backstepping sliding mode tracking control method for an underactuated unmanned surface vehicle. Adaptive backstepping is also adopted in nonlinear systems [23] and is designed for trajectory tracking and payload delivery in a medical emergency. In the literature [24], closed loop system characteristics with an incremental backstepping controller are investigated through theoretical analysis when both measurement biases and model uncertainties exist.

Adaptive control is also adopted to design the controller of the nonlinear air spring suspension. Adaptation is the ability of a system to change its behavior in order to adapt to a new environment. Therefore, adaptive control can be viewed as a feedback control system that can intelligently adjust its own characteristics in response to changes in the environment so that the system can work optimally according to some set criteria. The literature [25] presents a novel adaptive feedforward controller design for reset control systems. Furthermore, adaptive control has been applied in different fields and is used to study different objects [26,27].

From the above literature analysis, many references have proposed great control algorithms and have obtained excellent results. Although some reports have studied the air suspension system and have designed adaptive control algorithms; however, the uncertainties of nonlinear air suspension systems, which has become a difficult problem, are neglected by many designed control methods. Thus, this paper innovatively proposes an adaptive control algorithm to specifically address the problem of vehicle height regulation and ride comfort for nonlinear active air suspension systems with uncertainties. Under this control method, both ride comfort and vehicle height regulation can be taken into account when the uncertainty of a nonlinear system is considered.

The remainder of the paper is structured as follows. Section 2 established the controller based on adaptive backstepping. In Section 3, simulation is given to the controller. Two different road inputs are used to verify the controller effectiveness. Finally, Section 4 presents the conclusion of this research.

2. Problem Formulation and Controller Design

A physical model of automobile air suspension can be built as in Figure 1. Here, z_s is the vertical displacement of the sprung mass, z_w is the vertical displacement of the unsprung mass, z_r is the pavement vertical input, m_s is the sprung mass, m_w is the unsprung mass, c_s is the damping coefficient of the suspension shock absorber, c_w is the tire vertical damping, k_w is vertical stiffness of the wheel table, and Q is the air mass flow through the solenoid valve.

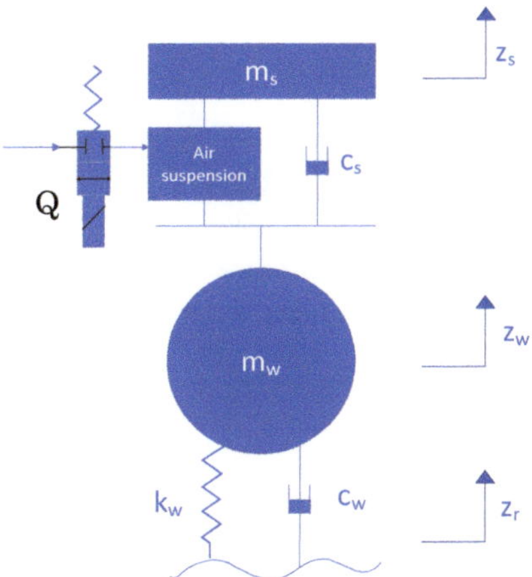

Figure 1. Physical model of air spring suspension.

According to the physical model shown in Figure 1, the dynamic model of sprung mass is established as

$$P_{as}A_{as} + c_s(\dot{z}_w - \dot{z}_s) + F_s = m_s\ddot{z}_s \tag{1}$$

where P_{as} is air spring chamber pressure, A_{as} is the effective cross-sectional area of the air spring, and F_s is the upper bound is known to be uncertain.

The dynamic model of the unsprung mass is

$$\begin{aligned} k_w(z_r - z_w) + c_w(\dot{z}_r - \dot{z}_w) - P_{as}A_{as} \\ - c_s(\dot{z}_w - \dot{z}_s) + F_w = m_s\ddot{z}_w \end{aligned} \tag{2}$$

where F_w is the upper bound is known to be uncertain. The dynamic model of the air pressure chamber of the air spring is

$$\dot{P}_{as}A_{as}(z_{a0} + z_s - z_w) = -KP_{as}A_{as}(\dot{z}_s - \dot{z}_w) + KRTQ + F_p \tag{3}$$

where z_{a0} is the air spring at the beginning of high degree, K is the variable index, R is the ideal gas constant, T is the gas temperature, F_p is the upper bound, a known uncertainty.

The above formula can be sorted out:

$$\begin{cases} \dot{P}_{as} &= \dfrac{KRT}{A_{as}(z_{a0}+z_s-z_w)}Q - \dfrac{KP_{as}}{z_{a0}+z_s-z_w}(\dot{z}_s - \dot{z}_w) \\ &\quad + \dfrac{F_p}{A_{as}(z_{a0}+z_s-z_w)} \\ \ddot{z}_s &= \dfrac{A_{as}}{m_s}P_{as} + \dfrac{c_s}{m_s}(\dot{z}_w - \dot{z}_s) + \dfrac{F_s}{m_s} \\ \ddot{z}_w &= \dfrac{k_w}{m_w}(z_r - z_w) + \dfrac{c_w}{m_w}(\dot{z}_r - \dot{z}_w) - \dfrac{A_{as}}{m_s}P_{as} \\ &\quad - \dfrac{c_s}{m_w}(\dot{z}_w - \dot{z}_s) - \dfrac{F_w}{m_w} \end{cases} \tag{4}$$

Let $x_1 = z_s$, $x_2 = \dot{z}_s$, $x_3 = z_w$, $x_4 = \dot{z}_w$, $x_5 = P_{as}$, $x_6 = \frac{A_{as}}{m_s}\dot{x}_5 + \frac{c_s}{m_s}(x_4 - x_2)$, $Q = u$, $\frac{F_s}{m_s} = F_1$, $\frac{F_s}{m_w} = F_3$, $\frac{F_p}{m_s(z_{a0}+z_s-z_w)} = F_2$.

$$\begin{cases} \dot{x}_1 = x_2 \\ \dot{x}_2 = x_6 + F_1 \\ \dot{x}_3 = x_4 \\ \dot{x}_4 = \frac{k_w}{m_w}(z_r - x_3) + \frac{c_w}{m_w}(\dot{z}_r - x_4) - \ddot{x}_{1r} + F_3 \\ \dot{x}_6 = \frac{kRT}{m_s(z_{a0}+x_1-x_3)}u + \frac{c_s}{m_s}(\dot{x}_4 - \dot{x}_2) + F_2 \\ \quad - \frac{k}{z_{a0}+x_1-x_3}(x_6 - \frac{c_s}{m_s}(x_4 - x_2))(x_2 - x_4) \end{cases} \tag{5}$$

The control objective is to design controller u, which can make $x_1 \to x_{1r}$ and stabilize the system. Let $z_1 = x_1 - x_{1r}$, $z_2 = x_2 - x_{2r}$; x_{2r} is a virtual control input. Design $x_{2r} = -\tilde{F}_1 - k_1 z_1 + \dot{x}_{1r}$, where $\hat{F}_1$ is the estimated value of F_1, and $\tilde{F}_1$ is the error between the true value and the estimated value, which can easily have $\tilde{F}_1 = F_1 - \hat{F}_1$

$$\begin{aligned} \dot{z}_1 &= \dot{x}_1 - \dot{x}_{1r} \\ &= z_2 + x_{2r} - \dot{x}_{1r} \\ &= z_2 - \tilde{F}_1 - k_1 z_1 \end{aligned} \tag{6}$$

Design the Lyapunov function $V_1 = \frac{1}{2}z_1^2 + \frac{1}{2}\gamma_1^{-1}\tilde{F}_1^2$

$$\begin{aligned} \dot{V}_1 &= z_1\dot{z}_1 + \gamma_1^{-1}\tilde{F}_1\dot{\tilde{F}}_1 \\ &= z_1 z_2 - k_1 z_1^2 - \tilde{F}_1(z_1 + \gamma_1^{-1}\dot{\hat{F}}_1) \end{aligned} \tag{7}$$

The dynamic equation of z_2

$$\begin{aligned} \dot{z}_2 &= \dot{x}_2 - \dot{x}_{2r} \\ &= x_6 + F_1 - \hat{F}_1 + k_1\dot{z}_1 - \ddot{x}_{1r} \end{aligned} \tag{8}$$

Let $z_3 = x_6 - x_{6r}$; x_{6r} is also the virtual control input.
Design

$$x_{6r} = -k_2 z_2 - z_1 - k_1\dot{z}_1 + \ddot{x}_{1r} - \hat{F}_1 - \tilde{F}_2 + \phi_1 \tag{9}$$

where ϕ_1 is a tuning function, which is undetermined, and $\tilde{F}_2 = F_2 - \hat{F}_2$. Design the Lyapunov function $V_2 = \frac{1}{2}z_2^2 + \frac{1}{2}\gamma_2^{-1}\tilde{F}_2^2 + V_1$

$$\begin{aligned} \dot{V}_2 &= z_2\dot{z}_2 + \gamma_2^{-1}\tilde{F}_2\dot{\tilde{F}}_2 + \dot{V}_1 \\ &= z_2 z_3 - k_2 z_2^2 - k_1 z_1^2 - \tilde{F}_2(z_2 + \gamma_2^{-1}\dot{\hat{F}}_2) + z_2\gamma_1(\phi_2\gamma_1^{-1} - \gamma_1^{-1}\dot{\hat{F}}_1) \\ &\quad + \tilde{F}_1(z_2 - z_1 - \gamma_1^{-1}\dot{\hat{F}}_1) \end{aligned} \tag{10}$$

Let

$$\phi_1 = \gamma_1(z_2 - z_1) \tag{11}$$

Combining $\phi_1 = \gamma_1(z_2 - z_1)$ and Equation (10), we can have

$$\dot{V}_2 = z_2 z_3 - k_2 z_2^2 - k_1 z_1^2 - \tilde{F}_2(z_2 - \gamma_2^{-1}\dot{\hat{F}}_2) + (\tilde{F}_1 + z_2\gamma_1)(z_2 - z_1 - \gamma_1^{-1}\dot{\hat{F}}_1) \tag{12}$$

The dynamic equation of z_3

$$\begin{aligned} \dot{z}_3 &= \dot{x}_6 - \dot{x}_{6r} \\ &= \frac{kRT}{m_s(z_{a0} + x_1 - x_3)}u + \frac{c_s}{m_s}(\dot{x}_4 - \dot{x}_2) + F_2 \\ &\quad - \frac{k}{z_{a0} + x_1 - x_3}(x_6 - \frac{c_s}{m_s}(x_4 - x_2))(x_2 - x_4) \\ &\quad - \dot{x}_{6r} \end{aligned} \tag{13}$$

Design

$$u = -\frac{m_s(z_{a0} + x_1 - x_3)}{kRT}\left(\frac{c_s}{m_s}(\dot{x}_4 - \dot{x}_2) + \hat{F}_2\right.$$

$$-\frac{k}{z_{a0} + x_1 - x_3}(x_6 - \frac{c_s}{m_s}(x_4 - x_2))(x_2 - x_4) + k_2\dot{z}_2 \tag{14}$$

$$+ \dot{z}_1 + k_1\ddot{z}_1 - \dddot{x}_{1r} - \dot{\phi}_1 + k_3 z_3 + z_2 - \phi_2 - \phi_3),$$

where ϕ_2 and ϕ_3 are also undetermined tuning functions. Plugging u into (13) yields

$$\dot{z}_3 = -\hat{F}_2 + \dot{\hat{F}}_1 + \tilde{F}_2 - k_3 z_3 - z_2 + \phi_2 + \phi_3 \tag{15}$$

Design $V_3 = \frac{1}{2}z_3{}^2 + V_2$

$$\begin{aligned}
\dot{V}_3 &= z_3\dot{z}_3 + \dot{V}_2 \\
&= z_3\gamma_2(\phi_3\gamma_2^{-1} - \gamma_2^{-1}\dot{\hat{F}}_2) + \tilde{F}_2(z_3 - z_2 - \gamma_2^{-1}\dot{\hat{F}}_2) \\
&\quad + z_3\gamma_1(\phi_2\gamma_1^{-1} + \gamma_1^{-1}\dot{\hat{F}}_1) + (\tilde{F}_1 + z_2\gamma_1)(z_2 \\
&\quad - z_1 - \gamma_1^{-1}\dot{\hat{F}}_1) - \sum_{i=1}^{3} k_i z_i^2
\end{aligned} \tag{16}$$

Let $\phi_2 = \gamma_1(z_1 - z_2), \phi_3 = \gamma_2(z_3 - z_2)$

$$\begin{aligned}
\dot{V}_3 &= (\tilde{F}_2 + z_3\gamma_2)(z_3 - z_2 - \gamma_2^{-1}\dot{\hat{F}}_2) \\
&\quad + (\tilde{F}_1 + z_2\gamma_1 - z_3\gamma_1)(z_2 - z_1 - \gamma_1^{-1}\dot{\hat{F}}_1) - \sum_{i=1}^{3} k_i z_i^2
\end{aligned} \tag{17}$$

Design $\dot{\hat{F}}_1 = (z_2 - z_1)\gamma_1$ and $\dot{\hat{F}}_2 = (z_3 - z_2)\gamma_2$, which leads to $\dot{V}_3 \leq 0$. According to Barbalat's lemma, we can have z_i approaches 0 when t approaches infinity.

When $\ddot{z}_1 = \dot{z}_2 = \dot{z}_3 = 0$, the system zero dynamics is

$$\begin{cases} \dot{x}_3 = x_4 \\ \dot{x}_4 = \frac{k_w}{m_w}(z_r - x_3) + \frac{c_w}{m_w}(\dot{z}_r - x_4) - \ddot{x}_{1r} + F_3 \end{cases} \tag{18}$$

it can be inferred

$$\ddot{x}_3 + \frac{c_w}{m_w}\dot{x}_3 + \frac{k_w}{m_w}x_3 + \ddot{x}_{1r} - \frac{c_w}{m_w}\dot{z}_r + \frac{k_w}{m_w}z_r - F_3 = 0 \tag{19}$$

The characteristic equation is

$$s^2 + \frac{c_w}{m_w}s + \frac{k_w}{m_w} = 0 \tag{20}$$

As $c_w > 0, k_w > 0, m_w > 0$, $\frac{c_w}{m_w} > 0$, $\frac{k_w}{m_w} > 0$ can be inferred. The coefficients of the characteristic equation of the second-order zero-dynamic system are all positive, so the zero-dynamic system is stable. x_3, x_4 is bounded when the road inputs that the value of $z_r, \dot{z}_r$, the reference signal $\ddot{x}_{1r}$ and uncertainty F_3 are bounded.

3. Simulation Verification

In order to verify the effectiveness of the adaptive control method, simulation verification is carried out. There are two scenarios. The first case is the pavement vertical input $z_r = 0.01\sin 2\pi t$ and $x_{1r} = 0.01\sin 2\pi t$. The other case is $x_{1r} = 0$, and the pavement vertical input is random. The vehicle parameters in simulation are shown in Table 1 below. The controller parameters are shown in Table 2 below [28].

Table 1. Vehicle parameters.

Parament	Value	Parament	Value
m_s	1535 kg	m_w	400 kg
c_w	10,000 Ns/m	k_w	650,000 Ns/m
c_s	11,086 Ns/m	K	1.4
T	293.15 k	R	287.1

Table 2. Controller design parameters.

Parament	Value	Parament	Value
k_1	100	k_2	100
γ_1	100	γ_2	100

3.1. Sinusoidal Road Input

In the sinusoidal road input simulation process, the parameters are set as follows. The vehicle height was adjusted under a vertical input of $z_r = 0.01 \sin 2\pi t$, the initial height of air sprung $z_{a0} = 0.03$ m, the uncertain outer boundary perturbation input $F_1(t) = F_2(t) = 0.01$, x_1 is initialized as 0.2 m, and other states are initialized to 0. The sampling time is 0.001 s and the simulation results are shown in Figures 2–7.

Figure 2 shows the tracing effect of the car body height on the reference trajectory in the process of vehicle height adjustment. Under control of the controller, the tracing curve of the car body height almost coincides with reference trajectory. As $z_1 = x_1 - x_{1r}$, $z_1 = 0$ can be inferred. Figure 3 is the curve of z_1, which confirms $z_1 = 0$. Compared with the PID controller, the designed controller can not only track the reference curve more accurately, but also make the error more inclined to 0.

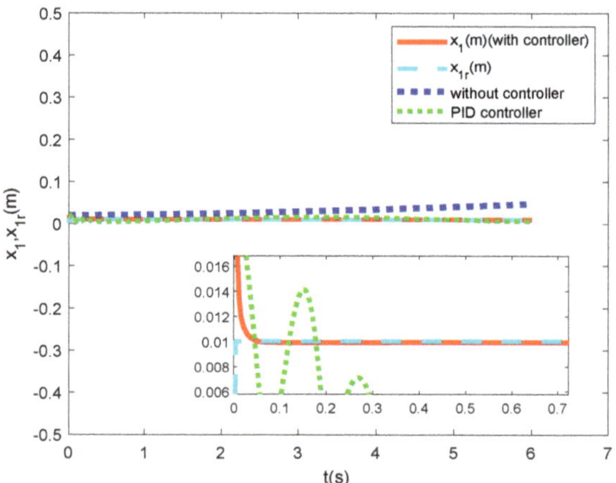

Figure 2. Tracing curve of vertical displacement of sprung mass.

Figure 4 is the state curve of car body speed. Compared with the design controller, the PID controller has greater fluctuation of the speed curve. The corresponding system state error under the proposed control algorithm is shown in Figure 5. Combining Figure 4 and Figure 5, the car body completes the car body height adjustment with a smooth curve under the proposed control algorithm. The value of the system state error z_2 approaches 0 after a very short period of fluctuation.

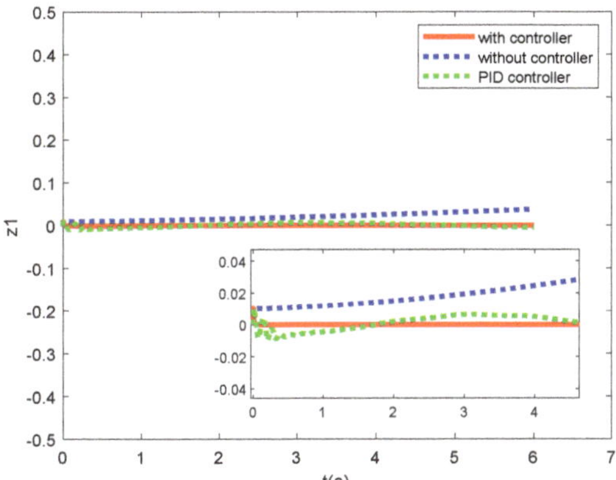

Figure 3. Tracing error curve of vertical displacement of sprung mass.

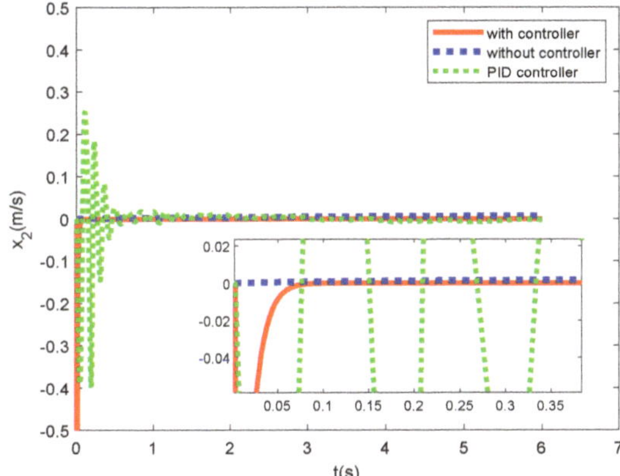

Figure 4. State curve of car body speed.

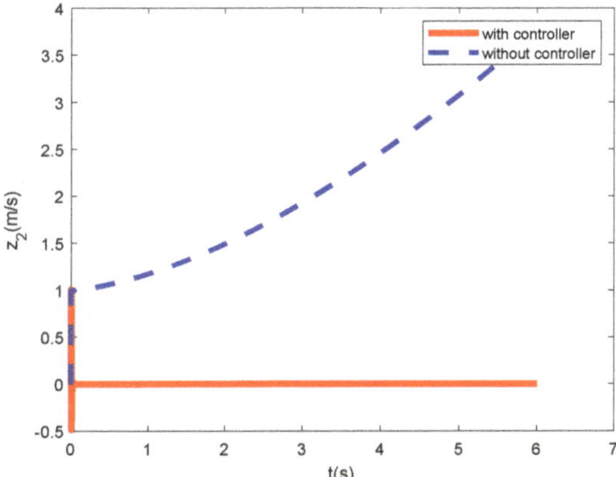

Figure 5. State curve of z_2.

Figure 6 is the state curve of car body acceleration. As shown in the picture, the value of x_6 approaches 0 and the fluctuation is small. Figure 7 is the state curve of the controller. However, in both figures, the PID controller takes longer to stabilize and has a larger fluctuation range. The simulation confirms that the controller can keep stable.

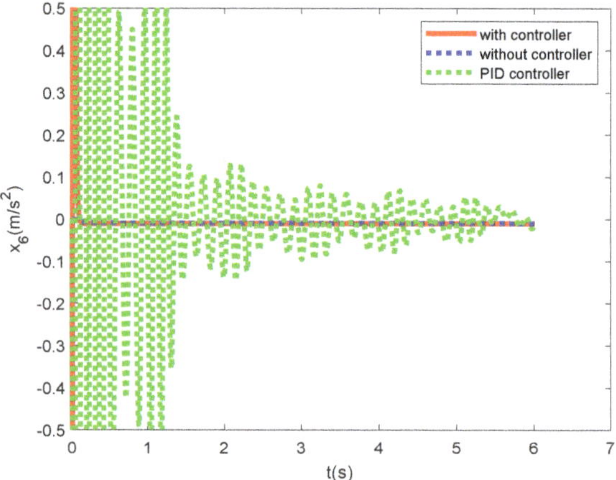

Figure 6. State curve of car body acceleration.

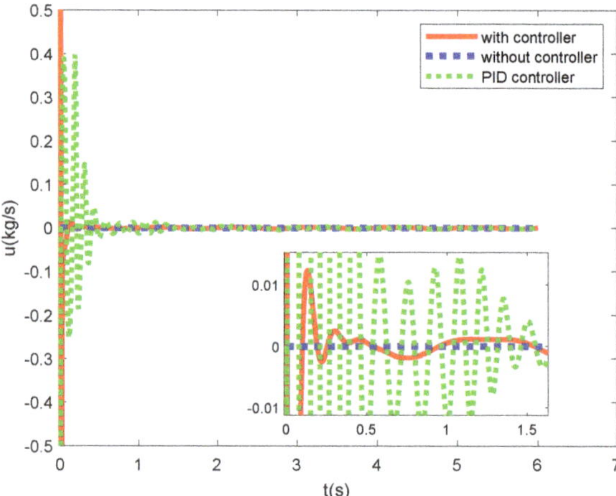

Figure 7. State curve of controller.

From Figures 2–7, the system remains stable under the control of the controller, which shows that the control algorithm is effective. Compared with the PID controller, the designed controller achieves better control effects.

3.2. Random Road Input

In the process of the random input of pavement simulation, the vertical input of the pavement is filtered white noise (Figure 8)

$$\dot{z}_r(t) = -2\pi n_1 v z_r(t) + 2\pi n_0 \sqrt{G_q(n_0)v} w(t) \tag{21}$$

The parameters are set as follows. n_1 is the lower cutoff frequency, v is speed of the car, n_0 is the spatial reference frequency, and $G_q(n_0)$ is the coefficient of road roughness. Class A uneven pavement is used in the simulation, where $n_0 = 0.1\,\mathrm{m}^{-1}, G_q(n_0) = 16 \times 10^{-6}\,\mathrm{m}^3, n_1 = 0.01\,\mathrm{m}^{-1}$, and $v = 10\,\mathrm{m}/s$.

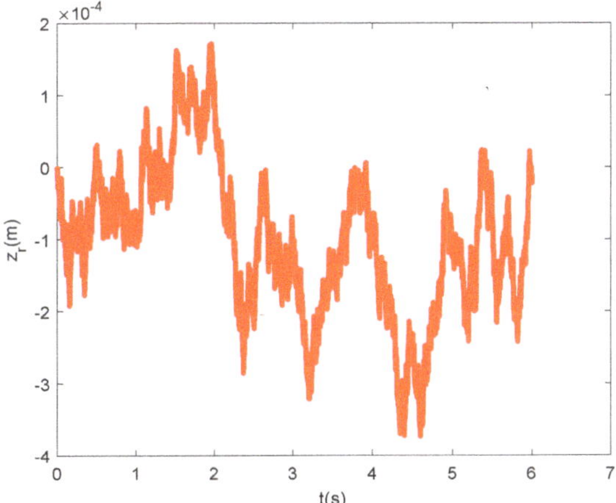

Figure 8. Vertical input for Class A uneven road surface.

The vehicle height was adjusted under a vertical input of $z_r = 0.01 \sin 2\pi t$ and an initial height of air sprung $z_{a0} = 0.03$ m; the uncertain outer boundary perturbation input $F_1(t) = F_2(t) = 0.01$, all states are initialized to 0, and the sampling time is 0.001 s.

The simulation results are shown in Figures 9–13. Figure 9 presents the difference between the state curves for the vehicle body height with and without the controller. Under the control of the controller, the state curves for the vehicle body height still have a certain level of fluctuation, but it is too small to be seen. Figure 10 shows the state curves for the vehicle body height tracking error. Combining the two figures, it can be seen that the controller can effectively reduce the variation range of the process of the car body height adjustment, which means that the controller reduces the car body vibration created by the road input.

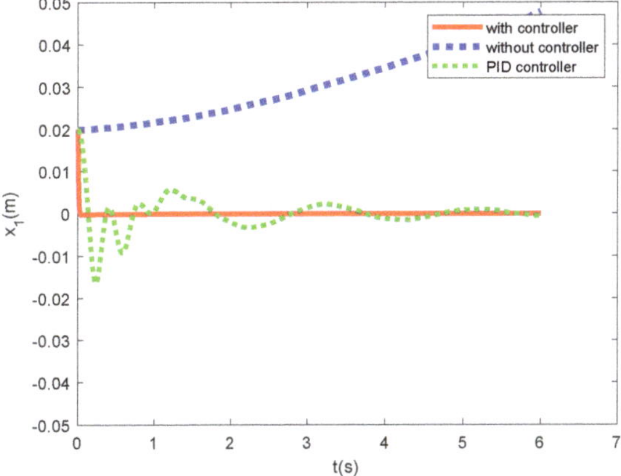

Figure 9. State curves for the vehicle body height.

Figure 11 shows the state curves for vehicle body velocity. During the process of car body height adjustment, the value of the vehicle body velocity increases and changes greatly. In contrast, the state curves for the vehicle body velocity keep stable under the control of the controller. However, like x_1, x_2 has small fluctuations but they are too small to be seen.

Figure 12 shows the state curves for the vehicle body acceleration. With the designed controller, the vertical acceleration of the body is reduced and thus, the comfort is improved. Under the condition of no controller, the fluctuation of the vehicle body acceleration state curve is large. The PID controller cannot reduce the fluctuation amplitude of the body acceleration curve. Compared with the PID controller, the designed controller is more efficient.

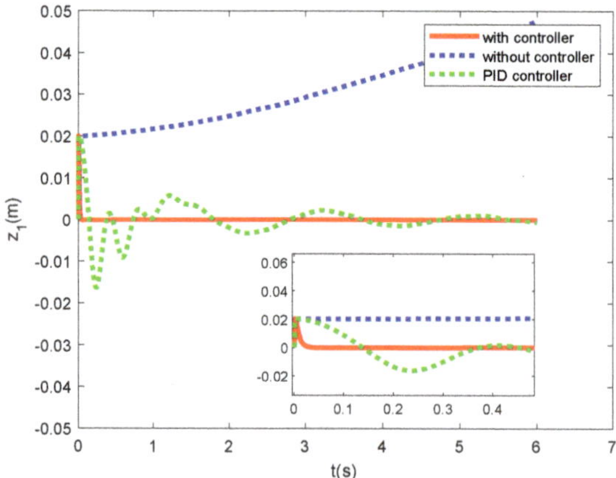

Figure 10. State curves for the vehicle body height tracking error.

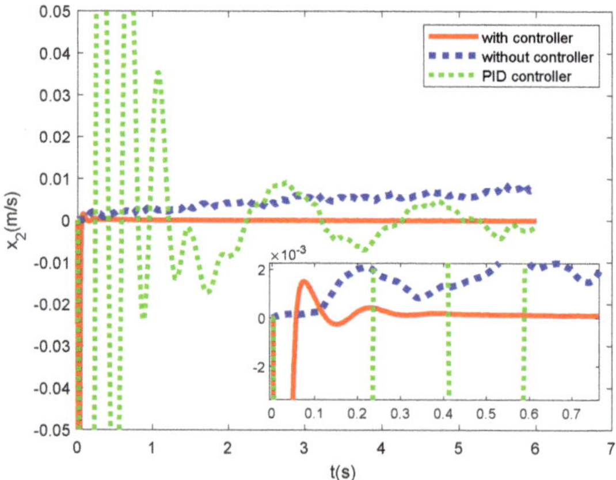

Figure 11. State curves for the vehicle body velocity.

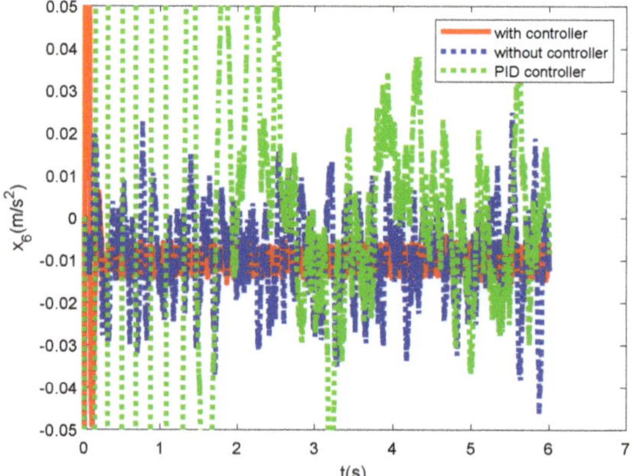

Figure 12. State curves for the vehicle body acceleration.

In the process of the vehicle body height adjustment, the state curves of the controller are shown in Figure 13. Compared with the PID controller, the designed controller has a shorter settling time and faster stabilization.

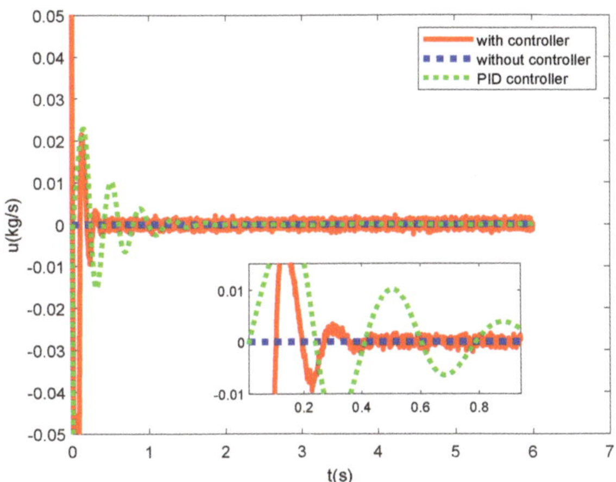

Figure 13. State curves of the controller.

4. Conclusions

In this paper, an adaptive control algorithm for the vehicle height adjustment of nonlinear air suspensions is proposed to improve the vehicle ride comfort. The designed algorithm can track the reference height curve, and the stability of the nonlinear air suspension systems with uncertainties is guaranteed by Lyapunov stability theory. Two different simulations are carried out to verify the effectiveness of the proposed controller. In the case of sinusoidal road input, the controller can track the reference value of body height well and make the corresponding error tend to 0. In the case of random road input, the controller reduces the fluctuation of the vertical parameters and improves the ride comfort. The following research will focus on the experimental verification of the proposed controller.

Author Contributions: Methodology, J.Z.; Writing—original draft, Y.Y.; Funding acquisition, C.H. All authors have read and agreed to the published version of the manuscript.

Funding: This research was funded by the Guangzhou Science and Technology Plan Project (202201010475, 202201020173) and the National Natural Science Foundation of China (52202492).

Data Availability Statement: The data used to support the findings of this study are included within the article.

Conflicts of Interest: The authors declare no conflict of interest.

References

1. Zhang, J.; Sun, W.; Du, H. Integrated Motion Control Scheme for Four-Wheel-Independent Vehicles Considering Critical Conditions. *IEEE Trans. Veh. Technol.* **2019**, *68*, 7488–7497. [CrossRef]
2. Jin, X.; Wang, J.; Sun, S.; Li, S.; Yang, J.; Yan, Z. Design of Constrained Robust Controller for Active Suspension of In-Wheel-Drive Electric Vehicles. *Mathematics* **2021**, *9*, 249. [CrossRef]
3. Jin, X.; Wang, J.; Yang, J. Development of Robust Guaranteed Cost Mixed Control System for Active Suspension of In-Wheel-Drive Electric Vehicles. *Math. Probl. Eng.* **2022**, *2022*, 4628539. [CrossRef]
4. Fu, Z.J.; Dong, X.Y. H infinity optimal control of vehicle active suspension systems in two time scales. *Automatika* **2021**, *62*, 284–292. [CrossRef]
5. Zhang, J.; Sun, W.; Feng, Z. Vehicle yaw stability control via H∞ gain scheduling. *Mech. Syst. Signal Process.* **2018**, *106*, 62–75. .: 10.1016/j.ymssp.2017.12.033. [CrossRef]
6. Veselov, G.; Sinicyn, A. Synthesis of sliding control system for automotive suspension under kinematic constraints. *J. Vibroeng.* **2021**, *23*, 1446–1455. [CrossRef]

7. Zhang, W.; Fan, X. Observer-based event-triggered control and application in active suspension vehicle systems. *Syst. Sci. Control Eng.* **2022**, *10*, 282–288. [CrossRef]

8. Unguritu, M.G.; Nichitelea, T.C.; Selisteanu, D. Design and Performance Assessment of Adaptive Harmonic Control for a Half-Car Active Suspension System. *Complexity* **2022**, *2022*, 3190520. [CrossRef]

9. Wu, K.; Ren, C. Control and Stability Analysis of Double Time-Delay Active Suspension Based on Particle Swarm Optimization. *Shock Vib.* **2020**, *2020*, 8873701. [CrossRef]

10. Zhang, J.; Sun, W.; Jing, H. Nonlinear Robust Control of Antilock Braking Systems Assisted by Active Suspensions for Automobile. *IEEE Trans. Control Syst. Technol.* **2019**, *27*, 1352–1359. [CrossRef]

11. Pan, F.; Luo, J.; Wu, W. Active Disturbance Rejection Control of Voice Coil Motor Active Suspension Based on Displacement Feedback. *Actuators* **2022**, *11*, 351. [CrossRef]

12. Fu, B.; Giossi, R.L.; Persson, R.; Stichel, S.; Bruni, S.; Goodall, R. Active suspension in railway vehicles: A literature survey. *Railw. Eng. Sci.* **2020**, *28*, 3–35. [CrossRef]

13. Jiang, H.; Xu, G.; Zeng, W.; Gao, F.; Chong, K. Lateral Stability of a Mobile Robot Utilizing an Active Adjustable Suspension. *Appl. Sci.* **2019**, *9*, 4410. [CrossRef]

14. Zhang, J.; Sun, W.; Liu, Z.; Zeng, M. Comfort braking control for brake-by-wire vehicles. *Mech. Syst. Signal Process.* **2019**, *133*, 106255. [CrossRef]

15. Zhang, J.; Wang, M. Integrated Adaptive Steering Stability Control for Ground Vehicle with Actuator Saturations. *Appl. Sci.* **2022**, *12*, 8502. [CrossRef]

16. Gao, S.; Zhang, B.; Sun, J. Research on the Design Method of a Bionic Suspension Workpiece Based on the Wing Structure of an Albatross. *Appl. Bionics Biomech.* **2019**, *2019*, 2539410. [CrossRef]

17. Rui, B. Nonlinear adaptive sliding-mode control of the electronically controlled air suspension system. *Int. J. Adv. Robot. Syst.* **2019**, *16*, 1729881419881527. [CrossRef]

18. Ha, D.V.; Tan, V.V.; Niem, V.T.; Sename, O. Evaluation of Dynamic Load Reduction for a Tractor Semi-Trailer Using the Air Suspension System at all Axles of the Semi-Trailer. *Actuators* **2022**, *11*, 12. [CrossRef]

19. Chen, B.; Dong, G.; Shi, Y.; Tan, X.Y. Research on Damping Mode of Passenger Vehicle Air Suspension System. In Proceedings of the 3rd International Workshop on Renewable Energy and Development (IWRED), Guangzhou, China, 8–10 March 2019; Volume 267. [CrossRef]

20. Sun, L.; Wang, Y.; Li, Z.; Geng, G.; Liao, Y.G. H-infinity Robust Control of Interconnected Air Suspension Based on Mode Switching. *IEEE Access* **2022**, *10*, 62377–62390. [CrossRef]

21. Li, Z.; Zhou, Y.; Zhang, X.; Jiang, H.; ; Xue, H. Interconnected State Control Method and Simulations of Four-corner Interconnected Air Suspension. In Proceedings of the 6th International Conference on Mechanical, Materials and Manufacturing (ICMMM), Boston, MA, USA, 12–14 October 2019; Volume 689. [CrossRef]

22. Zhao, Y.; Sun, X.; Wang, G.; Fan, Y. Adaptive Backstepping Sliding Mode Tracking Control for Underactuated Unmanned Surface Vehicle With Disturbances and Input Saturation. *IEEE Access* **2021**, *9*, 1304–1312. [CrossRef]

23. Qian, F.; Cai, J.; Wang, B.; Yu, R. Adaptive Backstepping Control for a Class of Nonlinear Systems with Unknown Time Delay. *IEEE Access* **2020**, *8*, 229–236. [CrossRef]

24. Jeon, B.J.; Seo, M.G.; Shin, H.S.; Tsourdos, A. Closed-loop Analysis with Incremental Backstepping Controller considering Measurement Bias. *IFAC Pap.* **2019**, *52*, 405–410. [CrossRef]

25. Brummelhuis, K.; Saikumar, N.; Van Wingerden, J.W.; HosseinNia, S.H. Adaptive Feedforward Control For Reset Feedback Control Systems—Application in Precision Motion Control. In Proceedings of the 2021 European Control Conference (ECC), Delft, The Netherlands, 29 Jun–2 July 2021; pp. 2450–2457.

26. Alwan, N.A.S.; Hussain, Z.M. Deep Learning for Robust Adaptive Inverse Control of Nonlinear Dynamic Systems: Improved Settling Time with an Autoencoder. *Sensors* **2022**, *22*, 5935. [CrossRef]

27. Quang, L.H.; Putov, V.V.; Sheludko, V.N. Adaptive robust control of a multi-degree-of-freedom mechanical plant with resilient properties. In Proceedings of the 14th International Symposium on Intelligent Systems, ELECTR NETWORK, Montreal, QC, Canada, 14–16 December 2020; Zelinka, I., Pereira, F., Das, S., Ilin, A., Diveev, A., Nikulchev, E., Eds., 2021; Volume 186, pp. 611–619. [CrossRef]

28. Sun, W.; Zhang, J. Heavy Vehicle Air Suspension Control Considering Ride Comfort and Height Regulation. *Control Theory Appl.* **2022**, *39*, 1002–1010.

MDPI
St. Alban-Anlage 66
4052 Basel
Switzerland
Tel. +41 61 683 77 34
Fax +41 61 302 89 18
www.mdpi.com

Mathematics Editorial Office
E-mail: mathematics@mdpi.com
www.mdpi.com/journal/mathematics

www.ingramcontent.com/pod-product-compliance
Lightning Source LLC
LaVergne TN
LVHW080456180726
843515LV00007BA/1746